DISCOVERING

DISCIPLESHIP
DYNAMICS OF
CHRISTIAN EDUCATION

DISCOVERING

DISCIPLESHIP
DYNAMICS OF
CHRISTIAN EDUCATION

BY
DEAN G. BLEVINS
MARK A. MADDIX

BEACON HILL PRESS
OF KANSAS CITY

ISBN 978-0-8341-2496-7

Printed in the
United States of America

Cover Design: Brandon Hill
Interior Design: Sharon Page

Disclaimer: The authors of *Discovering Discipleship* and Beacon Hill Press of
Kansas City are not engaged in rendering legal services or advice. Such services and
advice should be secured from a member of the legal profession. Where appropriate,
state and local laws and requirements should be consulted.

Library of Congress Cataloging-in-Publication Data

Blevins, Dean Gray.
  Discovering discipleship : dynamics of Christian education / Dean G. Blevins, Mark A. Maddix.
    p. cm.
  Includes bibliographical references.
  ISBN 978-0-8341-2496-7 (hardcover)
  1. Holiness churches—Education. 2. Discipling (Christianity) 3. Christian education.
I. Maddix, Mark A., 1965- II. Title.
  BX7990.H6B64 2010
  248.4'871—dc22

                                                                          2010003482

10 9 8 7 6 5 4 3 2 1

CONTENTS

Acknowledgments

No one writes a book without a lot of help. We both remain debtors to a number of people who worked to shape our understanding of Christian education and empowered us to put our thoughts into practice. We would like to take a moment to acknowledge with gratitude and humility those whom God used as means of grace in our lives.

Professionally, I (Dean Blevins) would like to thank five academic institutions that shaped and empowered my journey. I would like to thank John Wesley College whose faculty nurtured my first theological vision of Wesley, Nazarene Theological Seminary (NTS) whose faculty helped to shape and connect my passions for theology and Christian education, and Claremont School of Theology whose faculty forged those initial thoughts into a doctoral study of Wesley and his approach to Christian religious education. I would also like to thank Trevecca Nazarene University (TNU) who nurtured my early years as a university professor in Christian education and whose research committee provided valued financial resources when I first began this project. NTS again became my home, this time as academic faculty, where graduate students and colleagues graciously probed my ideas at a new level, and the institution provided much-needed sabbatical time for the writing of this volume. MidAmerica Nazarene University also deserves appreciation for providing needed resources and office space for writing, while I was a scholar-in-residence at that hospitable institution. Each of these institutions represents Christian charity as do those communities of faith that nurtured my faith journey: Calvary Church of the Nazarene, Anaheim First Church, Trevecca Community, and Kansas City First Church. Each church represents the Church of the Nazarene, a denomination I now call "home."

Personally, I have far too many people to mention. Early exemplars of faithful discipleship include John Smith, an elderly gentleman willing to teach an awkward junior high student; Bertha Eury, a matron who embraced a broken young man with Christian love and care; Mike McClure, Judy Wimmer, and Jerry and Linda Whittum, who shepherded a young man toward a call to ministry; and Dee and Dorothy Blevins, who loved a son through many strange turns and moments of grace. I would like to thank teachers who modeled faithful discipleship: Brian Donley, Karl Luff, John and April Lindsey, Chet Galloway, Ed Robinson, Rob Staples, Don Whitlock, Dee Freeborn, Frank Rogers, Jack Verheyden, and Mary Elizabeth Moore. Other leaders have

7

nurtured my journey as a minister and educator: Jarrell Garsee, Tom Goble, Ron Benefiel, and particularly Millard Reed, who proved to be as much my pastor as my president at TNU. I have had great colleagues who were ready to take extra time to discuss the task of faithful discipleship: Henry Spaulding, Rick Quinn, Tim Green, David Wesley, Vicki Copp, Doug Hardy, Jim Hampton, Mark Hayse, and, of course, my coauthor and deep friend, Mark Maddix. Finally I would like to thank my wife, JoAnn, and daughter, Rachel, both extremely patient with their husband/father (as long as I had time to mow the lawn and play a little basketball) and who continue to be means of grace in my life.

I (Mark Maddix) am deeply grateful for a rich Christian heritage. As a first-generation Nazarene, my roots are in a small rural church near Olive Hill, Kentucky. During these formative years, I saw faithful discipleship modeled by my parents, Amos and Janet Maddix, and the Globe Christian church community. I want to thank Timothy Thomas, my professor of Christian education at Asbury College, who introduced me to the Church of the Nazarene and to the discipline of Christian education. Dr. Thomas helped set my feet on a path of faithful discipleship and service to the Church of the Nazarene, which are foundational to my lifework and ministry. I want to thank the faculty at Asbury College who nurtured and developed my Wesleyan understanding of life and faith, transforming my understanding of faith and practice by opening up a world of new thoughts and ideas. I also want to thank the faculty at Asbury Theological Seminary who helped me integrate theology and ministry from a Wesleyan perspective, and the faculty at Princeton Theological Seminary and Trinity Evangelical Divinity School who created space for me to integrate the social sciences and Wesleyan theology as a framework for Christian education. I want to thank Nazarene Bible College (NBC), which provided my first opportunity to teach in Christian higher education. The time at NBC was significant as I developed several courses in Christian discipleship and completed my dissertation. I especially want to thank the administration and faculty of Northwest Nazarene University, who granted me a sabbatical to complete this book. The support of the university and my colleagues in the School of Theology and Christian Ministry was critical in completing this project.

I also want to thank the undergraduate and graduate students whom I have taught during the past ten years. These students have taught me much about life and faithful discipleship. I also want to thank students from several global contexts: Venezuela, Ecuador, Brazil, the Philippines, Korea, Australia, France, Switzerland, Bulgaria, England, Barcelona, and Africa. The example of faithful discipleship I witnessed in these settings challenged me to rethink my Western (North American) view of discipleship on several fronts. As a result of engaging with students in their own cultures, I have developed a richer and broader understanding of faithful discipleship.

The congregations in which I have served in full-time ministry gave me an opportunity to share with them in faithful discipleship. I want to thank the congregations of Lexington First Church of the Nazarene, Lexington, Kentucky; Fairview Village Church of the Nazarene, Fairview Village, Pennsylvania; College Church of the Nazarene, Nampa, Idaho; Community Chapel, Air Force Academy, Colorado Springs, Colorado; and Ephrata Church of the Nazarene, Ephrata, Pennsylvania. I especially want to thank the Ephrata congregation for seeing the broader vision of my life by allowing me to pursue a doctoral degree at Trinity. Their investment in my life made it possible for me to follow my call to teach in Christian higher education.

Personally, I want to thank the teaching faculty who modeled faithful discipleship for me: Timothy Thomas, Vic Hamilton, Owen Dickens, Donald Joy, Steve Seamands, Ted Ward, Linda Cannell, Perry Downs, and James Loder. Thanks, also, to pastors who invested in my life: Riley and Betty Laymon, Bruce Peterson, B. W. Hambrick, Larry Cook, and Daryl Johnson. I want to thank my colleagues who share life and ministry with me and are daily reminders of faithful discipleship: Jay Akkerman, Joe Bankard, Wendell Bowes, Rhonda Carrim, Ed Crawford, Mike Kipp, Diane Leclerc, George Lyons, Ralph Neil, Tom Oord, Brent Peterson, and Jim and Carol Rotz. I especially want to thank Dean Blevins, my coauthor and friend, for sharing this faithful journey of writing with me. And finally to the most important people in my life, my wife, Sherri, for her constant encouragement and support during this project and my children Adrienne Meier and Nathaniel who reminded me to "keep up the good work, Dad." The love and support of colleagues and family are constant reminders of God's love and goodness.

Together, our thanks go to Alex Varughese, Roger Hahn, and Bonnie Perry for their patient guidance of this effort as part of the Church of the Nazarene Centennial Project. We also offer many thanks to a number of our colleagues who read and responded to drafts of different chapters. Thanks to Barbara A. Dick and Richard Buckner for their editorial assistance.

We also want to express our appreciation to those journals and publishing houses who have graciously granted permission to summarize our earlier work for this book, particularly for the following works:

- Blevins, Dean G. "Learning Theories," *Evangelical Dictionary of Christian Education*. Grand Rapids: Baker, 2001. Used by permission.

- Blevins, Dean G. "Renovating Christian Education in the 21st Century: A Wesleyan Contribution," Christian Education Journal Series 3, vol. 2, no. 1 (Spring 2005), 6-29. Used by permission.
- Blevins, Dean G. "Take Five: Jumpstarting Your Child Safety Program," Children's Teacher, vol. 14, no. 1 (Fall 2006), 33-4. Used by permission.
- Blevins, Dean G. "Story Telling or Storied Telling? Media's Pedagogical Ability to Shape Narrative as a Form of 'Knowing,'" Religious Education, vol. 102, no. 3 (Summer 2007), 250-63. Used by permission.
- Blevins, Dean G. "Technology and the Transformation of Persons," Christian Education Journal Series 3, vol. 5, no. 1 (Spring 2008), 138-53. Used by permission.
- Leclerc, Diane, and Mark A. Maddix. "Wesleyan Integration: A Distinctive Philosophy of Education," Wesley Theological Journal, 45:2 (Fall 2010). Used by permission.
- Maddix, Mark A. "John Wesley and a Holistic Approach to Christian Education," Wesleyan Theological Journal 44:2 (Fall 2009), 76-93. Used by permission.

Finally, to God be the glory, Father, Son, and Holy Spirit, for the grace we receive and the hope we have in the fulfillment of the kingdom of God.

INTRODUCTION

Welcome to *Discovering Discipleship: Dynamics of Christian Education,* a Wesleyan approach to Christian education. When you think of Christian education in your church, what comes to mind? Where does discipleship occur and for what reason? How would you explain to someone in five minutes or less why Christian education is important to you? If you are interested in answers to questions like these, then we invite you to journey with us toward the goal of faithful discipleship.

We will introduce you to strategic theoretical principles that define discipleship, engage the current dynamics that influence Christian education, and suggest a design for discipleship in local ministries. We believe that our Wesleyan heritage offers a sound approach to discipleship for Christian communities of other traditions.

Our heritage does not place us in opposition to other traditions, but rather we remain Christians first and foremost, drawing from the resources of others across the history of the church. This ecumenical and evangelical awareness is reflected in our academic background and ongoing relationships with professional colleagues. As leaders in major academic guilds devoted to Christian and religious education, we are personally familiar with the passion and depth of many Christian educators in other denominations and social sciences. We are committed to incorporating their contributions in our own work to demonstrate the depth and wealth of discipleship within the kingdom of God.

While the kingdom of God is too rich and the church too diverse to limit discipleship to just one method, not every approach proves equally effective or faithful to God's desire and mission. We seek faithful discipleship—true to our convictions about God's work in Christ through the Holy Spirit, to our Christian heritage in the Wesleyan spirit, and to the contexts that challenge us—that will lead people to lives of holiness for the sake of others. We believe our Wesleyan heritage holds a key to this type of faithful practice, organized around the fundamental tasks of formation, discernment, and transformation. John and Charles Wesley's vision, articulated in the goal of holiness of heart and life and lived out through the process, the means of grace, offers just such an approach to discipleship. This Wesleyan approach seeks to honor God, to understand our role in contemporary context, and to guide persons and communities according to kingdom principles.

▶ WELLS AND MAPS:
  READING TO LEARN . . . NOT TO UNLEARN

We confess a deep concern that in offering this book for your reading and exploration we may contribute to your unlearning. Robert Boostrom (2005) observes that providing a comprehensive overview of material can lead to "non-thinking" (18-19) because the author has done your thinking for you. In other words, you might assume that we (the authors) have already given you (the reader) all you need to know, making further exploration or study unnecessary. If that sounds strange, then consider how many times you have taken a course and stopped learning about the subject once you passed the class. If you believe that in this book we have exhausted all possible disciplines on Christian education and organized the summaries into a comprehensive overview, you might study the text but not bother to learn the field. Reading in this way leads to unlearning, since you do not continue to think about, actively explore, or form your own ideas on the subject.

How do we address this concern? Does pursuing our passion to give you a comprehensive introduction to the world of discipleship, to introduce you to the field as we have known and taught Christian education for a number of years, and to frame key issues and provide helpful information for your benefit lead you to unlearn Christian education? Two metaphors, digging wells and charting maps, will help answer this question. Some subjects contain considerable depth, but we have only scratched the surface water table in this book. We have provided information, like water drawn from a shallow well, to satisfy your initial thirst for knowledge. As with a well, however, the more you dig and the deeper you go, the cooler and sweeter the water becomes. We hope you will continue to dig deep to find the true riches of Christian education for which we have given you a first sip. In a similar vein, we have charted the landscape, but you need to take the trip. Maps provide a two-dimensional overview of terrain. They point the way from one location to the next, but they rarely capture the full pictures of mountains, rivers, and deserts, much less the intimate experience of hills, streams, and woodlands. Mapmaking is only the start of the journey. Until you hike a wilderness, ride a river, or climb a mountain, you cannot truly know the story of the land. More important, until you chart your own course on the ground, you have not really traveled. It is one thing to approach the material as a tourist; it is quite another to become a pioneer.

We hope you will continue to read and continue to learn. We ask you to take what you read and dig deeper or chart new territory in the field of discipleship through Christian education. We will expose you to the "discipline" (Boostrom 2005, 48-50) of Christian education and invite you to allow this introduction to discipline your ongoing pursuit of faithful discipleship.

READING AND ORGANIZING

Four large domains form the four parts of this book: definitions, dynamics, design, and basic practices. Much of the material intersects with the life and thought of John Wesley, but we also lift up broader themes within Christianity that resonate with a Wesleyan perspective: the role of narrative in scripture, history, and personal lives; the nature of humanity and the important ways that people contribute to their own learning through the prevenient grace of God; communal as well as individual discipleship processes. Each of these themes, consistent with our Wesleyan heritage, emphasizes Christian practice, focuses on the goal of holiness of heart and life, and lifts up our missional roles as co-pilgrims on this journey as we all seek to become means of grace to others and to our world. We will note where these themes appear in other texts and sources. Three aspects of Christian practice—formation, discernment, and transformation—guide much of our work. We assert that faithful discipleship, that is, effective Christian education, organizes around these three fundamental components. If you are unfamiliar with this terminology, review chapter 5 and keep it as a reference point in your studies.

Part 1 defines the terms and basic concepts that shape our understanding of faithful discipleship (see chapter 1). As you begin to understand the state of Wesleyan Christian education, its value for local congregations, and its potential impact within larger evangelical and ecumenical contexts, you will see the source of our passion and form a point of reference for the rest of the work. We then move thematically through the role of scripture (chapter 2), the history of the church (chapter 3), and the place of theological convictions in shaping faithful discipleship (chapter 4). In each chapter, we explore these themes as methodological landscapes that inform our understanding of the process of Christian education. We then turn to the life of John Wesley, his efforts in Christian education (chapter 5), and an approach that arises from his use of the means of grace (chapter 6). These last two chapters are unabashedly Wesleyan, our response to the questions posed in chapter 1.

Readers familiar with the nature of foundational books in Christian education may ask how we address the role of philosophy, particularly different approaches to educational philosophy. Within the limitations of the size of this text, we have set forth our own philosophical and theological perspective. Contrary to some Christian education theorists, we believe John Wesley engaged a number of philosophical traditions: Locke's empiricism, the Neoplatonic thought of William Law and the Cambridge Platonists, mystical readings, and the implicit essentialist theory of the British schooling system of his day. His approach to knowledge might appear platonic, while his approach to experience could be quite pragmatic. His appropriation of different intellectual traditions was comprehensive, and his use of practices as well as his description of virtuous tempers was Aristotelian. Apparently, Rousseau receives the dubious distinction of being the only educational theorist Wesley openly disparaged in his day (Blevins 2005). Wesley's biblical and theological perspective incorporated a broad spectrum of disciplines, and we trust they infuse our approach as well.

Part 2 considers the dynamics of faithful discipleship. Christian education exists in changing contexts, and we need trustworthy guides to understanding the experiential world in which we live. Chapter 7 provides basic categories (development, learning, and faith) for this engagement, and reminds us that even our attention to dynamics can be active ministry. The following chapters explore these same contexts in depth, beginning with developmental processes (chapter 8), faith development (chapter 9), and learning theory (chapter 10). The section closes with another dynamic, shaping curriculum and teaching practices as our creative response to context (chapter 11). We see curriculum as a dynamic, interactive process rather than a static arrangement of content, a process that often resembles art more than science and one that complements the teaching/learning process.

This discussion on curriculum leads into part 3, where we begin to assist readers to faithfully incorporate the basic design of formation, discernment, and transformation within their own contexts. We believe that most sound Christian education surfaces from within congregations and ministries when core convictions encounter the unique conditions and circumstances of those communities. However, we do believe that we can rely on certain indicators, themes, and practices to help us identify and guide faithful efforts in discipleship. Rather than presenting a formula for success, these three chapters provide a framework for investigating and developing formative, discerning, and transformative practices that are consistent with the convictions that drive these efforts and pertinent to the local context. We suspect and trust that from this study of formation, discernment, and transformation, readers will identify other means and methods for practicing faithful discipleship in their congregations. The organization and interplay of these practices might be quite different from one community to another, but we believe that each ministry needs to incorporate all three approaches for faithful discipleship. Our goal is to equip readers with a working philosophy/theology of Christian education that allows them to respond to the questions we first posed about discipleship (When you think of Christian education in your church, what comes to mind? Where does discipleship occur and for what reason? How would you explain to someone in five minutes or less why Christian education is important to you?), and to help formulate effective and faithful Christian education systems for themselves and for the congregations and ministries they serve.

The final section, part 4, explores how the practice of faithful discipleship might be lived out in different educational environments and structures, through various age-level and family settings, and by shepherding others. The section is largely descriptive and practical; we recognize that our suggestions will be adapted and altered to particular cultural contexts and conditions. However, we felt it valuable to provide observations and principles that align with the philosophy and theology outlined in the text to guide faith practice.

The practice of faithful discipleship occurs in the daily life of Christian education in the local church, within its structures and developmental arenas and through faithful ministry. Christian educators spend much of their time and energy on developing practices that will foster faith and community formation. While no book can cover all aspects of ministry, the practices we have identified in part 4 provide an overview of the significant focus areas of faithful discipleship for Christian educators: context (learning environments, Sunday school, and small groups), development (age-level and family ministry), and ministry (administration, legal considerations, and leadership). We hope that these chapters will inspire readers to explore and develop practices and systems appropriate to their settings and that people will grow in their knowledge and relationship with Jesus Christ.

A WORD ON TEXTS AND CONTEXT

As you move through the book, you will recognize a wide range of references at the end of each chapter. Some of these writings hail from previous generations yet still serve as primary resources for the book. These texts might best be understood as classics, works whose intrinsic quality shapes a lot of what we know about Christian education. Authors like Augustine, Wesley, Comenius, Dewey, and even Erik Erikson represent substantive thought from which we all can benefit, even if we do not always agree with their perspectives. We draw from these significant, enduring resources much as Wesley drew from The Christian Library, the range of texts he edited and frequently cited as source material for his thinking.

Other listed texts represent both formative and informative sources from our own contexts as students and instructors in this discipline. Many of these are books we discovered during particularly rich periods of study in the areas of developmental theory, learning strategies, and curriculum development. These are texts that have survived the critical scrutiny of scholars and demonstrated their usefulness to practitioners. We suspect (and to some degree hope) that several of these books will become classics in their own right. Of course, not all of these will prove worthwhile in the long term, and we recognize our own context and preferences in their selection. I (Dean Blevins) remember reading a newly released book in which the author cited a famous theologian and commented that a particular quotation rang true—even twenty years later. A check of the reference, however, revealed that the comment by the famous theologian was now forty years old. Apparently the author worked out of a twenty-year-old paradigm! Hopefully, the resources we point to will prove a bit more immediate in application, even as they have borne the test of time.

The list of references also includes recent texts and articles. Christian education theory continues to move and shift over time. Often our own interests intersect with the edges of current research, where new knowledge appears to be created daily. We have chosen to act judiciously with these newer texts; they have yet to undergo the same range of measured critique and application as earlier materials, and we urge strategic consideration and use of these references.

A well-written book contains all three types of resources: perennial wisdom that stands the test of time, formative texts that have survived scrutiny and the tests of application, and recent, if untested, research that explores the boundaries of new knowledge and practice in our contemporary context. Our hope is that our own efforts prove faithful and enduring.

▶ REFERENCES

Blevins, Dean, contrib. 2005. Faithful discipleship: A conjoined catechesis of truth and love. In *Considering the Great Commission: Explorations for a Wesleyan Praxis of Mission and Evangelism.* Ed. W. Stephen Gunter and Elaine A. Robinson. Nashville: Abingdon Press.

Boostrom, Robert. 2005. *Thinking: The Foundation of Critical and Creative Learning in the Classroom.* New York: Teachers College Press.

DEFINING FAITHFUL DISCIPLESHIP

Where should one begin to understand the role of Christian education in the church? What is *Didache*? How does faithful discipleship occur in a Wesleyan tradition? These questions shape part 1. For our purposes, *Didache,* the Greek term for teaching, serves as a conceptual framework for discipleship that is both faithful to Christian convictions and representative of the Wesleyan tradition. Often we use the concepts of *discipleship* and *Christian education* interchangeably. *Discipleship* is the older concept of a particular way of living as learners and teachers in rhythm with the Holy Spirit. Many people associate Christian education with more recent approaches to teaching and learning, often anchored in approaches grounded in a modern understanding of educational theory and practice. While we validate many of these contemporary insights (as the book demonstrates), we also see Christian education as larger than modern educational methods. It includes spiritual formation, catechetical guidance, pastoral leadership, compassionate service, and missional engagement. These acts shape and form people as they grow in grace, which is the work of *discipleship.* God calls us all to practice faithful discipleship that includes specific Christian education efforts but implies a larger, holistic approach.

We begin with a rationale for a Wesleyan approach to Christian discipleship (chapter 1), the basics of scripture and basic methods of teaching the Bible (chapter 2), and the history of Christian discipleship through the church (chapter 3), often using resources from that history to guide this study. Chapter 3 addresses theological considerations of educating in a way that is both Christian and Wesleyan. Chapter 4 stays within the Wesleyan tradition to recount John Wesley's efforts in Christian education and provide a contemporary approach to organizing faithful discipleship true to the practice of the means of grace. Rather than present a traditional philosophy of Christian education, we have elected to provide a practical theological framework in chapter 5, one that reveals certain philosophical assumptions but also orients our approach in conversation with other efforts in contemporary Christian education. Chapter 5 actually serves as the orienting principle for the entire book. Students wishing to understand our particular passion for formation, discernment, and transformation (themes that run through other chapters) would be wise to review this material carefully.

We hope that this book on Christian education will guide faithful discipleship in any congregation or ministry that takes the Christian message seriously. The definition we give to *discipleship* should be broad enough to provide space for conversation in evangelical and mainline church traditions. We also recognize, however, that this book represents and resources a particular tradition focused on the vision of holiness of heart and life, anchored in the ministry of John Wesley. This is our context, and it frames our assumptions and passions as Christian educators. This book represents but one of many attempts to define and direct efforts at faithful discipleship throughout the church.

Nevertheless, the challenge remains to define faithful discipleship for a people who count themselves Christian and Wesleyan. John Wesley thought himself a Christian before he applied terms like *Methodist* to his movement. As Wesley was concerned with the renewal of the church and the redemption of a people, we take our clues from his efforts, our eyes focused upon Jesus Christ, by the grace of God and through the power of the Holy Spirit.

ONE

WHY DISCIPLESHIP FROM A WESLEYAN PERSPECTIVE?

▶ INTRODUCTION

Imagine you are interviewing for a youth ministry position in a local congregation anchored in the Wesleyan tradition. During the interview process one of the leadership asks you to describe your theology of Christian discipleship. What would you say? Another member of the leadership asks you to provide biblical foundations to Christian discipleship. What scripture passages would you use to describe Christian discipleship?

Imagine you are teaching a series on Christian discipleship. How would you compare a Wesleyan view of discipleship with those of other faith traditions? How would you describe Christian discipleship from a Wesleyan perspective?

To be a disciple is to be a follower of Jesus Christ. A disciple is a learner, a servant (*doulos*). Christians are called to lives of discipleship that emulate the life of Christ. Discipleship, regardless of the faith tradition, includes giving up your life in order to save it (Mark 8:34-38). The great commission given by Jesus to his followers was "to go and make disciples of all nations" (Matthew 28:19-20). This call is given to us as well. We are called to be Christ's ambassadors (see 2 Corinthians 5:20), to proclaim the good news to all nations.

▶ CHRISTIAN DISCIPLESHIP AND THE WESLEYAN CHALLENGE

All Christians hold to this biblical view of Christian discipleship; each faith tradition, however, gives specific expressions to what it means to be a follower of Jesus Christ. Some faith traditions place a strong emphasis on a contemplative life; some emphasize social justice and mercy, while others focus on moral behavior. Each is a valid expression of Christian discipleship, but none provides a complete view.

The Wesleyan faith tradition reflects one particular expression of Christian discipleship, rooted in the theology of John Wesley and in the American Holiness Movement. The Wesleyan tradition comprises several denominations, including the Church of the Nazarene, the Free Methodist Church, the Wesleyan Church, and the Church of God (Anderson). This book strives to develop a Wesleyan approach to Christian discipleship.

While the larger Methodist tradition has always focused on discipleship, there remains a tension between ongoing education and a prominent focus on revivalism and instantaneous experiences, often promoted by itinerant evangelists and others in leadership. These challenges affect our Wesleyan heritage in general and the broader Evangelical movement in North America. This chapter begins the process by providing a rationale for a Wesleyan approach to Christian discipleship and its value to the broader church today.

LACK OF LITERATURE

Wesleyan Christian educators have struggled to articulate the role of John Wesley's theology and Christian education in several settings (Blevins 1999; Maddix 2001). Even an emphasis in Wesleyan-oriented spiritual formation texts for lay discipleship (Tracy et al. 1994) must contend with explicitly non-Wesleyan, evangelical supplemental texts in Sunday school teacher training and a "generic evangelicalism" shaped by reformed educational paradigms from conservative evangelical traditions (York 1992; Gangel 1992).

There have been some responses to the disparity. Les Steele's book *On the Way* (1990) focuses on Christian formation, David Michael Henderson's book *John Wesley's Class Meeting* (1997) provides an educational framework for Wesley's small groups, and Sondra Matthaei's book *Making Disciples: Faith Formation in the Wesleyan Tradition* (2000) provides a strong argument for faith formation from the Wesleyan perspective. While these books offer a significant contribution to the field, none provides a comprehensive approach to Wesleyan Christian education for the twenty-first century.

LOSS OF THEOLOGICAL IDENTITY

The lack of a comprehensive approach to Wesleyan discipleship reflects another concern, that the reformed influence within American evangelicalism threatens Wesleyan identity (Benefiel 1996; Blevins 1998, 1999; Drury 1995; Hoskins 1997).

Steve Hoskins (1997) and Keith Drury (1995) suggest that the identity crisis indicates problems in the larger Wesleyan movement. According to Drury, a primary reason for the apparent death of the movement is that we have "plunged into the evangelical mainstream" (1995, 2):

> Over time we quit calling ourselves "holiness people" or "holiness churches" or "holiness colleges" or "holiness denominations." We began to introduce ourselves as "Evangelicals." We started becoming at home with NAE [National Association of Evangelicals] and CHA [Christian Holiness Association]. Local churches repositioned themselves as "evangelicals" in their communities . . . we gradually were assimilated into the evangelical mainstream. . . . The influence on our pastors [is from]

evangelical[s], not holiness leaders. Gradually the theology among our people became the same generic evangelical soup served at any other evangelical church. (Drury 1995, 2)

Until evangelicalism's collapse into fundamentalism in the twentieth century, the Wesleyan tradition was viewed within the broader Evangelical movement. *Evangelicalism* has been variously defined; according to American historian George Marsden, it refers to "a broad group of Christians who believe the same doctrines" or "a self-conscious inter-denominational movement, with leaders, publications, and institutions with which many subgroups identify" (1991, 5). The tension between interdenominational cooperation and doctrinal conflict occurs explicitly and implicitly between Wesleyan and evangelical concerns.

Has the tradition that seeks to be Wesleyan become more generally evangelical (and Reformed) to the neglect of its own distinctive theological heritage? Douglas Sweeney notes that American evangelicalism, in spite of its emphasis on revivalism, draws primarily from the Reformed church tradition and Calvinistic presuppositions, which often contradict Wesleyan theology (1991, 70-85). Wesleyan discipleship faces the challenge of differentiating between the implicit theology within the American evangelicalism subculture and a theology more consistent with the Wesleyan perspective.

For all of the theological distinctions between evangelicalism and Wesleyanism, the two traditions share a bit of history, including borrowed terminology. For instance, evangelicals claim Wesley as part of their common ancestry (Noll 2003), a particular point of departure that will be discussed later. Likewise, Wesleyans often adopt the modifier *Evangelical* to describe their actions and activities (Sanner and Harper 1978, 11). However, both traditions also assert that a "gap" (for some) or "chasm" (for others) remains between them.

Evangelicals (Noll 2004, 38) tend to be suspicious, if not actually dismissive, of the intellectual content within Wesleyan movements. Evangelicals also tend to misrepresent, if not completely misunderstand, the holiness doctrine of the Wesleyan tradition, often due to a lack of familiarity with current research (Geisler 2004, 238-40, 578-87). Wesleyans remain decidedly suspicious of Calvinist soteriology, be it substitutionary atonement or unconditional election (Dunning 1988, 378-79). Wesleyans note with alarm that appropriation of seemingly generic evangelical curriculum carries with it real soteriological risks (York 1992).

Other Wesleyan denominations also wrestle with the desire to be true to their Wesleyan roots. For example, David McKenna of the Free Methodist Church provides a link between the message of John Wesley and its relevance in our fast-paced, fluid, postmodern culture (1999). Theodore Runyon, a United Methodist, provides a sound description of John Wesley's theology as formulated in the eighteenth century and how it applies today to such issues as human rights, the problems of poverty and economic rights, and the rights of women (1998, 168). These world issues were concerns during Wesley's time that have new significance for today.

A strong Wesleyan voice within evangelicalism may prove beneficial for both traditions; each claims the brothers Wesley as part of its common ancestry (even if disputes began as early as Wesley's encounters with Puritan evangelicals). For instance, both Mark Noll (2000, 1-11) and Dallas Willard (2000, 30) claimed Wesley as each tradition's great-grandfather when an evangelical professorship was established at Yale University. George Marsden acknowledges the inclusion of Methodist, Pentecostal, and other movements as aids in diversifying the inauguration of the National Association of Evangelicals (1991, 28-31). The place of theologically sound Wesleyans within the Evangelical movement may ensure that a broader conversation continues within evangelical settings.

Wesleyans may also find new points of conversation and collaboration as evangelicalism changes in the face of new, postmodern adaptations. Henry Knight offers key comparisons between the emerging postmodern Christian consciousness and Wesleyan theology: "Wesleyans should support this new movement because the purposes and values that emerging churches seek to embody—their vision of discipleship, church, and mission—are highly congruent with those of the Wesleyan tradition" (Knight 2007, 34). Collaborations with new church leadership may open doors between Wesleyans and evangelicals that respect the contributions of both traditions.

These examples signify the emergence of a newly robust Wesleyan theology for the church. Therefore, a fresh attempt to recover a Wesleyan approach to Christian discipleship, based on John Wesley's theology, is a necessary and valuable contribution to this conversation.

▶ WESLEYAN THEOLOGY AND CHRISTIAN EDUCATION

Another rationale for a Wesleyan approach to Christian discipleship is the disconnection that often occurs between Wesleyan theology and Christian education. Theology should inform Christian education. What we believe about God, sin, and salvation should influence our educational practices. Randolph Crump Miller states, "The major task of Christian education today is theology, and in theology properly interpreted lies the answer to most of the pressing educational problems of the day" (1950, 4). Rediscovery of a relevant theology will bridge the gap between content and method, providing the background and perspective of Christian truth (15).

Historically, Christian education has been concerned with the knowledge of God (viewed through the lens of the tradition), the role of the church, the nature of human beings, the mission of the church in the world, and the method of theology (Seymour and Miller 1982, 10). By the end of the twentieth century, however, Christian education had been reduced to technique and skill development. Christian educators became more pragmatic, influenced by fads in Christian education, which resulted in a disconnection between their faith tradition and theology and their ministry practices. Pastors in the tradition may have a good understanding of Wesleyan theology, but they do not apply it in educational settings (Maddix 2001, 220). When pastors described how their theology influenced their educational practices, they used the language of Wesley's theology but did not connect it with their educational practices (ibid.). Pastors and Christian educators placed a strong emphasis on teaching and preaching a holiness message but were unable to see the impact of holiness on their practice of ministry. For a tradition to reflect John Wesley's theology, it must be seen in its ministry practice (25). Theology and practice inform each other; one cannot be divorced from the other. Mary Elizabeth Moore laments, "Theology remains little affected by educational practices," and educational practices are little affected by theological reflection. Moore calls for "theology and education to stand in relationship, to speak to one another, and to be reformed by one another" (1991, 1). Integration of theology and practice is central to a Wesleyan approach to Christian education.

▶ TOWARD A WESLEYAN APPROACH TO CHRISTIAN EDUCATION

A Wesleyan approach to Christian education will seek to recover Wesleyan theology and propose practices that are shaped by that theology. It will include a renewed focus on Wesley's view of sacramental theology, specifically the "means of grace"; Wesley's focus on Christian conferencing in small groups as an avenue for "growth in grace"; and a renewed interest in Wesley's view of holiness as a process of "growth in grace" (Maddix 2001, 225). These will be covered in detail in later chapters, but a brief overview is helpful here.

"MEANS OF GRACE"

John Wesley's theology and educational perspective were most clearly reflected in his view of the "means of grace" (Blevins 1999, 21-30). God ordains these outward signs, words, and actions as channels that convey his grace. The means of grace include practices that Christians associate with spiritual formation: the Eucharist, Bible reading and proclamation, prayer and fasting, worship, service and social ministry, church and small-group participation.

As described by Wesley, God conveys grace toward humanity through these educational and ministry practices, thus leading to spiritual maturity and holiness of heart and life. "For Wesley, the means of grace provide an inner logic that asserts that the means to Christian life (salvation) and the ends of the Christian life (holy living) are intertwined within the practices of the means of grace" (Knight 1992, 168-96).

The means of grace provide an orienting framework for Christian education. Undergirded by Wesley's sacramental theology and his desire for a transformative holiness of heart and life, the complementary approaches we have already identified as *formation, discernment,* and *transformation* constitute an authentic Wesleyan Christian education. Wesley's organization of the instituted and prudential means of grace, along with acts of mercy, corresponds with educational theories of formation, discernment, and transformation (see chapter 5).

SMALL GROUP FORMATION

A second aspect of a Wesleyan approach to Christian education includes the recovery of Wesley's small group formation. Wesley's development of interlocking groups of societies, classes, and bands provides the overall framework for accountability, relationships, and spiritual formation for Methodism (Henderson 1997, 83-126). Wesley's system of group formation is distinct and was the primary basis for the success of Methodism. His development of groups as a means for holy living is unparalleled in eighteenth-century England. It reflects his soteriological focus on "holiness of heart and life." D. Michael Henderson's groups, which emphasize cognitive (societies), behavioral (classes), and affective (bands) aspects of human development, fit naturally into Wesley's model. Henderson's system of group formation could be adapted for congregational use as a means of spiritual growth and discipleship (1997), reclaiming Wesley's distinctive approach to spiritual formation and discipleship.

"HOLINESS OF HEART AND LIFE"

The goal of Wesleyan educational ministry is "holiness of heart and life." Wesley's soteriological focus was most clearly reflected in his desire for holiness and sanctification of all humanity. Holiness of heart and life is the driving force behind all of Wesley's educational practices. It is the *telos* of all ministry and educational practices.

Christian educators and pastors differ in their views of *holiness.* Some believe that holiness of heart and life is a process of development, while others see holiness as an instantaneous event. A Wesleyan approach to Christian education includes the understanding of holiness as a process of growth through participation in the means of grace and a life of obedience to God, which is central to Christian discipleship.

▶ CONCLUSION

The need for a Wesleyan approach to Christian discipleship is evidenced by the lack of literature in the field of Christian education, the concern about a loss of theological identity within the Wesleyan tradition, and the significant role theology plays in informing Christian discipleship. Christian educators within the Wesleyan tradition have a renewed interest in John Wesley's theology and its relationship to Christian discipleship. This book develops a fresh approach to Christian discipleship from a Wesleyan perspective by focusing on the means of grace as an orienting framework for Christian education that incorporates Wesley's model of interlocking learning and formation groups, with the primary goal of holiness of heart and life.

▶ REFERENCES

Benefiel, Ron. 1996. The Church of the Nazarene: The fragmentation of identity. Paper presented at the Association of Nazarene Sociologists of Religion Annual Conference, Kansas City.

Blevins, Dean G. 1998. Denominational identity and higher education: Formation and discernment. In *Christian Education Journal* 2:111-22.

_____. 1999. *John Wesley and the Means of Grace: An Approach to Christian Education.* Ph.D. diss., Ann Arbor, MI: UMI / Claremont School of Theology.

Drury, Keith. 1995. What happened to the holiness movement? Paper presented at the conference for Holy Living in a Post-Christian Age, The Wesley Center for Applied Theology, Nampa, ID.

Dunning, H. Ray. 1988. *Grace, Faith, and Holiness.* Kansas City: Beacon Hill Press of Kansas City.

Gangel, Kenneth O. 1992. Ten steps to Sunday school revival. In *Preacher's Magazine* 68:4-6.

Geisler, Norman L. 2004. *Systematic Theology.* Vol. 3: *Sin/Salvation.* Minneapolis: Bethany House.

Henderson, D. Michael. 1997. *John Wesley's Class Meeting: A Model of Making Disciples.* Nappanee, IN: Evangel.

Hoskins, Steve. 1997. The Wesleyan-holiness movement in search of liturgical identity. In *Wesleyan Theological Journal* 31 (1-2): 121-39.

Knight, Henry H., III. 1992. *The Presence of God in the Christian Life: John Wesley and the Means of Grace.* Metuchen, NJ: Scarecrow.

_____. 2007. John Wesley and the emerging church. In *Preacher's Magazine* (Advent/Christmas): 34.

Maddix, Mark A. 2001. *Reflecting John Wesley's Theology and Educational Perspective: Comparing Nazarene Pastors, Christian Educators, and Professors of Christian Education.* Ph.D. diss., Trinity Evangelical Divinity School / Ann Arbor, MI: UMI.

Marsden, George A. 1991. Fundamentalism and American evangelicalism. In *The Variety of American Evangelicalism*, 22-35. Ed. D. W. Dayton and R. K. Johnston. Downers Grove, IL: InterVarsity Press.

Matthaei, Sondra H. 2000. *Making Disciples: Faith Formation in the Wesleyan Tradition*. Nashville: Abingdon.

McKenna, David L. 1999. *What a Time to Be Wesleyan*. Kansas City: Beacon Hill Press of Kansas City.

Miller, Randolph C. 1950. *The Clue to Religious Education*. New York: Scribner's Sons.

Moore, Mary E. M. 1991. *Teaching from the Heart: Theology and Educational Method*. Minneapolis: Fortress.

Noll, Mark A. 2000. Evangelicalism at its best. In *Where Shall My Wond'ring Soul Begin? The Landscape of Evangelical Piety and Thought*, 1-26. Ed. M. A. Noll and R. F. Thiemann. Grand Rapids: William B. Eerdmans.

_____. 2003. *The Rise of Evangelicalism: The Age of Edwards, Whitefield, and the Wesleys*. Downers Grove, IL: InterVarsity Press.

_____. 2004. The evangelical mind today. In *First Things* 146 (October): 34-39.

Runyon, Theodore. 1998. *The New Creation: John Wesley's Theology Today*. Nashville: Abingdon.

Sanner, A. Elwood, and Albert F. Harper, eds. 1978. *Exploring Christian Education*. Kansas City: Beacon Hill Press of Kansas City.

Seymour, Jack L., and Donald E. Miller, eds. 1982. *Contemporary Approaches to Christian Education*. Nashville: Abingdon.

Steele, Les L. 1990. *On the Way: A Practical Theology of Christian Formation*. Grand Rapids: Baker Books.

Sweeney, Douglas A. 1991. The essential evangelical movement and the observer-participant dilemma. In *Church History* 60 (1): 70-85.

Towns, Elmer L. 1993. *Ten Sunday Schools That Dared to Change*. Ventura, CA: Regal Books.

_____. 1994. *Characteristics of a Healthy Sunday School*. Sunday Ministries Division, Church of the Nazarene, Kansas City: Nazarene Publishing House, videocassette no. VA-603.

Tracy, Wes, et al. 1994. *The Upward Call: Spiritual Formation and the Holy Life*. Kansas City: Beacon Hill Press of Kansas City.

Welch, Don. 1984/1985. *American Adult Sunday School Leadership in the Church of the Nazarene, 1907-1994*. Ph.D. diss., Kansas Univ. / Ann Arbor, MI: UMI.

Willard, Dallas. 2000. Christ-centered piety. In *Where Shall My Wond'ring Soul Begin? The Landscape of Evangelical Piety and Thought*, 27-36. Ed. M. A. Noll and R. F. Thiemann. Grand Rapids: William B. Eerdmans.

York, Mark. 1992. Is your congregation a church at risk? In *Preacher's Magazine* 68 (1): 10-12.

TWO

THE STORY OF GOD

▶ INTRODUCTION

Imagine yourself in a meeting with two Sunday school teachers. The first states emphatically, "If we could just get back to the New Testament, then all of our problems would be solved in this church." The second responds, "That may work for you, but I don't know why we have to spend so much time in Bible study with youth when we know they really want time for fun and fellowship. If we just change our emphasis, we could double our youth group in a month!" How would you respond?

Faithful discipleship does not emerge from a vacuum but from the life of the Christian church and resonates with the sources of faith, particularly the scriptures and tradition. It springs from God's ongoing activity, revealed in scripture and demonstrated through the history that continues to shape and influence our assumptions about the nature of the church. This chapter explores the role of the preeminent source for discipleship, the Bible, in the history of Christian education as believers in each generation have used it to inspire and teach.

▶ SCRIPTURE: CONTENT, CONTEXT, AND COMPASS

What is the role of scripture in shaping Christian education? The Bible is fundamental to any effort in discipleship formation and offers us diverse yet rich responses to the question. We see the Bible as providing content, revealing context, and serving as a compass in Christian education.

CONTENT: THE FORMATIVE CENTER OF CHRISTIAN EDUCATION

The Bible provides specific content for Christian education, but it is not the only information the church communicates. From the early church forward, Christians have also learned the essentials of the faith through doctrinal statements such as the Apostles' and Nicene Creeds and through worship practices shaped by the Christian year. It should be no surprise that the church formalized its creeds and established many of its worship patterns and Christian festivals during the same time it was discerning the writings that would comprise the biblical canon (Johnson 2006). Nevertheless, scripture remains the primary resource for faithful discipleship, providing the formative foundation of saving faith and faithful principles for Christian living. The importance of scripture within a Wesleyan framework surfaces from John Wesley's own admission:

> I have thought, I am a creature of a day, passing through life as an arrow through the air. I am a spirit come from God, and returning to God: Just hovering over the great gulf; till, a few moments hence, I am no more seen; I drop into an unchangeable eternity! I want to know one thing—the way to heaven; how to land safe on that happy shore. God himself has condescended to teach the way: For this very end he came from heaven. He hath written it down in a book. O give me that book! At any price, give me that book of God! I have it: Here is knowledge enough for me. Let me be *homo unius libri* [A man of one book]. I sit down alone: Only God is here. In his presence I open, I read his book; for this end, to find the way to heaven. (Wesley 1984, 1:104-5)

Finding the "way to heaven" for Wesley included doing God's will on this earth ("on earth as it is in heaven" as the Lord's prayer states) in accordance with the lessons derived from scripture. Indeed, scripture invites teaching. The shape of the book of Deuteronomy assumes a literate audience; it served a Levitical teaching community and explained the processes required to be shaped into the people of God. The Psalms provide a basic guide to prayer and worship. The Gospel of Matthew includes large blocks of scripture arranged for memorization, and the Letter to the Ephesians was written to be circulated and studied throughout the region. Scripture invites discernment, encourages formation, and calls for continuous engagement and life application. Understanding the impact of scripture on the lives of the first readers and believers through the centuries aids our own experience of it as a guiding, formative presence.

Christian educator Donald Miller notes that people often approach scripture expecting the Bible to function in a particular manner, particularly when thinking about how the text intersects with life (1987, 103-5). Some people see scripture serving primarily as a source of *propositional* knowledge (i.e., information that provides, or proposes, a clear explanation and understanding of a subject; also known as informational knowledge). As in textbooks and technical manuals, biblical verses reveal abstract principles that simply need to be memorized and applied for the sake of personal salvation and Christian living. This approach relies on a critical mass of information that irrefutably proves God's truths and compels transformation. However, Les Steele notes that this view often detaches scripture from life and ends up dividing people over which statements have priority (e.g., dress, conduct, or the role of women)

(1990). Other people see scripture as a historical account of religious experience in the past. These persons view the Bible as a deposit of experiential knowledge that we can delve into and hopefully replicate in our daily practice by developing analogous experiences through activities (often fun activities) that prove the validity of God. Unfortunately, such a view often pits the experience of the past (in the Bible) with contemporary experience in a kind of tug-of-war over which is valid. A third approach primarily sees scripture functioning to facilitate an existential encounter with God. This view assumes that scripture speaks directly to our lives, challenges us moment by moment as we read, and calls us to response. Every time we pick up the text, we are reminded of Paul's admonition in 2 Corinthians 5:19 (ESV) that "in Christ God was reconciling the world [even YOU] to himself"! Rather than analyzing the text for guidelines, or probing for historical insight, we merely prepare ourselves to hear and respond through worship and obedient living. Miller notes that this in-your-face approach to Bible study anticipates change but often proves hard to maintain and tends toward manipulation over time.

Each of these approaches might serve a valid purpose in particular circumstances. There is, however, one additional approach that has broader application and resonates with Wesleyan perspectives. While scripture serves many different functions, the content of the Bible is a narrative, or story, leading readers to understand the nature of God and God's actions on behalf of creation, including humanity. Biblical scholar Tim Green notes:

> More than simply telling numerous disconnected stories, we recognize that for the people of God there exists a grand narrative, beginning with the earliest chapters of the Bible and extending through the history of the Christian church to the present day. It is a *megastory* with a grand plot: God is reconciling the world to himself through His people. In more recent years, such an approach to ministry that calls persons to find their identity within the grand Story of God has been given the name narrative. (2001, 26)

A narrative approach to reading (and living into) scripture connects the power of God to the daily lives of people throughout history. According to Les Steele, the Bible contains two major narrative acts (Old and New Testaments) that disclose in broad fashion the meaning of scripture. Act One includes accounts of the story of God and God's intimate relationship with creation, the implications of sin through the Fall, and God's repeated calls to return to covenant relationship. In these stories, one repeatedly senses the love of God, the beauty of creation, humanity's brokenness, and God's steadfastness in pursuing faithful relationship with humankind (1990, 17-22). Act Two includes the stories of incarnation and Christian identity. The Gospel narratives reveal

God's persistent love in the person and mission of Jesus Christ, inviting us to "come along" as disciples of Christ, from birth to ministry and from death to resurrection (22-35). The rest of the New Testament invites us to follow the Holy Spirit as God reveals Jesus again and again through the ministry of Peter, John, Stephen, and Barnabas, through the language of Paul and James, and the visions of John.

DIFFERENCE BETWEEN NARRATIVE AND EXPERIENTIAL

In experiential models, the Bible is simply an account of another's experience, read to inspire one's own experience; in narrative models, the Bible is shared story (so the Bible produces experience as well as describes it). The narrative approach overcomes issues of authority. Liberalism (grounded in experiential learning) tended to diminish the authority of scripture and emphasize contemporary experience. The narrative approach challenges this by showing the necessary link between story and experience in order to interpret, critique, or reexperience life through the story.

Like a jewel, scripture offers many individual facets that illuminate. Some offer straightforward assertions ("if Christ has not been raised, . . . your faith is in vain" [1 Corinthians 15:14, ESV]), some are descriptive accounts (the shaping of the nation of Israel and the early church), some boldly confront (God was and *is* in Christ reconciling the world . . . even you!). The true beauty and power of the Bible, however, is revealed when the jewel is viewed in its entirety; the master narrative, or *megastory,* of the Bible provides opportunity to teach the content of scripture as a living story wherein people can discover the "strange new world" (Barth 1928/1978, 28-50) of the Bible and their lives within it.

DISCERNING CONTEXT: SITUATING SCRIPTURE

While teaching the content *of* scripture is one aspect of the formative role of the Bible in Christian education, we must also learn *from* the scriptures to ensure that our discipleship proves faithful. Obviously, our approach to understanding the content will influence our choice of the methods we employ (the process). Does scripture offer counsel about the appropriateness of teaching? Are historical accounts or exhortations to teach revealed in the text? Do larger narratives provide themes to guide our efforts? Christian educators have drawn from all of these approaches in exploring the Bible for help. In one approach, we compare the historical accounts in the Bible with our larger understanding of education in the Old Testament and New Testament eras. We will cover this approach later in our own historical overview (see chapter 3). In another method, ministers cite specific passages as either abstract instructions or existential challenges to discipleship practice. These efforts can offer limited success, but sometimes cause major problems and misunderstanding. For instance, one workshop leader used John 8:6 (Jesus writing in the sand during the attempt to stone the woman caught in adultery) to indicate that Jesus endorsed the use of audiovisuals! While Jesus certainly employed imagery in his teaching, taking an incident out of biblical context does not make the case for the use of PowerPoint or screens in the church. In another setting, a youth leader used the Luke 2:41-52 passage (Jesus among the teachers in the Jerusalem temple) to infer that youth ministry's importance stems from Jesus' "teenage" years. Again, a little bit of contextual research concerning a Jewish understanding of childhood and adulthood would have saved some embarrassment down the road. As Donald Miller (1987, 108-9) and Robin Maas (1982, 58-90) note, we must approach scripture carefully, using the full range of scholarly studies available to us.

How can we appropriately draw on specific passages from the story of God? One faithful approach surfaces when we seek to discern the educational pronouncements and methods used in scripture. Through thoughtful reading, verses will surface that educators grasp to explain or justify their teaching. These are not abstract concepts; they are educational proverbs, short statements that serve as doorways to a wealth of God's wisdom. For instance, in Deuteronomy 6:1-9, verses 4-5 include the great *Shema* (Hebrew for "hear"), or commandment, that summarizes much of the teachings of the nation of Israel. "Hear, O Israel: The LORD our God, the LORD is one. Love the LORD your God with all your heart and with all your soul and with all your strength."

This creed is a powerful, straightforward statement that opens a door to God's intent for Israel. It is a doorway that opens to the Ten Commandments, to the entire book of Deuteronomy, and ultimately to the teachings of the first five books of the Bible, known as the Torah, or Law, to Jews. This simple, two-verse admonition also propels us into the rest of the Old Testament: the struggles of Israel in repeatedly breaking and reclaiming this commandment, the role of the prophets, the Exile and return to rebuild Israel. This small statement is the gateway to a big story. So what else do we find in this passage? A quick read reveals admonitions to receive this commandment as a family (verses 1-2) and to communicate the meaning of the Shema to everyone. Listen to the action verbs that follow in verses 6-9: *"Impress* them on your children. *Talk* about them when you sit at home and when you walk along the road, when you lie down and when you get up. *Tie them as symbols* on your hands and bind them on your foreheads. *Write* them on the doorframes of your houses and on your gates" (emphasis added).

If the Shema stands at the center of the entire message of the Old Testament, the commandment to teach occupies the same space as a response to God. The passage in Deuteronomy opens a door to countless activities related to teaching and learning: communicate, instruct, model, exhort, inscribe, interpret, and live out these commands as a person, as families, and as the people of God. Robert Pazmiño (2008, 54-55) notes that other passages open similar doors, some more familiar than others. Each provides proverbial wisdom through language; when we listen with discernment, they also offer existential encounters to challenge us as teachers.

> Deuteronomy 30:11-20—A doorway into shaping a community toward God, reminiscent of the shaping of the nation of Israel through various teachings, practices, symbols, even the actions of Moses.

> Deuteronomy 31:9-13—A doorway into discipleship for everyone, which begins in community but requires personal engagement.

> Psalm 78—A doorway into the world of worship and praise that moves a people toward the love of God. Revealing what Pazmiño (2008, 51) calls the "education of worship."

> Proverbs 22:6—A proverbial doorway into the need for patient instruction of children, true from the time of the patriarchs to the shaping of Christian parenting in the New Testament, and true today.

> Matthew 5—7—A doorway to the true model of teaching, Jesus Christ. Other aspects of Jesus' teaching will be noted, but Christ demonstrates the centrality of teaching in revealing the kingdom of God.

> Matthew 28:16-20—A doorway to the ongoing tasks of daily discipleship, including initiating people into the community, shaping them in the triune life of God, calling them to obedience to the commands of Christ, and assuring them of the ongoing presence of the Spirit of Christ. Jesus' post-Resurrection commission reaches back to the calling/sending of the disciples and the "seventy-two" of Luke 9 and 10, and forward to the call of the seven deacons in Acts 6. It evokes Paul's admission of Christ's call to him to be an "apostle" (Acts 22 and 26), and the call of Paul's companions (2 Timothy 3—4; Titus 1—2) and others.

> Luke 24:13-35—A doorway into the various ways that the resurrected Jesus Christ encounters people and the role of teaching in the "journey" of discipleship. Luke 24 may contrast with Acts 9, where Paul's conversion is more dramatic (an in-your-face moment rather than the gradual awareness of the Emmaus road). Yet even Paul

needs discernment and explanation from Ananias (verses 17-19*a*) before he can move on in his journey.

Acts 2:42-47—A doorway into the life of the church. Maria Harris (1989) asserts that these activities constitute Christian community and discipleship as the basic tasks of discipleship organized through the life of the congregation. Following Harris's use of Greek terms for each task, this passage, with others, reminds us that discipleship occurs through worship (*leitourgia*), service (*diakonia*), teaching (*didache*), fellowship (*koinonia*), and witness (*kerygma*). As the church engages in these ministries of formation, communal care, and missional transformation, it shapes disciples.

First Thessalonians 2:7-12; Hebrews 5:11—6:3—Doorways to the attitudes and dispositions of teachers as ministers who are careful to understand the nature of disciples, shape teaching to the "readiness of learners," and model Christlikeness in a way that the Christian life is both taught and caught by example.

Ephesians 4:1-11—A doorway into the life of the church as a whole, joined together in the tasks of becoming a community of disciples, engaged in pastoral teaching but also other works of ministry that lead to Christian unity and maturity, the goal of the entire teaching of the New Testament.

Undoubtedly, there are other proverbial passages in scripture that open up the importance and practice of discipleship. The Christian educator asks not "which scripture?" but "how does this passage open up, challenge, describe, or invite me into the task of discipleship?"

Beyond this proverbial approach are other methods of discerning the context of discipleship in the Bible. Following the work of Maria Harris (mentioned with Acts 2:42-47), other educators have pondered how the narrative flow of scripture reveals something of the role of discipleship. Scholar Walter Brueggemann surveys the literary genres in the Old Testament and notes that each literary type, as a given form of narrative, invites different roles and goals for teaching. The first five books of the Bible, the Torah, provide a deeply formational approach focused on tradition and a sense of continuity, while the prophetic books open up God's Word to radical and disruptive new interpretations. Psalms reveals the height of the transformative glory of God, particularly through special moments of worship, while the wisdom of Proverbs reminds the reader how to discern God in everyday life (1982, see appendix 2.2).

Each narrative form exposes an entirely different means of seeking and understanding God's will, collectively providing a larger, complementary view of discipleship practices. Robert Pazmiño (2008, 46-53) offers a New Testament version, with the life of the church as the locus for discipleship. Pazmiño argues that comprehensive Christian education occurs through an integrated model that incorporates five complementary (and complimentary) approaches to discipleship. These tasks include *koinonia:* education for and of community; *kerygma:* education for and of proclamation; *prophetia:* education for and of advocacy; *diakonia:* education for and of service; and *leitourgia:* education for and of worship. Much like Maria Harris, Pazmiño sees these various expressions as places where discipleship occurs in the daily life and practice of the church.

A COMPASS TO GUIDE TRANSFORMATIVE TEACHING

How do we see ourselves modeling Jesus in our teaching and discipleship efforts? Christian educator William Yount offers one set of observations drawn from scripture (1996, appendix 3.2) and organized around the ideas that Jesus embodied what he taught, that he varied his teaching but focused on relationships, and that he understood the limits and potential of his students. Yount's and other similar observations provide a good beginning. However, as we follow the organization of the narrative themes, we note that Jesus both modeled and reframed several key aspects of teaching expected of rabbis in the Old Testament, expanding this task to include prophetic and mediating roles.

Jesus was a teacher; "rabbi" served as a primary description by the disciples. Jesus called followers to him (people we would least expect) and invited them to be shaped and formed into the model of discipleship prevalent in Jesus' day. Jesus also participated in Jewish festivals and practices such as baptism, while instilling new practices, such as Communion, to shape a new community. In this sense Jesus' role as rabbi expanded to encompass the mediating and pastoral roles of the priests of the Old Testament in shaping the children of Israel into a new community. Jesus claimed he was not abolishing Torah but filling it to its true fullness as God's attempt to shape a people in authentic discipleship. His prayers, such as the high-priestly prayer of John 17, fueled a vision of the future of discipleship. It is not surprising that Jesus was compared to Moses by the writer of Hebrews (see 3:2-16).

Jesus also assumed a sagelike role as a teacher. As Charles Melchert notes, Jesus did more than just recite scripture, he drew powerful images from everyday life through the parables, revealing timeless wisdom as he used these narratives to overturn the expectations of the religious ruling class (1998, 205-7). Jesus' craft at exposing religious assumptions and reframing life in light of the kingdom of God created a new and dangerous mode of discipleship for those who opposed him.

Finally, Jesus taught through his prophetic presence, in speech and by example. In the Sermon on the Mount (Matthew 5—7) Jesus asserted, "You have heard that it was said . . . but I say to you" (5:21, ESV). His pronouncements, much like the prophets before him, revealed the disparity between assumed beliefs and God's expectations. Jesus demonstrated his prophetic and divine role throughout the Gospel of John. Jesus revealed his divinity through miraculous acts, but he often turned these actions into opportunities to call people to embrace his role as "the bread of life" (John 6:35), "the light of the world" (8:12), and "the resurrection and the life" (11:25). As the Son of God, Jesus need not prove his divinity; however, he used his divinity in a prophetic manner to reveal his purpose and to announce the kingdom of God for the sake of his disciples.

In short, Jesus used every aspect of his life—priestly acts, sage teachings, and prophetic actions—to express and teach the kingdom of God. We might attempt to emulate Jesus' teaching methods, but we would be wise to remember who the Master Teacher is. We may be one of the disciples on the road with the Rabbi of rabbis, a Pharisee shocked out of religious complacency by a simple story of a sinner's prayer, or merely a Jewish or Gentile member of the Palestinian countryside observing an amazing miracle. In each case, Jesus invites us into the great, redemptive story of God that he both authors and narrates as the consummate Teacher. Rather than aspire to be *master teachers,* we should seek to work as the *Master's teachers;* attending and appreciating, yet remaining humbled by Jesus' ability and compassion. This approach gives us a trustworthy compass for our teaching. It reminds us that we are, with our students, inside God's story. Its grand narratives shape us and outfit us with a large array of methods of discipleship and goals worthy of the kingdom of God—all at the feet of the Master Teacher, Jesus Christ, the only true Rabbi, Savior, and Lord.

Just as Jesus inspires and humbles us as servants, we discover what true, faithful discipleship looks like through the story of God. The very methods that invite our students to participate in God's story also provide us with goals and a compass that direct our efforts. For example, Robert Pazmiño's integrative model provides not only tasks but also aspirations for our teaching. Pazmiño uses the same categories to remind us that we teach for a reason and that our efforts should cultivate theological virtues like faith (*kerygma*), hope (*prophetia*), and love both within the community (*koinonia*) and outward to the world (*diakonia*), virtues all summarized in our worship (*leitourgia*) of God extending "honor, glory, praise and worth to God" (2008, 46). These elements provide touchstones to remind us of the appropriate outcomes for our teaching, expressed in the Wesleyan tradition as the pursuit of holiness of heart and life.

Our careful attention to the narrative themes of God's story provides a powerful reference for assessing our efforts. Scripture reminds us of God's great creativity and invites us to participate through new and innovative forms of teaching. The text also reminds us of our responsibility to love and make disciples of people born in the very image of God and living under God's ongoing grace. We seek to be faithful as we reflect and represent God in the world. While we must remain vigilant to how easily we might be seduced to manipulate our educational efforts for the sinful goals of personal gain rather than Kingdom values, we can rest that a covenant-keeping, holy God calls us to partner with God in redemptive action. For our covenant to remain anchored in the work of Jesus and the power of the Holy Spirit, we must ask how our efforts at discipleship reflect Christlikeness and demonstrate our willingness to follow the leading of the Spirit. Ultimately we must assess how our teaching methods redemptively emulate life inside God's story, inside the kingdom of God. When we ask these questions we turn once more to the story of God and to the Master Teacher as our compass and guide.

▶ CONCLUSION

In Christian education, scripture provides an indispensible role as content, context, and compass. The Bible remains crucial, but not as a mystical text that possesses talisman-like power in itself, for that would be idolatry. As text and readers come together, scripture serves God's gracious desire to reveal Jesus Christ by the power of the Holy Spirit. The scripture provides information necessary for the salvation of persons, communities, and the world. This information primarily comes through the *megastory,* God's story, which reveals to us God's creative and redemptive power, indicates the object of his love in creation and in humanity that bears his image, and demonstrates the possibility of redemption through the work of the Master Teacher, Jesus Christ, and through the ongoing direction of the Holy Spirit.

▶ REFERENCES

Barth, Karl. 1928/reprint 1978. *The Word of God and the Word of Man.* Glouchester, MA: Peter Smith.

Brueggemann, Walter. 1982. *The Creative Word.* Minneapolis: Fortress Press.

Green, Tim. 2001. Participating in the story of God: A narrative understanding of Christian ministry. In *Worship-Centered Teaching,* 23-34. Ed. Jim Hampton and Rick Edwards. Kansas City: Beacon Hill Press of Kansas City.

Harris, Maria. *Fashion Me a People: Curriculum in the Church.* Louisville, KY: Westminster/John Knox Press, 1989.

Johnson, Maxwell F. 2006. The apostolic tradition. In *The Oxford History of Christian Worship,* 32-69. Ed. Geoffrey Wainwright and Karen B. Westerfield Tucker. New York: Oxford Univ. Press.

Maas, Robin. 1982. *Church Bible Study Handbook.* Nashville: Abingdon Press.

Melchert, Charles. 1998. *Wise Teaching: Biblical Wisdom and Educational Ministry.* Harrisburg, PA: Trinity Press International.

Miller, Donald E. 1987. *Story and Context: An Introduction to Christian Education.* Nashville: Abingdon Press.

Pazmiño, Robert. 2008. *Foundational Issues in Christian Education.* 3rd ed. Grand Rapids: Baker Books.

Steele, Les L. 1990. *On the Way: A Practical Theology of Christian Formation.* Grand Rapids: Baker Book House.

Wesley, John. 1984. Preface. In *The Works of John Wesley,* Vol. 1. Ed. Albert Outler. Nashville: Abingdon Press.

Yount, William. 1996. *Created to Learn.* Nashville: B&H Academic.

Appendix 2.1
Scriptural Approaches

Approach	Propositional (Informational)	Experiential	Existential	Narrative
Scripture	Asserts	Describes	Encounters	Invites
Knowledge	Information directs action	Scripture illustrates religious experience	Existential encounter inspires belief	Storied lives reshaped by gospel story
Method	Memorize and consent	Express and act	Hear and encounter	Hear and reinterpret
Learning	Learn by reproducing	Learning by doing	Learning by confronting	Learning by reliving the story
Activity	Memorization and practical application	Games and dramatic replication	Study and worship	Naming, exploring story, and retelling
Aim	Datable conversion	Growth and development	Continual conversion	Living into story
Limitations	Tends to divide	Subject to experiential interpretation	Tough on continuity	Messy to implement

Appendix 2.2
Teaching as Jesus Teaches

William R. Yount, *Created to Learn* (B&H Academic, 1996), 354-62.

Observations of Jesus the Teacher:
- He was what He taught
- comfortable with people of all kinds
- compassionate toward learners
- possessed a strong Father-focused self-concept
- Man on mission
- dynamic humility
- calmness under attack
- patient with disciples
- identified with the Father through prayer
- knew His learners
- Master of the Old Testament

Also Jesus' teaching approaches included
- established relationships with people
- stimulated and maintained interest
- taught by example
- taught people, not lessons
- focused on ever-smaller groups
- recognized the worth of His learners
- emphasized character more than content
- emphasized quality of effort over quantity of learners
- emphasized action over knowledge
- focused on structure more than detail
- stressed long-term rather than immediate results

Jesus also recognized the disciples as
- imperfect (met them where they were but did not leave them there)
- slow to learn (required patience)
- self-centered (had to break them out of their world)
- teachable (learning always a possibility)

THREE

DISCIPLESHIP THROUGH THE CENTURIES

▶ INTRODUCTION

Imagine yourself in a home where children and parents engage in this series of questions and answers:

Question: Why is this night different from all other nights of the year? On all other nights we eat with either leavened or unleavened bread. Why, on this night, do we eat only unleavened bread?

Answer: We eat unleavened bread to show how we hurried out of Egypt. There was no time to wait for bread to rise. This was the command of God.

Question: On all other nights we eat all kinds of herbs. Why, on this night, do we eat especially bitter herbs?

Answer: We eat bitter herbs to show the bitterness we experienced in Egypt.

Question: On all other nights we do not dip herbs in any condiment? Why, on this night, do we dip them in salt water?

Answer: The salt water represents our tears and misery in Egypt.

Question: On all other nights we may sit at the table erect. Why, on this night, do we recline?

Answer: Kings and emperors recline at the table to show their freedom. We do the same on this night because God has made us free.

Now imagine yourself in a small discipleship class, preparing for your baptism into the faith, hearing for the first time:

I believe in God, the Father Almighty,
Maker of heaven and earth;
And in Jesus Christ, His only Son, our Lord;
Who was conceived by the Holy Spirit,
Born of the Virgin Mary,
Suffered under Pontius Pilate,
Was crucified, dead, and buried;
He descended into hades;
The third day He rose again from the dead;

He ascended into heaven,
  and sits at the right hand of God the Father Almighty;
  from there He shall come to judge the living and the dead.
I believe in the Holy Spirit,
  the holy catholic (universal) Church,
  the communion of saints,
  the forgiveness of sins,
  the resurrection of the body,
  and the life everlasting.
Amen.

What makes these exercises educational? What difference do experiences like these make in our study of Christian education? What should we hope to learn from studying the past?

Christian education does not begin in a vacuum. We live in a given time in history with particular struggles and challenges, but teaching the story of God requires that we understand the stories of faithful discipleship from different eras of our history. We can learn from earlier efforts to form people as disciples, to lead them in discernment and empower them to act to transform the world. This is our heritage, and it provides fresh insights to our roles and responsibilities in Christian education today.

Scripture begins the grand story of God, the road to faithful discipleship. That story exists in, and comes to us through, a given history. As philosopher George Santayana reminds us, "Those who cannot remember the past are condemned to repeat it" (1905/1980, 122). However, our study of history does more than help us avoid the mistakes of the past. The stories of our heritage also help guide our present practice and shape future efforts in faithful discipleship. Traditionally, three approaches have shaped how scholarship presents the people and stories of history:

Romantic Biography or Hagiography: Eyewitnesses or early followers present historical figures and movements as larger than life and without flaw. Such efforts often stem from a desire to retain the best of the movement for future generations.

Honest Accounting: Later scholars revisit original materials to interpret more critically (and accurately) the real person or the movement's strengths and limitations. This usually includes situating the person or movement within the context of the historical forces that influenced them.

Replication of Intent: In a final phase, scholars reassess the person or movement in light of contextual realities, highlighting the original insights (limitations and all) and discovering their implications for the current context.

This approach represents a fairly sound model of learning: first, fascination with a subject forges deep bonds; second, engagement in a disciplined exploration of the subject (the good and the bad) encourages the critical thinking skills necessary for true understanding; and third, bringing the subject into conversation with present issues and concerns reinforces and secures both understanding and relationship. When true learning occurs in this way, the subject can then be integrated into current and future practice. All historical study should evoke these stages of respect, understanding, and application. The historical movements and persons we will cover in this chapter warrant such consideration, but we have space for only a brief review of believers who sought to disciple future generations based on their learning.

▶ ORGANIZING TIME

Any review of history raises the problem of organizing the efforts of discipleship into particular eras. The history of the church has several marker events or periods that have assisted other theorists writing Christian education histories (Pazmiño 2008, 133-66). However, we may include additional frameworks to help us understand and appreciate the efforts of each era, theoretical principles that surfaced, and the people or movements that gave life to those principles. While several strong historical overviews already exist (Estep et al. 2003; Reed and Prevost 1993), this chapter's brief chronology uses a unique set of criteria related to Christian education. The survey of each era will use the three primarily educational approaches of *formation, discernment,* and *transformation.* In a later chapter related directly to the Wesleyan tradition, we will explore these three approaches in greater detail. For now they will help to organize our historical review of faithful discipleship both topically and chronologically. We will review seven dominant eras of church development: (1) the historical forces that influenced and interacted with the Old Testament, (2) the New Testament (particularly Greek and Roman themes, (3) the early church, (4) the established church, (5) the Reformation era, (6) the modern church, and (7) contemporary Christian education.

We offer one early caution: while the study of the history of Christian education often names particular persons and movements as instrumental, the overall power of Christian discipleship rests in the gradual, formative processes of the church in general. Marianne Sawicki notes that the gospel story cannot be separated from the "portrait" of the life of the church. Local congregations exist as the result of the gospel, as the agent of the gospel, and as the primary medium and message by which the gospel represents God's redemption in and for the world (1988, 5-10). Historically, faithful discipleship must ask how the principles and practices of each era shaped and informed the people of God, particularly (for our task) as congregations within the history of Christianity.

OLD TESTAMENT ERA

Capturing the historical forces that shaped early civilization, which includes the patriarchs and the children of Israel, is a large task. These forces include the children of God living as a nomadic people in the midst of other larger cultures, escaping from slavery, establishing a monotheistic nation in the midst of polytheistic beliefs and practices, and later maintaining and reestablishing identity and tradition during exile, return, and occupation by the Babylonians, the Persians, and ultimately the Romans.

Formation: Early formative influences must include the family. Primarily nomadic during the time of Abraham, the family remained a primary agent in shaping children's lives. Family practices included both rituals and worship. As the children of Israel escaped Egypt and began their journey through the wilderness, formation took place at the community level. Many of the Levitical laws incorporated practices specifically intended to shape the twelve tribes into a coherent community. Ritual space like the tabernacle, priestly activities, and religious ceremonies and festivals extended as Israel became a nation with a temple and a formal system of worship (Estep et al. 2003, chapter 2). Later, during the Exile, the family would return to the center of religious life and practice. By the beginning of the New Testament, with the dispersion of the Jewish people throughout the ancient Near East, both family and synagogue collaborated as formative communities with specific stories, rituals, and festivals to guide formation within shifting contexts.

Discernment: As much as the Old Testament focused on God shaping his people into a particular community, the Jewish people were called to discern his ways. Discernment included literacy training, primarily for boys and men; some women were educated but only the aristocracy (Crenshaw 1998, 14-15, 168-69). Models of schooling began as early as the Babylonian teachers of cuneiform and extended to the education of the royal court by the time of Solomon. The emergence of wisdom literature and the role of sages in early Israel also expressed and influenced the desire to understand and appreciate God's work in the world. With the Exile and return of Israel to a decimated homeland, the role of the Torah quickly filled the absence of the temple. Study surfaced as a devotional process equal to worship. Jewish schooling following the Exile began as early as age five and proceeded through three levels of instruction: basic literacy, academic investigation, and advanced training (Estep et al. 2003, 3:9). The mere presence of the writing Prophets, along with expansion of the Hebrew scriptures to include both history and wisdom writings, gestures toward the growing emphasis of understanding God's intent for the Jewish people.

Transformation: While considerable emphasis may be placed on family formation and instruction of Torah, we must not forget that God had a particular purpose for Israel—to live out his promise for the sake of the world. Israel consistently failed in this, from Abraham's deception of Sarah to Moses' failure to possess the Promised Land, and on to the failure of judges and kings to keep Israel away from idolatry and political dependence on other cultures. Yet the prophets continually proclaimed that Israel should learn from its errors and should attempt to engage others as God's people. Israel's nomadic nature, from its tribal beginning to the Exile and return, is powerful evidence that Israel served to engage the larger culture, not escape from it.

NEW TESTAMENT ERA

Educational processes in the New Testament and early church eras drew heavily from both Jewish and Greek cultures. Paul was not only a rabbi (a Pharisee) but also a Roman citizen and probably received basic, if not advanced, Roman education. We will focus on the cultural expectations of education in this era, not only in and around Palestine but also throughout the Greek and Roman Empires that shaped this period.

Formation: With the rise of Greek education, a new formative emphasis stressed *padeia* (Greek for teaching) for the sake of citizenship. Greeks placed considerable emphasis on the city-state, and education shaped the soldiers and civic leaders who protected and governed the cities. Cultivation included training the body as well as the mind in gymnasiums. Many Greeks passed through three levels of learning: tutoring, elementary school (covering grammar, music, and physical education), and advanced lessons in philosophy and rhetoric. Collectively these educational schools sought to create literate, cultured, physically sound citizens who could reason clearly and argue forcefully for the sake of their cities.

Discernment: The emphasis on well-rounded, reasoned education ushered in several key subjects that later would form the liberal arts tradition of contemporary education. The Greek understanding of a well-rounded education introduced the trivium of grammar, rhetoric, and dialectic (reasoning) as well as the quadrivium of geometry, arithmetic, music theory, and science. These seven subjects cultivated basic intellectual abilities (trivium) and perennial cultural capacities (the quadrivium served travel, commerce, art, and technology) necessary for any good citizen. Greek education also sought to assist youth in the pursuit of virtues—truth, fidelity, beauty, and goodness—that were the ultimate goal of *padiea* (Estep et al. 2003, 4:16).

Transformation: Education for transformation took two distinct routes. Roman culture expanded the Greek process to prepare people not only for local citizenship but also for global engagement as the empire expanded. In a sense the Greco-Roman educational process prepared soldiers and citizens to expand the reach of Roman culture (Estep et al. 2003, 5:1-16). However, another form of transformation occurred through the life and ministry of Jesus. Jesus' engagement, teaching, and compassionate care modeled a different empire or Kingdom that also prepared its citizens to engage the world, not through control, but through proclamation and compassion. Paul modeled both routes of teaching. Utilizing both his rabbinic and Greek heritage, Paul used reasoning and rhetorical skills to argue the meaning of Jesus' life, death, and resurrection, and he proclaimed the message of the gospel to new and growing faith communities (Estep et al. 2003, 4:17).

THE EARLY CHURCH

The early church emerged from the preaching of the gospel. It lived first as a minority religion in a hostile culture, sought to distinguish itself from Judaism, endured persecution, and ultimately reframed itself as the state religion under the emperor Constantine. Discipleship practices shifted as the movement grew in respectability, but circumstances did not alter the challenge to develop faithful disciples.

Formation: Early church tasks included more than establishing the canon of the Bible (the books within it). The early church also established basic forms of worship, including the celebration of the Lord's Supper and the major festivals we call the Christian calendar (Advent, Christmas, Lent, Easter, etc.). Engaging scripture, worship, and celebrative life allowed Christians to "live into" the story of God (Johnson 2006). Early Christians often participated in an ongoing formational process, resembling the spiritual formation practices that occur in and through the church today: prayer, worship, devotional reading of scripture, service to others, and so forth.

Discernment: In addition to broad formative practices, a more formal process included preparation for church membership through baptism. This catechetical process involved specific stages of preparation, running up to two years before acceptance into the church. *Catechetical* and *catechumenate* both spring from the idea of catechesis or "echoing" the gospel (Harmless 1995, 39-69). This formal process might include specific instruction in the basics of the Christian faith, with the Bible and the Apostles' Creed serving as primary resources. As students progressed, they were allowed to stay longer in worship before being excused for instruction. "Hearers" stayed through the service of the word so they might hear the gospel preached before returning to instruction. "Kneelers" were allowed to remain for prayer so that they might participate in the life of the congregation. After being baptized, "The Chosen" participated in the Lord's Supper as full members of the congregation (Estep et al. 2003, 6:1-4). While this introduction to worship proved formative, its primary role was discernment. The persecuted church needed to be able to discern friend and foe, guarding against disclosing too much information, like the names of parishioners, to a stranger who might be a government spy. Provisional Christians needed to know enough about the faith of the church to be accepted as believers.

Transformation: Catechesis, however, stood not only for instruction but also for evangelism. Augustine, in his sermon "On the catechesis of the uninstructed," included strong injunctions to vary teaching based on the person's ability to understand and willingness to receive the gospel (Harmless 1995, 113-23). Educating people about the gospel remained a part of the missional life of the early church. During persecutions, the witness of the church stretched to include the martyrdom of early Christians, which often shaped the church's self-understanding of public evangelism (Harmless 2003, 50-51).

THE ESTABLISHED CHURCH

This period, which overlaps the early church, incorporates the longest Christian era. One might begin as early as Constantine's incorporation of the church into Roman culture and conclude with the divisions of the church, first the Greek Orthodox and Roman churches and later the Reformation. This period resembles, in part, the Old Testament; the church is at the center of power (in Rome and during the medieval era) and on the margins of power (after the empires in Rome and Constantinople fell). Whatever the challenges, Christian education often served the church by preserving or perpetuating faithful discipleship in the midst of changing historical forces (Sawicki 1988, 112).

Formation: Two eras of formation, often contrasted, served the church through this long period. The first surfaced just after the fall of the Roman Empire. Monastic orders, some of which sprang up in protest when the church served primarily as a civic religious institution under Rome, continued to develop under the names of Benedict, Augustine, Francis and Clare, Ignatius of Loyola, John of the Cross, and Teresa of Avila. These orders preserved the faith through disciplined living and daily devotion, serving as the formative presence of the church in the midst of despair or during periods of excess in the Middle Ages. Second, the church continued to shape Christian life through pastoral oversight. Leaders, like Rome's Gregory the Great and the Byzantine patriarchs of Eastern Orthodoxy, shaped pastoral roles and authority. They also established formal processes of worship that included artistic imagery, music, and pageantry to captivate worshippers and reinforce Christian concepts as they sought to provide an alternative, heavenly world to counteract the overwhelming struggles of daily living.

Discernment: Monasteries served as locations for the preservation of scripture and theology during the collapse of Rome (Reed and Prevost 1993, 111-19). Often these centers of learning collected and preserved the writings of the early church fathers (key leaders like Clement of Alexandria, Origen, Athanasius, and Augustine, who provided the key doctrinal teachings of the developing church). After the turn of the first millennium (A.D. 1000), as the church's influence grew again across the Western world, cathedral schools provided basic leadership education in key areas of church law, doctrine, and church governance. Cathedral schools later gave way to the rise of universities where the academic study of theology as the queen of the sciences and the emergence of the first doctors of the church established the official teaching office (magisterium) of the church (Osmer 1990, 73-83). Augustine and Origen gave way to the work of Lombard, Anselm, and Aquinas as the church sought to deepen and widen its understanding of the faith.

Transformation: Monks served not only monasteries but also the world. Throughout the darkest times the church continued to move and expand its influence in England, Germany, Russia, and other world regions. Some, such as Egypt's Coptic Christianity, established early. Other areas, such as Spain, struggled to remain Christian with repeated Islamic incursions. Discipleship often grew where the church encountered opposition (one must know what one believes in the face of suffering). But faith also developed through evangelism. Cathedrals stood in the centers of towns, providing needed services and guidance. Entire villages and regions embraced a church that influenced almost every aspect of personal life (Gonzales 1984/2007, 301-23).

THE REFORMATION

In some sense the Reformation can only be understood with the Renaissance as prologue. The incorporation of Erasmus' Christian humanism in northern Europe derives from the desire to return to original sources and the rediscovery of humanistic teachings from Greek and Roman times, as well as the celebration of innovation and learning (McGrath 2001, 39-44). At the same time, the period included growing distrust, manipulation, and layers of unreflective teaching that often strangled any sense of learning. In a desire to reform the church, Luther, Calvin, and others challenged the Christian faith with diverse, emerging traditions that demanded fresh approaches to faithful discipleship.

Formation: As with any new movement, the church (now denominationally oriented) faced the need to fashion new traditions and practices. New worship guidelines surfaced within each tradition, often combining a particular view of the Lord's Supper with specific church practices. New prayers and prayer books were written, either as devotional guides or as examples for the elect. Scripture was rehabilitated as a central focus for the church and provided in local languages, thanks to the development of the printing press. The ability to read scripture for oneself shifted formation from a congregational process to a personal or family endeavor.

Discernment: The desire to return to the Bible prompted Luther and other Reformers to push for education for all children (boys and girls). With a renewed interest in the Bible came the need for new commentaries and theological treatises. Protestant churches soon developed their own academic centers, and new church doctors (protestant ministers preached in academic gowns rather than priestly vestments during this era). Basic catechisms were written to be used in church or in homes, including Martin Luther's "Table Talks," *The Westminster Catechism,* and the Anglican Church's "Articles of Religion." In response the Catholic Church set forth a Counter-Reformation movement that included not only a rebuttal of Protestant thought but also a cleansing of Catholic excesses of the previous era (Haugaard 1981; Thompsett 1981). Christian educators faced the daunting task of sorting through the myriad theological claims to find the true way forward to faithful discipleship.

Transformation: If one wants to start a revolution (or a Reformation), one must convince the people of the need for drastic change. The printing press provided a powerful tool for getting positions circulated, thus helping to secure the success of the Reformation and establishing the need for universal education. As in earlier movements, Christian education proved important not only in spreading the gospel but also in distributing corrective interpretations to new members of upstart churches. Teaching was seen as both heroic and subversive, depending on the perspective of the teacher. Writings from independent movements, some suppressed by the institutional church (Catholic and Reformed), surfaced to provide a rich view of the Christian life. Christian education was exciting and dangerous, depending on which theological view prevailed with the political and religious leadership. In England alone, massive shifts during this period marked the rise of Anglican, Catholic, and Puritan leadership that rocked the religious and educational landscape for nearly two hundred years.

THE MODERN CHURCH

If the Renaissance served the Reformation, the Enlightenment of the eighteenth century shaped the modern church. Disillusioned by the religious and political strife of the previous era, intellectuals began to focus on the reasoning individual as the source of knowledge rather than on religious or institutional authority. This turn to the individual included a new emphasis on individual religious experience (also known as Pietism) and fresh insight into the education of children. The church faced new challenges in reasserting the gospel in an age of reason in which faith and thought seemed pitted against each other.

Formation: Concurrent with the Enlightenment, a number of dedicated educators and theorists opened the door to the world of children and learning. Controversial theorist Jean Jacques Rousseau suggested that children, as "noble savages," merely needed to be freed from adult intervention to excel. Others, such as John Amos Comenius, Johannes Pestalozzi, and Friedrich Froebel (founder of the Kindergarten), discovered that children excelled in the world of experiential learning. Formation, far from controlling children's development, became a means to help children engage and flourish as they explored the world through their senses. Early educational efforts in the United States included the creation of the McGuffey Reader, which shaped a generation of young learners. A uniform Sunday school curriculum often circulated in local churches and town newspapers at the turn of the twentieth century (Estep et al. 2003, 11:1—13:10). Religious experience itself provided a powerful formative influence. The great awakenings of the eighteenth and nineteenth centuries, characterized by large interdenominational meetings and expressive religious actions (revival movements), shaped youth and adults through demonstrative altar calls and small-group Bible studies focused on cultivating personal religious experience. With the focus on individual change through personal devotional practices, demonstrative worship and small-group accountability marked the life of the church and most private Christian schools.

Discernment: Focus upon the individual provoked an incredible range of studies on personality and learning. One of the earliest changes included in-depth study of curriculum and the shift to a graded lesson plan for different age-groups. The emerging discipline of psychology included theorists such as Jean Piaget, Erik Erikson, and James Fowler, whose insights into learning, human development, and faith deeply influenced the development of contemporary Christian education. In time, Christian education became a professional field, first through the Religious Education Association and later with the development of church-related departments of Christian education and the North American Professors of Christian Education (Maddix 2003, 14:1—15:31). As a specialized field that served both churches and Christian schools, the discipline of Christian education (CE) investigated a number of specialized domains within psychology, sociology, and education that informed in-depth attempts to connect the Bible and doctrine to daily life for the sake of faithful discipleship (CE20 Project 1998).

Transformation: Robert Raikes' founding of the Sunday school in England took root in the United States as a primary agent of education on the frontier (Lynn and Wright 1971). Christian education had already served the early colonies through mandated schooling acts and the efforts of the Society to Promote Christian Knowledge (Reed and Prevost 1993, 293-99). However, the rise of industrialization and shifts in population resulted in the creation of organizations to advocate on behalf of youth, including the YMCA, YWCA, and Christian colleges. Later efforts included local church youth groups modeled after the nineteenth-century youth organization Christian Endeavor. The stratification of youth through the public school system in the twentieth century resulted in a number of relationally based, experientially focused youth programs like Youth for Christ and Young Life, which continue to influence youth ministry approaches (Senter and Kesler 1992, 71-106). The modern church enjoyed the rise of an experiential Christianity that reached generation upon generation of new believers through discipleship efforts.

THE CONTEMPORARY CHURCH

Beginning with the late twentieth century, the world began to see new shifts in both intellectual approaches and in gospel expansion. With the rise of multiple cultural perspectives, the monolithic view of individual reason has begun to break down. Churches suddenly find they are freed from strategies focused on proving the gospel, and they might proclaim and make disciples again. In addition, the rapid expansion of Christianity in the southern hemisphere presents incredible challenges in teaching entire regions of new and emerging Christians while ensuring that people engage the gospel in light of their own cultures. Even where Christianity serves as the predominant (but not necessarily dominant) faith tradition, new trends in proclamation and learning often surface simultaneously. What does the future hold for faithful discipleship? The following tentative observations offer some clues to the future.

Formation: Future generations of Christians find themselves facing a world deeply pluralistic and fragmented. A return to basic Christian practices that shape and give life to Christian faith seems to be the direction of the future (Bass 1998). Rather than a potpourri of specialized studies for personal development, recent initiatives advocate for a church anchored in prayer, worship, study, and ministry; in other words, a church that returns to the basic formational practices that deepen Christian lives.

Discernment: New technologies, particularly in media, call for ongoing discernment in developing the best educational practices (Hipps 2006). With the recognition that social context influences personal development, greater attention is being given to discipleship that is anchored less in developmental psychology and more in cultural analysis and multicultural engagement. The rise of neuroscience, however, promises to create new interest in the nature of learning and personal transformation, which could yield a healthy balance between communal and personal factors that shape Christian education.

Transformation: Recent interest in the meaning of *missional* seems to be raising evangelistic endeavors beyond personal engagement (Guder and Barrett 1998). The idea that the church serves as God's agent in the world should shift the focus away from Christian education as a means of inviting people *into* the church through educational, age-specific events. Instead, congregations will explore new modes of discipleship and leadership development that empower people to live out the gospel in local and global communities *as* the church.

▶ CONCLUSION

Each historical era included a number of influences that shaped educational principles and practices. Those influences included social/cultural assumptions, economics, political influences, technological advances, and philosophical insights. Faithful discipleship always attempts to bring enduring gospel principles to light within a particular historical setting. Understanding the strengths and limits of each era requires greater attention than this chapter can give, but the innovation and determination to provide Christian education throughout the church's history demands our attention and appreciation if we desire to be as faithful in our efforts today and into the future.

▶ REFERENCES

Bass, Dorothy, ed. 1998. *Practicing Our Faith: A Way of Life for a Searching People.* San Francisco: Jossey-Bass.

CE20 Project: Christian Educators in the Twentieth Century. Talbot School of Theology/ Lilly Endowment 1998, available online, http://www.talbot.edu/ce20 (accessed May 28, 2009).

Crenshaw, James L. 1998. *Education in Ancient Israel: Across the Deadening Silence.* New York: Doubleday.

Estep, James Riley, Jonathan Hyungsoo Kim, Alvin Wallace Kuest, and Mark Amos Maddix. 2003. *C.E.: The Heritage of Christian Education.* Joplin, MO: Teacher's College Press.

Gonzales, Justo L. 1984/2007. *The Story of Christianity: Complete in One Volume, The Early Church to the Present Day.* Peabody, MA: Prince Press.

Guder, Darrell L., and Lois Barrett, eds. 1998. *Missional Church: A Vision for the Sending of the Church in North America.* Grand Rapids: William B. Eerdmans.

Harmless, William. 1995. *Augustine and the Catechumenate.* Collegeville, MN: Liturgical Press.

Haugaard, William P. 1981. The continental reformation of the sixteenth century. In *A Faithful Church: Issues in the History of Catechesis*, 109-73. Ed. John H. Westerhoff III and O. C. Edwards Jr. Wilton, CT: Morehouse-Barlow Co.

Hipps, Shane. 2006. *The Hidden Power of Electronic Culture: How Media Shapes Faith, the Gospel, and Church*. Grand Rapids: Zondervan.

Johnson, Maxwell F. 2006. The apostolic tradition. In *The Oxford History of Christian Worship*, 32-69. Ed. Geoffrey Wainwright and Karen B. Westerfield Tucker. New York: Oxford Univ. Press.

Lynn, Robert W., and Elliot Wright. 1971. *The Big Little School: Two Hundred Years of the Sunday School*. New York: Harper and Row.

Maddix, Mark A. 2003. The "early days" of religious education, and The rise of evangelical Christian education: 1951-2000. In *C.E.: The Heritage of Christian Education*. Ed. James Riley Estep, Jonathan Hyungsoo Kim, Alvin Wallace Kuest, and Mark Amos Maddix. Joplin, MO: Teacher's College Press.

McGrath, Alister. 2001. *Christian Theology: An Introduction*. 3rd ed. London: Blackwell Press.

Osmer, Richard. 1990. *A Teachable Spirit: Recovering the Teaching Office in the Church*. Louisville, KY: Westminster/John Knox Press.

Pazmiño, Robert. 2008. *Foundational Issues in Christian Education*. 3rd ed. Grand Rapids: Baker Books.

Reed, James E., and Ronnie Prevost. 1993. *A History of Christian Education*. Nashville: Broadman and Holman.

Santayana, George. 1905/reprint 1980. *Reason in Common Sense*. New York: Charles Scribner and Sons; New York: Dover Publications. Available online at http://d.scribd.com/docs/19ni7uc21cghl782f1ce.pdf (accessed February 24, 2009).

Sawicki, Marianne. 1988. *The Gospel in History*. New York: Paulist Press.

Senter, Mark, III, and Jay Kesler. 1992. *The Coming Revolution in Youth Ministry: And Its Radical Impact on the Church*. Wheaton, IL: Victor Books.

Thompsett, Fredrica Harris. 1981. Godly instruction in reformation England: The challenge of religious education in the Tudor commonwealth. In *A Faithful Church: Issues in the History of Catechesis*, 174-203. Ed. John H. Westerhoff III and O. C. Edwards Jr. Wilton, CT: Morehouse-Barlow Co.

FOUR

WESLEYAN THEOLOGICAL FOUNDATIONS

▶ INTRODUCTION

Imagine you are a Sunday school teacher in a local congregation. You have a new student who has never been in a Wesleyan-oriented church before. She asks you, "What do Wesleyans believe?" and "How is being a Wesleyan similar to or different from being a Baptist, Presbyterian, or Pentecostal? Is being Wesleyan any different from being a Christian?" How do you summarize the commonalities and differences of these belief systems in the few minutes you have? How do your Wesleyan, Christian beliefs shine through your educational ministry?

Now imagine you are attending a Sunday school training seminar. The presenter argues that, since people remain constantly sinful, we need strong behavioral approaches to curb their sinful appetites. The presenter argues for a curriculum that emphasizes the struggle of the Christian life in contemporary society. One of the participants states, "It sounds like you don't trust people," and the presenter responds, "Until they make a decision for Christ, no . . . and then I think the best we can hope for is occasional obedience to God between failure and proclivity for sin." The presenter concludes by encouraging teachers to work hard since "God helps those who help themselves." One of the participants stops you on the way out and asks, "How can I help myself when all I can do is constantly fight sin in and through my teaching?" How do you respond?

Theology plays an important role in shaping our faith and our views of Christian education. Christian education that does not reflect our core Christian convictions is no longer Christian, and theology is the foundation for Christian educational practices. What the church believes about God, humanity, sin, and redemption remains important in both the content we teach and the methods we employ. It is especially important to understand the distinctly Wesleyan theological foundations of Christian discipleship, which inform our theological and philosophical approaches to teaching methods. This chapter focuses on the Wesleyan theological convictions and methodologies for Christian discipleship.

▶ CHRISTIAN FAITH AND DOCTRINE

Defining *faith*, a human disposition that exists only through the grace of God, has never been easy. Too often people reduce faith to cognition only, a major mistake for Christian educators. A more comprehensive definition includes objective and subjective elements of faith: Christian faith is a gracefully sure and profound response to, and trust in, the grace of God revealed in Jesus Christ (objective). Faith defines a mutual relationship that, while based in the gracious initiative of God through the Holy Spirit, invites a quite human response (subjective). This human response includes cognitive, affective, and volitional dimensions out of which we demonstrate our faith in what we do (behavior). However, faith is more than the sum of these human dimensions; it is part of the mystery we acknowledge as a gift of grace. Therefore, an appropriate "faith that seeks understanding" includes not only a depth of conviction (the ability to believe and yet struggle with doubt on occasion) but also consistent belief (*orthodoxy,* right belief), consistent behavior (*orthopraxis,* right behavior), and a consistently loving attitude (*orthopathy,* right heart) in regard to God and neighbor.

FAITH AND DOCTRINE

Faith and doctrine are related but not the same. Perhaps one way to understand their relationship is through a marriage analogy. When a couple marries they usually exchange vows in a wedding ceremony. Obviously the vows are insufficient to describe the totality of their love (much as specific doctrines do not adequately express the totality of our faith or of God's revelation). However, the vows remain extremely important. Sometimes those spoken commitments (the vowed relationship) can sustain a marriage during tough times, when feelings of love alone are not enough. Vows remind us to "love, honor, and obey" even when we do not feel like it. Ultimately, vows alone cannot make a marriage work (there must be love), but they give direction and purpose, and sometimes serve as a reminder of that love between two people. Faith and doctrine work the same way, particularly when doctrine reminds us of God's love for us even when we do not feel like loving God (or demonstrating our faith). Doctrine provides direction and shape in the relationship. If the doctrine is bad (like poorly constructed marriage vows), the relationship may fail when faith falters.

Doctrinal statements go beyond this analogy, particularly since they attempt to describe not only our relationship with our marriage partner (the Triune God) but also the nature of our relationship (salvation) from our perspective and even from God's perspective—no easy task. Fortunately we have resources to help resolve the issue, in scripture and from the history of Christian thinkers who have reflected and struggled hard before us. John Wesley is one such thinker that our tradition takes seriously, for both his synthesis of scripture and Christian tradition and for his attention to reason and experience of the world around him in fashioning his theology. To be "Wesleyan" requires attending to Wesley's distinctive contributions on the nature of doctrine and to his application of doctrine to the practice of daily living, including our task of discipleship.

Doctrine is particularly important in Christian education as these disciplines are symbiotically related. Luke Timothy Johnson argues that most religions seem satisfied focusing on right behavior (personal and liturgical actions), while Christianity emphasizes the necessity of right belief to guide purpose and conduct (2003, 9-11). Christians acknowledge that the creed (statement of doctrine) provides a beginning point for "professing" our conviction, our faith; and the creed provides a standard, "rule," or norm for Christian identity (40-49). Initially, most doctrinal statements, or creeds, were written to guide the church and, in particular, to teach the faith to its people. Guidance occurs through the teaching/learning process; learning doctrine always includes ongoing reflection on the meaning of the doctrine for our lives today. We teach theology, and we also reflect theologically to ensure that *how* we teach reinforces *what* we teach.

THEOLOGY AS PROCESS AND PRACTICE

The "how" question becomes important since Christian education serves not only as a carrier of theological doctrine but also as a theological exercise. Theology originally served as a reflective process to deepen our understanding of God (a goal often associated with spiritual formation). Ultimately, due to the changing role of education in teaching specializations, theology divided into various disciplines, such as systematic theology, biblical theology, historical theology, and practical theology (Farley 1983). Each specialization implies different points of departure (doctrine, scripture, church history, or contemporary practices inside and outside the church), and some adaptation of method. Each discipline, however, shares the common goal of a more faithfully informed approach to the Christian life.

For the church, theology is never an abstract exercise; we engage in theological reflection to better articulate, via preaching and teaching, the Christian faith. However, as Karl Barth notes, theology also provides a process by which the church discerns whether its preaching (and teaching) remains faithful to the gospel. We hope our teaching does something more than pass along facts. Teaching should engender faith, bringing about transformation in the student.

In summary, theology defines a disciplined discernment of the nature of God and also a reflective process of understanding just who "I" am (creation) in relation to him (salvation). Embedded in every question concerning the nature of God is the implicit question of our relationship with him. As our teaching in community raises these issues and questions, we engage in theology. Christian education represents a theological *practice* among Christians as well as a reflective *process* within each Christian. Theology defines our content for teaching (doctrine), our compass (showing our true direction), and our context (Christian teaching as a theological endeavor).

▶ WESLEYAN THEOLOGICAL CONVICTIONS

Our basic faith, broad doctrinal beliefs, and reflective practices coalesce into a particular picture of the Christian life and what we think it ought to be based on our understanding of God's perspective. That picture, or perspective, of the Christian life often shapes and is shaped by a tradition. In our circumstance the tradition that guides our theological reflection originates in the perspective of the Christian life asserted by John Wesley.

HOLINESS OF HEART AND LIFE

Wesleyan Christian education takes seriously the kind of dynamic, transformative life Wesley believed God made available for Christians. Wesley's concept, holiness of heart and life, represents a perspective, or tradition, that shapes the convictions of our writing and, we believe, one that demands faithful teaching. A deep understanding of scripture and doctrinal readings from the early church shaped John Wesley's view, which then spoke to the needs of the Christian and non-Christian world around him.

HISTORY OF THE WESLEYAN TRADITION

From the broad standpoint of the history of Christianity, the Wesleyan denominations often (but not always) arise out of the conservative American Holiness Movement, tracing their theological roots to eighteenth-century Anglicanism and their historical roots to the nineteenth-century American holiness movement. The Wesleyan tradition remains committed to the historic Christian faith, as expressed in the Nicene and Apostles' Creeds, and to the key doctrines of the Protestant Reformation, such as justification by faith, the supremacy of the scriptures, and the universal priesthood of believers. However, the Wesleyan tradition senses a special calling to stress the biblical teachings of original sin, prevenient grace, the new birth, Christian perfection, and the Spirit-filled life as articulated in John Wesley's theology. It is the aim of the Wesleyan tradition to walk in the Spirit, to exemplify the fruits of the Spirit, and to seek the glory of God and the redemption of humanity in a spirit of perfect love. All of these theological factors are foundational for a Wesleyan approach to Christian discipleship. The following theological statements demonstrate how Wesleyan theology affirms the doctrines of the church universal and stands in the broader Evangelical ethos. We will also highlight distinctive elements that make a Wesleyan paradigm unique in the context of Christian education.

▶ THE HOLY LOVE OF THE TRIUNE GOD

Wesleyan theology affirms that the primary characteristic of the Triune God is holy love. God is the Creator of all that is and remains lovingly related to creation. God offers a particular love for humanity and desires communion with us. Theorists note Wesley's Trinitarian dispositions (Anderson 1999; Collins 1998; Wainwright 1995). Wesley systematically elaborates on the presence of the Three-One God (his preferred term) in 1 John 5 in his sermon "Spiritual Worship" (1780/1986, 3:88-97). Wesley writes that the original purpose for writing 1 John was not faith or holiness "but of the foundation of all, the happy and holy communion which the faithful have with God the Father, Son and Holy Ghost" (89-90). God's being incorporates holiness and relationality simultaneously. God's holy sufficiency in triune relationship extends outward to humanity. The three members of the Godhead remain in perfect relationship and express holy love toward one another. This love manifests itself, not merely in therapeutic terms, but primarily in moral terms such as complete truth and justice. God's moral purity is not something God must exert; it stems naturally from the relationships shared within the Triune Godhead. Human beings always seem to struggle in three-way relationships (say between two parents and a child), always privileging one of the relationships (Thatcher 2007, 78-108). The Three-One God exhibits a unique love that does not need to privilege one relationship in favor of the other (so the Son is not privileged by the Father over the Holy Spirit though the Son is "beloved"). This means that God's relational love toward humanity extends out of the very being of the Trinity. While the Trinity describes the essence of God, aspects of the Triune Godhead give insight into the nature of God's character.

▶ JESUS CHRIST

God is revealed most definitively in the person of Jesus Christ, and thus Wesleyan theology remains thoroughly Christocentric. God cares deeply about the redemption of all persons, which comes out of his relational character and is manifested through the humble, self-giving love Jesus Christ expressed on the cross. *Christology,* simply defined, is the study of the person and mission of Jesus Christ. As Luke Timothy Johnson states, the Apostles' Creed makes clear that we should not separate these two names, since they indicate that the Son of God was truly human and divine simultaneously. Likewise, there is no simple distinction between who Jesus is (incarnation) and what Jesus came to do (atonement); they always inform each other, though material often remains divided between the doctrine of Christ and the work of salvation (soteriology).

Invariably, Christian educators must address the key questions: Who is Jesus? and What is Jesus' relation to God? They usually approach these questions from four perspectives:

1. What Jesus thought and taught about himself
2. What New Testament writers affirmed
3. What tradition (both Christian history and current Christian theology) affirms
4. What Christian educators acknowledge is the result of the first three perspectives

These questions have been revisited over time, but they carry with them certain implications concerning Jesus and ourselves as Christians.

JESUS IS GOD

John 1 affirms that Jesus, as the Word of God, is eternal (giving structure and meaning to creation from its beginning), distinct (with God, but not identical in all ways), and yet totally affirmed as being God. Jesus' godhood leaves us with certain other implications: (1) God can reveal himself to humanity in a very specific way. Jesus is not just the Word *of* God but the Word *disclosed by* God. Jesus both announces and actualizes God's grace, so we can see God's redemptive activity in history. (2) God can fully identify with humanity and thus enter into the world and redeem it from sin. Here we get close to the mission of Jesus. The mere presence of Jesus, the Incarnation, announces God's intent to enter history for the sake of our salvation. The Incarnation demonstrates God's ability to overcome sin within our world (breaking the bondage of sin) and overcome sin for our ultimate future (providing eternal life). Long before the passion, God exhibited the depths of his love as eternity entered into history in the form of a child.

JESUS IS HUMAN

John 1:14 states "and the word became flesh" (*incarne* = enfleshment). The idea of total humanity is further stressed in Philippians 2:6-9 (NRSV) in the famous kenotic hymn.

> Who, though he was in the form of God,
>> did not regard equality with God
>> as something to be exploited,
> but emptied himself [kenosis],
>> taking the form of a slave,
>> being born in human likeness.

And being found in human form,
>   he humbled himself
>   and became obedient to the point of death—
>   even death on a cross.
Therefore God also highly exalted him
>   and gave him the name
>   that is above every name.

Jesus exhibits the qualities of complete humanity. Such an observation raises even more implications. (1) This affirmation overcomes the other great theological struggle, If God is so radically different, then how can we ever apprehend his self-disclosure of the intended salvation of humankind? The self-disclosure comes to us through human means and in historical time via the humanity of Jesus. God can communicate with us because he totally identifies with humanity, though we may not understand the totality of that identification. We view Jesus through the lens of the Resurrection, which causes us to focus on his exalted deity (the other half of the Philippians hymn) and miss the reality of his humanity. (2) God *assumes* (takes in or puts on) what God saves (known normally through the negative: what God does not assume, God cannot save). Jesus' total identification with humanity leads to two major affirmations: the original goodness of creation and creation worthy of redemption.

JESUS HAPPENED

Often overlooked, the simple fact that Jesus occurred in history provides a sometimes startling perspective. We are a community of people grounded in the assertion that God has acted in a specific way in this world, which gives us a memory or story of redemption and a call to understand the implications of the God who became Man. This assertion of the God/Man who existed comes with difficulties: trying to understand how eternity can coexist with humanity. William Greathouse and H. Ray Dunning stress that there is no official doctrine of Christ, no formal attempt beyond the creeds to explain how these two natures coexist (1989, 35). Nevertheless the grounded reality of Jesus in history provides the foundation for the reality of God's love in Christ for living a life of discipleship shaped by Jesus' life and teachings.

▶ THE HOLY SPIRIT

Two biblical terms are used to identify the Holy Spirit. The Old Testament term, *Ruach,* describes both a child's breathing as well as a whirlwind. The activity of the Spirit of God proves unpredictable, the Spirit seizes people, invades them, and shakes them, giving them power to do mighty deeds or say perceptive things. Yet the Spirit often bestows power to particular people, like the judges of Israel. In the New Testament a new term, *Pneuma,* reveals activity that may be personal (i.e., human), corporate (community), or unique (as in "Holy" Spirit). The Greek understanding could at times seem abstract, but at Pentecost the Holy Spirit ultimately came to be understood as a uniquely different manifestation of God, poured out and promised to all (the democratization of the Holy Spirit).

The presence of this third member of the Godhead raises questions concerning God's transcendence and immanence. We recognize God as transcendent. God remains distinct from the creation and exceeds the grasp of any created intelligence. Yet the presence of the Holy Spirit also forces us to acknowledge God's immanence, permeating the world in sustaining creative power, shaping and guiding creation, if not actually controlling every moment. John Wesley's assertions concerning the independence of the Holy Spirit and the interdependence of the same Spirit within the Trinity maintains both the freedom and the relationality of the Spirit as indicated in scripture. "For Wesley the main point of such scriptural teachings is not merely that the Spirit is a person in relation to the Father and to the Son, but that the Spirit is a person in relation to us! When the Spirit deals with us, it is not some impersonal 'influence' with which we have to do. It is none other than the personal God himself in his outgoing relational activity" (Staples 1986, 201-2).

The ministry of the Holy Spirit may be perceived in direct activity with individuals, but the Holy Spirit is also free to operate quietly in sustaining all of creation. This form of "imperceptible" activity includes a preliminary "universal operation of the Spirit which on the grounds of the atonement, gives all men freedom and moral conscience" (Starkey 1962, 77). In all of these ministries, the Holy Spirit works to enable humanity. The Trinitarian perspective emphasizes, perhaps to a different degree than other traditions, the work of the Holy Spirit in the world, in the life of the church, and in individual lives (Leclerc and Maddix 2010).

▶ CHRISTIAN ANTHROPOLOGY

The Wesleyan tradition believes that humanity is uniquely created in the image of God, and that this image was not entirely obliterated by the Fall, but only distorted. Goodness remains in all of humanity, particularly because of the ongoing, prevenient grace of God in the world. Wesleyans believe that one of the primary goals of salvation, and particularly of sanctification, is the full renewal of the image of God and the actualization of Christlikeness. This is possible in this life through the grace of God and by the power of the Holy Spirit. In sum, Wesleyan theology views humanity in a more positive light than many other traditions. It specifically affirms human free-will and the role of humanity as cocreators with God (Leclerc and Maddix 2010).

Wesleyan theology affirms a strong doctrine of sin and acknowledges that sin is inherited from our first human parents. But again, unlike many other traditions, Wesleyan Christians are optimistic about living a victorious life in God and overcoming the power of sin through grace. For Wesleyans, sin describes a willful act (or the omission of good acts). Human limitations (e.g., emotional or mental disabilities or a lack of wisdom), however, are not seen as sins, but as infirmities for which we are not (eternally) responsible. This again leads Wesleyans to a very hopeful stance toward God's transforming grace in human life here on earth. Sin, when emphasized, is expressed in relational terms. Sin negatively affects a person's relationships with God, with others, with oneself, and with the earth. Similarly, holiness defines "perfect love" (1 John 4:18) expressed in the context of these same relationships. Holiness expressed in love provides sin's cure (Leclerc and Maddix 2010).

▶ SOTERIOLOGY

Wesleyan theology in regard to salvation (soteriology) affirms that Jesus is "the way and the truth and the life" (John 14:6), and that all grace—saving and sanctifying—remains available because of his death and resurrection. This includes prevenient grace, which describes the grace that draws us, even before we recognize it, into choosing a relationship with God and into our new birth. This grace also covers those who remain irresponsible, such as young children, those with mental or emotional infirmities, and, according to Wesley, those who have not had the opportunity to hear the good news of the gospel (see Romans 2:12-16). Prevenient grace also gives us access to general knowledge. Wesleyan theology affirms that all truth is God's truth. Grace, through Jesus Christ, reconciles sinful humanity to God so that we are saved by grace through faith in Christ alone. Jesus' life of willful obedience and love, compassionate death, and bodily resurrection provide the means of salvation for all who accept him (Leclerc and Maddix 2010).

Wesleyan theology affirms that the purpose of humanity, as God created us, is to live holy lives and to fulfill the two greatest commandments—love of God and love of others. Indeed, all the points above are directed toward the message of holiness. Wesleyan-Holiness theology is firmly committed to the doctrine of entire sanctification and spiritual growth in Christlikeness through the indwelling power of the Holy Spirit. Yet, the essence of the Wesleyan message of holiness is never "holiness for holiness' sake" or "sinlessness for sinlessness' sake." Grace-enabled holiness empowers us to love God and others, especially those who need Christ. Thus, the Great Commandments remain closely connected to the Great Commission as the church's mission (Leclerc and Maddix 2010).

▶ CHURCH AND SACRAMENT

Wesleyans embrace the role of the church and the sacraments as core convictions. Among the many biblical metaphors for the church, a few stand out as particularly appropriate for Wesleyan theology. *People of God* served as the earliest and most inclusive term. In the Old Testament it describes a particular ethnic and national group. By New Testament times, it is more universal (without boundaries), yet still describes a particular people. *Body of Christ* surfaces as a more particular description. The phrase so often used in the Pauline Epistles reveals diversity within the church while adhering to the centrality of Christ. The next metaphor, *communion,* suggests that each individual finds identity and fulfillment through Christ while *fellowship* suggests a relational dimension with other Christian people and in Christ. Finally terms such as *charismatic, spiritual,* or *in the power of the Spirit,* acknowledge both the force that holds the church together (through the indwelling of the Holy Spirit) and the ongoing, outward call into mission (through the empowerment of the Holy Spirit).

Beginning with the Nicene Creed, the church has also been characterized by the "marks" or "notes" of the church: *one, holy, catholic, apostolic.* Alister McGrath remarks that each of these terms indicates something of the nature of the church (2001, 494-505).

ONE

This term emphasizes unity, but not necessarily uniformity. Traditional responses to the idea of *one* included an imperial view, in which the hierarchy of the church determines who is in or out, and a Platonic view, which creates a dualism between the ideal (invisible) church versus the real (visible) church comprised of both true Christians and unbelievers. Other interpretations include an eschatological view that the church today is imperfect but will be purified during Christ's return, and a biological view of the New Testament church's confession of Christ as the tree trunk that has branched into the various churches. The key to unity appears to be the confession of Jesus Christ as Lord, the single unifying factor until the return of Christ.

HOLY

This term might be translated "separated," originally implying "purity from" (the world) or "dedication to" (God). This mark also implies an ethical nature and witness to grace. Holiness also means the ability to function according to the purpose and mission the community of faith is called to fulfill.

In a sense it is the call to each congregation to join the process of sanctification as a collective people in the world, becoming a community of integrity and Christlikeness.

CATHOLIC

Often translated as *universal,* this term also connotes a community in transition. This descriptive term implies all churches that manifest within the Christian family. While the term has gone through different phrases of meaning, it primarily asserts the diversity of the church without giving up on the commonality that holds these different churches together as part of the church universal.

APOSTOLIC

This term evokes both history and mission (*apostolos* means "to send"). We are an apostolic church in that we have a particular connection to apostles (New Testament figures or more contemporary ones such as Luther, Wesley, or Bresee). Their apostolic missions are part of our heritage and call us to our own mission to proclaim the gospel of Christ to the world.

WESLEY'S MARKS OF THE CHURCH

John Wesley had his own version of the "marks of the church." A "saved and saving community" demonstrated living faith, biblical preaching and sacraments, disciplines of the Spirit and Christian mission, all through the power of the Holy Spirit. These marks give clues to the nature of what the church is called to be and do. Wesley's emphasis on activity—preaching and sacraments (word and table)—reveals both his appreciation for traditional sacraments and his broader category of the means of grace.

SACRAMENT

Theologian Rob Staples identifies a *sacrament* as a sign or symbol of a previous pledge between two people and the promise represented in that pledge (1991, 85-86). Wesley, following Augustine, acknowledges *sacrament* as "an outward sign of an inward work of grace." Exactly how the sacraments communicate grace changes with different traditions, but Wesley seemed to resist the idea that a sacrament possesses the power to convey grace on its own (*ex opere operato*) regardless of the faith of the minister administering the sacrament or the one receiving (*ex opere operantis*). Wesley seemed to embrace the idea of sacrament embodying a virtual presence. In this sense the sacrament serves to incarnate grace through the activity of the Holy Spirit, transforming not the elements in particular but persons and the broader life of the church into the body of Christ as they participate (Blevins 2003).

Wesley acknowledged baptism and Communion as true sacraments (and advocated both). However, he also provided a larger rubric to help us understand how any act might be considered sacramental through his use of the term *means of grace*. Wesley's emphasis on the means of grace provides both as referents for our understanding of Christian practices (including Christian education) and an opportunity to see how the Trinity is at work in the world. More will be said in later chapters.

▶ EDUCATIONAL METHODOLOGIES: THEOLOGICAL AND PHILOSOPHICAL ASSUMPTIONS

The Wesleyan perspective not only supports particular understandings of theological doctrines but also represents a certain method of theological inquiry, and by implication, some methodological insights for education as well. The following is a list of educational methodologies that are informed by a Wesleyan theological perspective.

SEEKING TRUTH

The word *truth* in today's secular and religious vernacular has taken on weighty, yet diverse meanings. In the secular realm, truth has become relative and purely contextual in the postmodern era. In response, the religious world has sometimes pressed truth into a box, so to speak, and viewed it as something not to be explored, but only defended. Truth is thus reduced to religious presuppositions that some consider absolute. Wesleyan theology tends to transcend these extreme positions. For Wesley, truth is primarily embodied and not abstract. Specifically, truth is the person of Jesus Christ whom we encounter. Thus, when we refer to "seeking truth," we mean nothing more or less than seeking personal engagement with God through Christ as enabled by the Spirit. This does not mean that there are not truths to which we hold. But it does imply, in a Wesleyan paradigm, that genuine relationship takes precedence over religious statements or propositions (Leclerc and Maddix 2010).

According to Wesley, one can intellectually affirm belief statements without truly being Christian in the world. When John Wesley explores being Christian, he focuses on living out "faith filled with the energy of love." Christian education is best viewed as the joining of knowledge and vital piety. It seeks knowledge and affirms excellence in intellectual pursuits. It also seeks to integrate faith and learning. What makes education Christian is that it seeks not only to be informative but also to be formative and transformative through engagement with the living God.

INDUCTION AND KNOWLEDGE

One aspect of a Wesleyan philosophy/theology of education includes the fact that the Wesleyan approach begins, not with an indoctrination of deductive presuppositions, but rather with creative engagement and inductive thinking about real life situations and contexts that allow students to engage materials on deep levels. That said, the Wesleyan approach, particularly in a liberal arts context, does pursue knowledge through all of the traditional academic disciplines of the university and in all parts of God's creation, whether religious or secular. All truth is God's truth. Wesleyan Christian education focuses on the integration of scripture, tradition, reason, and experience. Christian educators also remain contextually and existentially engaged, correlating biblical truth with every new generation and cultural context.

QUADRILATERAL

While Wesley affirmed the Reformation idea of *sola scriptura* ("scripture alone") and placed the authority of scripture above all else, he did modify some of the implications of this doctrine. Wesley believed that the Bible is the primary source of authority but not necessarily the only religious authority. As Donald Thorsen states, "John Wesley's most enduring contribution to theological method stems from his . . . [inclusion] of experience along with Scripture, tradition, and reason as genuine sources of religious authority. While maintaining the primacy of Scripture, Wesley functioned with a dynamic interplay of sources in interpreting, illuminating, enriching, and communicating biblical truths" (2004, 81). This perspective does not imply that tradition, reason, or experience can stand alone as authorities. The Bible stands above these three helpers.

Tradition, particularly from the early church period, requires serious consideration. One must understand how the church interpreted the Bible, particularly in the development of orthodox beliefs such as the nature of the Trinity and the nature of Jesus Christ as both human and divine. Seeing how ministers interpreted the Bible through the centuries remains important. People must also use reason in understanding how the biblical message is discerned, formulated, and communicated. Wesley did not suggest that we can reason our way to God, but that God gave us rational faculties to use. Experience also serves in confirming the truth of scripture. If Christians do not experience the scriptural message, then we should question our interpretation of the message. Wesley is known for reexamining and subsequently reinterpreting scripture in light of some of the experiences of his Methodist people. Tradition, reason, and experience provide crucial insights into biblical understanding (Leclerc and Maddix 2010).

CATHOLIC SPIRIT

Wesleyans often focus attention on those things essential to our salvation. On nonessentials we are to give liberty of thinking in areas not addressed in scripture or in the articles. For example, one denomination has refused to bind its people to particular beliefs about the beginning or the end of the world, following Augustine's dictum: "In essentials unity; in non-essentials liberty; and love over all." Wesley's sermon "The Catholic Spirit" expresses this same theme, defending core theological convictions yet leaving considerable space for differences of worship, practice, and polity. Thus, when we speak of a catholic spirit, we show openness to hearing other perspectives with respect and love. This ethos should enter every classroom and meeting. This approach does not imply that persons cannot have strong opinions but that persons must agree to disagree with love in a healthy learning community (Leclerc and Maddix 2010).

▶ CONCLUSION

John Wesley's theology represents one system of belief within the Christian tradition, a belief system that informs discipleship in Wesleyan-based congregations. A Wesleyan approach to Christian discipleship begins with understanding John Wesley's theology and key doctrinal beliefs. These doctrines provide the foundation for faithful teaching and practice. Being a Christian consists of consistent orthodoxy (right belief) with consistent orthopraxis (right practice and behavior) and a consistent orthopathy (right heart with God and neighbor). We study theology to know more about who God is and how God works in the world. The result is faithful discipleship, living a life of Christlikeness, which Wesley believed would lead to "holiness of heart and life."

▶ REFERENCES

Anderson, E. Byron. 1999. Trinitarian grammar of the liturgy and the liturgical practice of the self. In *Wesleyan Theological Journal* 34, no. 2 (fall): 152-74.

Blevins, Dean G. 2003. A Wesleyan view of the liturgical construction of the self. In *Wesleyan Theological Journal* 38, no. 2 (fall): 7-29.

Collins, Ken. 1998. Reconfiguration of power: Basic trajectory of John Wesley's practical theology. In *Wesleyan Theological Journal* 33, no. 1 (spring): 164-72.

Farley, Edward. 1983. *Theologia: The Fragmentation and Unity of Theological Education.* Philadelphia: Fortress Press.

Greathouse, William, and H. Ray Dunning. 1989. *Introduction to Wesleyan Theology.* Kansas City: Beacon Hill Press of Kansas City.

Johnson, Luke Timothy. 2003. *The Creed: What Christians Believe and Why It Matters.* New York: Doubleday Books.

Knight Henry H., III. 2007. John Wesley and the emerging church. In *Preacher's Magazine* (Advent/Christmas): 34.

Leclerc, Diane, and Mark A. Maddix. 2010. Wesleyan integration: A distinctive philosophy of education. In *Wesleyan Theological Journal* 45 (fall): 2.

McGrath, Alister E. 2001. *Christian Theology: An Introduction.* 3rd ed. Oxford: Blackwell.

Meeks, M. Douglas, ed. 2000. *Trinity Community and Power: Mapping Trajectories in Wesleyan Theology.* Nashville: Kingswood Books.

Staples, Rob L. 1986. Wesleyan perspectives on the doctrine of the Holy Spirit. In *The Spirit and the New Age,* 199-236. Ed. Alex R. G. Deasley and R. Larry Shelton. Anderson, IN: Warner Press.

_____. 1991. *Outward Sign and Inward Grace: The Place of the Sacraments in Wesleyan Spirituality.* Kansas City: Beacon Hill Press of Kansas City.

Starkey, Lycurgus M., Jr. 1962. *The Work of the Holy Spirit: A Study in Wesleyan Theology.* Nashville: Abingdon Press.

Thatcher, Adrian. 2007. *Theology and Families.* Malden, MA: Blackwell.

Thorsen, Donald. 2004. Interpretation in interactive balance: The authority of scripture for John Wesley. In *Reading the Bible in Wesleyan Ways,* 81-106. Ed. Barry L. Callen and Richard P. Thompson. Kansas City: Beacon Hill Press of Kansas City.

Wainwright Geoffrey. 1995. Why Wesley was a trinitarian. In *Methodists in Dialogue,* 261-74. Nashville: Abingdon Press.

Wesley, John. 1780/1986. Spiritual worship. In *The Works of John Wesley: Sermons,* Vol. 3: 88-102. Ed. Albert Outler. Nashville: Abingdon Press.

_____. 1872. *The Works of John Wesley,* 3rd ed. Ed. Thomas Jackson. 14 vols. London: Wesleyan Methodist Book Room. Also see http://wesley.nnu.edu.

_____. 1984-1995. *The Works of John Wesley,* bicentennial ed. Ed. Reginald Ward and Richard Heitzenrater. Nashville: Abingdon Press.

FIVE

WESLEY THE EDUCATOR

▶ INTRODUCTION

Imagine you live in eighteenth-century England. What challenges might you face as a Christian educator in light of the view of children in that day? What educational obstacles would you need to overcome when working with the poor?

Consider your life today as a minister. What is the main thing that guides your educational ministry? If you want to seek total Christlikeness for people, where will you put your best efforts; what is your orienting concern? Why?

John Wesley was a practical theologian. He lived out his theology in his ministry. He understood the need to establish educational ministry practices that aided people to grow toward "holiness of heart and life" (Blevins 1999). He was very influential in the development of educational practices that fostered transformation of human persons and society. In particular Wesley employed four primary arenas—childhood education, adult education (formation), social reform of individual lives and social structures, and evangelism (personal conversion)—that reveal his educational ministry perspectives and the theological influence of his primary orienting concern of holiness of heart and life.

▶ CHILDHOOD EDUCATION

Wesley's approach to the Christian education of children follows logically from his theology. He believed in the fall of the human race from birth, including its youngest members. Sin dislodged the moral and natural image of God in all humanity and brought alienation from God for young and old. Wesley was deeply concerned about the salvation of children and saw Christian education as a primary means to this end. In his sermon "On the Education of Children," Wesley states, "Now, if these are the general diseases of human nature, is it not the grand end of education to cure them? And is it not the part of all those to whom God has entrusted the education of children, to take all possible care, first, not to increase, not to feed, any of these diseases (as the generality of parents constantly do)" (1975/2003, 3:352).

BAPTISM

Wesley spent much of his ministry educating children, and he believed that the first step in their redemption was baptism (Wesley 1872/1986, 10:188). Adults reached the new birth, the beginning of spiritual transformation, through baptism, but only on the condition that they repented and believed the gospel. Children reached spiritual life through an outward sign of baptism without condition, however, for they could neither repent nor believe (5:38). Infants remained in a state of original sin, and ordinarily they could not be saved unless washed by baptism. Baptism regenerates, justifies, and gives infants the privileges of the Christian religion.

People often misunderstand Wesley's theological view of infant baptism. As a result, infant baptism is often not practiced in the Wesleyan traditions. "In perhaps no other aspects of their sacramental practices have the churches in the Wesleyan/holiness tradition strayed from their classical Wesleyan heritage more conspicuously than in the matter of infant baptism" (Staples 1991, 161).

One of the primary reasons for the void in practicing infant baptism is the theological misconception of infant baptism as a regenerative sacrament (Blakemore 1996, 179). Most people ask how the transformation Wesley describes occurs in an infant who, so the argument goes, lacks the cognitive abilities necessary for this experience. Wesley replies, "Neither can we comprehend how it is wrought in a person of riper years" (Wesley 1872/1986, 6:74).

Rob Staples provides a good summary of Wesley's rationale of infant baptism: (1) The benefit of baptism is the washing away of the guilt of original sin; (2) baptism is proper for children because of the continuity of the covenant of grace God made with Abraham; (3) small children should be brought to Christ and admitted into the church, based on Matthew 19:13-14 and Luke 18:15; and (4) Wesley found support for infant baptism in the practice of the church "in all ages and in all places" (1991, 167-72). Wesley saw infant baptism as an important step in the spiritual development of the infant and the child's entrance into the faith community.

Wesley taught that through baptism "a principle grace is infused" (Wesley 1872/1986, 10:192) and "that infants need to be washed from original sin; therefore they are proper subjects for baptism" (10:193) If a child lives, he or she never passes again through the door of repentance to faith, unless he or she commits sin. However, it is natural for children to commit sin, for the principle of nature is still at work in the child (Towns 1975, 320). The only way to conserve the innocence of children is to guard them completely against contamination during their helpless years and at the same time build character. As a result, they may resist evil by their own strength when they become of age (Prince 1926, 95). This, Wesley argued, is the task of education,

"The grand end of education is to cure the diseases of human nature" (Wesley 1872/1986, 2:310).

CONVERSION

Wesley saw conversion as the next step in the Christian education of children. He believed that anyone who had sinned after baptism had denied the rightness of baptism and, therefore, must have recourse to a new birth for salvation. Wesley felt conversion to be universally necessary for children as well as for adults. Prince states, "Wesley did not hold that Christian education makes conversion unnecessary, but that Christian education and conversion supplement each other" (Prince 1926, 96). In his sermon "On the Education of Children" (1975-2003, 3:347-360), Wesley stated that training children in the way they should go equates curing the disease of nature with training the individual in religion. Prince's seminal work on Wesley and childhood education states Wesley's idea of the purpose of Christian education:

> The goal of all work with children at home, in the schools, in the Methodist society is to make them pious, to lead to personal religion, and to insure salvation. It is not merely to bring them up so that they do no harm and abstain from outward sin, not to get them accustomed to the use of grace, saying their prayers, reading their books, and the like, nor is it to train them in right opinions. The purpose of religious education is to instill in children true religion, holiness and the love of God and mankind and to train them in the image of God. (1926, 87-88)

PRACTICES

This education to make children Christians, both inwardly and outwardly, began with the parents and continued in schools by instructors and in the societies (Naglee 1987, 228-37).

Educational assessments of Wesley's approach with children vary (see Blevins 2005, 2008; Estep 1997, 43-52; Felton 1997; Heitzenrater 2001; Prince 1926, 103-36; Seaborn 1985, 30-59; Stonehouse 2004). All educators, however, remain indebted to Prince, for he was the first to explore Wesley's approach to education (Hall 1998, 12). John Gross notes that some of Wesley's early experiences may have influenced his curricular design for higher education (1954, 13-14). Stonehouse argues that Wesley's theology was central to his educational perspective and provided a driving force in his educational ministry practices (2004, 133-48). Wesley himself provides one summary of his theological foundations for educating children: "The bias of nature is the wrong way: education is designed to set it right. This, by the grace of God, is to turn the bias from self will, pride, anger, revenge, and the love of the world, to resignation, lowliness, meekness, and the love of God" (1872/1986, 13:476).

Wesley's educational practices with children were certainly influenced by his theological convictions, but we must remember that he viewed children through the lens of eighteenth-century England. First, as John Gross states, "He [Wesley] never considered a child as a child, but rather as a unit for salvation, bred in sin, apt to evil, and altogether as a 'brand to be plucked out of the burning'" (1954, 9). Second, Wesley firmly believed that a genuine and deeply religious life was possible in childhood (Prince 1926, 82). This belief proved most evident in the childhood conversions at Kingswood school. Reports indicate that children at Kingswood experienced salvation between the ages of six to fourteen years of age. Wesley believed children remained ripe for spiritual change up to age ten. By age ten, the child's sins had nullified the "Washing of the Holy Ghost" received at baptism (Wesley 1872/1986, 2:465). Third, Wesley felt that the beginning of conscious religious instruction should coincide with the dawn of reason in the child (13:476).

Fourth, the child must be educated out of the disease of sin. As we have seen, Wesley's view of original sin was the foundation of his concept of Christian education. Fifth, the will of the child must be broken. Wesley's discipline of children was harsh and severe at times, especially when it came to this point. This is not to suggest, however, that he advocated a totalitarian or unrestrained form of child discipline (Estep 1997, 49). In *A Thought on the Manner of Educating Children*, Wesley stated,

> Even religious masters may not have the spirit of government to which some even good men are stranger. They may habitually lean to this or that extreme, of remissions or of severity. And if they give children too much of their own will, or needlessly and churlishly restrain them; if they either use no punishment at all, or more than is necessary, the leaning either to one extreme or the other, may frustrate their endeavors. (1872/1986, 13:474)

Wesley's view of childhood discipline explains his rejection of play as being detrimental, both educationally and spiritually: "We have no play on any day; for he that plays as a child will play as a man" (285). Wesley's view of play differed from that of his predecessors (Reed and Prevost 1993, 319). Sixth, Wesley spoke to his teachers about pedagogical practices and techniques that included such things as how to talk, how to develop a relationship of love, and how to educate children through repetition (Towns 1975, 325).

SCHOOLS

The development of the Kingswood and Charity schools also illustrates Wesley's strong theological conviction about Christian education and grew from his scorn for public education. He believed the public schools of his day were "nurseries of all manner of wickedness" (1872/1986, 2:301). As Alfred

Body states, "Public education was a total lack of religion and religious motive, and it is this which gives us at once the clue to his chief educational idea: religion and education go together" (1936, 47).

Jim Estep (1997, 51) provides a list of Wesley's criticisms of public education in England, to which he regarded Kingswood as the solution:

1. Most schools were located in "great towns" wherein children could be distracted from their studies by the activities of the community.

2. Most schools admitted students indiscriminately, with the worst corrupting the better.

3. Defective religious education, and hence the aim of education, in Wesley's opinion, was misguided.

4. Basic study skills, such as reading and writing, were neglected for more formal educational pursuits, such as classical languages.

5. Finally, when classical education is provided, the order of instruction and flow of curriculum is arbitrarily arranged (see Wesley 1872/1986, 13:289-301).

Wesley's concerns about public education moved him to action. He spoke to parents and schoolmasters, supplying them with useful resources as outlined in "Instructions for Children" (1872/1986, 14:217-18) and other publications (Felton 1997). Wesley remained deeply committed to providing an educational environment that fostered religious growth and development, as realized in the Kingswood school. Wesley did not maintain that all contemporary forms of Christian education proved beneficial. In fact, he thought that false religions, poor instruction, and undisciplined teachers did "more harm than good." Therefore, he argued that family and professional instructors must provide sound education for children that ensured not just a religious education but a Christian one (Wesley 1872/1986, 14:474-77).

Alfred Body observes that the boarding school at Kingswood served as an idealized form of education, though it struggled as an institution (1936, 84-130). Body reveals what he believes were the two major features of Wesley's educational philosophy: "religious training and perfect control of the children" (94). In spite of struggles with staff and various financial concerns at Kingswood, Body's investigation of the school frames Wesley's work in the humanitarian spirit of the eighteenth century (39-40). For Wesley, as for Whitefield, religion and education belonged together: "The purpose of education was that it should be a means to the great end of saving the souls of the children" (74). Nevertheless, Wesley's schools reflected a number of assumptions consistent with other British educational systems of the era, particularly compared to the Charity schools and Grammar schools of Wesley's day (Blevins 2008; Heitzenrater 2001).

The rise of Sunday schools in 1780 marked another important educational development. Though chief credit for the development of the Sunday school belongs to Robert Raikes, Methodism's impact cannot be dismissed. Methodists developed Sunday schools for children of poor families (Marquardt 1992, 54). Sunday schools opened doors to all children, unlike the regular grammar schools. Children learned the basics of reading, writing, arithmetic, and the most important portions of the catechism. Also, Bible study served as the primary focus of the Sunday school (54-55). Wesley advanced the establishment of the Sunday schools with a goal of evangelizing the lost. Sunday school meant more than the impartation of knowledge; children needed to develop into Christians who might lead a renewal of the entire nation.

The foundation of Wesley's educational work, as of his evangelical mission, was primarily humanitarian, and his early schools were established for the poorer class. He observed the poverty and misery of the poor, and his heart was stirred to give them a better existence, even providing clothes in needy cases (Body 1936, 133). Body's understanding "that service to humanity was to Wesley only a visible manifestation of his service to God" fuels his assessment of all of Wesley's educational efforts (134).

In summary, Wesley's emphasis on childhood education remains closely linked to his anthropological and theological foundations. The emphases on infant baptism, the conversion of children, and spiritual formation of children all reveal the influence of his theological understanding of humanity.

▶ ADULT EDUCATION

Wesley's writings and their assessment by scholars indicate that Wesley provided more clearly defined educational practices for adults than children. Evidence of Wesley's focus on adult formation includes recent studies of his early personal devotional life and study of mystical classics in spiritual formation (Harper 1983a; Tuttle 1989) as well as Wesley's approaches to spiritual direction, seen in his letters to followers (Tracy 1987). Further, scholars conclude that Wesley's concept and practice of group formation was a key feature in his educational practices and provides a guide for contemporary ministry. Wesley's philosophy of group formation clearly guided his development of small groups.

The formation of Wesley's thinking in regard to small groups began with his childhood education experiences at home, where his mother, Susanna, played a key role:

> Family devotions were held not only for us but for the servants as well. Devotional meetings were frequently held in the rectory kitchen on Sunday evening. When my father was away my mother took charge. Once when my father was spending time in London . . . some members

of the congregation joined our meetings. At first there were thirty or forty [people] but by the time my father returned the attendance had reached more than 200. (Tuttle 1978, 44-45)

Wesley's experiences at Oxford also contributed to his disciplined methods (Tyerman 1872/1986, 69-70).

A more significant stage in the development of Wesley's small-group practice, however, occurred after his Aldersgate experience in May 1738. Three weeks after his conversion, Wesley set out to visit the Moravian settlements in Saxony. At the first settlement, Marienborn, he met with the Moravian leader Count Zinzendorf. At the settlement at Herrnhut, Wesley observed the Moravian community with great fascination. Count Zinzendorf had arranged the community into compact cells, or "bands" as he called them, for spiritual oversight and community administration (Henderson 1997, 59). The Moravians' example became one of the hallmarks of Methodism: the separation of instruction from edification as two distinct functions. The instructional sessions were called "choirs," given entirely to teaching. Edification groups, called "bands," were for personal encouragement. No teaching was allowed during these meetings, only intimate sharing, confessions, and personal reporting of spiritual experiences (60-61).

When Wesley returned to England, he was eager to experiment with his newfound knowledge and within three weeks he had organized bands of believers after the Moravian/Herrnhut model. Despite his enthusiasm, Wesley eventually separated himself from the Moravians because of doubts about their doctrine and practices. It was a painful separation, but one that he deemed necessary. Nevertheless, Wesley gained valuable insights that provided the impetus for his group formation (Outler 1964, 353-76).

Wesley shared leadership of new societies he formed with Moravian Peter Bolher, gathering together forty or fifty men who met for prayer and group encouragement (Simon 1923, 150). The meetings included a list of thirty-three articles, consisting mostly of rules for group admission, function, cohesion, expulsion, and order (Wesley 1872/1986, 97). The development of these groups marked a critical shift in Wesley's adult educational practices; the groups were not associated with the Church of England. Also, Wesley had been dissatisfied with his participation in other religious societies because of their lack of opportunity to bare one's soul and to share one's spiritual struggles in a secure and accepting group (Henderson 1997, 65).

The Fetter Lane Society experienced difficulties in 1739. Many of the members were losing interest in the groups. Factions were developing between the Moravians and the Anglicans. As a result of Wesley's dissatisfaction with the group, he held a meeting at the nearby Foundry, which was under construction.

Wesley's success resulted in more than three hundred people attending the opening of the Foundry, and Wesley decided to break from the Fetter Lane Society to begin a new group called the Foundry Society (Henderson 1997, 76-77).

The Foundry Society was a great success and grew to more than nine hundred members by 1741. The bands, however, were not increasing in number as rapidly as the societies, and Wesley was concerned about the need for better supervision. The result was the development of class meetings. The class meetings filled the critical gap between the society and the bands. It was through the class meetings that Wesley created an environment of acceptance for people from widely different social backgrounds. They met in homes, shops, schoolrooms, attics, and even coal bins. Groups called penitent bands, which were designed for rehabilitation, were also formed at this time. They included people who had severe social and moral problems, who required more stringent and forceful treatment (Henderson 1997, 80).

The development of the societies, the bands, and the class meetings provided a comprehensive educational system for adults. Twentieth-century educators and pastors have adapted Wesley's group formation to reflect more current educational practices. David Michael Henderson developed a taxonomy (or system of classification) that provides an external framework of identification for Wesleyan groups (1981). Henderson's system is based upon instructional aims rather than psychological functions (Drakesford 1978, 104). He provides a list of underlying principles on which Wesley's educational philosophy is based. They include three primary "modes" or "appropriate method[s] of procedure" that include societies (cognitive mode), class meeting (behavioral mode), and bands (affective mode) (Drakeford 1978, 187-88). Henderson's assessment of Wesley's group formation provides a philosophical basis for small groups today. Congregations can use Wesley's groups to evaluate the primary purposes of their small groups.

David Lowes Watson made the most significant contribution to contemporary approaches in Wesleyan group formation (1985, 1990, 1991). Watson developed a framework for discipleship groups in local congregations, particularly United Methodist churches. His work is helpful in providing practical application of Wesley's group formation. More recently, David Hunsiker linked Wesley's group formation to current cell-group developments in American Protestantism. He dubbed Wesley "the father of the modern small group movement" (1996, 210).

Wesley's approach to adult education is reflected most clearly in his formation of groups. Group formation represented his theological convictions. Wesley believed that spiritual growth and holiness of heart and life require discipline, nurture, and accountability. His small groups provide the primary avenues for persons to grow toward holiness of heart and life (Henderson 1997; also see chapter 16).

▶ SOCIAL REFORM

Wesley's development of schools for children, his evangelistic efforts, and the formation of adult groups comprised an educational system that stemmed from his theological convictions. Wesley's impact on eighteenth-century England cannot be overlooked. Some people prospered in the early eighteenth century. Population grew slowly, while commerce grew rapidly. Those who owned land or had skill and the means of production had opportunities for economic growth. During this time of economic boom, however, more than half of England's workers were becoming increasingly poor (Tyson 1997, 176). The economic situation of the lower classes was worsened by legislation designed to maintain the income and interests of the upper classes.

The Methodist movement was strongest in the emerging manufacturing and industrial centers. The Wesleys were most effective in places where the established Church of England was weak and where they were able to consolidate societies that had already been established by others (Armstrong 1973, 68). The genius of the Wesleys and early Methodism, given the socioeconomic situation of the 1740s, lay in the liberating and empowering structures of the societies (Tyson 1997, 179).

Groups were lay-led, which fit well with the individualism of the emerging working class. The fact that Methodism stood outside the spheres that undergirded the older, repressive social order, made it an attractive alternative to those whose interests did not coincide with those of the clergy or landowners (180-91). Methodism styled itself as a reforming movement in an era that was beginning to agitate for social reform. The Methodist societies were the chief vehicle for implementing Wesley's "evangelical economics" (180). Wesley's desire to reach the poor and to resist social evil were cardinal tenets of his approach to Christian education (199). Wesley's compassion for the poor led to the development of school, which provided the poor with education and even clothing.

Manfred Marquardt makes a strong argument for Wesley's social reform. He develops the relationship between Wesley's educational efforts with his theological ethic focused on transforming social structures (Marquardt 1992, 199-204). Marquardt's primary focus is the social concern that prompted Wesley's pedagogy and the results of that pedagogy in empowering the poor (103-22). He even concludes that "one of the prominent parts of Wesley's life work, subordinate to evangelism and social service, was his role as founder, promoter, and theoretician for various diverse educational projects, especially to groups: the poor, who were excluded from the existing means of education; and the recently-converted Methodist society members, for whom Wesley felt highly responsible" (49). "The primary reason for the development of schools within his sphere of influence was primarily a religious and humanitarian one" (52).

Scholars disagree about the impact of Wesley's social reform on eighteenth-century England. Some historians assert that Methodists remained primarily concerned with the salvation of the soul. Methodist emphasis on social reform was purely in the stream of the "Protestant ethic" and is overly exaggerated (Madron 1981, 109). Other scholars consider Methodism to have had a pivotal influence in social reform. They assume that the democratic practices and philanthropy of the Methodist societies were automatically translated into the larger public sphere. Wesley is a hero to these scholars, who credit him and the Methodists with keeping England from experiencing a revolution like the one that occurred in France (Keefer 1990, 11). Most historians position themselves between these two extremes (Armstrong 1973). They recognize the extensive influence that Wesley's spiritual revolution had on English history, which includes the gradual improvement of the country's social condition. Methodism's achievements in philanthropy, the extension of education reform, and the abolition of slavery are all aligned with Wesley's positions and focus.

Scholars do agree that Wesley's social reform was intentional; he established definite structures and enlisted others to continue the work beyond the scope of his life. His life proved a model for all Methodists. He wanted to model how others might apply themselves to similar projects within their spheres of ministry. His concern for doing good was multiplied many times over in the lives of those influenced by his work (Keefer 1990, 8). Henry Abelove provides a detailed rationale for Wesley's success. One primary reason was that Wesley provided medical services without charge wherever he traveled (Abelove 1990, 8). The poor could seldom afford a physician or an apothecary. Instead they would go to the back door of a nearby rectory or great house, where they could get broth, wine, common drugs, advice, or a favor (9). Wesley deployed genteel and open-handed charity, providing not only coal, bread, and clothes for the needy—especially among his followers, whom he visited house-to-house and oversaw closely—but also creating make-work for the unemployed and, on one occasion, assuming responsibility for an orphaned child (9). Wesley's concern for social reform cannot be overlooked as one of his primary educational perspectives.

▶ EVANGELISM

John Wesley desired "to cure the diseased soul." John Prince offers a view of Wesley as primarily an evangelist whose efforts with adults and children were energized by his focus on salvation. Most of Prince's work attempted to link Wesley's adult evangelistic efforts with his teaching on the Christian nurture of children: "Many evangelists have preached with great power, but only a few of the greatest have combined with it an eagerness to spread education" (1926, 10). For Prince, Wesley's educational goals included his theological and pedagogical analyses, which were interconnected and reciprocal. He viewed Wesley's educational emphasis with children primarily as preparation for conversion. "He [Wesley] gives the concept of training and education a wider connotation than they actually carry. He uses them to include not only the bringing of children to a knowledge and appreciation of the condition of salvation, but also to their personal appropriation of salvation" (99-100).

In his sermon "On Family Religion" (1872/1986, 7:76), Wesley speaks about the importance to "train up a child in the way he should go." For him, this means to lead children into the experience of salvation in much the same way as adults. In his tract *A Thought on the Manner of Educating Children* (1872/1986, 7:458-59), Wesley identifies conversion with at least a part of the educative process (Prince 1926, 101): "Education is designed to set aright the bias of nature, to cure the disease of self-will, pride, and so on" (Wesley 1872/1986, 7:458-59).

The evangelistic efforts of John Wesley, Charles Wesley, and George Whitefield are impressive. Nearly everywhere Wesley preached, his hearers were convicted of their sinfulness. He traveled some twenty-five thousand miles and preached about forty thousand sermons (Abelove 1990, 2-3). The primary focus of his preaching, development of schools for children, and his group formation was his passion for souls to be saved. These educational practices are incomplete in themselves, however. While they develop an aspect of Wesley's theology and educational perspective, they do not contain his entire purpose, and they can limit practices that might be needed in contemporary Wesleyan studies. As applied in his time, Wesley's educational practices are not broad enough to satisfy his understanding of Christianity focused on holiness of heart and life.

▶ WESLEY'S THEOLOGICAL FOUNDATION: "HOLINESS OF HEART AND LIFE"

Scholars have developed themes that attempt to unify Wesley's theological approach. For example, Randy Maddox uses "responsible grace" as a connecting thread for the individual doctrinal themes that Wesley developed early to those that came later in his life (1994, 15-19). Knight (1992) and Blevins (1999) use the "means of grace" as a unifying theme to bridge Wesley's theology with his wide range of educational practices. Blevins asserts that three approaches—formation, discernment, and transformation—provide a framework for educational practice and a unified approach to Wesley's educational perspective (362-80). The primary theological focus and singular emphasis of Wesley's educational perspectives remains "holiness of heart and life" (Maddox 1994; Collins 1997; Grider 1994; Dunning 1988). As a broad description of transformation, holiness of heart and life encompasses Wesley's objectives in evangelism, social reform, and educational practices for children and adults. It is a phrase used repeatedly in Wesley's sermons and writings, including his sermon "The Righteousness of Faith":

> One thing more was indispensably required by the righteousness of the law, namely, that this universal obedience, this perfect holiness both of heart and life, should be perfectly uninterrupted also, should continue without any intermission, from the moment wherein God created man, and breathed into his nostrils the breath of life, until the days of his trial should be ended, and he should be confirmed in life everlasting. (1872/1986, 5:67)

He also addressed this theme in his sermon "On Perfection": "St. Peter expresses it in a still different manner, though to the same effect: 'As he that hath called you is holy, so be ye holy in all manner of conversation' (1 Peter 1:15). According to this Apostle, then, perfection is another name for universal holiness: Inward and outward righteousness: Holiness of life, arising from holiness of heart" (6:414).

Wesley's educational practices all derive from this universal theological truth. Holiness of heart and life proceeds from Wesley's views on the sinfulness of humanity and the need for restoring the *imago dei* (political and moral image of God). Wesley developed this idea in his sermon "The Image of God" (1872/1986, 4:293-95). Of three aspects of the image of God—natural, political, and moral—Wesley designated the last as the principal image: "So God created man in his own image . . . but chiefly in his moral image" (ibid.). The reason for this distinction, according to Ken Collins, is that the moral image contains both true righteousness and holiness; it is the context for the possibility of sin and is intimately related to the moral law (1997, 24-25). Because of this, scholars (Lindström 1980; Williams 1960; Outler 1964; Collins 1997) place Wesley's *ordo salutis,* or order of salvation, at the core of his theology. Through the empowering grace of God, an individual realizes and experiences the promise of the restored image of God, which will not occur without human cooperation with and response to the grace of God.

Thus, the transformational and lifelong experience of holiness of heart and life best expresses Wesley's conviction about salvation and forms the primary theological framework for his educational perspective. Each of Wesley's educational avenues—childhood education, adult education, evangelism, and social reform—derive from this theological framework.

▶ SUMMARY

Wesley's educational perspectives provide a holistic approach to Christian education that fosters spiritual growth toward holiness of heart and life. Wesley focused on development of the individual learner, both children and adults. Nurture and development were the emphases in providing educational opportunities for oppressed children and class meetings (small groups) for adults. The development of societies, classes, and bands, unique to Wesley, is the primary educational approach that actualizes his theological conviction of holiness of heart and life. His ultimate goal was to see human persons transformed by the grace of God through the power of the Holy Spirit. Wesley's educational perspectives, undergirded by his theological foundations, provide a holistic approach to Christian education that fosters holiness of heart and life.

▶ REFERENCES

Abelove, Henry. 1990. *The Evangelist of Desire: John Wesley and the Methodist.* Stanford, CA: Stanford Univ. Press.

Armstrong, Anthony. 1973. *The Church of England, the Methodists and Society 1700-1850.* London: Univ. of London.

Blakemore, Stephen G. 1996. By the Spirit through the water: John Wesley's "evangelical" theology of infant baptism. In *Wesleyan Theological Journal* 31, no. 2: 167-91.

Blevins, Dean. 1999. *John Wesley and the Means of Grace: An Approach to Christian Religious Education.* Ph.D. diss., Claremont School of Theology. Ann Arbor, MI: UMI Microfilms.

———. 2005. Faithful discipleship: A conjoined catechesis of truth and love. In *Considering the Great Commission: Explorations for a Wesleyan Praxis of Mission and Evangelism.* Ed. W. Stephen Gunter and Elaine A. Robinson. Nashville: Abingdon Press.

———. 2008. To be a means of grace: A Wesleyan perspective on Christian practices and the lives of children. In *Wesleyan Theological Journal* 43, no. 1 (spring): 47-67.

Body, Alfred H. 1936. *John Wesley and Education.* London: Epworth.

Collins, Ken. 1995. The soteriological orientation of John Wesley's ministry to the poor. In *Asbury Theological Journal* 50, no. 1: 75-91.

———. 1997. *The Scripture Way of Salvation: The Heart of John Wesley's Theology.* Nashville: Abingdon Press.

Drakeford, John W. 1978. *People to People Therapy.* San Francisco: Harper and Row.

Dunning, H. Ray. 1988. *Grace, Faith, and Holiness.* Kansas City: Beacon Hill Press of Kansas City.

Estep, James Riley. 1997. John Wesley's philosophy of formal childhood education. In *Christian Education Journal* 1, no. 2: 43-52.

Felton, Gayle Carlton. 1997. John Wesley and the teaching ministry: Ramifications for education in the church today. In *Religious Education* 92, no. 1 (winter): 92-106.

Grider, J. Kenneth. 1994. *A Wesleyan-Holiness Theology.* Kansas City: Beacon Hill Press of Kansas City.

Gross, John. 1954. *John Wesley: Christian Educator.* Nashville: Board of Education, The Methodist Church.

Hall, Elaine Friedrich. 1998. *Pedagogical and Andragogical Principles of John Wesley's Anthology.* Ph.D. diss., Univ. of North Texas.

Harper, Steve. 1983a. *The Devotional Life in the Wesleyan Tradition.* Nashville: Upper Room.

_____. 1983b. *John Wesley's Message for Today.* Grand Rapids: Francis Asbury Press.

Heitzenrater, Richard P. 1984. *The Elusive Mr. Wesley.* 2 vols. Nashville: Abingdon Press.

_____. 1989. *Mirror and Memory: Reflections on Early Methodism.* Nashville: Kingswood Books.

_____. 1995. *Wesley and the People Called Methodist.* Nashville: Abingdon Press.

_____. 2001. John Wesley and children. In *The Child in Christian Thought,* 279-99. Ed. Marcia J. Bunge. Grand Rapids: William B. Eerdmans.

Henderson, David Michael. 1981. *John Wesley's Instructional Groups.* Ph.D. diss., Indiana Univ.

_____. 1997. *John Wesley's Class Meeting: A Model of Making Disciples.* Nappanee, IN: Evangel Press.

Hunsicker, David. 1996. John Wesley: Father of today's small group concept? In *Wesleyan Theological Journal* 31, no. 1: 192-211.

Hynson, Leon O. 1995. Wesley, Jennings and the poor. In *Evangelical Journal* 13 (spring): 39-44.

Jennings, Theodore W. 1990. *Good News to the Poor.* Nashville: Abingdon Press.

Keefer, Luke L. 1990. John Wesley, the Methodists and social reform in England. In *Wesleyan Theological Journal* 25, no. 1: 7-20.

Knight, Henry Hawthorn. 1992. *The Presence of God in the Christian Life: John Wesley and the Means of Grace.* Metuchen, NJ: Scarecrow Press.

Knowles, Malcolm S. 1980. *The Modern Practice of Adult Education: From Pedagogy to Andragogy.* Chicago: Follett.

Lawson, John, and Harold Silver. 1973. *A Social History of Education in England.* London: Methuen.

Lindström, Harold. 1980. *Wesley and Sanctification: A Study in the Doctrine of Salvation.* Grand Rapids: Zondervan.

Maddix, Mark A. John Wesley and a holistic approach to Christian education. In *Wesleyan Theological Journal* 44, no. 2: 76-93.

Maddox, Randy. 1994. *Responsible Grace: John Wesley's Practical Theology.* Nashville: Kingswood Books.

Madron, Thomas. 1981. John Wesley on economics. In *Sanctification and Liberation,* 102-15. Ed. Theodore Runyon. Nashville: Abingdon Press.

Marquardt, Manfred. 1992. *John Wesley's Social Ethics: Praxis and Principles.* Trans. John E. Steely and W. Stephen Gunter. Nashville: Abingdon Press.

Naglee, David I. 1987. *From Font to Faith: John Wesley on Infant Baptism and the Nurture of Children.* New York: Peter Lang.

Outler, Albert C., ed. 1964. *John Wesley.* New York: Oxford Univ. Press.

Prince, John Wesley. 1926. *Wesley on Religious Education: A Study of John Wesley's Theories and Methods of the Education of Children in Religion.* New York: Methodist Book Concern.

Reed, James E., and Ronnie Prevost. 1993. *A History of Christian Education.* Nashville: Broadman and Holman.

Runyon, Theodore. 1998. *The New Creation: John Wesley's Theology Today.* Nashville: Abingdon Press.

Seaborn, Joseph. 1985. *John Wesley's Use of History as a Ministerial and Educational Tool.* Th.D. diss., Boston Univ. School of Theology.

Simon, John S. 1921. *John Wesley and the Religious Societies.* London: Epworth Press.

———. 1923. *John Wesley and the Methodist Societies.* London: Epworth Press.

Staples, Rob. 1991. *Outward Sign and Inward Grace.* Kansas City: Beacon Hill Press of Kansas City.

Stonehouse, Catherine. 2004. Children in Wesleyan thought. In *Children's Spirituality: Christian Perspectives, Research and Applications,* 133-48. Ed. Donald Ratcliff. Eugene, OR: Cascade Books.

Towns, Elmer. 1975. John Wesley. In *A History of Religious Educators.* Grand Rapids: Baker.

Tracy, Wes. 1987. *The Wesleyan Way to Spiritual Formation: Christian Spirituality in the Letters of John Wesley.* St.D. diss., San Francisco Theological Seminary.

Tuttle, Robert G. 1978. *John Wesley: His Life and Theology.* Grand Rapids: Zondervan.

———. 1989. *Mysticism in the Wesleyan Tradition.* Grand Rapids: Francis Asbury Press.

Tyerman, Luke. 1872/1986. *The Life and Times of the Reverend John Wesley, M.A.* New York: Harper and Brothers.

Tyson, John R. 1997. Why did John Wesley "fail"? A reappraisal of Wesley's evangelical economics. In *Methodist History* 35, no. 3: 176-87.

Watson, David Lowes. 1985. *The Early Methodist Class Meeting.* Nashville: Discipleship Resources.

———. 1990. *Forming Christian Disciples.* Nashville: Discipleship Resources.

———. 1991. *Covenant Discipleship: Christian Formation Through Mutual Accountability.* Nashville: Discipleship Resources.

Wesley, John. 1872/1986. *The Works of John Wesley.* 3rd ed. 14 vols. Ed. Thomas Jackson. London: Wesleyan Methodist Book Room; reprint, Peabody, Mass.: Hendrickson. Also see http://wesley.nnu.edu.

———. 1975-2003. *The Works of John Wesley.* 16 vols. Ed. Albert Outler, Richard P. Heitzenrater, and Frank Baker. Nashville: Abingdon Press.

Williams, Colin. 1960. *John Wesley's Theology Today: A Study of the Wesleyan Tradition in the Light of Current Theological Dialogue.* Nashville: Abingdon Press.

SIX

THE MEANS OF GRACE

▶ INTRODUCTION

Imagine you have just ten minutes between Sunday school hour and worship. A parent stops you in the church foyer and asks, "Why in the world are we putting so much effort into (children's/youth/adult) ministry? What are you trying to accomplish in Christian education anyway?" How would you respond?

Imagine, during a church interview, a leader asks, "We have a number of skilled teachers at the church, why should we hire you? How would you organize our discipleship ministries any differently than the local grade school? What difference will it make to have a minister lead our Christian education ministries? What would you say?

Every serious Christian educator implicitly or explicitly seeks to organize educational activities around a common approach or theme. This effort often reveals the theological and educational assumptions that guide attempts at faithful discipleship. These assumptions guide curricular and program choices and provide a rationale for the program itself. Articulating our approach reveals our philosophy of Christian education, though we may not have time in a five-minute foyer conversation to say everything we think is important. So what do you say about your purpose, mission, and approach to Christian education? Is it important to teach the Bible, to shape people through the community of faith, to reach people and nurture them based on where they are in life, to make a difference in the community? Is it a combination of these or all of them; what do you think? Understanding your enduring mission can help overcome the terror of peer pressure, congregational demands, and countless changes in ministry that may be based on recent fads. This understanding also provides the vision needed to adapt and innovate without losing your core focus.

Maintaining continuity while adapting to changing times is an enduring problem (M. E. Moore 1983). Some approaches favor continuity, stressing the need to either teach the *content* of the faith (scripture and Christian doctrine) or encourage regular *participation* in faith communities that instill steady faith in difficult times. Other approaches favor strategic response to *dynamic changes in persons* (developmental or life experience) or *shifts in the social fabric*. These discipleship approaches identify engagement and adaptation as key virtues in Christian education, focusing on the needs of individuals or society (Seymour

1997). All four approaches have been applied at various times in the history of Christian education, often with an accompanying challenge to interpret the times and discover what is most meaningful for Christians in a given context or historical situation. The challenge often rests in recognizing the strengths and limits of each approach when applied in isolation. What approach is consistent with a Wesleyan perspective, any of these or something else?

▶ RETURNING TO WESLEY THE EDUCATOR

Discovering an approach consistent with Wesleyan convictions and practice begins with the theological assumptions and educational passions already covered in the previous chapters. As noted in chapter 5, John Wesley's understanding of Christian education began with the discipline of his mother, Susanna, and the intellectual passion of his father, Samuel. Wesley's methodical approach was shaped at his mother's knee, while his ministerial sensibilities grew from his father's vocation as a minister. Wesley focused on the education of children and youth and the needs of adults who joined the Methodist societies and bands. In some ways, Wesley merely perpetuated the educational systems of the culture, particularly in fashioning the Kingswood school for young students and endorsing a growing interest in Sunday instruction that was modeled on the charity schools of his day (Blevins 2005). Wesley was also an innovator, adapting his understanding of Anglican religious societies and Moravian bands to create Methodist societies and class meetings (Blevins 2002/2003). Wesley's desire to provide educational materials (written sermons, tracts, and edited volumes) for young and old proved invaluable, then and now. His efforts to lift up the religious experience of young people alongside the lives of adults provided a living witness to the power of the Wesleyan message (Blevins 2004). As noted, his efforts at traditional schooling and accountable discipleship surface in various academic treatments as he sought to create a community shaped in devotion and discipline, a community of faithful disciples focused on holiness of heart and life (Chilcote 2004; Henderson 1997).

Wesley also encouraged personal and social Christian practices intended to foster deeper growth in grace. His advocacy and organization of these practices, known as the "means of grace," provide the best organizing principle for faithful discipleship from a Wesleyan perspective. Many ministers and laypeople appreciate Wesley for his theological contributions, particularly his emphasis on holiness of heart and life. Wesley knew that such holiness found its life and expression only through forms of discipline that take the source of holiness, the sacramental love of God, seriously. The result was Wesley's call for Christians to practice the means of grace, a set of enduring and yet flexible Christian practices that shape a life of holiness. As we will see, the means of grace also provide a framework for exploring and organizing contemporary Christian education practices.

▸ The Means of Grace

Wesley's most explicit definition for the means of grace appears in his sermon of the same title: "By 'means of grace' I understand outward signs, words, or actions, ordained of God, and appointed for this end—to be the *ordinary* channels whereby he conveys to men, preventing, justifying or sanctifying grace" (1975-2003, 1:381).

The term *means of grace* originated during a controversy with the Moravians over the Fetter Lane Society and culminates with Wesley's instructions to ministers to utilize various practices (and dispositions) for godly living. Wesley's detailed argument for the means of grace at Fetter Lane set the stage for his continued use of this term to emphasize an increasing number of sacramental practices. Wesley actually described the various practices of the means of grace in sermons and other writings, using different categories, particularly in key documents of Methodist polity and those that focus on the practice of Communion (Blevins 1999, 136-227). But in this first, key sermon Wesley includes three "chief means"—prayer, searching the scriptures, and participating in the Lord's Supper (1975-2003, 1:381). Another list of practices appears in "The Scripture Way of Salvation":

First, all *works of piety,* such as public prayer, family prayer, and praying in our closet; receiving the Supper of the Lord; searching the Scriptures by hearing, reading, meditating; and using such a measure of fasting or abstinence as our bodily health allows.

Secondly, all *works of mercy,* whether they relate to the bodies or souls of men; such as feeding the hungry, clothing the naked, entertaining the stranger, visiting those that are in prison, or sick, or variously afflicted; such as the endeavoring to instruct the ignorant, to waken the stupid sinner, to quicken the lukewarm, to confirm the wavering, to comfort the feebleminded, to succour the tempted, or contribute in any manner to the saving of souls from death. (2:166)

The *means of grace* also served as a standard Wesleyan phrase in polity and ministry. Wesley, in "The Nature, Design and General Rules of the United Societies," stressed that society members should evidence their desire for salvation in three ways: by doing no harm and avoiding evil, by doing good, and by attending upon all the ordinances of God (1872/1986, 9:69-73).

The means of grace surface in other locations where Wesley includes practices such as reading, meditation, and prayer as well as providing additional emphasis on compassionate acts . . . all reminiscent of traditional Anglican nomenclature in his day (1975-2003, 3:340, 343, 385-89). In 1781, with his sermon "On Zeal," Wesley described a series of concentric circles around the love of God. The first circle contains the holy tempers: "Long-suffering, gentleness, meekness, goodness, fidelity, temperance" (3:313). Additional circles included works of mercy followed by works of piety, all encapsulated by the church "a little emblem of which, of the church universal, we have in every particular Christian congregation" (3:314). Wesley elaborated on works of piety and established a relationship between the two sets of practices and their influence on the dispositions (or tempers) within the believer.

The "Larger" Minutes of 1778 may serve as one of the most important documents to demonstrate how Wesley incorporated the means of grace as a part of the regular examination of all lay ministers (1872/1986, 13:299, 322-24). Wesley encouraged his ministers to view their "helpers" as pupils and to encourage them in using all the means of grace (13:322). In this document, Wesley revealed new language to describe the means of grace. Rather than works of mercy and works of piety, Wesley now used the language of *instituted* and *prudential* means of grace. The *instituted means* (very similar to Wesley's understanding of ordinances or acts of piety) include prayer (private, family, and public), searching the scriptures (by reading, meditating, and hearing), the Lord's Supper, fasting, and Christian conference (13:322-23). The *prudential means* include rules, arts of holy living, acts of ministry, and larger attitudes toward daily living under the headings of watching, denying ourselves, taking up our cross, and exercising the presence of God (13:323-24).

▶ THE MEANS OF GRACE AS FORMATION, DISCERNMENT, AND TRANSFORMATION

Wesley was certain about the effects of faithful practice of any means of grace: "Never can you use these means but a blessing will ensue. And the more you use them, the more will you grow in grace" (13:324). When combined and compared, Wesley's categories of the instituted and prudential means of grace, along with the acts of mercy, suggest a way of ordering educational practices into three complementary, mediating, approaches for Christian education— formation, discernment, and transformation—that respect both the intent of the practices and the larger goal of faithful discipleship.

FORMATION AS CHRISTIAN EDUCATION

Wesley's understanding of the instituted means of grace suggests an approach to Christian education best described as *formation,* where grace is mediated by assimilating persons into the Christian culture through a series of established Christian practices. Individuals are formed and transformed as they participate in the total life of the faith community, through the discrete practices that identify that community. By faithful (i.e., intentional) participation, persons are shaped in Christian character and transformed by their new identity.

The instituted means of grace form a series of interdependent practices that, if followed faithfully, result in experienced grace. Wesley believed that people should use the practices "with a constant eye" toward the renewal of their souls in "righteousness and true holiness" (1975-2003, 1:545). He insisted that these practices would not automatically evoke grace, yet he was confident that grace was possible if the means were practiced with a sense of trust and expectation. Henry Knight argues that, in practicing the means of grace, persons were exposed and ultimately shaped into the character of God (1988, 185-240). Formation occurs as persons are socialized into the Christian faith through the life and practices of the faith community (Foster 1982). People are transformed, personally and communally, through the traditional practices of the Christian faith.

As demonstrated earlier, formative practices, throughout the history of Christian communities, were anchored within the Christian narrative and influenced by the culture, which provided the deep structures that shaped practicing Christians (Engen 2004, 20-22). Recent Christian educators who stress the need for formation often associate the term with the writing of C. Ellis Nelson and his thesis that we live into the culture of the Christian faith through a series of practices (1967, 35-66). John Westerhoff calls for intentional assimilation into the Christian worldview via eight aspects of communal life:

1. Communal rites (repetitive, symbolic, and social acts that express and manifest the community's sacred narrative along with its implied faith and life)
2. Church environment (including architectural space and artifacts)
3. Time (particularly the Christian calendar)
4. Communal life (polity, programs, and economic life as well as support behaviors)
5. Discipline (structured practices within the community)
6. Social interaction (interpersonal relations and motivations)
7. Role models (exemplars and mentors)
8. Language (which names and describes behavior). (1992, 272-78)

Through the intentional employment of these aspects in distinctly Christian ways, Westerhoff believes we can induct children into a Christian community and culture, which are the basic forms of discipleship for Christians. Westerhoff champions his approach (1987) and later offers the following reason:

"For Christians, the integrity of the church assumes an alternative community alongside and within a society where intolerance and interference are accepted. Christian families need to be able to shape the convictions by which they are to live and by which they hope their children will live" (1992, viii).

Westerhoff's concern echoes efforts by evangelical Christian educators like Larry Richards in the intentional nurture of children into the life of the church (1983, 17-83). Westerhoff's corporate approach may be more intentional than Richards', but they share similar goals.

The instituted means of grace, as an approach to education through formation, suggest a repertoire of Christian practices that collectively shape an understanding of God. The practices provide a way of responding to God's active presence by rehearsing a way of life that is Christian. The practices also provide an opportunity to connect faith with daily life (Bass 1997, xiii, 6-11). Wesley himself encouraged an ongoing observance of the ordinances. The repetitive use of these practices can shape Christian character and provide continual transformation into holiness of heart and life (Markham 2007).

Obviously worship stands at the center of this formative practice (Murphy 2004). While a necessary beginning point, worship is only one part of a larger ecology of church practices, including the broader domains of ministry, discipleship, outreach, and polity. Each domain of congregational life includes a formative process, and the collective interplay of all these domains (like that of the means of grace) reveals either a deliberate formative system or dissolves into a confusing array of contradictory practices. Determining how to arrange the practices requires an approach that complements formative Christian education. This second form of discipleship, discernment, emerges through the prudential means of grace.

DISCERNMENT AS CHRISTIAN EDUCATION

The prudential means of grace include a large array of contextual practices that may also become means of grace for the practitioner. Discerning which practices are truly means of grace involves both critical investigation and a constructive (or imaginative) appreciation of God's ongoing activity. Discerning the appropriate context and quality of formative practices, their relationship to basic beliefs, and their location in each historical period is a key challenge (Engen 2004, 3). Community practices are not "generic"; they are weighted with cultural implications (20-21). Determining their validity as means of grace is an act of discernment. Wesley's provision for a contextual set of prudential practices invites ministers to an ongoing task of discerning what practices truly convey grace.

Discernment has a long history within Christianity (McIntosh 2004) as both an individual and communal practice (Rogers 1997, 107-13). Wesley often engaged in practices of discernment in shaping the devotion and discipline of the Methodist people (Blevins Fall 2002/Spring 2003, 88-92). Wesley also exercised discernment as a spiritual director to others (Tracy 1987, 44-186) and through a series of instructions for practices designed to foster accountability among Methodists involved in class meetings and band meetings (Henderson 1997). Surveying the history of spiritual discernment, theologian Mark McIntosh notes five basic movements:

> 1) Discernment as faith, spiritual discernment as grounded in a loving and trusting relationship with God; 2) Discernment as distinguishing between good and evil impulses that move people; 3) Discernment as discretion, practical wisdom, moderation, and generally good sense about what to do in given practical situations; 4) Discernment as sensitivity to and desire to pursue God's will in all things; and 5) Discernment as illumination, contemplative wisdom, a noetic relationship with God that irradiates and facilitates knowledge of every kind of truth. (2004, 5)

Many of these descriptions apply to Wesley's personal life and ministerial practice as he sought to balance both faith and vision with instructions for educating and guiding Methodist devotion and discipline (Chilcote 2004). Discernment includes a deep understanding of scripture as well as honest engagement with Christian conduct. Wesley's instructions include the following questions to be asked at every class meeting:

1. Have you the forgiveness of your sins?
2. Have you peace with God, through our Lord Jesus Christ?
3. Have you the witness of God's Spirit with your spirit, that you are a child of God?
4. Is the love of God shed abroad in your heart?
5. Has no sin, inward or outward, dominion over you?
6. Do you desire to be told of your faults?
7. Do you desire to be told of all your faults, and that plain and home [to the point]?
8. Do you desire that every one of us should tell you from time to time, whatsoever is in his heart concerning you? (1872/1986, 8:272-74)

The queries could include what class members had heard that needed verification as well as open, frank, and cutting statements concerning a member's current faults. Questions include: "1) What sins have you committed since our last meeting? 2) What temptations have you met with? 3) How were you delivered? 4) What have you thought, said or done, of which you doubt whether it be sin or not?" (273).

Specific directions concerned avoiding certain "sinful" behavior, including profaning the Lord's day, drinking, dishonesty in business, gossip, and so forth. The combination of questions and actions also helped Methodists engage in at least the first four movements described by McIntosh. Henry Knight classifies several of Wesley's admonitions as "general means of grace," listing them as: obedience, keeping commandments, watching, denying self, taking up the cross daily, and exercising the presence of God (1992, 5). Knight notes that these collectively relate directly to the Methodist dictums of "do no harm, do good, attend the means of Grace" (122-26). These practices reflect not only the distinguishing of good and evil (McIntosh 2004, 13-16) but also provide a type of daily wisdom that combines virtue with common sense in the seeking of God's will (16-20). It is also helpful to note that Wesley's later conjectures on the "New Creation" as individual, and finally, cosmic transformation (Runyon 1998, 7-12) reflect McIntosh's fifth stage in which contemplation on the transformation of the whole of creation draws one closer to God (2004, 20-22). Wesleyans are challenged to teach the complete range of discernment as part of their heritage.

Discernment, following its Latin root, *discerner,* is an activity of shifting and distinguishing (Wood 1985, 68). As an aural activity, discernment implies a type of hearing that invites closer attention, in order to appreciate the intricate harmonies within a musical score. Discernment not only involves discrimination among options but also embraces an imaginative appreciation of the possibilities available from the various options presented. Discernment, in this sense, includes critical and creative components. Critical thinking can be a difficult task for students and teachers. It takes courage to release one's control of knowledge and trust the Holy Spirit to guide Christian educators and parishioners in the pursuit of truth. This type of thinking begins by questioning the historical, cultural, and psychological assumptions that influence Christian life and practice. It means allowing students to develop questions rather than teachers always providing the answers (Kasachkoff 1998). Teachers must make students aware of the framework of any good argument and of how often students—and their teachers—tend to miss the small inconsistencies of their lives.

Critical discernment occurs as practitioners investigate the possibility of any new practice becoming a prudential means of grace. Practices do not automatically qualify as means of grace. God's transformative grace must be evident within the practice, particularly manifested in holiness of heart and life. Each practice, within its context, must be analyzed to determine not only if it mediates grace but also whether it impedes God's gracious activity. Critical discernment engages the world to determine how practices might be used for evil as well as for good. Approaches to liberative Christian education (Moore 1982; Schipani 1988), which challenge structures and practices in the world that oppress persons and impede God's gracious activity, model this aspect of discernment. The very process of critical discernment itself can become a sacramental act (Warren 1994a). Ultimately, formation efforts must first discern the life of the congregation to ensure faithful practice. This leads to congregational leadership strategies that regard discernment as primarily a congregational task (Hawkins 1997).

Self-reflection becomes a part of the critical process as well. Christian educators must explore their own heritage and training. They must learn how to affirm the positive aspects of their history while becoming alert to poor influences and faulty assumptions. They must distinguish between their own felt needs (often desires) versus the real needs of their lives. Most of all, they must become aware that thinking is an active process rather than a passive reception of information.

Educators recognize that discernment requires more than critical analysis. Theorists practicing discernment must include imagination and constructive thought to embrace Wesley's openness to new practices and to the potential for grace in these practices. Theologically, creative discernment acknowledges the power of the Holy Spirit to empower new structures for the sake of conveying God's free grace so that the presence of Jesus Christ might be revealed in the most remarkable places and during the most mundane practices. Creative discernment is an interpretive practice of naming God at work in the world and also seeking the means to God's gracious activity (Seymour et al. 1993). Anchored in the hope of Christ's return, the practice of creative discernment also anticipates the promises of God evident in the practices (Schipani 1988, 68-100).

Discernment is an ongoing task of faithful discipleship. Continual openness to practices that might, for a time, reveal God's grace is encouraged by the prudential means of grace. Identifying such practices is the task of constructive discernment, and determining their validity requires critical assessment. Cultivating the capacity to discern God's activity in new practices also helps the participant appreciate God's grace at work within formative practices. Discernment increases the faithfulness of participants as they expectantly seek God's transforming grace through Christian practice. The means of grace also suggest activities that seek to create as well as identify transformation. Works of mercy encourage participants to *become* a means of grace as well as to *use* them.

TRANSFORMATION AS CHRISTIAN EDUCATION

Scholars list the works of mercy alongside the prudential means of grace, but they deserve separate consideration. Wesley confirmed his emphasis on works of mercy by his own discipleship practices for those on the margins

(Blevins 1999, 87-93, 114-18). As an educational approach, the purpose of transformation is to heal and liberate persons, Christian communities, society, and ultimately all of creation. Wesleyans seek to accomplish these goals through educationally transformative activities.

Education for the sake of transformation has a long history in religious education (Seymour et al. 1984), including the progressive education movement of Dewey, Coe, and Harrison Elliot (Moore 1989). These early movements sought to engage the public in order to bring about educational and religious transformation. Contemporary attempts to transform social structures and the environment include Paulo Freire's *conscientização* or "conscientization" (Freire 1988, 19, 75-118; M. E. Moore 1991, 166-74). *Conscientization* describes an educational process that not only critically discerns the existing social order but also seeks to reform it. A number of Christian educators use this approach, even in youth ministry (Warren 1994a; White 2005). Evangelical educators also embrace Freire within certain limits (Pazmiño 1997, 75-80). There have been other approaches to transformative education. Liberative approaches lift up the role of women (Harris 1988) or empower poor people who are often held captive to an unjust social order (Evans et al. 1994). Christian discipleship includes efforts for peace and justice, visits or relocations to impoverished areas for deeper understanding of the human condition, and service learning and alternative Bible studies that explore real life situations in dynamic interplay with the Bible.

Similar transformation approaches surface in evangelical Christian education through mission efforts (Habermas and Issler 1992, 50, 52-53) or evangelism efforts always tempered with aspects of compassion or humility (Root 2001, 55-57). Often such strategies require discernment as well as action, but the results may be quite transformative (Pazmiño 2001, 130-31). Educators often address ecological as well as individual needs for the sake of transformation (Habermas and Issler 1992, 52). Ultimately, transformation includes the acts of witness and testimony for the church and the larger community (Long 2004, 3-20). Formative acts can "translate" into engaging moments of transformational conversation.

As noted earlier, Wesley's efforts do not always lend themselves to a pure understanding of liberative teaching, though there was a social quality to many of his efforts with children and adults (Marquardt 1992). His desire to transform others spiritually and materially coincides with a broad view of social transformation, including the transformation of all creation (Runyon 1998, 8). The goal of Wesley's educational efforts, holiness of heart and life, may actually hold a clue for a Wesleyan understanding of transformative Christian education. Holiness of heart and life can be part of the process of education as well as its goal. This is clear from Wesley's understanding of Christian conference. Wesley understood that holiness of heart and life was an ongoing goal to be lived out each day. As persons sought to live a life of holiness, they were changing the world around them as well as being changed by their own participation in the means of grace. Stated another way, Methodists participated in the means of grace in order to become a means of grace to the broader society.

Discernment, as critical thinking and heightened imagination, joins with liberative practice to create what Peter Hodgson terms a transformative pedagogy or *padeia* of God's wisdom (1999, 114). New learning emerges from the attempts to create transformation, which in turn reenergizes and refocuses transformative efforts. As Wesleyans engage the world as "means of grace," their efforts provide a transformative framework for their own lives. The result is that Wesleyan transformational practices also "form" the practitioners.

▶ CONCLUSION

The three approaches of formation, discernment, and transformation provide a broad understanding of Wesleyan discipleship, particularly through the means of grace. These approaches are interactive, much like various practices of the means of grace that work together for the sake of discipleship. Formative practices shape new ways of discerning the world. Critical and constructive discernment invites participants to see not only the urgent necessity for transformation but also the creative possibility of a transformed world. Transformative practices, which rely upon discernment, are themselves formative, socializing persons into a community that believes and works for transformation. Together these three approaches reveal common tasks, though the approaches remain discrete enough to organize our ministry around the larger categories: formation engages us in the continuity of our Christian faith, transformation calls us to respond to the changing environment, while discerning the relationship between our past heritage and our future vision maintains our integrity as a people of God. Collectively, these approaches guide persons and communities into a new way of living and engaging in faithful discipleship that is consistent with our Wesleyan roots yet open to hope for God's continual accomplishments in this world. The next time someone asks you why he or she needs educational ministry, you can readily respond: "We need to form persons into the people of God, guide them to discern the direction of God's work in the church and the world, and empower them to be transforming agents for the sake of the gospel." Or, you might say, "We participate in the means of grace, the faithful discipleship of Jesus, in order, by the power of the Holy Spirit, to become means of grace, the agents of God's reconciliation, in and for our world." May our educational ministry be worthy of such goals and organized to respond to them by God's grace.

▶ REFERENCES

Bass, Dorothy. 1997. *Practicing Our Faith: A Way of Life for a Searching People.* San Francisco: Jossey-Bass.

Blevins, Dean G. 1999. *John Wesley and the Means of Grace: An Approach to Christian Education.* Ph.D. diss., Claremont School of Theology. Ann Arbor, MI: UMI.

_____. 2002. Educating the liturgical self: A sacramental view of pedagogy. In *Journal of Christian Education: Australian Christian Forum on Education* 45 (December) (3), 7-20.

_____. Fall 2002/Spring 2003. Practicing the new creation: Wesley's eschatological community formed by the means of grace. In *Asbury Theological Journal* 57 (2) and 58 (1), 81-105.

_____. 2004. Holy church, holy people: A Wesleyan exploration in congregational holiness and personal testament. In *Wesleyan Theological Journal* 39, no. 2 (fall): 54-73.

_____. 2005. Faithful discipleship: A conjoined catechesis of truth and love. In *Considering the Great Commission: Explorations for a Wesleyan Praxis of Mission and Evangelism.* Ed. W. Stephen Gunter and Elaine A. Robinson. Nashville: Abingdon Press.

Chilcote, Paul W. 2004. *Recapturing the Wesleys' Vision: An Introduction to the Faith of John and Charles Wesley.* Downers Grove, IL: InterVarsity Press.

Engen, J. V. 2004. Introduction: Formative religious practices in premodern European life. In *Educating People of Faith: Exploring the History of Jewish and Christian Communities.* Ed. J. V. Engen. Grand Rapids: William B. Eerdmans.

Evans, A. F., R. A. Evans, and W. B. Kennedy. 1994. *Pedagogies for the Non-Poor.* Maryknoll, NY: Orbis Books.

Foster, Charles R. 1982. The faith community as a guiding image for Christian education. In *Contemporary Approaches to Christian Education,* 53-71. Ed. J. L. Seymour and D. E. Miller. Nashville: Abingdon Press.

Freire, Paulo. 1988. In *Pedagogy of the Oppressed.* Trans. M. B. Ramos. New York: Continuum.

Gardner, Howard. 1982. *Art, Mind & Brain: A Cognitive Approach to Creativity.* New York: Basic Books.

Habermas, Ronald, and Klaus Issler. 1992. *Teaching for Reconciliation: Foundations and Practice of Christian Educational Ministry.* Grand Rapids: Baker Books.

Harris, Maria. 1988. *Women and Teaching: Themes for a Spirituality of Pedagogy.* New York: Paulist Press.

Hawkins, Thomas R. 1997. *The Learning Congregation: A New Vision of Leadership.* Louisville, KY: Westminster/John Knox Press.

Henderson, D. Michael. 1997. *John Wesley's Class Meeting: A Model of Making Disciples.* Nappanee, IN: Evangel.

Hodgson, Peter C. 1999. *God's Wisdom: Toward a Theology of Education.* Louisville, KY: Westminster/John Knox Press.

Kasachkoff, Tziporah, ed. 1998. *In the Socratic Tradition: Essays on Teaching Philosophy.* Lanham, MD: Rowman and Littlefield.

Knight, Henry H. 1988. *The Presence of God in the Christian Life: A Contemporary Understanding of John Wesley's Means of Grace.* Ph.D. diss., Emory Univ. Ann Arbor, MI: UMI.

Long, Thomas G. 2004. *Testimony: Talking Ourselves into Being Christian.* San Francisco: Jossey-Bass.

Markham, Paul N. 2007. *Rewired: Exploring Religious Conversion.* Eugene, OR: Pickwick Publications.

Marquardt, M. 1992. *John Wesley's Social Ethics: Praxis and Principles.* Trans. John E. Steely and W. Stephen Gunter. Nashville: Abingdon Press.

McIntosh, M. A. 2004. *Discernment and Truth: The Spirituality and Theology of Knowledge.* New York: Herder and Herder, Crossroads.

Moore, Allen J. 1982. Liberation and the future of Christian education. In *Contemporary Approaches to Christian Education,* 103-22. Ed. J. L. Seymour and D. E. Miller. Nashville: Abingdon Press.

———. 1989. A social theory of religious education. In *Religious Education as Social Transformation,* 103-22. Ed. A. J. Moore. Birmingham, AL: Religious Education Press.

Moore, Mary Elizabeth. 1983. *Education for Continuity and Change: A New Model for Christian Religious Education.* Nashville: Abingdon Press.

———. 1991. *Teaching from the Heart: Theology and Educational Method.* Minneapolis: Fortress Press.

Murphy, Deborah Dean. 2004. *Teaching That Transforms: Worship as the Heart of Christian Education.* Grand Rapids: Brazos Press.

Nelson, C. Ellis. 1967. *Where Faith Begins.* Richmond, VA: John Knox Press.

Pazmiño, Robert W. 1997. *Foundational Issues in Christian Education: An Introduction in Evangelical Perspective.* 2nd ed. Grand Rapids: Baker Books.

Richards, Larry. 1983. *Children's Ministry: Nurturing Faith Within the Family of God.* Grand Rapids: Zondervan.

Rogers, Frank. 1997. Discernment. In *Practicing Our Faith: A Way of Life for a Searching People,* 105-18. Ed. Dorothy Bass. San Francisco: Jossey-Bass.

Root, Jerry. 2001. Evangelism and discipleship. In *Introducing Christian Education: Foundations for the Twenty-first Century,* 53-59. Ed. M. J. Anthony. Grand Rapids: Baker Books.

Runyon, Theodore. 1998. *The New Creation: John Wesley's Theology Today.* Nashville: Abingdon Press.

Schipani, Daniel S. 1988. *Religious Education Encounters Liberation Theology.* Birmingham, AL: Religious Education Press.

Seymour, Jack L., ed. 1997. *Mapping Christian Education: Approaches to Congregational Learning.* Nashville: Abingdon Press.

Seymour, Jack L., Robert T. O'Gorman, and Charles R. Foster. 1984. *The Church in the Education of the Public.* Nashville: Abingdon Press.

Seymour, Jack L., Margaret Ann Crain, and James V. Crockett. 1993. *Educating Christians: The Intersection of Meaning, Learning, and Vocation.* Nashville: Abingdon Press.

Tracy, Wes D. 1987. The Wesleyan way to spiritual formation: Christian spirituality in the letters of John Wesley. St.D. diss., San Francisco Theological Seminary.

Tracy, Wes D., E. D. Freeborn, J. Tartaglia-Metcalf, and M. Weigelt. 1994. *The Upward Call: Spiritual Formation and the Holy Life.* Kansas City: Beacon Hill Press of Kansas City.

Tracy, W. D., G. Cockerill, D. Demaray, and S. Harper. 2002. *Reflecting God.* Kansas City: Beacon Hill Press of Kansas City.

Volf, M., and D. Bass, eds. 2002. *Practicing Theology: Beliefs and Practices in the Christian Life.* Grand Rapids: William B. Eerdmans.

Warren, Michael. 1994a. *Youth, Gospel, Liberation.* 2nd ed. New Rochelle, NY: Don Bosco Multimedia.

_____. 1994b. The sacramentality of critique and its challenge to Christian educators. In *Christian Education Journal* 15 (fall) (1): 42-52.

Wesley, John. 1975-2003. *The Works of John Wesley.* 16 vols. Ed. Albert Outler, Richard P. Heitzenrater, and Frank Baker. Nashville: Abingdon Press.

_____. 1872/1986. *The Works of John Wesley.* 3rd ed. 14 vols. Ed. Thomas Jackson. London: Wesleyan Methodist Book Room; reprint, Peabody, Mass.: Hendrickson. Also see http://wesley.nnu.edu.

Westerhoff, John. 1987. Formation, education and instruction. In *Religious Education* 82 (fall) (4): 578-91.

_____. 1992. Introduction, and Fashioning Christians in our day. In *Schooling Christians, "Holy Experiments" in American Education,* v-xx, 262-81. Ed. Stanley Hauerwas and John Westerhoff. Grand Rapids: William B. Eerdmans.

White, David. 2005. *Practicing Discernment with Youth.* Cleveland: Pilgrim Press.

Wood, Charles M. 1985. *Vision and Discernment.* Atlanta: Scholars Press.

PART 2

THE DYNAMICS OF
FAITHFUL DISCIPLESHIP

Providing a definition for faithful discipleship serves as a necessary first step for any Christian education text. However, our task would be incomplete if we did not move from conceptual perspectives to practical considerations. Discipleship occurs within a dynamic context that includes the biological and developmental changes of people's lives as well as the shifts in social context that often frame our educational ministry.

This section begins with a brief overview of the dynamics that, as ministers, we must attend to for the sake of faithful discipleship: learning, growing, and coming to faith within specific cultural settings (chapter 7). Chapters 8 to 10 review the various developmental theories that shape our general knowledge of people and research that helps us understand their ability to learn. We recognize that our knowledge of people always intersects with our desire to teach them; content and context merge when we begin to think through how we will fashion a curriculum for faithful teaching (chapter 11). Faithful educational effort incorporates dynamic understanding of the learner, the social environment, and desired outcomes. Even the design and delivery of a curriculum remains dynamic as we adapt our teaching methods to the tasks at hand.

Didache, or faithful discipleship, emerges when defined convictions interact with dynamic engagement of context. With these tasks accomplished, we will then reorient our Christian education in a framework that respects both concepts and contexts as we shape a faithful approach to Christian discipleship.

97

SEVEN

PAYING ATTENTION TO PEOPLE AND CULTURE

▶ INTRODUCTION

Imagine yourself in a church foyer. A new couple arrives for worship. As you introduce yourself, what questions would you ask? What basic information would you seek and how well would you know these people after three to five minutes? How would this information help you determine who they are from a spiritual perspective?

Imagine you are a local youth worker. You invite the youth group to attend a nearby restaurant—a pizza parlor or other popular gathering place—as part of a Sunday night gathering. Afterward a dedicated layperson in your congregation confronts you about the event: "How can you call this gathering an opportunity for ministry? You should be teaching the Bible, engaging in prayer, or at least helping others in the congregation rather than consuming pizza!" How would you respond?

Faithful discipleship entails shaping people into the kingdom of God, helping them discern God's direction, and empowering them for faithful, missional engagement in the world. What difference do these scenarios make in our role as Christian educators, as educational ministers? Faithful discipleship, authentic Christian education, must also be understood through the lens of ministry.

▶ MINISTRY: PAYING ATTENTION TO PEOPLE

How do we define *ministry*? Concepts of "service" and "care" come to mind, but not as recipients of these loving acts. *Ministry* is action, the extension of God's love toward and with others. The terms *minister* and *ministry* describe, not domains ("I" am a minister or "this" is my ministry), but actions (I *minister*, we *minister*). Ministry should be understood more as a verb than a noun.

In the larger life of the church, *ministry* describes the interpersonal actions that surface out of the *koinonia* life of the church. *Koinonia*, the Greek term for community or fellowship, implies a "sharing with" or participation with others in caring love (Hauck 1984, 797-809). The concept of ministry probably best describes the interpersonal, loving actions that occur among participants in Christian community and as the Christian community in the world. One of the terms we use for the Lord's Supper is *Communion,* an intimate sharing with Christ and with one another. Our dispositions and actions toward one another define our Christian relationships. When we as Christians share, care, and serve in love, we minister as the body of Christ. When such actions become the primary role in our lives; when we say yes to God's call, through the life of the church, to ensure that such caring action occurs, then we are *ministers.*

If caring for others defines ministry, how does this change when we add the adjective "educational"? Christian educator Daniel Aleshire summarized this particular role best when he described educational ministry as "paying attention" to people. Aleshire does not mean to define all of ministry this way; in fact, he writes, "Paying attention to people provides the information required for articulate expressions of ministry" (1988, 15). In other words, paying attention, or discerning, prepares us to provide appropriate ministry, whether our intent is specific care or simply to "bless" people in their journey (23).

What should we "pay attention" to? Where should we focus our discernment and place our attention? Aleshire offers three key areas of attention for educational ministers: how people grow, how they learn, and how they come to faith. Aleshire notes that such discernment, or attentiveness, is not always easy, due to the complexity of people's lives, the complexity of our ministry, and our complex perceptions of people (24-27). Too often we focus on basic information. Remember the foyer scenario? We normally attend to basic information about occupation, family relationships, geographic location, and denominational background. We might also listen for immediate life experiences—certain crises or celebrations. Aleshire argues that we need to look deeper and pay closer attention to the core developmental concerns associated with where people are in their life journeys. Attending to these issues helps us fashion sustained ministry, particularly educational ministry, to, for, and with people.

HOW PEOPLE GROW: NATURE OR NURTURE?

When we pay attention to how people grow, we develop a clear sense of their capabilities and needs at various stages of the life span. In this regard, the field of developmental psychology provides a helpful baseline for educational ministry. We will draw deeply from that material.

One ongoing struggle about development resides in how we resolve the nature/nurture continuum: are people who they are because of genetics, or is it social context that shapes them? Almost all developmental theories revolve around these concerns. Do people have natural impulses that influence their every decision, a basic drive, or a natural desire? Do people have innate capacities for continual learning and adaptation to environment? If you said yes to these questions, you are influenced by the *nature* side of the continuum. However, if you believe that context shapes people's lives, you might find yourself closer to the *nurture* camp. You believe that broad social forces, including culture and personal experiences (e.g., the death of a parent or success in vocation), shape people more than genetic dispositions.

New research in neuroscience is breaking down the nature/nurture divide. According to neuroscientist Joseph LeDoux, people begin to develop at the synaptic level, at the points where neurons, or nerve cells, connect. Nerve cells provide the basic genetic framework, the blueprint for human life. At birth, many cells are predisposed to move to very specific places in the human body to provide connection points and influence other cell movement. The energy that crosses from one neuron to the next, that sends signals designed to spark human action, proceeds across these connections, or synapses. Synapses define the specialized junctions where electrochemical impulses guide human experiences and result in human responses. Neuroscience is discovering that, even at this very basic level, the quality of personal experience literally shapes synaptic connections in very specific ways: nature and nurture coincide. As LeDoux comments, "Nature and nurture are really two ways of doing the same thing—wiring up synapses—and both are needed to get the job done" (2002, 66). Nature (our biological and genetic predispositions) and nurture (social and relational influences) combine to reveal both specific habits and broader tendencies. In the following chapters, we will share several developmental theories that reinforce just how important it is to pay attention to the ways people grow and change through their lives.

HOW PEOPLE LEARN: PERCEPTION AND PROCESS

Learning is a crucial aspect of God's "creation" gift to human life. We utilize our capacity for learning in negotiating daily tasks, adapting to people, adopting new processes in family and work, responding to challenges, and entertaining ourselves. "How" we learn, the cognitive processes we go through and the physical and emotional adaptations we make, varies in both method and intensity from one person to the next.

What affects the ability and readiness, or tendency, to learn? Obviously, an affirming context, conducive to learning, is important; we will explore environment in future chapters (see chapters 15—16). When it comes to paying attention, however, we need to consider personal tendencies as well as context. What is it about the nature of people that shapes the way they learn? We will survey individual learning styles, but first we must address the larger question of how to categorize and organize various learning styles. Let's look at perception and process.

Perception describes the way people take in information—how they initially grasp or apprehend experiences and intentions, as well as how they comprehend data and concepts—that surfaces in everyday life and through intentional learning strategies. Unless we understand how people stop long enough to capture an idea, a concept, an event, or a practice, we cannot determine how they transfer this information into learning. Once we grasp information, gain a perspective of data, or see what is going on, we process that information into knowledge.

For instance, people often employ one of the major senses (touch, taste, sight, smell, hearing) when they connect with new information. Researchers have explored what happens as people tend to lean into one sense more than others in gathering information. Question: Do you prefer to see a visual outline of information as it is presented, or would you rather close your eyes and listen deeply to what the presenter is saying? Do you appreciate artwork and graphs in a book; would you rather have white space in the margins for taking notes when you read; would you be happiest with an audiobook? How you answer these questions demonstrates how you tend to connect with information as you learn. One learning style model based on these perceptual tendencies is the VAKT, or VAK(t), learning profile, based on the original research of Grace Fernald (1943). The "V" stands for *visual,* which describes people who tend to prefer a visual connection with the material they are learning. Slides, outlines, even stick figures help these people grasp information. The "A" stands for *auditory* and points to people who learn best when they can hear a presentation or explanation of key concepts. In many societies oral learning remains a key approach, not just a technological limitation (LCWE/ION 2005, 18-27). The symbol K(t) stands for *kinesthetic* and/or *tactile* learning. Learners in this category tend toward hands-on learning, either directly experiencing the event or employing some means of manipulating the information as they engage it. Do you doodle when you are listening to someone? Do you tend to create an outline or sketch a picture of the information being presented? Would you prefer to actually experiment with a task and see if you can learn how to install or fix something without reading the instructions first? Our tendency for hands-on activity often indicates our preference for this way of initially perceiving or grasping information.

In addition to perception, Christian educators must also explore how we *process* experiences, information, and data into new knowledge. Studies of learning styles often explore the more interior processes of reflection or the tendency to externalize and experiment with information to see the implications. With the rise of neuroscience, particular attention is being given to how learning occurs. Researchers remain amazed at how certain pathways, not

only in the brain but also throughout the body, guide information and transmit decisions. The implications of specific chemicals that communicate and
store information, even at the synaptic level, are beginning to emerge (Wolfe
2001). Discovering and charting specific processes at the microscopic level will
take a generation, though we are already gaining insights into how this type
of information shapes interpersonal contact (Goleman 2006) and even split-
second decision making (Gladwell 2005). At the same time, more macroscopic
studies at the cultural level indicate that we tend to process information quite
differently based on cultural and biological tendencies. Richard Nisbett notes
Western and Asian cultures approach language and other cultural processes
quite differently. Asian culture tends to view the world more holistically, while
Western thinkers tend to be more linear and analytical (2003, 44-45).

Perhaps the most famous example of diverse learning processes surfaced
with the work of Howard Gardner. Gardner, who teaches at Harvard University, posited a series of multiple intelligences. Gardner defines intelligence
as "a biopsychological potential to process information that can be activated
in a cultural setting to solve problems or create products that are of value in
a culture" (1999, 34-35). This process potential often relies upon a given cultural value (if the culture does not value the process, people tend not to use it).
Originally Gardner listed seven intelligences:

Linguistic: being sensitive and adaptive to spoken language

Logical-Mathematical: analyzing, investigating, and operating with logical and mathematical precision

Musical: recognizing, performing, and composing musical patterns

Bodily-Kinesthetic: using portions or the whole body to solve problems or
fashion products (including arts and sports)

Spatial: recognizing, judging, and manipulating wide spaces or specific
objects

Interpersonal: engaging and understanding interpersonal intentions, motivations, and desires

Intrapersonal: self-reflective capacity to understand oneself. (41-43)

In addition, Gardner now suggests at least one additional intelligence: the
naturalist intelligent person "demonstrates expertise in the recognition and
classification of the numerous species—the flora and fauna—of his or her environment" (48). Gardner also appears to be exploring two other intelligences:
spiritual (relating to and understanding a transcendent dimension to life) and
existential (engaging with the "ultimate" issues in life). However, unlike the
naturalist intelligence, Gardner remains reluctant to give either of these last
two categories a special capacity; probably for good reason, since it would im-

ply that some people are not as inclined to be as spiritual or philosophical as other people (53-66).

Gardner's work has resulted in a number of books on multiple-intelligence learning styles and assessments: some of which have no resemblance to what Gardner had in mind (79-92). Gardner does admit that the contemporary schooling paradigm tends to privilege people who demonstrate linguistic or logical-mathematical intelligences more than other intelligences (41). Overall, Gardner's typology helps us understand how and why different people tend to respond better to, and process differently, the information they grasp.

Gardner's work also points to the fact that the categories of perception and process often overlap. The intersection of these two domains of learning

Figure 7.1

Visual Representation of Kolb's Model

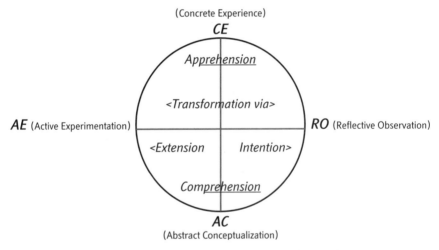

(Concrete Experience)
CE
Apprehension
<Transformation via>
AE (Active Experimentation)   *RO* (Reflective Observation)
<Extension   *Intention>*
Comprehension
AC
(Abstract Conceptualization)

Cycle moves clockwise from *CE* (Concrete Experience) to *RO* (Reflective Observation) to *AC* (Abstract Conceptualization) to *AE* (Active Experimentation). These four learning processes begin with a *concrete experience (CE)*. As a person experiences life, he or she reflects on these experiences, which Kolb calls *reflective observation (RO)*. These reflections begin to develop into concepts and judgments, or *abstract conceptualization (AC)*. The concepts or ideas that have been formulated from reflection result in doing or acting: *active experimentation (AE)*.

Processing knowledge also includes dialectical intersections between gaining *(prehending)* experience and transforming experience into knowledge

CE—AC continuum   "prehending" experience through perception (apprehension) or insight (comprehension)

RO—AE continuum   "transforming" experience through internal organization ("intention") or external manipulation ("extension")

can influence the ways we pay attention to how people learn. For instance, David A. Kolb (1984) uses a particular process to indicate our ability to "transform" what we have received into new learning (51). Drawing from research by Jean Piaget, John Dewey, and Kurt Lewin, Kolb argues that we tend to process experience into knowledge through a given cycle (figure 7.1) that begins when we apprehend a new experience, transform that information via reflection into concepts, check our concepts against key information that we already comprehend, and then extend our learning by experimenting with the new information to bring about new learning. For Kolb this type of learning appears to be cyclical, moving from experience to knowledge back into experience. Our use of perception (or perhaps *prehension*) and process indicate a similar cycle.

HOW PEOPLE COME TO FAITH:
HUMAN ACTIVITY AND RESPONSE TO GOD

Defining faith (a human disposition that exists only through the grace of God) has never been easy. Generally we understand that human faith entails our awareness and trust in something larger than ourselves, often something of transcendent value and power. In this general sense we might talk about our faith in our families or our country, in particular values that drive our lives, or even in allegiances to groups, movements, and persons. Sports fans may have faith that their favorite team will perform better the next year. Patriots might have faith in their country. Children have faith in their family's ability to care for them. Too often theorists reduce faith to cognition only, a major mistake particularly for educators.

Christian faith begins with the human capacity for faith, much like other interpersonal emotions (born out of God's creative presence in our lives). However, Christian faith is much more because of God's continuing relationship with and love for us. We know that God's desire for a deep awareness and growing relationship precedes our understanding or awareness of the need for this loving presence. God's second gracious movement in revealing God-self through Jesus Christ by the power of the Holy Spirit allows us to awaken a second time to awareness of the love of God and to respond by faith. Perhaps the best human analogy is the birth of a child. A newborn may only be aware of our presence without knowing who we are (our personality, our formal relationship to the child, even our particular skin tone or body type). Yet the child remains dependent upon us and gradually becomes aware of our loving presence in meaningful ways. James E. Loder provides the excellent example of exploring the importance of a face (1981, 165-73). He notes that the first real image that emerges with a newborn's sight is that of a round oval with eyes and a smile, the mother's face. That image is often accompanied by food, warmth, caress, loving sounds, and a general sense of well-being. From a newborn's perspective, when the face is gone, it is gone from the world since the child cannot conceive of a person in another room or place. The first real test for the child is to trust, to have faith that the loving face will return to the world. It is small wonder that God instructed the tribe of Aaron to give this "blessing" to the children of Israel.

> "The LORD bless you and keep you;
> the LORD make his face shine on you and be gracious to you;
> the LORD turn his face toward you and give you peace."
> (Numbers 6:24-27, TNIV)

Faith describes our knowledge that God looks upon us and smiles, calling us into relationship with God's presence.

Christian faith is a gracefully sure and profound response to, and trust in, the grace of God revealed in Jesus Christ (the objective side of faith). Faith also describes a mutual relationship that, while based in the gracious initiative of God through the Holy Spirit, invites a human response (the subjective side of faith). This human response includes cognitive (reason), affective (emotion), and volitional (choice) dimensions out of which we demonstrate our faith through our actions (behavior). Faith, however, proves more than the sum of these human dimensions (the same way bread is more than grain, yeast, and milk). Faith remains, in part, a mystery, which we also acknowledge as a gift of grace. Therefore, an appropriate "faith which seeks understanding" includes not only a depth of conviction (the ability to believe even as we struggle with doubt), but also consistent belief (orthodoxy), consistent behavior (orthopraxis), and a consistent loving attitude (orthopathy) in regard to God and neighbor (Steele 1990, 102-5). Such faith defines what we pay attention to in our own lives and in the lives of others.

Beyond knowing the basic categories of growing, learning, and coming to faith, what else do we need to discern or pay attention to?

▶ PAYING ATTENTION TO CULTURAL CONTEXT

We live in a culturally diverse world. People of various ethnicities and cultural perspectives gather physically (and virtually, thanks to Internet technologies). Christianity is increasingly diverse as well. Christianity is strong and growing quickly in many settings that North American Christians often took for granted as foreign mission fields, particularly in the southern hemisphere (Jenkins 2002). Nevertheless, our context and cultural assumptions guide how we understand people. We must discern how people grow, learn, and come to faith; we must also pay attention to cultural context.

Contextual differences often revolve around key characteristics that define a culture or subculture. We can organize our discernment through these categories that guide our attention. For instance, using the LASTS Cultural Guide (see appendix 7.1), we can focus on a culture's Language, Actions (and key Actors)—use of Space, conceptions of Time, and core Symbols. Sherwood Lingenfelter and Marvin K. Mayers note that cultures differ on several key value systems: our understanding of time (clock or event), how we make decisions (either/or or both/and), how we handle crises (anticipating or innovating), goals (accomplishing tasks or relating to people), what gives us a sense of self-worth (status or achievement), and expressions of vulnerabilities (concealing or revealing) (1986, 2003). How different cultures live out and validate each value system tells us a lot about their contextual expectations and behaviors.

Elizabeth Conde-Frazier, S. Steve Kang, and Gary A. Parrett note that attention to context often includes controversial issues that require us to acknowledge how people categorize, and sometimes caricature, others through domains like race (which is a social construct), ethnicity, social class, and gender (2004, 17-20). People have often been excluded from learning, and even from Christian fellowship, because of prejudice and fear. Part of our attention to others includes being aware of our own insecurities and opening our lives to allow the Holy Spirit to give us a spirit of openness and humility (Law 1993). James A. Banks, a leader in multicultural education, notes that our attention must rest not only on cultural differences but also on how those differences prevent people from being empowered when they are the minority (2008, 15-16). Banks calls for people, as global citizens, to live in the delicate intersection of their global, national, regional, and cultural identification (29) yet value others who come from different perspectives (particularly national, regional, and cultural differences). As Christians with a "kingdom of God" perspective, we must value what it means to live as Kingdom citizens (Kang 2004, 79-104) exploring the boundaries of our own cultural expectations and crossing those boundaries to understand other people, their struggles and joys. We can do this only as we cultivate knowledge of other cultures, adopt an attitude of openness, and engage with different cultures to experience people in their contexts (Kim 1992).

▶ CONCLUSION

Ministry requires serious discernment. Beyond simply gathering information in the church foyer, we must "pay attention" to how people grow and learn and come to faith, as we also acknowledge the culture and context that shape their lives. As we allow the Holy Spirit to guide our attention and reduce our assumptions and prejudices, we can begin to imagine approaches to Christian education that will truly make a difference, that is, to engage in faithful discipleship.

▶ REFERENCES

Aleshire, Daniel O. 1988. *Faithcare: Ministering to All God's People Through the Ages of Life.* Philadelphia: Westminster Press.

Banks, James A. 2008. *An Introduction to Multicultural Education.* 4th ed. Boston: Pearson.

Conde-Frazier, Elizabeth, S. Steve Kang, and Gary A Parrett, eds. 2004. *A Many Colored Kingdom: Multicultural Dynamics for Spiritual Formation.* Grand Rapids: Baker Academic.

Fernald, Grace M. 1943, 1971. *Remedial Techniques in Basic School Subjects.* New York: McGraw Hill Book Company.

Gardner, Howard. 1999. *Intelligence ReFramed: Multiple Intelligences for the 21st Century.* New York: Basic Books.

Gladwell, Malcolm. 2005. *Blink: The Power of Thinking without Thinking.* New York: Little, Brown and Company.

Goleman, Daniel. 2006. *Social Intelligence: The New Science of Human Relationships.* New York: Bantam Books.

Hauck, Friedrich. 1984. Koinos, Konineo, Koinonia. In *Theological Dictionary of the New Testament,* vol. 3, 797-809. Ed. Gerhard Kittel. Grand Rapids: William B. Eerdmans.

Jenkins, Philip. 2002. *The Next Christendom: The Coming of Global Christianity.* New York: Oxford Univ. Press.

Kang, S. Steve. 2004. Salient theoretical frameworks for forming kingdom citizens. In *A Many Colored Kingdom: Mutlicultural Dynamics for Spiritual Formation,* 79-104. Ed. Elizabeth Conde-Frazier, S. Steve Kang, and Gary A. Parrett. Grand Rapids: Baker Academic.

Kim, Young-Il. 1992. Identifying and communicating God's presence in the cross-cultural context. In *Knowledge, Attitude and Experience: Ministry in the Cross-Cultural Context,* 7-20. Ed. Young-Il Kim. Nashville: Abingdon Press.

Kolb, David A. 1984. *Experiential Learning: Experience as the Source of Learning and Development.* Englewood Cliffs, NJ: Prentice Hall Books.

Law, Eric H. F. 1993. *The Wolf Shall Dwell with the Lamb: Spirituality for Leadership in a Multicultural Community.* St. Louis: Chalice Press.

LCWE/ION: Lausanne Committee for World Evangelization and International Orality Network. 2005. *Making Disciples of Oral Learners.* New York: International Orality Network with Elim.

LeDoux, Joseph. 2002. *Synaptic Self: How Our Brains Become Who We Are.* New York: Penguin.

Lingenfelter, Sherwood G., and Marvin K. Mayers. 1986, 2003. *Ministering Cross-Culturally: An Incarnational Model for Personal Relationships.* 2nd ed. Grand Rapids: Baker Press.

Loder, James E. 1981. *The Transforming Moment: Understanding Convictional Experiences.* New York: Harper and Row.

Nisbett, Richard. 2003. *The Geography of Thought: How Asians and Westerners Think Differently . . . and Why.* New York: Free Press.

Steele, Les L. 1990. *On the Way: A Practical Theology of Christian Formation.* Grand Rapids: Baker Books.

Wolfe, Patricia. 2001. *Brain Matters: Translating Research into Classroom Practice.* Alexandria, VA: ASCD.

Appendix 7.1
LASTS Cultural Guide

LASTS: *Exploring and Explaining Youth Culture*

Have you ever wanted to help someone understand your world or felt like you needed to be a cultural guidebook for someone so he or she could better understand what is meaningful for your generation? Here is your chance. You are about to become both a cultural anthropologist and cross-cultural guide to help other people take your world seriously. For instance, if you are a young person, think about the five categories that often describe the lasting aspects of a culture (what gives the culture enduring meaning): Language, Actions (and Actors), Space, Time, and Symbols. How a given group of people uses these categories tells a lot of about what is lasting and enduring about their culture.

L *anguage*

Language communicates key thoughts and ideas. Sometimes we use code language or slang (a type of insider language) that is important for our friends. At other times language communicates central concepts and values (e.g., security, compassion, friendship) that are meaningful to our lives. Can you identify either code language or valued concepts that are important in your world?

A *ctions (and Actors)*

Actions (and the people who perform the actions) often tell us what is meaningful in what we do in our day-to-day lives. They may involve a simple process (shaking hands) or complex activities (playing sports). Some actions have a ritual quality (a particular way of greeting someone), other actions help us just get through the day. Often we associate different types of activity with different people (sports/athletes, academics/intellectuals, relationships/dates, etc.). What are some key activities you engage in daily or at specific times of the week and with whom?

S *pace*

We often associate certain aspects of our lives with particular spaces. We have buildings dedicated to education, to religion, to sports, to business, to legal activities, and so forth. Sometimes we divide up a building into social, private, and even safe spaces. Think about your week; where are some key spaces that you spend time and why? Where do your friends get together? Where do you spend most of your time each day or during key times of the day?

T *ime*

If space identifies our physical presence, time identifies both our needs and desires. Often time identifies how we order and prioritize our activities and relationships. Sometimes the most important things in our lives are not necessarily the things we spend the most time doing, so timing is important as well. How do youth around you spend most of their time? What are some key moments or times that are especially important?

S *ymbols*

Every culture has certain concrete images/symbols that convey meaning (e.g., art forms or commercial products). These images do not need explaining within the culture; instead they ignite our passion and imagination. Advertisers understand this as well as governments and churches. If you could name three or four images/symbols that are meaningful to your culture, what might they be?

LASTS Journal

Take a couple of minutes to identify key components of your culture under each domain, strictly from memory. Feel free to include anything you like from the profound to the ridiculous (you can change it later). Then keep an eye out during the day for new entries for each category and add them in when you have the chance. You will be surprised at what you notice each day.

LANGUAGE:

ACTIONS (and actors):

SPACE:

TIME:

SYMBOLS:

LASTS Intersections

Obviously there are moments when these five domains intersect. Think it through and see what is important. Do certain actions occur at certain times? Are key symbols associated with selected spaces? Try to sift through and identify what is crucial about your culture if you tried to explain it to someone else.

	Language	Action	Space	Time	Symbols
Language	LASTS				
Action		LASTS			
Space			LASTS		
Time				LASTS	
Symbols					LASTS

EIGHT

DEVELOPMENTAL THEORY

▶ INTRODUCTION

Imagine you have been asked to teach a youth Sunday school class for the first time. You are aware that teenagers are at a particular stage of development, but you are not sure how to relate to them. You ask your Christian education director for information regarding how teens grow and develop intellectually, socially, and morally. What do you expect to hear?

Imagine you are leading a Bible study with a group of senior adults. Your only experience with senior adults is interaction with your grandparents, and you have never taught a class to this age-group. In preparing for the Bible study you ask your pastor to advise as to what to expect in teaching senior adults. What are your assumptions about development at later stages of life?

Faithful teaching includes understanding how God has made and created us. God has created us in his image and likeness with the capacity to learn, grow, and develop. Just as we study the human body to understand the stages of physical growth throughout our life span, we can also understand how the human person grows and develops cognitively, morally, and socially. When we understand growth more fully, we can teach more faithfully.

This chapter explores the relationship of theology and the social sciences in regard to Christian discipleship. The chapter also provides an introduction to *developmentalism,* a holistic approach to Christian discipleship, and a summary of the development theories of Jean Piaget, Lawrence Kohlberg, and Erik Erikson with an analysis of their strengths and weaknesses.

▶ THEOLOGY AND SOCIAL SCIENCES

As a discipline, Christian education falls under the rubric of practical theology, which also includes such disciplines as mission, preaching, worship, evangelism, and discipleship. Practical theology is an interdisciplinary approach that incorporates both theology and the social sciences. Christian education also combines a strong theological framework, in our case a Wesleyan theological framework, with an understanding of the social sciences. Theology provides the lens through which ministers view and evaluate the social sciences. People tend to focus more on one side of this equation than the other. Either they have a strong theological and biblical foundation without understanding how their view applies to ministry, or they have a deep understanding of how people grow and develop without a clear theological lens through which to focus their work. Both theology and the social sciences are integral to the interdisciplinary study of Christian education.

One framework for joining these disciplines comes from understanding the two ways in which God the Creator reveals truth: the scripture (specific revelation) and creation (general revelation). We must study both respected sources of divine revelation in order to comprehend the wonders of God's wisdom and expression. Truth, wherever it is found, has its source in God and therefore should be valued (Downs 1994, 14). Within this framework, *theology* is the systematic inquiry into God's specific revelation through scripture, using human reason, experience, and church tradition; *science* is the systematic inquiry into God's general revelation through creation (15; see figure 8.1). Scientists make sense of creation by applying the rules of scientific inquiry to empirical data. The study of creation includes such disciplines as psychology, sociology, biology, and the humanities. As we study creation, we gain a greater understanding of the nature of human life.

Figure 8.1: Theology and Social Science (Downs 1994, 14)

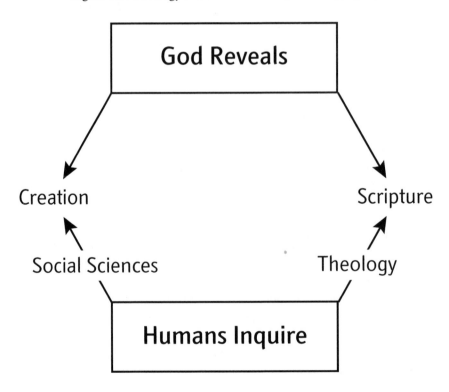

This framework, which values both general and specific revelation, guides faithful discipleship. There is no conflict between the sciences and theology; we must maintain an integrated approach. Understanding of both humanity and God is crucial to our Christian discipleship and our ministry of Christian education.

▶ HOLISTIC CHRISTIAN DISCIPLESHIP

Ted Ward compared the process of spiritual maturation to an ecological system of human development. He asserts that five empirical domains of human development—physical, intellectual, emotional, social, and moral—serve as "input and output functions to and from the spiritual core" (1995, 16). Each component contributes to an interrelated system of development. Ward uses the illustration of the human hand to identify the five dimensions that represent the human person (16; see figure 8.2). These five dimensions give us some solid empirical information about the complex factors that form us.

Figure 8.2: Aspects of the Human Person (Ward 1995, 16)

The thumb represents the physical dimension with particular attention to the human body. The index finger represents the emotional dimension, or the affective domain. The middle finger represents the social dimension and our ability to communicate and interact with others in a variety of social settings and social roles. The ring finger represents the intellectual dimension, or cognitive function, that enables us to think. The little finger represents the moral dimension where matters of morality and ethics are entertained and considered. The palm of the hand represents the spiritual dimension that is made alive through a personal encounter with Jesus Christ but is potentially present in every human being as a consequence of having been created in the image of God and sustained by prevenient grace (Lowe and Lowe 2008, 13-15).

The hand illustrates a holistic approach to Christian education. God works through our natural aspects, or personality, to form us into the image of Christ. Spiritual maturation includes each individual aspect, but it is impossible to separate one aspect from the other. This model leads us to think about spiritual development as the central integrating dimension of human personhood, nested within the other developmental capacities as all follow the same patterns of growth.

> Although the evidence is incomplete, [we] hypothesize that spiritual development is a dimension of human life and experience as significant as cognitive development, emotional development, or social development. All of these dimensions of development are interrelated. It is the spiritual dimension that is most involved in a person's effort to integrate the many aspects of development. (Roehlkepartain et al. 2006, 9)

Spirituality, as one significant dimension of human development, follows the same processes of maturation across the span of human life as the other dimensions. It is significant that we place the spiritual dimension in the palm of the hand; it cannot be separated from the rest of the hand and treated as if it operates from different laws of growth. The biblical foundation for teaching about spiritual development confirms this conclusion; Scripture begins each passage on how things grow in the spiritual realm with an illustration of how things grow in the natural realm (Lowe and Lowe 2008, 13-15; see, e.g., Deuteronomy 5:1; 6:4; 1 Thessalonians 5:23).

Developmental systems theories identify the whole person in terms of "biological, psychological, and behavioral characteristics" (Lerner 2002, 176) or through the perspective of "biology, cognition, personality, and behavior" (178). Some more elaborate lists include "biology, mental system, subconscious processes, values, norms, motives, and goals; self-structures and self-perceptions; and behavioral characteristics" (178). However one dissects the various dimensions of the whole person, all theories attempt to view the individual "as an integrated, complex, and dynamic totality" (178).

A holistic approach to Christian discipleship cannot ignore or neglect any of the six aspects if the goal is transformation into the "whole measure of the fullness of Christ" (Ephesians 4:13). A halt to intellectual, physical, emotional, social, or moral growth has an impact on spiritual formation. All six aspects must be nurtured and developed in order for a person to grow toward spiritual maturity.

The New Testament offers useful examples of this principle. For instance, Paul calls upon the Christian community to "offer your *bodies* as living sacrifices" (Romans 12:1, emphasis added). On another occasion he calls the church to be "renewed in the spirit of your *mind*" (Ephesians 4:23, KJV, emphasis added). Jesus reminds us of the summary of the Old Testament law: "Love the Lord your God with all your heart and with all your soul and with all your mind and with all your strength. . . . Love your neighbor as yourself" (Mark 12:30-31). This command calls for commitment of the whole person, not a dissection of the various ways in which we are to love God and neighbor.

When we attend to and nurture all six aspects of human development, we come closer to being fully human, formed into the image and likeness of Christ. God works through the natural aspects of humanity to facilitate our spiritual formation. Approaches to spiritual formation often negate the importance of these natural aspects. Effective spiritual formation requires the development of all of them.

▶ DEVELOPMENTAL THEORY

Christian education includes God's revelation as revealed in scripture and God's design of human person as revealed in studying creation. Developmental theory provides a framework for understanding the process of human growth and development throughout the life span. *Developmentalism* helps the Christian educator understand the process of educating people for spiritual growth, assuming that learning is an integral part of becoming spiritually mature (Downs 1994, 69).

Contributions to understanding human development come from the social-science disciplines of cultural anthropology (the study of human developmental process), sociology (the study of the role of family, church, and education, and their impact on individuals), and the natural science of biology (genetic and cellular development and the study of aging). Developmental theorists deal not only with changes in behavior as people develop but also with individual differences in these changes (Pullman 2001, 63). In other words, an effective theory should be able to describe and explain the general course of development as well as specific aspects of that development over the course of a human life.

There are various approaches to developmental psychology, with specific emphases in each approach. However, all developmentalists hold certain presuppositions in common. Donald E. Miller has identified five such presumptions in a developmental approach to Christian education.

   1. *Development presumes a ground plan, a preexistent structure through which persons move.* Our genes carry this structure. Human beings are more than a product of environmental stimuli; they are genetically unique creatures.

2. *Development presumes an invariable sequence.* Development is linear. Each stage presumes the previous stage and leads to the next stage. We are genetically programmed to move through predictable patterns in our development. All people go through the same stages in the same order, although some people move through stages more quickly than others (Downs 1994, 74). Furthermore, no stage can be skipped, and difficulties in one stage may cause difficulties in later stages.

3. *Development presumes the integration of increasingly complex elements.* Often this integration or synthesis remains stable until challenged by new experiences that do not fit the current schema. Confronted with new experiences, the individual faces a personal crisis, which leads toward a new developmental integration.

4. *Development assumes persons interact with their environment.* Active integration with the physical environment provides a sense of reality; active interaction with social, cultural, and religious environments provides a sense of selfhood, identity, and responsibility.

5. *Development has a goal and an end.* Development does not just terminate, but rather moves toward a final level of integration that is usually referred to as maturity (Miller 1982, 76-77; see also Pazmiño 1997, 214-15).

As Christian educators gain understanding of the presuppositions of developmentalism, the natural human processes of growth and development, they can begin to see how developmental theory relates to spiritual growth and maturation.

▶ DEVELOPMENTAL APPROACHES

Developmental psychology has been historically viewed in three camps: behaviorism, psychoanalysis, and humanistic or integrative psychology. The following provides a summary of each of these developmental approaches and their impact on Christian education.

BEHAVIORISM

The primary assumption of behaviorism is that human behavior is explained in terms of environment stimuli. First introduced by Russian physiologist Ivan P. Pavlov, and then applied to psychology by John B. Watson and Edward L. Thorndike, this psychological approach came to the forefront under the influence of B. F. Skinner (1904-90). The behaviorist perspective provides an empirical approach to psychology. How does this relate to Christian education? It helps us understand that behavior modification, such as rewarding children or teens for positive or negative behavior, can be an effective means of learning.

Behaviorism is inadequate, however, as the only means of learning because its underlying assumptions fundamentally disrespect human beings. Practitioners attempt to control the behavior of others. Christian educators must adopt a more comprehensive approach to understanding people.

PSYCHOANALYSIS OR DEPTH PSYCHOLOGIES

The primary approach here is a mode of therapy that emphasizes unconscious forces in the mind. Sigmund Freud developed the theory of psychoanalysis by focusing on the unconscious in the development of the individual. Psychoanalysis assumes that human beings are primarily proactive toward their environment. Human behavior is understood as a force that is driven from within and includes emotions and their influence on personality. Other key influences in the field are Carl Jung, Anna Freud, and Erik Erikson. In one way or another, they are concerned with the various internal forces that shape the personality and activity of an individual.

The primary contribution of psychoanalysis to Christian education is its attempt at understanding the inner workings of the human personality. While more beneficial when it comes to therapeutic care than education, Erikson's eight stages of psychosocial development assist educators in understanding childhood development and adolescent changes (see below).

HUMANISTIC OR INTEGRATIVE PSYCHOLOGY

The humanistic approach focuses on the affective dimension of the learner and offers a more balanced perspective than either psychoanalysis or behaviorism. Humanist psychologists value human beings as thoughtful and purposeful. They understand that people interact with their environments; they not only are influenced by environment but also exert influence on it. Developmentalism, as an integrative psychology, is highly compatible with a Christian perspective and offers helpful insights for the educational ministry of the church. Primary influences include Jean Piaget, James Fowler, Lawrence Kohlberg, Carl Rogers, and Abraham Maslow.

Humanists base learning on self-perception. Learning is self-directed, with the teacher acting as a facilitator in the process. Theorists agree that the learning environment should promote and encourage discovery; they also advocate attending to learners' emotional needs and orientations. Integrative psychology is compatible with a Wesleyan approach to Christian education because it focuses on the individual's free interaction with the environment and promotes integration of internal and external factors of environment and will. Developmental psychology embraces a complex formula of social/environmental influences, personal drives, and human participation working in an integrative fashion as people grow.

COGNITIVE DEVELOPMENT THEORY: JEAN PIAGET

Spiritual maturity includes the development of the mind. Historically, the Wesleyan-Holiness tradition has given more emphasis to development of the heart through its pietistic tradition, but development of the mind is an essential aspect of discipleship. Evangelicalism has been charged with anti-intellectualism, neglecting to recognize or nurture reason as a significant aspect of human nature (Marsden 1991, 72). Scripture, however, gives testimony to the importance of the mind. For example, Romans 12:2 calls us to be "transformed by the renewing of [the] mind"; 1 Corinthians 2:16 assures us that "we have the mind of Christ"; Matthew 22:37 commands us to "love the Lord . . . with all [our] heart . . . soul and . . . mind." Perry Downs states, "When people learn to think in new ways, with new values and new categories in place, their minds are renewed. The task of Christian education is to teach so that people's minds may be renewed" (1994, 62). The development of the mind includes not only the acquisition of knowledge but also the transformation of the mind so that people can apply Christian thinking to all matters of life and faith.

Jean Piaget (1896–1980), a Swiss genetic epistemologist, studied genetics and knowledge to learn how people achieve knowledge (epistemology). He was concerned with finding a biological explanation for knowledge. He was the first to describe cognitive process in children. Piaget developed a theory of cognitive development that explained how children develop. He arranged his stage theory into cognitive schemes, organized patterns of behavior or ways of interacting with the environment.

Central to Piaget's theory was his view of *adaptation*. He believed it to be the essence of how people function cognitively. *Adaptation* defines the capacity to organize the sensory stimuli we receive into some sort of order and then adapt to our context. Adaptation consists of two processes, *assimilation* and *accommodation*. *Assimilation* defines the processes by which we incorporate ideas, people, customs, manners, and so forth, into our own activities. *Accommodation* describes how we balance assimilation, adjusting how we reach out to our environment and reordering our filing system of stimuli and response. Humans learn to accommodate and assimilate their environments; we adapt to the things we learn.

The force that regulates assimilation and accommodation is *equilibration* (Downs 1994, 84). The human mind seeks to understand, to keep ideas in balance. Piaget believed that three factors stimulate cognitive development: maturation, experience, and social transmission. *Maturation* defines the process by which the mind grows and matures. Humans develop the mind through exercising it, just as we exercise our physical bodies. *Experience* is the active process of engaging the environment. As we are actively engaged in our surroundings, we take in new information and experience new realities. *Social transmission* takes place as we interact with other people, such as parents, friends, or peers. These social interactions provide stimulation for cognitive growth.

The key to learning and transformation is disequilibrium, when a change occurs in either the organism or the environment. Piaget believed this was required for growth. In Christian discipleship this is a necessary part of the process of learning, growth, and transformation.

Piaget's theory of cognitive development includes four stages. He developed these by observing children to describe patterns that all children share. He believed that in all ages and in all cultures children follow predictable patterns to make sense of their environment (Downs 1994, 85).

Stage 1: Sensorimotor (birth to two years). Children develop intelligence through sensory input and motor activity. Children need a safe environment in which adults provide sensory input through holding and touching the child. Children need to explore the world at this stage, not receive content.

Stage 2: Preoperational (two to seven years). The primary task of this stage is to learn to use symbols as replacements for actual objects. Children begin to make-believe as a means of making objects stand in for other objects. They dress up, pretending to be someone else. Children will often talk more to themselves than to others, providing commentary on their own actions and thoughts. It is normal and healthy for a child to develop an imaginary world, to believe in Santa Claus and the Tooth Fairy. This process is necessary for children to move to the next stage of cognitive development.

Stage 3: Concrete Operations (seven to eleven years). The concrete operational stage is an exciting time of intense learning. As Downs states, "Children are no longer limited to perceptual data to make judgments regarding concrete, real problems; they now can use logical operational thinking that is capable of reversible, decentered perceptions" (1994, 87). Children begin intense learning as they can now employ logic and handle more than one concept (decentered perception). Children are able to number and place things in logical order. When teaching children at this stage, it is important to recognize that they view the world, including the Bible and God, in concrete, black-and-white terms.

Stage 4: Formal Operations (twelve to fifteen years). This is the last stage of cognitive development. This person can now imagine possible realities and solutions other than those that actually exist. They begin to think in new, abstract ways. For example, teenagers will begin to question lessons they once accepted at face value. This questioning is good because it means they are thinking, and thinking is necessary for spiritual growth.

The implications of Piaget's cognitive development theory for Christian discipleship include viewing teaching as a means of stimulating equilibration. Teachers introduce new concepts that challenge existing cognitive structures, but teachers must remember that cognitive structures determine what a child can or cannot learn. Teaching needs to be developmentally appropriate to the age of the child. Faithful teaching for young children includes active participation and using the senses in learning. Concrete thinking is necessary for the development of formal operational thinking, and it is important that teachers not try to rush children through this stage of development. Abstract ideas need to be connected to concrete examples; otherwise the child will not be able to understand the concepts. Finally, faithful teaching of teenagers requires creating a safe context where students can ask tough questions. Fostering dialogue and discussion will help students develop their thinking skills and lead to maturity.

MORAL DEVELOPMENT THEORY: LAWRENCE KOHLBERG

A holistic approach to Christian discipleship includes education that helps people grow morally and make good moral decisions. The church provides a context to teach and model moral behavior. Morality consists of developing values. What a person values will shape how that person acts and behaves. Some people within the Wesleyan tradition primarily view morality as adherence to "rules and regulations," which has often led to legalistic practices. The church remains concerned about what people *ought* to do, the content of moral judgments, but people often do not give adequate attention to the *reasons* for moral actions (Stonehouse 2000, 18). Rules and regulations have often been seen as a means of character development. However, imposed character development is not effective in indoctrinating behavior; rather, effective character education is concerned with passing on certain values and beliefs. One of the primary tasks of Christian discipleship is to provide a context in which persons develop moral thinking and moral judgments. A Wesleyan approach to morality includes both personal and social holiness. Morality is the responsibility of the individual and the community. Our morality is shaped and formed through our interaction with parents, the church community, and society.

Lawrence Kohlberg (1927-87) builds his theory of moral development by following Jean Piaget's *Moral Development of the Child* (1965). Kohlberg served as the director of the Center of Moral Development at Harvard University for more than twenty years. He was the first to apply stages to the development of moral reasoning. His study was conducted over a thirty-year period and consisted of men only. Kohlberg's theory is critical to our understanding of development, but the fallacy in his argument was the separation of morality and ethics. For Kohlberg, morality deals with "what is," which is relative to the culture, and ethics deals with what "ought to be" (absolutes); he does not hold the two together.

Kohlberg distinguished between moral judgment (beliefs) and moral action, recognizing the possibility of a discrepancy between belief and action. Moral judgment is what a person believes to be right and wrong and includes moral content and moral structure. Moral content focuses on *what* a person believes to be right or wrong. Moral structure focuses on the reasoning supporting moral content, stating *why* particular content is right or wrong (Downs 1994, 99). Kohlberg identified three levels of moral reasoning, which includes six stages of development. A summary of his theory is given here (see the theory applied to the concept of justice in appendix 8.1).

Level 1: Preconventional Morality. Moral reasoning is egocentric, drawing moral judgment from individual needs. It is focused on reward and punishment. *Congregational example:* People follow God because of what they can gain or avoid by means of their obedience.

- *Stage 1: Heteronomous Morality.* Morality is based on physical consequence of a person's actions, seeking primarily to avoid punishment. The rightness and wrongness of an act is determined by the consequence it may bring to the individual. No matter what the adult values in an action, the child sees only approval or disapproval. Fear of punishment serves as a practical deterrent. People avoid theft based on the assumption that "if you steal, you will get in trouble."

- *Stage 2: Individualism, Instrumental Purpose, and Exchange.* Moral judgment at this stage is still egocentric, but external; authorities are no longer considered all-powerful. Fairness is expressed as an exchange: "You scratch my back, I'll scratch yours." Reciprocity guides honesty; people avoid stealing based on the assumption that "if you steal, people will probably steal from you, and you'll lose everything anyway."

Level 2: Conventional Morality. Moral reasoning is based on the shared values and beliefs held by the group, community, or society. There is a strong attitude of loyalty and conformity to personal expectation and social order and strong identification with those involved in maintaining, supporting, justifying the order of things. Congregational example: The Bible appeals to people at this level because it teaches that God is to be obeyed because he is God. Here people move beyond "what it is for me" to accepting external authority, either from the church or from God.

- *Stage 3: Mutual Interpersonal Expectations.* This stage is characterized by the "good boy/nice girl" orientation to morality. The expectation of others becomes very important. A new awareness of relationship with others now means that issues of loyalty, respect, and gratitude must be considered. Actions are evaluated by how well they fill expectations of a group beyond pragmatic back-scratching. A person maintains expectations of the community, in this case the church, in order to receive approval from God and others. Avoiding theft now follows the assumption, "If you steal, everybody will think you are a crook."

- *Stage 4: Social System and Conscience.* Here a person considers the welfare of society as a whole, with a high regard for maintaining the authority of societal rules. The rules are binding and serve to prescribe the nature and extent of one's moral obligation. It is the duty of the person to follow the social order. Stage four heroes include someone who upholds the law when others disagree with him or her. People assume stealing is wrong "because stealing is against the law, and if it was allowed, it would cause anarchy."

Level 3: Postconventional Morality. Moral judgment takes a prior-to-society perspective, drawing on principles that have universal application. Effort is made to define moral values and principles that have validity and application apart from the authority of groups or persons; individuals also hold these principles apart from individual and group identification. *Congregational example:* People move beyond regulations, internalizing scripture and applying it to daily life.

- *Stage 5: Social Contract and Individual Rights.* This stage marks a transcendence of societal expectations through the discovery of universal ethical principles. Individuals are now aware that certain rights, such as those of life and liberty, must be upheld in any society, regardless of majority opinion. Here stealing may be permissible if it serves the greater good. The principle of the greatest good supersedes the law. The person is no longer searching for what the social system is; rather, now persons postulate principles to which self and society ought to be committed. The move to postconventional morality requires questioning received traditions and standards. Personal autonomy means freedom from society's views. The most adequate moral position means something like "making up one's own mind about what is right and wrong."

- *Stage 6: Universal Ethical Principles.* Moral judgment is determined on the basis of personal obligation to self-chosen ethical principles that apply to all humankind regardless of race, sex, nationality, or socioeconomic status. Universal ethical principles do not tell one specifically how to act but challenge one at every level. Stealing is wrong because it violates the rights of others and therefore is unjust. People cannot be capable of understanding postconventional morality until they are capable of understanding formal operations. Kohlberg's understanding of moral development is contingent upon Piaget's stages of cognitive development.

The implications of Kohlberg's moral development theory for Christian discipleship are significant. Christian educators can develop educational avenues that enhance moral development. It is important for Christian educators to ask the "why" questions in order to stimulate moral growth. Structures of moral development improve when students are given opportunities to experience and solve problems. The use of dilemmas, case studies, and world events provide an avenue for wrestling with moral questions and problems. Faithful teaching will require teachers to adjust their moral appeals to the developmental level of the student. Focus level one morality of reward/punishment on children; focus level two moralities of modeling and imitation on adolescents; level three moralities based on dialogue and discussion are appropriate for adult learning. It is very important not to rush people through these developmental processes. Faithful teaching includes creating a context of mutual respect and openness to new ideas. Moral development will be hindered if students feel threatened or judged when making moral judgments.

CRITIQUE OF KOHLBERG'S MORAL DEVELOPMENT THEORY

Lawrence Kohlberg's theory of moral development has received considerable critique since it first appeared some thirty years ago. One of the strongest voices of criticism has come from Kohlberg's colleague, Carol Gilligan (1993), whose primary argument rests upon the fact that both Piaget and Kohlberg biased their theories by focusing primarily on men. Gilligan argues that women view morality differently than men. Her research, based on interviewing women, shows that women are intrinsically "subjectively attached"—men's moral judgment rests in logic and law, whereas women focus on relationships (29). Gilligan reframes women's psychological development by focusing on interpersonal relationships, which she calls an "ethic of care" as compared to Kohlberg's focus on logic and reason. For Gilligan, the ethic of care resolves moral dilemmas by deciding what care and responsibility are called for in a given situation. This approach contrasts with Kohlberg's ethic of justice in which people resolve moral dilemmas on the basis of what one believes is right and moral.

Gilligan's ethic of care includes three stages: (1) care for self (egocentric). The primary element is, *"I don't want to be hurt."* (2) Care for others (maternal morality). The focus is *"I don't want others to hurt."* (3) Caring for truth (morality of nonviolence). The focus here is a balance between care for self and others, *"I don't want anyone hurt"* (1993).

Similar to Gilligan's critique is the recent book by Martin Hoffman, *Empathy and Moral Development* (2001). Hoffman argues that Kohlberg's view of justice as the primary motivation for morality, being right (justice), is limited. He argues, in the same vein as Gilligan, that morality is motivated by empathy or care. John Gibbs' *Moral Development and Reality* (2003) goes a step further by stating that the most plausible position of moral motivation is neither "affective primacy" (empathy) nor "cognitive primacy" (justice) but "*co*primacy" (both empathy and justice as primary motives). Gibbs argues that pro-social behavior includes moral self-relevance or "moral identity," which achieves a life characterized by total integration of self and morality (10).

Vanessa Walker and John Snarey have followed Gilligan's thesis by arguing that African-Americans come to moral judgments in a unique way. Their "ethics of care" relate to the influence of the family in making moral decisions (2004). Donald Joy argues that Kohlberg was influenced by Immanuel Kant's separation of fact and value for epistemological purposes, stating that fact (reason) is more important than value (experiences). Joy shows that Kohlberg's "one-sided" focus on facts needs to include a focus on values (1983, 42).

These critiques provide a helpful corrective to Kohlberg's theory. The focus on co-primacy (empathy and justice) offers a particularly balanced view of morality. As Christian educators, we are concerned about issues of justice (righteousness), but we are also concerned about care and empathy (love and mercy). This balanced view of morality is much closer to the biblical view of a Triune God.

PSYCHOSOCIAL STAGES OF DEVELOPMENT: ERIK ERIKSON

A holistic approach to Christian discipleship includes understanding how we grow and develop as we interact with societal demands and expectations. God has created us as social beings that enjoy relationships. The Triune God's very nature, three interrelated persons, is relational. Our sense of being and personhood is defined by our relationship with God, others, and society. As we grow and mature, our sense of self, body, and role in society intersect and connect at different levels. Erik Erikson, a psychoanalyst and professor of developmental psychology at Harvard University, developed the theory of psychosocial stages of development, described as *epigenesis,* that follow a process of conflict and resolution throughout the life span. Erikson, drawing heavily on Sigmund Freud, places emphasis on the role of sexuality (libido) and on the importance of the role of conflict involving the id (instinct), ego (sense of self that mediates between instinct and society), and superego (social conscience) in determining personality (Pullman 2001, 64). While Freud's view of human beings is largely negative, Erikson's is more positive because he is concerned with the healthy development of the self.

Erikson's developmental theory focuses on the social, affective, and differential aspects of the human personality. Erikson, following Piaget's structural approach, assumes that human personality develops according to predictable patterns. Personality is shaped as people interact with society, either positively or negatively. He also views society as primarily cooperative; social/ personal interactions are mutually supportive at each stage of crisis (Pazmiño 1997, 201-2). Erikson does not regard each stage as an achievement; the negative response to crisis provides a dynamic counterpart. Issues of life will resurface later and require attention. The positive resolution of each stage results in various virtues or elements of ego strength that foster individual development within the wider community (202).

Erikson's model of psychosocial development originally included eight stages, but more recently eleven stages of development have been identified. This revised theoretical construct takes into consideration the emergent changes in society and how they impact human development (Pullman 2001, 64). Erikson identified a series of conflicts or crises that must be encountered and resolved at each stage of development if a person is to mature. The word *crisis* refers, not to an extraordinary event, but to the normal process of understanding and adjusting to a new set of expectations. In each stage, Erikson believed that people experience a conflict or crisis that serves as a turning point in development.

Les Steele describes three aspects of each stage of development (1998). First, each stage includes its own psychosocial crisis. Second, each stage includes what Erikson first called ego strengths but later called virtues. These are the strengths that develop with the healthy resolution of each stage. Negative virtues, which Erikson calls antipathies or vices, accompany unresolved conflicts (79). Third, each stage includes what Erikson calls ritualization, ways in which individuals interact or socialize with those around them. Rituals provide familiar patterns of human interaction that allow us to be with others (80). Here are Erikson's original eight stages of psychosocial development (also see appendix 8.2):

- *Stage 1: Infancy (birth to two years): Trust vs. Mistrust.* The infant crisis exists between trust and mistrust, which is dependent on the quality of relationship with the quality of a material relationship. If the resolution results in mistrust, then there is anxiety.
- *Stage 2: Toddler (two to four years): Autonomy vs. Shame.* The child begins to develop freedom and autonomy as physical and mental abilities develop. If the child is encouraged to explore this new freedom, he or she grows more confident. However, if parents disapprove, the child can harbor doubts and shame.

- *Stage 3: Preschool (four to six years): Initiative vs. Guilt.* The child has increased capacity for taking responsibility and self-initiation. Parental support and encouragement increases initiative, but a lack of parental approval can promote guilt.
- *Stage 4: Middle Childhood (six to twelve years): Industry vs. Inferiority.* The child begins to develop the capacity for industry through skill development. These new skills bring the child closer to adulthood; however, inferiority may result if adults perceive such behavior as childish.
- *Stage 5: Early Adolescence (twelve to eighteen years): Identity vs. Identity Confusion.* This is probably the most popular concept of Erikson's theory. Adolescents have a growing sense of identity development characterized by questions about their role in the world. More recently this stage of development has expanded with research on delayed adolescences. Teenagers are now developing slower than previous generations.
- *Stage 6: Early Adulthood (twenty-four to thirty-five years): Intimacy vs. Isolation.* The emerging adult will develop meaningful relationships with others, including marriage in some cases. The negative result can lead to isolation.
- *Stage 7: Middle Adulthood (thirty-five to sixty years): Generativity vs. Stagnation.* The adult who has developed a strong sense of self will share his or her life with others through giving and productivity. Those who are not productive stagnate, which can lead to self-absorption and a sense of emptiness.
- *Stage 8: Late Adulthood (sixty to seventy-five years): Integrity vs. Despair.* The adult who has integrity can assess his or her life with a sense of satisfaction and fulfillment. Despair comes to adults who have feelings of regret and frustration as they realize they cannot change the past or believe they cannot influence the future in a positive way.

Erikson's stages of development provide the Christian educator a pathway to understand how a person grows and matures in a given context of life. Psychosocial theory contributes significantly to Christian discipleship. The development of the self is formed and shaped through the crisis or conflict of each stage of development. The faith community provides a context for nurturing and growth at each stage and can aid the process of formation as persons either progress or decline through each stage. The Christian community can assist persons in the search for meaning and significance in their lives.

The development of virtue, according to Erikson, implies a quality that develops the Christian's sense of self. Christian faith adds to this idea of soulfulness, a quality of character that motivates and points the person in the proper direction (Steele 1998, 131). The gathered Christian community—for worship, learning, or service—is a natural context for ritualization.

▶ CONCLUSION

A holistic approach to Christian discipleship includes understanding the natural stages of human development. Just as we grow physically, we also grow cognitively, morally, and socially. Developmental theory provides the Christian educator a pathway to enhance spiritual growth and maturation. God works through the aspects of the human person to form and shape us into his image and likeness. Holistic Christian discipleship would not be complete without a discussion on faith development, to which we turn next.

▶ REFERENCES

Downs, Perry. 1994. *Educating for Spiritual Growth*. Grand Rapids: Zondervan.

Fowler, James. 1995. *Stages of Faith: The Psychology of Human Development and the Quest for Meaning*. San Francisco: HarperOne.

Gibbs, John C. 2003. *Moral Development and Reality: Beyond the Theories of Kohlberg and Hoffman*. Thousand Oaks, CA: Sage Publications.

Gilligan, Carol. 1993. *In a Different Voice*. Cambridge, MA: Harvard Univ. Press.

Hoffman, Martin T. 2001. *Empathy and Moral Development: Implications for Caring and Justice*. Cambridge: Cambridge Univ. Press.

Joy, Donald. 1983. *Moral Development Foundations: Judeo/Christian Alternatives to Piaget/Kohlberg*. Nashville: Abingdon Press.

Lerner, R. M., ed. 2002. *Concepts and Theories of Human Development*. Mahwah, NJ: Lawrence Erlbaum Associates.

Lowe, Stephen, and Mary Lowe. 2008. Spiritual formation in theological distance education: An ecosystems model as paradigm. Unpublished paper for National Consultation on Spiritual Formation in Theological Distance Education.

Marsden, George M. 1991. *Understanding Fundamentalism and Evangelicalism*. Grand Rapids: William B. Eerdmans.

Miller, Donald E. 1982. The developmental approach to Christian education. In *Contemporary Approaches to Christian Education*, 73-102. Ed. Jack L. Seymour and Donald E. Miller. Nashville: Abingdon Press.

Pazmiño, Robert W. 1997. *Foundational Issues in Christian Education: An Introduction in Evangelical Perspective*. 2nd ed. Grand Rapids: Baker Books.

Piaget, Jean. 1965. *The Moral Judgment of the Child*. New York: Free Press.

Pullman, Ellery. 2001. Life span development. In *Introduction to Christian Education: Foundations for the Twenty-First Century*, 63-72. Ed. Michael J. Anthony. Grand Rapids: Zondervan.

Roehlkepartain, Eugene, et al. 2006. *The Handbook of Spiritual Development in Childhood and Adolescence*. Thousand Oaks, CA: Sage Publications.

Steele, Les. 1998. *On the Way: A Practical Theology of Christian Formation*. Eugene, OR: Wipf and Stock.

Stonehouse, Cathy M. 2000. *Patterns in Moral Development.* Eugene, OR: Wipf and
    Stock.
Walker, Vanessa Siddle, and John R. Snarey. 2004. *Race-ing Moral Formation: African
    American Perspectives on Care and Justice.* New York: Teachers College Press.
Ward, Ted. 1995. Foreword. In *Nurture That Is Christian: Developmental Perspectives on
    Christian Education,* 7-17. Ed. James C. Wilhoit and John M. Dettoni. Whea-
    ton, IL: Victor Books.
Wilhoit, James C., and John M. Dettoni, eds. 1995. *Nurture That Is Christian: Devel-
    opmental Perspectives on Christian Education.* Wheaton, IL: Victor Books.

Appendix 8.1
Kohlberg's Moral Development

"Justice"

				4½		
I **PRECONVENTIONAL**		**II** **CONVENTIONAL**			**III** **POSTCONVENTIONAL**	
Ego-centric *Focus:* Physical results of action. Avoid punishment/achieve reward.		Others-oriented External motivation: to please others *Focus:* Loyalty and conformity to external expectations Need to be competent draws individual to observe others		Do what I want—let everyone else do what they want.	Principled Internal motivation *Focus:* Validity of rule/law Evaluated in terms of: Universality Motivation Common good	
Golden Rule:		*Golden Rule:*			*Golden Rule:*	
Do to others what will make them reward and not punish me.	Do things for others that will cause them to do nice things for me.	Do things for others that will make them pleased with me.	Do things for others in my group that they expect me to do as one of them.		Do for others what we have decided is the greatest good for everyone.	Do for others what I would have them do for me if I were the least advantaged of all people.
1	2	3	4	4½	5	6

Appendix 8.2
Erik Erikson's Psychosocial Stages of Development

VIII. Late Adulthood								Integrity vs. Despair
VII. Middle Adulthood							Generativity vs. Stagnation	
VI. Early Adulthood						Intimacy vs. Isolation		
V. Early Adolescence					Identity vs. Identity Confusion			
IV. Middle Childhood				Industry vs. Inferiority				
III. Preschool			Initiative vs. Guilt					
II. Toddler		Autonomy vs. Shame						
I. Infancy	Trust vs. Mistrust							

NINE

FAITH DEVELOPMENT

▶ INTRODUCTION

Imagine you are a senior high youth pastor. You have observed that several teens who attend the youth group have a vibrant faith; however, when they are with their non-Christian friends at school their faith seems to be absent. What does this tell you about your teen's faith development?

Imagine being a parent of a junior high student. You have nurtured him in a Christian environment. He is active in the church and responsive to the Christian faith. However, as a parent you are concerned that he has not made a commitment of faith or a decision to follow Christ. Should you be concerned? What does this tell you about his faith development?

At the very core of Christian discipleship is faith. As Christians we find our identity in having faith in the ancient truths of scriptures, and in the life, death, and resurrection of Jesus Christ. Being a follower of Jesus Christ includes having faith in the message of the living Christ. A Wesleyan approach to Christian discipleship places a greater emphasis on living "the way" of Christ than believing in propositional truths. Jesus calls us to be a people of the way. Discipleship is marked by emulating the life of Christ as we love God and neighbor completely.

▶ WHAT IS FAITH?

As we saw in chapter 4, faith is not something that we possess but is a gift from God. We have faith because of God's grace working in our lives. For Wesleyans, the divine initiative of faith always includes a human response. Faith is God's first activity toward us, initiating a faithful response. This divine-human synergy is always in operation as we respond to God's grace. The human side of faith includes three primary aspects: belief, behavior, and attitude (Steele 1998, 102).

First, Christian faith includes believing correctly (orthodoxy). This is the cognitive side of faith. What we believe matters to how we live out our faith. Faith in Christ is not blind. It is informed by scripture, reason, and tradition: "Now faith is being sure of what we hope for and certain of what we do not see" (Hebrews 11:1). Faith is always "seeking understanding." Faith is always compatible with knowledge.

Second, faith includes right behavior or practice (orthopraxy). The New Testament understanding of faith includes more than mere ascent to belief; it means being moved to take action on what one believes. Faith is a verb. It is active. Having faith in Jesus Christ means living a life of obedience to the gospel message: "Faith without works is dead" (James 2:20, KJV). Christian discipleship includes living a life of faith that is always growing, dynamic, and active. In other words, right belief (orthodoxy) without right practice (orthopraxy) is an incomplete, dead faith!

Third, faith includes having a right heart (orthopathy). As Steele states, "It is important not only that we believe correctly and act correctly but also that we act and believe correctly for the right motives" (1998, 104). Faith is our willingness to trust God with our lives, surrendering completely to him. This aspect of faith is not easy. It may require sacrifice and call on us to stay the course, to continue to choose faith when faith does not feel good.

Faithful discipleship includes the integration of all three aspects: belief (knowing), behavior (doing), and passion (being). When too much emphasis is placed on one aspect to the neglect of the others, then our faith formation is out of balance. Christian educators must give focus to each of these three aspects of faith.

▶ FAITH DEVELOPMENT THEORY: JAMES FOWLER

One of the most significant books on faith development is James Fowler's *Stages of Faith* (1994). Fowler was influenced by the cognitive development theory of Jean Piaget, the cognitive/moral development theory of Lawrence Kohlberg, and the psychosocial development theory of Erik Erikson. A contemporary of Kohlberg, Fowler adapts stage theory as a way to view faith. Fowler was also heavily influenced theologically by H. Richard Niebuhr, Paul Tillich, and Wilfred Cantwell Smith (Dirks 2001, 83).

Fowler's view of faith is different from an evangelical or Wesleyan view. Faith development theory is designed to present "the way people understand and experience faith emerging through predictable stages" (Fowler 1981). Fowler believes that "faith is the way we make meaning out of life." He believes that everyone has human faith that can be measured. Faith is a person's or community's "way-of-being-in-relation to an ultimate environment." This definition of faith indicates that all persons live out of faith, whether or not they consider themselves to be religious or belong to a religious tradition (Miller 1982, 86). According to Fowler: "Faith, rather than belief or religion, is the most fundamental category in the human quest for relation to transcendence . . . Faith, it appears, is generic, a universal feature of human living, recognizably similar everywhere despite the remarkable variety of forms and contents of religious practice and belief" (1981, 14).

Fowler's theory focuses on the human side of faith, but he also acknowledges the importance of a divine transcendence, or the "ultimate conditions of existence." These terms, which can correspond to God, allow his theory to be applied to faith of any kind (Dirks 2001, 84). Fowler does not claim, however, that faith is universal in all contexts and cultures.

Since Fowler's human view of faith is generic, his content of faith is incomplete from our perspective, but we can accept the structure of faith he outlines. The content of faith can then be understood through the proposed structures of thinking, valuing, and knowing. These structures undergo change as faith development occurs (Dirks, 84). For example, the structure of a child's faith is different from an adult's faith. Each structure provides a stable pathway by which to deal with the issues of life in the midst of change.

STAGES OF FAITH DEVELOPMENT

Fowler's model, based on those of Piaget, Erikson, and Kohlberg, proposes that stages describe the way we live our faith. They provide the forms of faith by which we make meaning in our lives. He holds that stages are hierarchical (each stage builds on and adds to the previous stage), sequential (stages occur in the same order in each person), and invariant (each person progresses through the same stages). The journey through the stages can be repeated and revisited, but the capacities of each stage are retained. Each stage of development affects one's ability to relate to self, others, and God (see appendix 9.1).

- *Primal Faith (birth to infancy)*. Fowler calls this a "pre-stage" because it is not accessible to the normal modes of empirical inquiry used for faith-development research. Before the development of language, from birth to age two, an infant's predisposition to trust is formed through parents. Seeds of faith are developed.
- *Stage One—Intuitive/Projective Faith (early childhood)*. Faith develops through stories and symbols coupled with imagination. Children learn from their parents about God. This is an intuitive and highly imaginative stage, usually ages four to eight years old, when children are controlled by stories, symbols, and images, but not yet by logical thinking. Children develop either a positive or negative view of God from their parents.
- *Stage Two—Mythical-Literal Faith (childhood and beyond)*. Emerging concrete operations allow the person to think logically and order the world by means of categories of causality, space, and time, usually around age seven to eleven. This stage is characterized by the emergence of mutual interpersonal perspectives: "I see you seeing me; I see me as you see me; I see you seeing me seeing you" (Fowler 1981, 150). Children

understand faith in literal terms. They are learning to sort out reality from make-believe, but they may believe in Santa Claus or the Tooth Fairy. Children tend to have a sense of lawfulness and loyalty in their view of God and faith. As they mature, this view will be challenged.

- *Stage Three—Synthetic/Conventional Faith (adolescence).* Adolescents see themselves in relationship with others. The beliefs and values of the previous stages are synthesized into some sort of coherent perspective. It is conventional in that the perspective adopted tends to be the belief systems and forms of the community. Relationships play a large role in shaping faith and identity. For teenagers at this stage the church becomes an extended family. Faith is not shaped independently, but rather by the relationships with peers or even the faith of the church. Youth groups can offer positive peer pressure, but they can also prevent teens from moving on in their faith development because of strong community and pressure to identify with the group. Teenagers often compartmentalize their faith because of group influence. At church they can express a vital faith, but they may neglect their faith with non-Christian friends. The group can have positive or negative impact on teen decisions about faith.

- *Stage Four—Individuative/Reflective Faith (young adulthood).* Here the person makes decisions based on the self, apart from the expectations of the group. Self now stands outside of the group, questioning why the group believes and acts as it does. A person begins "to take seriously the burden of responsibility for his or her own commitments, lifestyles, beliefs, and attitudes" (Fowler 1981, 182). The desire to fit in is replaced with criticism. The individual establishes his or her own identity and reflects on the actions of the group. This is a very significant stage of faith formation as young adults reflect critically on and take ownership of their faith. This can be a very painful stage of development because young adults must deconstruct their faith in order to make it their own. They question and struggle with the security and stability of faith, which is now in question. This is why it is critical to create safe places for young adults to ask hard questions and to help them internalize their faith.

- *Stage Five—Conjunctive Faith (mid-life and beyond).* Here the truth is multidimensional, and it becomes reasonable to assume that other people have insights we do not have. Adults see their own limitations as well. The individual values ideas and thoughts of other groups and accepts a new quest for understanding. People "earn" this stage by living reflectively through the earlier stages. This stage requires that a person become receptive to the "voices of one's deeper self, composed of the ideals and prejudices that we absorb from our families and cultures" (Fowler 1981, 198). Persons at this stage feel comfortable with paradox and conflicting views. They can become cynical and complacent because of the relative nature of their worldview (Kelcourse 2004, 46). Some, however, have a strong desire to assist others in faith development (Dirks 2001, 85).

- *Stage Six—Universalizing Faith.* This requires a radical decentralization of self and a fundamentally new quality of participation with God. At this stage, communion with the "ultimate conditions of existence," or God, develops. There is a new focus on matters of love and justice. People are willing to spend their lives for the sake of others. People at this stage are open to other religious beliefs and truths, willing to interact with persons from all faith and religious traditions.

Fowler believes that very few people reach this final stage of faith development. He reserved stage six for people such as Martin Luther King Jr., Mother Teresa, and Mohandas Gandhi. "These persons embody costly openness to the power of the future; they are ready to spend and be spent in making the Kingdom actual" (Fowler 1981, 211). A Wesleyan understanding of sanctification and Christian perfection could be included at this stage. It can be closely associated with a biblical view of holiness and living a sanctified life of love and justice toward all of humanity, which is our primary goal in Christian discipleship.

WEAKNESSES OF FAITH DEVELOPMENT THEORY

Fowler's theory does have critics, who raise specific concerns worth considering. First, Christian educators recognize the limitations of Fowler's broad, generic view of faith that is inherent in all persons. As discussed above, we cannot accept his *content* of faith, but a focus on the *structure* of faith is beneficial to the Christian educator. It provides a pathway to understanding how people process faith.

Second, since Fowler believes that only a few people will achieve the highest stages of development, it raises questions about the ability to reach this stage at all. In other words, his final stage seems unattainable for most people. Third, though Fowler argues that his theory is universal, his view of development is focused through a North American perspective that does not have meaning in many cultural contexts. Fourth, Fowler's theory, influenced by Piaget's cognitive development, places more emphasis on cognition than on emotion and affection.

Finally for us, faith remains the work of the Sprit of God in Christ. It is a gift related to salvation, a gift we cannot achieve or earn. Fowler's theory cannot deal with these aspects of faith since, in his view, children have less faith than adults, which reflects on the adequacy of their salvation (Krych 1992, 71).

BENEFITS OF FAITH DEVELOPMENT THEORY

In spite of all the concerns just mentioned, the benefits of Fowler's faith development theory are significant for the purposes of faithful discipleship.

First, faith is relational and dynamic. Fowler's theory focuses on faith as relationship to self, others, and God, which is consistent with a Christian understanding of faith. Christians are called to worship and serve in faith communities with other members of the family of God. Faith is not static belief in a creed but grows dynamically throughout life. Also, faith development takes place through interaction with the environment, whether or not it is faith-based. A Wesleyan view of prevenient grace focuses on the work of the Spirit in all aspects of life, drawing all persons to God, whether or not they believe.

Second, faith development includes struggle and crisis. Faith develops in stages, a process that requires struggle and crisis, which are necessary for Christian formation. A Christian crisis of faith can help one become more aware of the reality of God. Christians recognize that growth requires working through difficult issues of life, depending on God's sustaining grace and holding onto the assurance that God is with us. Through these struggles we receive illumination and faith emerges in new forms.

Third, faith development's goal is maturity. Faith development is a journey that leads to maturity. Obviously Fowler's view of maturity differs from a biblical view of sanctification. Fowler views faith as a human experience, which neglects the word of God. The goal of Christian discipleship is maturity of faith, or holiness of heart and life. Fowler's theory outlines a pathway to spiritual growth and maturation. Christian educators can use this pathway to design educational opportunities and experiences that assist individuals in spiritual growth and maturation.

Fourth, faith development includes transformation. Growth through the stages of faith involves changing the way one views his or her relationship with God and others. Moving through the stages of development includes conversion and transformation. Each successive stage brings added potential for partnership with God or alienation from God, depending on the decision of the individual (Dirks 2001, 86).

▶ JOHN WESTERHOFF AND FAITH DEVELOPMENT THEORY

John Westerhoff III makes a significant contribution to faith development through his classic text *Will Children Have Faith?* Westerhoff addresses the nature of faith and how faith relates to education. For him, faith describes a way of behaving that involves knowing, being, and doing. Terms like *world-view* or *value system* describe the content of faith, but faith itself remains something we do. Faith is an action (1976b, 89). James Fowler's work on faith development influenced Westerhoff's early work; however, Carl Jung's developmental approach opened "a whole new way to understand faith" (Westerhoff 1992, 130). According to Westerhoff, faith becomes meaningful through the community of believers and must be experienced within the body of believers. "No one can determine another's faith and no one can give another faith, but we can be faithful and share our life and our faith with another. Others, regardless of age, can do the same with us, and through this sharing we each sustain, transmit, and expand our faith" (1976b, 91). The education of the church must proceed on the assumption that the life and work of the congregation is the curriculum.

FAITH STAGES

Westerhoff describes four kinds of faith that correlate with the major developmental stages (see appendix 9.2). First, during preschool and early childhood years, children typically act with *experienced faith*. Children explore and test, imagine and create, observe and copy, experience and react (1976b, 91). "A person learns Christ not as a theological affirmation but as an affective experience" (92).

Second, *affiliative faith* occurs in childhood and early adolescence. During this period, persons seek to act with others in accepting community with a clear sense of identity. Westerhoff notes that "all of us have a need to belong to a self-conscious community and that through our active participation we can make a contribution to its life" (1976b, 94).

Third, *searching faith* continues into adolescence. Young people probe previous assumptions and explore new conceptions of what life is all about. Searching faith includes experimentation and the need to commit one's life to a cause and persons. Fourth, *owned faith* begins sometime in early adulthood.

According to Westerhoff, "This movement from experienced and affiliative faith through searching faith to owned faith is what historically has been called *conversion*" (1976b, 98). *Conversion* may be sudden or gradual, dramatic or quiet, emotional or intellectual, but the transformation always involves a major change in the person's thinking, feeling, and will—in short, in their total behavior (98). After conversion, people desire to put their faith into personal and social action (Maddix 2009, 185).

FAITH AND CATECHESIS

For Westerhoff, faith is primarily nurtured through the pastoral activity of catechesis. His thesis of catechesis is best expressed in his book *A Faithful Church: Issues in the History of Catechesis* (1992). Berard Marthaler, a Roman Catholic, influenced Westerhoff by enlarging his understanding of religious socialization and helping him understand the history and nature of catechesis. According to Westerhoff, *catechesis* describes the process by which Christians are developed, and it indicates all intentional learning within a community of Christian faith and life. We are made a Christian at baptism. We spend the rest of our lives involved in the process of becoming more Christian. That lifelong process is catechesis. Catechesis and Christian education are not synonymous, however. *Catechesis* describes an essentially pastoral activity intended to transmit the church's tradition and to enable faith to become living, conscious, and active in the life of maturing persons and a maturing community. It is concerned not only with conversion and nurture, commitment and behavior, but with aiding the community to become Christian (Maddix 2009, 186). It involves passing on living tradition in the form of a story and vision to all those who share in the life and mission of the Christian faith community (Neville and Westerhoff 1978). Westerhoff affirms that "catechesis is the deliberate (intentional), systematic (related) and sustained (lifelong) process within community of Christian faith and a life process which establish, build up, equip, and enable it to be Christ's body or presence in the world to the end that all people are restored to unity with God and each other" (1987b, 582).

Westerhoff provides three aspects of catechesis: *formation, education,* and *instruction. Formation* implies shaping and refers to intentional, relational, experiential activities within the life of a story-formed faith community. *Education* implies reshaping and refers to critical reflective activities related to communal experience (Maddix 2009, 186). And *instruction* implies building and refers to the means by which knowledge and skills useful to communal life are transmitted, acquired, and understood through a teaching process. These three distinct aspects are interrelated processes in catechesis. Formation forms the body of Christ, education reforms it, and instruction builds it up (1987b, 581). Catechesis is a process that is, without apology, value-laden; a process that aims to introduce persons into a community of Christian faith with its distinctive values, understandings, and ways; a process that aims to aid persons to internalize and adopt the community's faith as their own and to apply that faith to life in the world. A primary function of catechesis is to help the faithful, individually and corporately, meet the twofold responsibilities that faith asks of them: communion with God and communion with one's fellow human beings—that is, to nurture the intimacy of spiritual life that expresses itself in social justice, liberation, and the political struggle for whole community, peace, and the well-being of all persons (1987a, 13-14).

▶ CRITIQUE OF FAITH DEVELOPMENT THEORY (STRUCTURALISM)

Developmental theory, built on a modernistic structural approach, dominated developmental psychology for several decades. As discussed in these last two chapters, its influence on faith development theory and practice in Christian discipleship is formative and cannot be overlooked. Christian educators can learn much about the process of spiritual maturation from developmental theories. They have, as we saw in chapter 9, been critiqued on several levels. First, James Loder (1931—2001), former professor of the philosophy of Christian education at Princeton Theological Seminary, provides an alternative approach to Fowler's stage development theory in *The Transforming Moment* (1981). Like Fowler, Loder is interested in transformations in human faith. But rather than argue for a generic series of stages through which all persons move, Loder focuses on what he calls "convictional knowing," life-changing events through which ways of knowing, believing, feeling, and acting are radically altered. Unlike Fowler and Kohlberg, Loder focuses on the dynamics of Christian transformation. He wants to discern how Christ, through the Holy Spirit, transforms the human spirit. Both Fowler and Kohlberg provide a more general view of human transformation, though Loder does provide an overview of how stages change when people encounter transformation (269-92).

Loder's five-stage "logic" of the human spirit includes: conflict, scanning, insight, release, and interpretation/verification (see appendix 9.3). Through this process the human spirit is reconstructed by the work of the Holy Spirit. This logic permeates every aspect of human development as a pattern that governs the stage transition process (1981, 128). According to Loder, the process of transformation is not limited to developmental stage transitions but takes in a variety of life experiences (Dykstra 1982, 61). Loder's description of the impact of the Holy Spirit in human transformation, as the power of convictional knowing in the Spirit, provides Christian educators with a credible alternative to Fowler's faith development theory.

Second, as we have already noted, most developmental theories are based on studies of middle-class Caucasian males who are assumed to represent the norm of human development. The study of women by Carol Gilligan (1993) and Mary Belenky (1986) endeavor to correct this imbalance by attending to women's experiences and articulating the meanings implicit in what women say. Also, Robert Coles (1967) has reported the life experience of persons living in minority, poor white, and migrant-worker communities, whose voices would not normally be heard in scholarly discourse (Kelcourse 2004, 7). Christian educators who work in multicultural or global contexts will have to recognize the limitations of the theories, which stem from the biased nature of the studies.

Third, research in the fields of neuroscience and brain research has significant impact on the basic assumptions of developmental theory. A new alliance among certain approaches to philosophy, psychology, and biology creates a new and productive, though sometimes odd, field (Damasio 1999, 13). Many of the new insights surface through the field of brain studies, particularly neuroscience and social neuroscience. Already preliminary insights in popular overviews (Damasio 1994; Gladwell 2005; Goleman 2006) and undergraduate textbooks (Santrock 2007, 115-23) describe and explain human behavior through neural mechanisms and social interaction. Specialists continue to study both large processes within the brain and specific transformations at the synaptic level (LeDoux 2002), which impact the quality of growth and development. For example, it is obvious that children from newborn to toddler undergo a phenomenal range of biological and mental development. In recent years, neuroscience studies have revealed that youth also incur a broad range of mental growth as certain neural pathways undergo rapid expansion. These studies provide a stronger biological base for the concept of adolescent abstract thinking (what Piaget called formal relations). Similar studies, however, have identified certain portions of the brain, particularly associated with judgment, that lag behind other developmental processes (Giedd 2009; Santrock 2007, 121-22). This information prompts developmental theorists to acknowledge both the risk-taking tendencies in youth and the need for authoritative (not authoritarian) communities to shape youth development (Boisture 2003). These relatively new insights are already shaping developmental theory and public policy. The more we know about biological change (including neurobiological processes) the more we can learn about and adapt developmental theory. Initial observations from these fields require further exploration and integration, and the impact of neuroscience research on developmental theory is yet to be fully realized. The next decade could bring an entirely new understanding of how we grow and develop.

▶ CONCLUSION

The faith development theories of Fowler and Westerhoff provide the Christian educator with a deeper understanding of the processes of faith formation. How our faith grows and develops is a central focus of Christian discipleship, with the goal of being like Christ. Faith is developed as we go through predictable stages of life, leading toward a life of spiritual maturity.

Faith development requires our ability to learn new understandings about God as we move through these stages. Faith formation requires our interaction with others and with God. As Westerhoff reminds us, faith formation takes place in the context of Christian community. Effective Christian discipleship includes recognizing these stages of development in the development of educational activities that foster faith formation.

▶ REFERENCES

Belenky, Mary F., et al. 1986. *Women's Ways of Knowing: The Development of Self, Voice, and Mind.* San Francisco: HarperCollins.

Boisture, Robert A. 2003. Hardwired to connect: The new scientific case for authoritative communities. YMCA, Dartmouth Medical School, and Institute for American Values.

Coles, Robert. 1967. *Children of Crisis,* Vol. 1. Boston: Atlantic-Little Brown.

Damasio, Antonio. 1994. *Descartes' Error: Emotion, Reason, and the Human Brain.* New York: Penguin Book.

_____. 1999. *The Feeling of What Happens: Body and Emotion in the Making of Consciousness.* San Diego: Harvest Book, Harcourt.

Dirks, Dennis. 2001. Faith development. In *Introducing Christian Education: Foundations for the Twenty-first Century,* 83-90. Ed. Michael Anthony. Grand Rapids: Zondervan.

Dykstra, Craig R. 1981. *Vision and Character: A Christian Educator's Alternative to Kohlberg.* New York: Paulist Press.

_____. 1982. Transformation in faith and morals. In *Theology Today* 39:1, 56-64.

Fowler, James. 1981. *The Stages of Faith: The Psychology of Human Development and the Quest for Meaning.* San Francisco: Harper and Row.

Giedd, Jay N. 2009. The teen brain: Primed to learn, primed to take risks. In *Cerebrum Journal,* February. The Dana Foundation, http://www.dana.org/news/cerebrum/ (accessed online April 2, 2009).

Gladwell, Malcolm. 2005. *Blink: The Power of Thinking Without Thinking.* New York: Back Bay Books.

Gilligan, Carol. 1993. *In a Different Voice.* Cambridge, MA: Harvard Univ. Press.

Goleman, Daniel. 2006. *Social Intelligence: The New Science of Human Relationships.* New York: Bantam Books.

Kelcourse, Felicity B., ed. 2004. *Human Development and Faith: Life-Cycle Stages of Body, Mind, and Soul.* St. Louis: Chalice Press.

Krych, Margaret A. 1992. Faith and cognitive development. In *Christian Perspectives on Human Development,* 65-76. Ed. LeRoy Aden, David G. Benner, and J. Harold Eilens. Grand Rapids: Baker Books.

LeDoux, Joseph. 2002. *Synaptic Self: How Our Brains Become Who We Are.* New York: Penguin.

Loder, James E. 1981. *The Transforming Moment.* San Francisco: Harper and Row.

Maddix, Mark A. 2009. John Westerhoff III: historical and theological aspects of Christian nurture. In *Journal of Christian Education and Information Technology* 16 (October): 183-201.

Miller, Donald E. 1982. The developmental approach to Christian education. In *Contemporary Approaches to Christian Education,* 73-102. Ed. Jack L. Seymour and Donald E. Miller. Nashville: Abingdon Press.

Neville, Gwen K., and John Westerhoff. 1978. *Learning Through Liturgy.* New York: Seabury Press.

Santrock, John W. 2000. *The Psychology or Religion Module.* 6th ed. New York: McGraw Hill.

———. 2007. *A Topical Approach to Life-Span Development.* 3rd ed. Boston: McGraw Hill.

Steele, Les. 1998. *On the Way: A Practical Theology of Christian Formation.* Eugene, OR: Wipf and Stock.

Westerhoff, John. 1976a. *Tomorrow's Church: A Community of Change.* Waco, TX: Word Books.

———. 1976b. *Will Children Have Faith?* New York: Seabury Press.

———. 1982. A catechetical way of doing theology. In *Religious Education and Theology.* Ed. Norma Thompson. Birmingham, AL: Religious Education Press.

———. 1983. A journey into self-understanding. In *Modern Masters of Religious Education.* Ed. Marlene Mayr. Birmingham, AL: Religious Education Press.

———. 1987a. A discipline in crisis. In *Religious Education* 74:1, 7-15.

———. 1987b. Formation, education, instruction. In *Religious Education* 52, no. 4 (fall): 578-91.

———. 1992a. *A Faithful Church: Issues in the History of Catechesis.* Wilton, CT: Morehouse-Barlow.

———. 1992b. The shaking of the foundation. In *A Reader in Christian Education.* Ed. Eugene Gibbs. Grand Rapids: Baker Book House.

Appendix 9.1

Summary of Fowler's Stage Theory of Faith Development*

Stage	Relative Age	Characteristics
Stage 1: Intuitive-Reflective Faith	Early Childhood	• Intuitive images of good and evil • Fantasy and reality are the same
Stage 2: Mythical-Literal Faith	Middle/Late Childhood	• More logic and concrete thought • Literal interpretation of religious stories; God is like a parent figure
Stage 3: Synthetic-Conventional Faith	Early Adolescence	• More abstract thought • Conform to religious beliefs of others, particularly peers
Stage 4: Individuative-Reflective Faith	Late Adolescence or Early Adulthood	• For the first time, individuals are capable of taking responsibility for their own religious beliefs • In-depth exploration of one's religious belief is carried out
Stage 5: Conjunctive Faith	Middle Adulthood	• More comfortable with paradox and opposing viewpoints • Stems from awareness of one's finiteness and limitedness
Stage 6: Universalizing Faith	Middle/Late Adulthood	• Transcending belief system to achieve a sense of oneness of being • Conflictual events are no longer seen as paradoxical.

*Adapted from John W. Santrock, *The Psychology or Religion Module,* 6th ed. (New York: McGraw Hill, 2000), 16.

Appendix 9.2
John Westerhoff, Stages of Faith Development*

	Observe and Copy	Act and React	Explore/Test
Experienced Faith (Early Childhood)	Acquiring role models and foundations for the integrity of belief and action	Formation of trust	Roots of openness or closeness
Affiliative Faith (Childhood)	Belonging, participation, and engagement	Affections; religion of the heart dominate	Authority; our story and way; a search for conviction
Searching Faith (Adolescence)	Commitment to ideology; engagement in related action	Intellect; religion of the head dominates	Critical judgment of the tradition nurtured in community
Mature Faith (Adulthood)	Personal belief; clear sense of personal identity with openness to others	Witness; religion of the will dominates	Centeredness; integrity of belief and action

*Adapted from Gwen Kennedy Neville and John Westerhoff III, *Learning Through Liturgy* (New York: Seabury Press, 1978), 163.

Appendix 9.3
James Loder, *The Logic of Transformation**

The logic of transformation occurs in a series of consequential steps in which there are continuity and discontinuity:

1. Conflict. Conflict occurs wherever there is discontinuity in our lived world. It may be an adverse incident such as an accident, an illness, loss of a loved one, or a sense of restlessness that threatens the continuity or stability of our lived world. Such a conflict may arise out of our consciousness or unconsciousness. The conflict provokes painful anxiety.

2. Interlude for Scanning. The self cannot live with this painful anxiety. As a *knower* it is not comfortable with not knowing. Therefore it begins scanning for possible ways to resolve the conflict and reduce the anxiety level. This scanning may involve both conscious and unconscious acts occurring concurrently. This period of scanning may last moments or years.

3. Insight. A solution is provided, which may not be due to logical reasoning but by a constructive act of imagination. Two or more noncompatible solutions may come together to produce a workable resolution to the conflict. This is the key process in transformation.

4. Release. The appearance of the solution, sometimes known as the aha moment, is accompanied by the release of energy, which is the response of our unconscious and reduces the anxiety level. Simultaneously there is the opening of the knower to new and expanded knowing or consciousness. This opening is a response of our conscious mind. Our knowing is expanded by this opening, resulting in a transformed lived world where we are able to see things clearer than before. It involves renewal in self-identity and relationship to our lived world.

5. Interpretation/Verification. In the final stage of interpretation, we used our transformed knowing to rebuild or improve upon our lived world. In reworking our lives forward, which Loder named "correspondence," we now live our lives with a renewed sense of identity and purpose. In reworking backward, or "congruence," we are able to understand our past experiences in a new light because of our new understanding.

---

*Adapted from James E. Loder, *The Transforming Moment* (San Francisco: Harper and Row, 1981), 99-122.

TEN

LEARNING THEORIES

▶ INTRODUCTION

Imagine you are leading a youth group in a lesson on loving your neighbor. You motivate the teens by external behavior, providing a prize of fifty dollars to the teen who brings the most new people to the group. Is this motivational approach consistent with Christian discipleship?

Imagine you are the Sunday school director of your local church. You have been asked by the senior pastor to review all the teachers. You attend an elementary age Sunday school class and you find that the teacher primarily teaches through lectures. What advice will you give her?

Christian education includes understanding how people appropriate, comprehend, and retain new information. Studying learning theories may help facilitate more faithful teaching. The long tradition of learning theory includes ancient and modern approaches. Augustine, in his sermon *The Teacher* (A.D. 389), emphasized the nature of the learner. John Amos Comenius (seventeenth century), through his writings and his textbook *Orbis Pictus,* and Johann H. Pestalozzi (eighteenth-century father of progressive education), both emphasized forms of teaching that took seriously the learners' need to connect knowledge with personal sense experience. Philosophers, such as John Locke and Immanuel Kant (eighteenth century), struggled over a definition of knowledge derived from external empirical data or internal presuppositions. Learning theory, as a psychological discipline, surfaced in the late nineteenth and early twentieth centuries with the work of pioneers Hermann Ebbinghaus, Edward Thorndike, and the creators of the Stanford-Binet test of IQ in individuals. Theoretical perspectives emerging from B. F. Skinner, Jean Piaget, Jerome Bruner, Albert Bandura, Erik Erikson, and Lev Vygotsky demonstrate the ongoing complexity and seriousness of this discipline.

Learning theories attempt to address a number of key questions concerning how we receive and retain personal and objective knowledge. The central issues often include:

1. How we receive and discriminate between different types of information (data) as we engage it through our senses
2. What conditions (internal and external) enhance our ability and desire to learn

3. How we process new information along with previous information and incorporate it all into our lives

4. How we retrieve and utilize information when it is needed

Each deals with major concerns that learning theories attempt to address through the studies of sensory perception, association, information processing, memory, and motivation.

Specific learning theories tend to fall into broad categories that share similar assumptions about the nature of people and the importance of the surrounding environment. The largest families lie along a continuum that stresses either the impact of the environment in shaping how we act (behavioral learning) or our individual ability to filter and organize received information (primarily cognitive learning). Many theories combine these two emphases, acknowledging the influence of society (either certain communities or particular people) in dialogue with the individual's personal abilities; these theories are often grouped into social or relational learning theory.

▶ BEHAVIORAL LEARNING THEORY

Behavioral learning theories emphasize how external stimuli (S) can cause a reflexive response (R) within a living organism. Living organisms, including humans, can then be conditioned to associate certain stimuli with a pattern of similar responses (S-R). "S-R conditioning" may be described in a number of forms including classical conditioning, operant conditioning, and reinforcement theory. The primary warrants supporting these theories assume that external forces can be manipulated to the point that the person learns, by association, to respond or behave in a predictable manner. Psychologists such as Ivan Pavlov, B. F. Skinner, and John Watson have championed this approach. Skinner advocated an approach called operant learning, learning determined progressively through scheduled exercises that reinforced certain responses by the learner. Motivation was determined by either creatively rewarding the learner (positive reinforcement) or intentionally eliminating obstructions to learning (negative reinforcement). Personal punishment as a form of reinforcement was discouraged.

IMPLICATIONS FOR CHRISTIAN DISCIPLESHIP

Behavioral theories tend to have a rather passive or antagonistic view of persons, one often contradictory to Christian anthropology. As noted in chapter 8, extreme behaviorism contradicts a Christian's value of the worth of individuals based on God's continuing love for people. Beyond this limitation, certain important aspects require our consideration for Christian education. Behavioral models take seriously the power of actions, such as worship or patterned prayer, to shape our understanding and practice of the Christian life. The recognition that teachers need to remove environmental barriers to learning (negative reinforcement) and praise students (positive reinforcement) are sensible insights from behavioral learning. Behavior modification, far from manipulation, may help persons stop destructive behaviors by helping them act into new, healthier ways.

▶ COGNITIVE LEARNING THEORY

Cognitive learning theories tend to emphasize the individual's capacity to selectively accept and organize information in the mind. Cognitive theories vary according to the theorist's conception of how the information is processed and stored. Motivation for learning, determined less by external factors, surfaces more through personal curiosity and the pleasure (or frustration) that occurs in understanding new information. Theorists assume that emotion, as a personal trait, either encourages or prohibits the learning process.

The most prominent cognitive theory, information processing, treats the mind like a computer or huge filing system. Sensory information is sorted, processed, stored, and retrieved in cognitive association with other similar bits of data. Learning occurs best when new information is well organized so that it connects (is cognitively associated), through an appropriate mental structure, with previous data that the learner already knows. Learners receive information as major concepts then attach new information that flows out of those concepts (deduction). Theorists like Robert Gagne advocate advanced organizers to assist guided learning, such as a comprehensive introductory outline, fill in the blank guides, or simple alliteration.

Another learning theory, *gestalt* (German for "form" or "shape"), assumes that different lines of association may emerge as the learner creates a new, larger pattern based upon seemingly disparate units of thought. Theorists advise persons to bring smaller ideas together to determine the larger concepts (induction). Learners may also use inquiry or problem solving as a strategy to allow different ideas to form around a central issue. Discovery learning, another strategy, is similar to problem solving and assumes that new knowledge can be discovered or even created through exploration and analysis (see below).

One prominent theorist, Jean Piaget, linked cognitive learning to personality development. Piaget noted that new information may be stored in older, familiar patterns of thinking (assimilation) or require new structures of thought to adapt to the new data (accommodation). The learner's ability to assimilate or accommodate new information is often connected to age and level of maturity (Gallagher and Reid, 1981). Theorists like Piaget and Roger Keagan see the abilities to think and to learn as basic forms of human development. The learner's ability to accept data and create new mental structures becomes an indicator of maturity (see chapter 8 for more on Piaget).

CATEGORIZATION AND DISCOVERY LEARNING: JEROME BRUNER

Jerome Bruner's work on categorization in learning is a significant contribution to understanding higher levels of cognitive process. Bruner's famous idea that "any subject can be taught effectively to a child at any stage of development" remains rooted in his understanding of perception and models of education (Downs 1994, 171). Bruner focuses on how a person thinks, particularly through the categorization of concepts developed in our minds. When we think, we fit concepts into categories formed in our mind. In order to fit into a category a concept must have a similar attribute and value as those concepts already included in the category (ibid.).

Bruner believes his theory of categorization proves necessary for thinking and functioning cognitively. Perry Downs identifies five critical functions of Bruner's theory. First, it serves to reduce the complexity of the environment. Second, categorization allows us to recognize objects and ideas we have never previously encountered. Third, categorization reduces the necessity for constant learning since we can recognize new objects without having to go through new learning. Fourth, categorization reduces the complexity of the environment by allowing us to relate objects or classes of events in categories using (fifth) a coding system (172).

The implication of Bruner's theory for Christian discipleship includes helping people develop new categories of thinking about scripture and theology. The Christian educator can provide a context in which people can develop lower levels of biblical and theological ideas in order to develop categories of understanding. In teaching the Bible and theology, the Christian educator can focus on helping the student know what information is included in each category.

Jerome Bruner also suggests that students discover learning by themselves, making their own cognitive categories. Discovery learning implies less directive teaching methods, such as questions and discussion. The motive to learn comes from intrinsic rewards, the student's desire to find information. As learners progress and develop higher cognitive processes, they discover answers, concepts, rules, or associations with less direct assistance from the instructor. The beauty of inductive teaching is that learners are given responsibility for their education and draw their own conclusions.

Discovery learning assumes that the learning process involves the whole person; it therefore nurtures the cognitive, affective, and behavioral domains of the human personality. It is an important alternative to the schooling-instruction paradigm that employs traditional methods, such as lecture, and nurtures only the cognitive domains of human development. Since discovery learning expects the learner to establish a personal structure, the process can be relatively unguided. It is characterized by varying degrees of trial-and-error; the method intentionally allows the learner to pursue blind alleys and find negative instances so that an incorrect response spurs the learner to discover the correct response (Glaser 1966, 13-26).

IMPLICATIONS FOR CHRISTIAN DISCIPLESHIP

Christian educators, when dealing with cognitive learning, must first balance their understandings of human limitations (due to sin and human finiteness) with their understandings of human capabilities (creation in the image of God, living within God's grace and influence). Cognitive theories assist in Christian belief and discernment. Data, whether from the Bible or from other sources of Christian thought and practice, can be analyzed, organized, stored, and used to inform and enrich Christian discipleship. Information processing provides a way to develop structures of thought known as convictions, beliefs, or doctrines. These represent God's expansive and complex revelation in concise forms, so that people can have a more coherent understanding of God. One caution is that these formulations cannot replace fully God's revelation, since they are created by human effort and are thus limited. Analytical skills are helpful here, in analyzing and comparing current beliefs and formative practices with the Bible, Christian history, and contemporary experience to make sure that those doctrines and practices are consistent with the purposes of the gospel.

▶ RELATIONAL LEARNING THEORY

The third, large learning-theory family is social or relational learning theory. A reaction to didactic approaches such as behaviorism and programmed instruction, relational learning theorists state that learning is an active, contextualized process of constructing knowledge (Piaget) rather than merely acquiring it. Relational learning theorists respect both the intellectual and emotional perspectives of the learner in relation to the teacher. Knowledge is constructed using personal experiences and the environment. Learners continually test these experiences through social negotiation. Each person has a different interpretation and construction of the knowledge process. The learner is not a blank slate (tabula rasa) but brings past experiences and cultural factors to a situation as well as a desire to learn. Relational learning includes theories often associated with humanistic learning perspectives.

Theorist and psychologist Carl Rogers, for instance, stressed facilitating a learning environment that affirmed the learner's efforts and encouraged self-discovery. For Rogers, learning was primarily an individualized process in search of personal meaning. This view, which emphasizes the student over the instructor, stresses attention to student abilities and efforts in an open yet collaborative environment. The approach provided a corrective to previous learning theories that tended to view the student as a passive object rather than active subject in learning. Relational learning theory understands that personal meaning emerges through relationships that value both teacher and learner in a mutual exchange, and it acknowledges the need to respect the learner as an active participant in the learning process. Relational learning theorists assume that all knowledge is constructed from the learner's previous knowledge, regardless of how one is taught.

The primary learning theories associated with social or relational learning theory include integrative developmental theories such as Erik Erikson's psychosocial stages of development (see chapter 9). Erikson emphasized that affective learning occurs in relationship to the broader culture. Social institutions (parents, school, church, etc.) often influence our ability to emotionally learn from and cope with internal stresses (crises). In addition, Lev Vygotsky's sociocultural development theory provides a contrasting approach to Jean Piaget's insular cognitive development theory, while Albert Bandura's social learning theory focuses on modeling and imitation as central to learning.

▶ SOCIOCULTURAL DEVELOPMENT THEORY: LEV VYGOTSKY

Lev Vygotsky (1896—1934), a Russian psychologist, developed a social development theory that proved foundational to *constructivism;* an approach that allows learners to set goals, solve problems, engage meaning, and engage metacognitive skills (thinking about thinking) as participants in the learning process (Santrock 2007, 345-47). For Vygotsky social interaction plays a fundamental role in the process of cognitive development. In contrast to Jean Piaget's understanding of child development (in which development necessarily precedes learning), Vygotsky felt that social learning precedes development. He argued that development takes place on the social and individual level, first between people and then within the child. His theory focused on the Zone of Proximal Development (ZPD), which describes the distance between a student's ability to perform a task under adult guidance and/or with peer collaboration and the student's ability to solve the problem independently. According to Vygotsky, learning occurs within this zone. He focused on the connections among people and the sociocultural context in which they act and interact in shared experiences. The role of the teacher is critical for development. According to Vygotsky, humans use tools that develop in a culture, such as speech and writing, to mediate their social environments. Children initially develop these tools to serve purely social functions, to communicate needs. Vygotsky believed that the internalization of these tools led to higher thinking skills.

One of the primary implications for faithful teaching is the replacement of traditional forms of teaching, which strictly focus on transmitting information, with active forms of learning. Vygotsky's theory promotes learning contexts in which students play an active role. Teacher and student roles shift, as teachers collaborate with students to facilitate meaning construction. Learning becomes a reciprocal experience for students and teachers.

Vygotsky's theory also asserts that social context is critical for development. Christian formation is not simply an internal process; it includes acquisition from the community of faith (Estep 2002, 160). The words, symbols, and language of individuals and the faith community have a formative impact on the life of the person (162).

SOCIAL LEARNING THEORY: ALBERT BANDURA

Social learning theory assumes that people learn in community as they observe, copy, and replicate the explicit behaviors of others as expressions of thought and emotion. Scholars believe that this theory, advocated by Albert Bandura, mediates between behavioral and cognitive learning, respecting both external influences (particularly people as role models) and internal thinking processes. Persons may perceive and choose to imitate behaviors based on personal preference, but their imitations are reinforced in personal interactions with the role model or in public interactions within the community. Teaching emphasizes a form of modeling, where the whole person or the collective actions of a community are seen as a source of learning.

The church applies social learning theory when it passes on the faith tradition through imitation and modeling. Christian nurture takes place as a child is informally socialized into the Christian culture and faith. The process of modeling is a powerful avenue of learning and development. Downs argues that Christians have two types of models. First, symbolic models are people we read about in books or see on television and in sports. Symbolic models do not represent actual relationships, but someone to whom others look as a model or hero. Second, an exemplary model is an actual living person with whom the student has a close relationship as a model or mentor (1994, 157). Christian educators, pastors, teachers, parents, peers, and colleagues can all serve as exemplary models. Through both symbolic and exemplary models, students imitate and reinforce behavior.

IMPLICATIONS FOR CHRISTIAN DISCIPLESHIP

Christian formation, as a broad category of Christian discipleship, recognizes that many behaviors may be taught or modified through personal or group relationships. Social learning, combined with theories of behavioral and cognitive learning (see above), shapes or patterns Christian behavior. Significant role models and larger communities have deep influence on personal responses to religious experience and assumptions about spirituality and worship. Christian educators must take seriously and utilize every activity within the church for the process of discipleship. Christian educators must also be aware of the dangers of formation approaches that are inconsistent or even contradictory to the gospel. The shaping process of authentic formation can help learners respond to new situations in ways that are consistent with the Christian message.

▶ A HOLISTIC APPROACH TO CHRISTIAN TEACHING/ LEARNING

The three primary learning theories—behavioral, cognitive, and social—provide a holistic approach to learning. Each theory is limited on its own, but together they provide a complete view of learning. Effective teaching will recognize and apply the value in each of the three families of theories to the teaching/learning context.

Christian educators (Yount 1996; Downs 1994) have viewed these three learning theories as a triad of human experience (Yount 1996, 250). These three domains of learning theory provide a holistic approach to learning that values doing, knowing, and being. The first aspect of the triad is behavioral, the doing side of learning. Cognitive learning is second, focused on thinking and the development of knowledge (knowing). And third is social learning, focused on feelings, values, and relationships (being). Effective Christian teaching includes each of these domains of learning (figure 10.1).

Christian educators can be tempted to gravitate toward the learning theory they find most comfortable; however, learning becomes unbalanced when Christian discipleship places too much emphasis on one domain over the others. Effective learning includes all three domains in teaching.

▶ ALTERNATIVE LEARNING THEORIES

Beyond the larger learning families, developments in learning theory and the varying needs of educators prompt consideration of alternative approaches. Some educators have advocated for alternative ways of knowing that resist conventional structure, such as intuitive, aesthetic, or even spiritual modes of knowing (Eisner 1985). The basic learning theories and these alternatives must

Figure 10.1: Holistic Approach to Learning

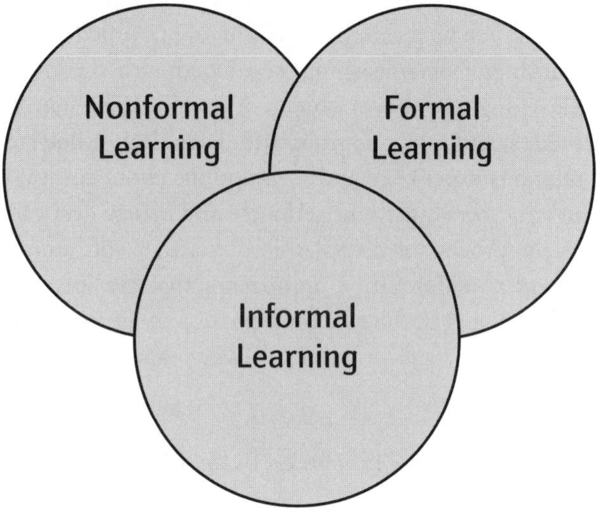

Formal education (knowing) includes teaching and learning carried out through formalized teaching, particularly in schools, which are linked to academic accomplishments. The primary focus of formal education is the developing of knowledge and theories. The development of formal thinking is necessary for higher forms of learning.

Informal education (being) is the natural socialization process that takes place through human interaction in families, schools, churches, and societies. Learning takes place primarily through interaction with the social context.

Nonformal education (doing) includes deliberate teaching and learning, not casual or merely circumstantial, not linked too tightly to the formal social ladder of schooling. Nonformal learning generally includes greater flexibility and freedom using experiential learning methods.

dialogue with and be tested against issues as specific as particular learning styles, as broad as influences shaped by gender and culture, and as rigorous as new insights in neuroscience.

▶ LEARNING STYLES AND CULTURAL EMPHASES

Learning theorists produce a large body of literature on individual learning preferences or styles. Learning styles may be based upon our preferences for receiving data (visually, aurally, kinesthetically, or even intuitively) or on how much data we prefer to receive (large blocks or smaller units).

David Kolb (see chapter 5) also provides several approaches to learning styles. Kolb theorized that people did not negotiate his cycle of learning (CE/RO/AC/AE) equally. The four quadrants that exist within the intersections of Kolb's prehension and transformation of knowledge reveal a vast array of learning preferences and approaches to life. Kolb's original descriptions noted that people tend to privilege a particular quadrant, which results in different learning styles and even worldviews that dictate specific interests (professions) and perspectives in understanding how reality works (see appendix 10.1).

Diverging (CE/RO): Focus on openness to different or divergent experiences

Assimilating (AC/RO): Focus on taking diverse material and incorporating into thought

Converging (AC/AE): Tendency to engage in specific knowledge around a subject

Accommodating (CE/AE): Tendency to seek applicability of ideas through adaptation

Bernice McCarthy (1980) adapted Kolb's experiential learning model and the work of Carl Jung into four learning styles: imaginative learner (Why learn this?), analytic learner (What is this?), the common sense learner (How does it work?), and the dynamic learner (What can this become?). Marlene LeFever popularized McCarthy's model for Christian audiences, incorporating McCarthy's terminology (1995, 15-16, 19-21) and formalizing Kolb's approach to experiential learning as a curricular plan (25-28). LeFever acknowledges that faithful teaching requires a variety of teaching methods in order for people to learn best. She argues that we tend to teach from our own learning style and miss connecting with people with different learning styles.

Learning theorists also explore how certain approaches to learning may be emphasized by certain cultures, often in issues of gender and power. These cultures influence what people value as authentic knowledge (the sociology of knowledge) and as appropriate ways of knowing or learning. For example, women's psychology, through theorists such as Mary Belenky et al. (1986), notes that women generally value relational learning that helps to connect people with the subject they are studying, whereas other learning theories favor a more detached, scientific stance.

Theorists have noted that some cultures see knowledge as a gradual yet steady accumulation of data while others value learning through conflict resolution (Pazmiño 2008, 198-200) or through sudden leaps of insight and imagination (Loder 1981). In addition, theorists give particular attention to issues of power. Paulo Freire, a Brazilian educator, developed a critical pedagogy focusing on liberating learners through a dialogic, problem-posing style that challenges students to become aware of their thoughts and recognize their power to change the world (1973). Freire combines individual and social transformation in a method he terms *conscientization,* achieved through a combination of action and reflection, a practical (*praxis*) approach. Education seeks to raise the critical conscience of the learner through experiential encounters with the realities of the culture. Freire is concerned that all learners have equal access to learning (1970, 53). He opposed the formal education model of his day, a "banking education" that deposited information from the teacher to the learner, which resulted in the student being simply "filed away" through a lack of creativity, transformation, and knowledge (58). Freire's approach to learning provides a counter to the oppressive nature of formal education in some cultural settings. He places strong value on human persons and their ability to grow and learn, as the subjects, rather than objects, of education.

▶ NEUROSCIENCE AND LEARNING THEORY

As noted in chapter 9, new insights in biology, cognitive processes, and brain studies are reshaping much of our understanding of how we grow, learn, and come to faith. For instance, grassroots approaches to dealing with trauma often struggle with how much the victim should discuss or process a dramatic event. However, recent studies in brain chemistry note that it may be best to delay direct engagement of traumatic events, since talking about these powerful moments can reinforce the trauma. Counselors should instead encourage patients to take beta-blockers to diminish the impact of negative environments (Johnson 2004, 200-203). However, these strategies of restorative intervention can also be used to move beyond therapy to enhance learning in questionable ways, either through parental manipulation of children (Kass 2003, 27-94) or through the use of attention-deficit drugs to optimize normal learning (Dana Foundation 2009; Pentilla 2009).

Beyond these ethical issues, neuroscience informs a host of key educational concerns, particularly basic studies in language acquisition, reading, mathematics, sleep, emotion, and processing experience (Goswami 2004, 6-10). New insights have helped educators understand the nature of human ability to catalog and adapt to experience at the synaptic level (LeDoux 2002, 134-73). Brain learning incorporates the use of neural circuitry, indicating that various portions of the brain work in tandem to address specific challenges (61-64). Contrary to the popular notion that the brain's emotional seat rests in the limbic system, LeDoux's research suggests that emotion incorporates more complicated neural circuitry and involves more than just this region (210-12).

Educators argue that due caution must be given in relating brain research to educational theory and practice (Hall 2005; O'Boyle and Gill 1998). In particular, early adopters of brain-based learning can apply incomplete, if not inaccurate, knowledge concerning neuroscience and learning. Many of these neuro-myths remain, such as the persistent misuse of left brain/right brain learning styles; brain imaging studies have revealed that learning is "far too complex to be controlled by a single hemisphere" (Willis 2008, 425). Multidisciplinary teams of researchers within education and neuroscience have begun new studies, some funded by the United States National Science Foundation (Gura 2005), which seek to determine the relationships between brain and learning. Research needs to continue to fully understand the relationship of not only neuroscience to learning but also the matrix of successful teaching methods (Goswami 2004, 2), which will be discussed in chapter 11.

Theologians, philosophers, counselors, and neuroscientists engage in conversations regarding neuroscience and the role of religion and religious experience (including the Wesleyan tradition; see Strawn and Brown 2004). These theorists posit new ways of understanding the self that retains an integral relationship between body and soul (Green and Palmer 2005; Murphy and Brown 2007). Paul Markham recently incorporated studies of Wesleyan theology and neuroscience in his exploration of the nature of conversion or religious transformation (2007). Following the work of Methodist theologian Randy Maddox (1998), Markham develops a Wesleyan theological anthropology in which God's grace transforms persons as their affections are shaped into moral tempers such as love and holiness (2007, 37-72, 130). First, Markham stresses the continual nature of this change as an ongoing process of conversion or sanctification (one and the same for Markham) that still allows for significant moral transformation (68-72). Second, Markham develops a neurobiological approach that resists viewing humanity as dualistic (body/mind, body/soul, or material/immaterial), yet also retains a view of the mind as an emerging entity that cannot be reduced to particular biological functions. Markham's third emphasis rests on the need for Christian praxis in congregations (not just cognitive understanding of salvation) that both shapes and encourages practices that serve as means of grace (152). Markham concludes that authentic transformation occurs through gradual participation within the means of grace. Such a view may help Wesleyans understand the importance of formation not only within a Wesleyan theological perspective but also from a growing understanding of neuroscience. Additional work will need to be done to account for other, more dramatic, transformations that require careful discernment (Blevins 2009); however, Markham provides at least one approach that takes seriously neuroscience, learning, and faithful discipleship. Undoubtedly other approaches will follow.

▸ CONCLUSION

Christian educators can appreciate the variety of learning theories, but individual approaches have limitations that urge caution in evaluation and use. Certain assumptions behind each theory, when not subjected to Christian discernment, may actually prove detrimental to the gospel. Christian educators must maintain a balanced view of the learner and a complex understanding of God's revelation. Often the role of the Holy Spirit is least understood in the process of learning. In some settings, problems arise from the view that the Holy Spirit is completely independent of the learning process; attention to the variety of learning styles and a positive learning environment are seen as irrelevant. At the other end of the spectrum, the Holy Spirit might be considered only after employing all other learning strategies (like bringing in a relief pitcher at the end of a baseball game) so that the Spirit's role is not incorporated into the entire learning process. A better way is to see the Holy Spirit participating and working through the various approaches and styles. Learning then becomes a means of grace by which the Holy Spirit may truly communicate grace through existing human structures and practices.

The diversity of learning theories reveals the complexity of God's creation (including human beings) and the variety of ways to approach God's truth. Careful attention to these theories will help Christian educators broaden their teaching methods to reach more people for the kingdom of God and deepen the faith of existing believers.

▶ REFERENCES

Belenky, Mary F., et al. 1986. *Women's Ways of Knowing: The Development of Self, Voice, and Mind.* San Francisco: HarperCollins.

Blevins, Dean G. 2009. Neuroscience, John Wesley and the Christian life. In *Wesleyan Theological Journal* 44, no 1 (spring): 219-47.

Dana Foundation. 2009. The neuroethics of enhancement: How smart are smart drugs? *The Dana Foundation* (February), http://www.dana.org/events/detail.aspx?id=7854 (accessed April 2, 2009).

Downs, Perry. 1994. *Educating for Spiritual Growth.* Grand Rapids: Zondervan.

Eisner, E., ed. 1985. *Learning and Teaching the Ways of Knowing.* Chicago: Univ. of Chicago Press.

Estep, James R. 2002. Spiritual formation as social: Toward a Vygotskyan developmental perspective. In *Religious Education* 97:2, 141-64.

Freire, Paulo. 1970. *Pedagogy of the Oppressed.* New York: Seabury.

_____. 1973. *Education for Critical Consciousness.* New York: Continuum.

Gallagher, J. M., and D. K. Reid. 1981. *The Learning Theory of Piaget and Inhelder.* Monterey, CA: Brooks/Cole.

Gardner, Howard. 1983. *Frames of Mind, the Theory of Multiple Intelligences.* San Francisco: Basic Books.

_____. 1993. *Multiple Intelligences: The Theory in Practice.* San Francisco: HarperCollins.

Glaser, Robert. 1966. Variables in discovery learning. In *Learning by Discovery: A Critical Appraisal,* 13-26. Ed. Lee S. Shulman and Evan R. Keisler. Chicago, IL: Rand McNally.

Goswami, Usha. 2004. Neuroscience and education. *British Journal of Educational Psychology* 74:1-14.

Green, Joel E., and Stuart L. Palmer. 2005. *In Search of the Soul: Four Views of the Mind-Body Problem.* Downers Grove, IL: InterVarsity Press.

Gura, Trisha. 2005. Big plans for little brains. In *Nature* 435, no. 7046 (June 30): 1156-58.

Hall, John. 2005. Neuroscience and education. In *Education Journal* 87 (March), 27-29.

Johnson, Steven. 2004. *Mind Wide Open: Your Brain and the Neuroscience of Everyday Life.* New York: Scribners.

Kass, Leon. 2003. *Beyond Therapy: Biotechnology and the Pursuit of Happiness,* The President's Council on Bioethics. New York: Regan Books/HarperCollins Publishers.

Kolb, David. 1984. *Experiential Learning: Experience as the Source of Learning and Development.* Englewood Cliffs, NJ: Prentice Hall.

LeDoux, Joseph. 2002. *Synaptic Self: How Our Brains Become Who We Are.* New York: Penguin Books.

LeFever, Marlene. 1995. *Learning Styles: Reaching Everyone God Gave You to Teach.* Colorado Springs: David C. Cook.

Loder, James E. 1981. *The Transforming Moment.* San Francisco: Harper and Row.

Maddox, Randy. 1998. Reconnecting the means to the end: A Wesleyan prescription for the holiness movement. In *Wesleyan Theological Journal* 33, no. 2 (fall), 29-66.

Markham, Paul N. 2007. *Rewired: Exploring Religious Conversion.* Eugene, OR: Pickwick Publications.

McCarthy, Bernice. 1980. *The 4Mat System.* Arlington Heights, IL: Excel.

Murphy, Nancey, and Warren S. Brown. 2007. *Did My Neurons Make Me Do It? Philosophical and Neurobiological Perspectives on Moral Responsibility and Free Will.* Oxford: Oxford Press.

O'Boyle, Michael W., and Harwant S. Gill. 1998. On the relevance of research findings in cognitive neuroscience to educational practice. *Educational Psychology Review,* vol. 10, no. 4: 397-409.

Pazmiño, Robert W. 2008. *Foundational Issues in Christian Education.* 3rd ed. Grand Rapids: Baker Books.

Pentilla, Nicky. 2009. How smart are we about smart drugs? Using "brain" pills to improve on normal leads to new questions of ethics. *The Dana Foundation* (February). http://www.dana.org/events/detail.aspx?id=7854 (accessed online April 2, 2009).

Santrock, John W. 2007. *A Topical Approach to Life-Span Development.* 3rd ed. Boston: McGraw Hill.

Strawn, Brad, and Warren Brown. 2004. Wesleyan holiness through the eyes of cognitive science and psychotherapy. In *Journal of Psychology and Christianity* 23, no. 2: 121-29.

Vygotsky, Lev S. 1978. *Mind and Society: The Development of Higher Mental Processes.* Cambridge, MA: Harvard Univ. Press.

Wills, Judy. 2008. Building a bridge from neuroscience to classroom. *Phi Delta Kappan* (February), 424-27.

Yount, William R. 1996. *Created to Learn.* Nashville: B&H Academic.

Appendix 10.1
Knowledge and Learning Approaches
Based on Kolb's Model
(Bernice McCarthy Categories included)
Synthetic/Qualitative (Humanistic)

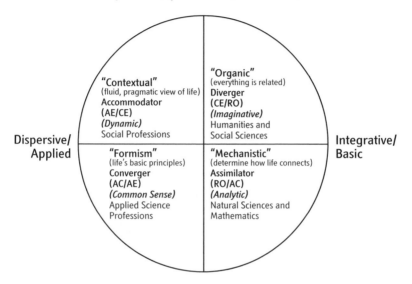

Analytic/Quantitative (Scientific)

Kolb's Styles	Diverger	Assimilator	Converger	Accommodator
Worldviews and Orientation	Organic	Mechanistic	Formism	Contextual
Inquiry Questions	Why?	What?	When and Where?	How?
Inquiry Strategy	Integrative Synthesis	Integrative Analysis	Discrete Analysis	Discrete Synthesis
Units of Knowledge	Processes	Underlying Structures	Natural Laws	Events
Method of Portraying Knowledge	Images	Symbols	Things	Actions
Theory of Truth	Coherence: how things hold together	Finding the primary cause(s)	How things correspond	Verifying the validity of "what works"
McCarthy's Version	Imaginative	Analytic	Common Sense	Dynamic (Application)

ELEVEN

TEACHING THAT MAKES A DIFFERENCE: CURRICULUM DESIGN AND DELIVERY

▶ INTRODUCTION

Imagine you have accepted leadership in a church that currently uses seven different Sunday school curriculums, including different resources for children, youth, and adult classes. How would you ensure that the quality of the resources being taught was consistent with your Wesleyan roots? What criteria would you use to help Sunday school teachers select quality resources for their classes?

Imagine you get a call from the pastor who is planning a six-week series on Old Testament motifs about holiness. The pastor wants the entire church to study the same passages, beginning with the role of the "Ruach" (Spirit) of God leading the children of Israel. He wants to know how long it will take to create support lessons for the first through third grade Sunday school classes. What would you recommend?

One of the primary challenges of faithful discipleship is the organization of the teaching ministry of the church. Each week we must decide not only what to teach but also how to structure the content (curriculum) and teaching, based on student readiness and ability (instructional strategies). Do we teach the Bible (content) or do we teach people? The answer, obviously, is "both." Our goal, however, is to understand how to arrange our teaching efforts so that people have a reasonable chance to learn.

▶ CURRICULUM DESIGN

Theories on the design of curriculum encompass a large array of issues. The term *curriculum* (derived from the Latin *curere,* which means to run) emerged from the idea of running on a racetrack. One must satisfactorily complete the course in order to complete the mission. Curriculum theory describes the arrangement or ordering of specific tasks used to teach people. First, curriculum includes explicit tasks that tell students exactly what teachers expect them to accomplish. Second, curriculum includes implicit or tacit strategies or goals that educate as well. For instance, the arrangement of a room so that all the students face the teacher rather than one another, may implicitly teach that only the teacher knows anything of value. A curriculum, however, that not only includes class discussion but also arranges the room so that students can see and talk together, tacitly teaches that students have knowledge. Curriculum that explicitly includes discussion questions, but then implicitly arranges students in rows facing the teacher, sends conflicting messages. The third primary curricular consideration is the material left out of a teaching plan, or null curriculum. Null curricular theory states that teachers often teach based on what they exclude, intentionally or not, from a course of study. For instance, if sermons regularly come from the New Testament, people may soon assume that the Old Testament is irrelevant to their lives. No pastor teaches this explicitly, but the absence of the material implicitly communicates a lack of concern. The classic example of this approach rests in illustrations. Early Sunday school materials incorporated pictures of dominant ethnic groups while excluding drawings or photographs of people of other cultures or ethnicities. Over time, many curriculum producers recognized this problem and diversified their resources. Nevertheless, the absence of particular ethnic faces influenced a generation in determining who should and should not receive the gospel. Learning to balance explicit curricular strategies with implicit (and sometimes unintended) curricular results, as well as recognizing what might be conveyed through null curriculum, remains one of the primary challenges of faithful discipleship.

MICRO OR MACRO CURRICULUM DESIGN

Historically people have associated the term *curriculum* with print resources used to assist in teaching. In reality this view of lesson plans or handouts represents only the micro version of curriculum theory, and the smallest unit of curriculum. Educators often struggle with the macro view, which includes the entire learning environment that teaches particular content or shapes personal perspectives. Parents visiting a college campus might ask how students learn relational skills or leadership methods. They might look for a particular course designed to accomplish these tasks but overlook the fact that student government and other student organizations exist to provide leadership training and that living in campus dormitories offers the opportunity to develop relational skills. In other words, the total life of the college campus works at a macro-curricular level to teach certain skills and abilities, whether or not the school has a specific class on the subject. Churches, too, teach through their overall life at a macro-curricular level. The way people conduct themselves at informal gatherings, how leadership models decision making, and what values surface regularly in classrooms and during community meals all contribute to the macro level view of the church. Understanding this level of often tacit or implicit teaching strategies has led some congregational specialists to note family resemblances among certain churches (Dudley 1988). Some churches, regardless of denominational ties, appear more family oriented, while others may be more institutionally minded when working relationally across the church. Some churches stress evangelism, while others stress compassionate ministry as a way to engage the world. Certain congregations prefer in-depth biblical preaching and teaching, while others stress experiential, lively worship as a means for encountering God. The range of explicit, implicit, and even null practices create an environment that shapes peoples' expectations of church life and daily discipleship.

Whether dealing with macro environments or micro units of resources and lesson plans, every curriculum designer follows the race course by establishing certain content boundaries and sequences for learning. Curricular theorists discuss this as the scope and sequence of curriculum. The *scope* describes the total learning content or total learning environment. Whether the scope of the study incorporates the Gospel of John for a small-group Bible study or the academic and social life of the college for an entering freshman, both content and environment define the boundaries of learning. *Sequence* describes how the curriculum negotiates or delivers the content to ensure a logical and consistent approach. With the Gospel of John, curriculum writers may sequence the material based on chapter headings or special theme studies, such as the "I am" statements of Jesus. Educators at a university order classes according to academic difficulty or encourage participation in certain internships or student activities based on academic year. Determining the scope and sequence of a particular study provides valuable insight into what a student might accomplish.

APPLIED CURRICULUM

Curricular designers also investigate the applicability of learning activities and their ability to ensure that learning occurs. Applied curriculum theory argues that attention must be given to the connection between teaching goals and activities, as well as the learning outcomes that emerge from students as they engage learning strategies. Every educational plan begins with some goal in mind or envisions particular outcomes for the sake of the students. These are usually expressed in terms of what students should know (head/cognitive), do (hands/behavioral or psychomotor), or value (heart/affective or volitional). Each of these large domains (head, hands, and heart) often includes specific levels of intensity (Bloom 1956; Yount 1996, 140-53).

Levels of Outcomes

Head/Cognitive
- Knowledge: memory, being able to recall information
- Comprehension: understanding the original meaning of the information
- Translation: being able to restate original meaning in another context
- Interpretation: unpacking the original meaning in regard to other knowledge
- Application: showing how the information shapes continued learning
- Analysis: critical assessment, breaking down the information into parts and comparing to other information
- Synthesis: demonstrating appropriate integration with other information
- Evaluation: judging the quality of the information in light of the other processes

Hands/Psychomotor or Behavioral
- Perception: seeing what is happening in order to replicate an action appropriately
- Set: performing a particular, fundamental action (with knowledge, confidence, and poise) so as to repeat it (for example, shooting a basketball or passing a soccer ball)
- Guidance: following a model or allowing a coach to direct actions
- Mechanism and complex response: Repeating an action with regularity and success
- Adaptation: changing actions in the face of new contexts and challenges
- Origination: creating a new move/skill based on what one has learned

Heart/Affective or Volition
- Receiving: demonstrating a willingness to listen
- Responding: indicating some personal response to the presented information or challenge
- Valuing: accepting and appreciating information given
- Organizing: making a commitment to the information given that changes how one thinks, acts, or judges
- Characterizing: allowing the information to change one's lifestyle in a regular manner

The nature of the students and the context determine the level of intensity of any expected outcome. For instance, students must be able recall a key concept before they can analyze its meaning. Similarly, students must be able to practice the fundamentals of a particular action (shooting a basketball or playing chopsticks on the piano) before they are able to adapt or improvise on those actions. And finally, students must be willing to at least receive and respond (e.g., to a gospel appeal) before they can commit and change their lives. Each of these processes indicates different depths of outcomes that any curriculum may attempt to engage. Too often, teachers push for a depth of intensity without asking what might be reasonable to expect first. Christian educators may need to accept that they have to earn the right to be heard several times (receiving and responding to the presented content) before they can expect people to make deep commitments to reorganizing their lives and changing their lifestyles. Appropriating the right goals and outcomes provides a stronger curricular design.

Activities without intention may serve as entertainment, but they are not education. Not all goals or intentional outcomes can be anticipated, however. Following the work of Elliot Eisner, curriculum not only employs specific objectives but also incorporates expressive outcomes designed to encourage student creativity (2002, 118-22). Eisner argues that curriculum should serve as a dynamic resource, allowing students to surface positive and creative outcomes that designers did not originally foresee. However, all theorists agree that every good curriculum begins with stated goals for the student or with a vision of the outcomes a student will receive or accomplish.

CURRICULAR DESIGN QUESTIONS

As we have seen, curriculum design, for small-group Bible resources or a large arrangement of ministries within the church, must deal with a number of key considerations. When organizing the material, one must address a series of curricular assumptions based on the six questions journalists use in news gathering: who, what, when, where, why, and how.

- Who: who are the learners, and what are their abilities?
- What: what is the content, and how does that influence the structure of the lessons?
- When: when will the material be taught and for how long?
- Where: where is the learning environment, and how conducive will the context be for learning?
- Why: why teach the material, and what is the goal of the lesson plan and anticipated outcomes from the learning?
- How: how should we structure the lessons so that there is flow among the various learning activities?

Obviously, these questions may be answered in different sequences. We often need to ask who, what, and why before we consider when, where, and how. For instance, sound learning theory reveals that people need to connect content with personal experience for meaningful learning to occur. In dealing with the "who" questions, different people bring different levels of experience to the learning task. Educators generally understand that children's curriculum must include experiences that reinforce the teaching outcomes. Children may not have a rich diversity of experience to draw from, but they love experiential events (one reason that sensory learning is so important for children). Similarly, educators know that youth like lessons that relate concepts and experiences with their rapidly growing cognitive and experiential encounters, while adults prefer lessons that reflect upon the experiences they have amassed over the years. Simply understanding the relationship between the learners and their levels of experience can shape the rest of the curricular design.

▶ CURRICULUM DELIVERY

While curriculum designers select the scope and sequence, as well as employ educational goals or intended outcomes, theorists also consider the overall approach or style of the curricular design. Who drives the lesson? What is the role of the student? How does learning occur? Our assumptions about the teaching/learning process are revealed in how the lesson guides the learning.

Theorists have identified at least three metaphors for curriculum design and delivery. The first design follows the production metaphor for education. Drawn from the industrial world of production lines that provide goods of consistent quality, this approach envisions *the teacher* as a social engineer producing students through set curriculum. Students move through the learning process in a logical, uniform manner that ensures that each component of learning prepares students for the next task with a predetermined outcome. Championed by theorists such as Ralph Tyler (1949), the approach often feels mechanistic, yet it underlies a number of strategies that use sequential learning to elicit specific behaviors.

The second approach is the growth metaphor, drawing from a greenhouse approach. The *student* dictates learning through life experiences (the teacher provides resources). While there may be a fixed scope to this type of learning (even a greenhouse has boundaries to protect plant life), the sequence of learning rests with the curiosity and drive of the student. Educators like A. S. Neill (1960/1995) associated this type of curricular design with open educational settings like Summerhill, where students often selected their own learning activities each day; but the approach often includes hot-topic approaches to study or student-driven learning models.

A final approach attempts to employ the best of the previous approaches through a travel metaphor that stresses *mutual interaction* between the teacher (as guide) and student (as traveler), with both supplying mutual support in negotiating the curriculum. Like fellow travelers on a pilgrimage, both teacher and learner engage and explore a given subject, allowing the contours of the topic to guide the journey as student and teacher both discover new insights and make meaning together as they process information into new learning. Theorists draw from the work of educators John Dewey (1938), Jerome Bruner (1963), and others who encourage a sense of mutual discovery often shaped by the implicit design found *within* the subject itself.

As noted, journalist questions often help in determining the intended outcomes and structure of curriculum design. These same questions can shape the teaching strategies employed in curriculum delivery. Every curriculum must address the "how" question in selecting learning activities that will engage the learner and interact with the content, objectives, and environment. A lesson may employ a number of learning activities: problem solving for small-group investigation, frenetic activities to encourage interpersonal support, or quiet reflection to promote discovery of personal meaning. While lessons may use a vast array of activities, they often employ teaching strategies from a larger family of teaching methods that reveal a specific teaching style, or methodology. Sara Little engages the work of several educational theorists in identifying five of these learning families (1983, 40-85):

- Information Processing
- Group Interaction
- Indirect Communication
- Personal Development
- Action/Reflection

Each of these approaches (or families of learning strategies) influences the method of curricular instruction, so curriculum design must also include delivery.

INFORMATION PROCESSING

Sara Little describes information processing as "faith asking the intellect for help" (1983). Information processing often incorporates intellectual activities: *acquiring* names and facts, *storing and organizing* the information, *restating* the information as concepts (summaries, synthesis of information, integration), and *relating* the information to other concepts and experiences (larger integration and evaluation). The scientific method serves as a prime example of this process as experience is gathered, organized, and stored as data for comparison and adaptation. Information processing places an emphasis on the student's cognitive ability to structure and retrieve important information. Several instructional strategies illustrate this approach:

1. As noted, the *scientific method* incorporates several logical steps: the presentation of a problem or puzzle leads to observation of phenomena; using reason, a hypothesis is developed, which calls for testing via experimentations, which then leads to new data (that either confounds or validates) and often results in a final answer to the problem—or a new puzzle that starts the process again.

2. Educators might use an *advance organizer* to guide information processing. This intellectual scaffold helps with sorting data through the use of an initial outline, a study guide, and an opening summary statement or merely the use of alliteration (e.g., the peril, pursuit, and promise of salvation).

3. Educators often rely on the *inductive strategy* to sort out major themes through disciplined observation and analysis. This approach follows three basic steps:

   a. Concept Formation: listing separate themes, grouping into categories, and labeling

   b. Interpretation: inferring and generalizing from the categorized data

   c. Application: making a general statement (hypothesis) that is explored and verified from earlier information

4. Certain schools and classes place an emphasis on *programmed instruction,* a popular, often self-guided approach to learning. At each step of the learning process students encounter an opportunity to test their knowledge of a subject before moving forward. This instructional strategy places emphasis on immediate feedback. The curriculum emphasizes repetition and the use of a term or concept in a variety of settings to insure understanding. Students must pass one level to progress to the next, and often the class includes a "pretest" to determine previous knowledge that may be used for comparison at the end of the course.

The information processing family is important for shaping experience into something students can utilize, and it often serves as a means for differentiating between personal reactions, which express values or feelings without knowledge, and informed comments, in which values or feelings include informed, reflective opinions.

GROUP INTERACTION

Take a moment to list all of the different groups in a given church and ask: Do all of them teach? Perhaps learning goes on, but do groups actually manifest a particular, intentional, educational strategy? If you can say yes, then you are on the way to identifying the second major instructional strategy.

The basic assumption in this family revolves around the conviction that learning occurs best as groups participate together rather than in individualistic endeavors. This approach incorporates more than interpersonal practices or group-building skills and challenges the traditional schooling model. Group interaction draws upon a combination of cognitive and affective learning processes with the goals of exploring, testing, and sharpening our beliefs in the company of people we trust. There is always the danger of this group process becoming mere therapy (sharing emotions but not ideas) or shared ignorance (a battle of anecdotal experiences); however, with proper guidance, this approach proves to be particularly powerful.

The size of the group may vary (the optimum range is four to twelve people), but group process is always highly interactive. Such groups share similar presuppositions: the smaller unit mirrors the larger community (consistency within the church), knowledge is constructed (built) through interpersonal interaction rather than appropriated from beyond the group out there, motivation rests less with individual desire than with group need. Outcomes may be hard to predict or control, but the interaction will affect both cognitive and affective areas when the teacher serves as a skilled resource and guide. Several approaches illustrate this strategy.

1. The most general approach occurs anytime a group takes on a particular educational task using group investigation to accomplish a project. Regardless of the challenge, when the group engages in planning, delegation, and leadership, they model group learning as well.

2. A second approach surfaces when groups decide to learn through simulation or case studies. Rather than attacking an existing problem, the group constructs a scenario or uses a previous or imaginary event in this learning strategy. Usually this approach incorporates several discrete steps:

   a. *Orientation and preparation:* linking the scenario to the larger unit of study; laying out rules for presentation and interpretation as well as the various roles assumed; carry out study or research

   b. *Introduction and enactment* of the simulation or case study

   c. *Debriefing:* often focused toward both presenter and participants, questions may include affective as well as problem-solving issues; it may be as appropriate to ask "what did you feel?" as "what did we learn?"

3. Group process can also occur around a particular study, including in-depth Bible study. Individual preparation is helpful (each member agrees to read the selected passage three to four times in advance, and the passage is marked by individuals with insights and ques-

tions). The truly constructive learning process occurs, however, as the group meets to discuss insights and investigate questions. In addition, leaders often provide supplemental resources to be used during actual group study. If resources are not available on site, members may engage in advance research. A summary of individual studies are given and explored at the beginning of meeting; the group then works toward general consensus about the passage and moves to potential application of the passage.

As you can see, a number of approaches to small groups may be employed. Roberta Hestenes noted that small groups may be utilized for in-depth study, for guiding personal sharing and development, for ministry to others, or for accountable discipleship (1983, 25-26). While different groups may have different goals, the quality of interaction guides the process so that intentional learning can happen in each of these settings.

INDIRECT COMMUNICATION

Educational strategies within the family often rely on "aha!" moments of encounter in which we are confronted or captivated by belief, similar to the discovery process discussed in chapter 9. Christian educators attempt to cultivate knowledge that penetrates to the very depths of our being and results in new self-awareness. The indirect method intentionally fosters moments of gestalt when various parts come together as a whole picture with a rich sense of oneness and harmony. Teachers will employ parabolic teaching (teaching in parables) or create environments that encourage serendipity (happy accidents). Teaching strategies often focus on aesthetic exercises of discovery, like figures emerging from a block of granite through the sculptor's efforts. Christian educators recognize that they possess no assurance that indirect methods will lead to encounter. Uncertainty and risk are a part of this teaching process, yet educators are willing to engage in a method that emphasizes intuition, imagination, and feeling because the learning that occurs through this method carries personal meaning for the student. This approach may use several strategies:

1. Clay sculpting (sometimes have students sculpt blindfolded)
2. Writing/drawing with our alternate hand
3. Storytelling with parabolic or surprising qualities: for instance, starting an open-ended story that students finish
4. Using artistic representations (song or painting) that portray traditional ideas in uncharacteristic ways
5. Using surprising stories and accounts (e.g., Søren Kierkegaard's writings)

When engaging in these strategies, teachers sometimes wonder, "Are we teaching?" The response, of course, should be yes. Although they cannot predict outcomes using the indirect process, educators are intentional in creating the opportunity for unexpected moments of discovery. In fact, attempting to control the outcome would reflect manipulation more than teaching. The key to this educational family rests in creating space for moments of awakening and encounter. Often associated with multiple intelligences, the approach stresses the many alternative ways of knowing (Bruner 1970; Eisner 1985) that may result in heightened awareness of self and world.

PERSONAL DEVELOPMENT

The personal development family of instructional strategies engage people who are being and becoming aware of their personal existence and vocational call. The implicit goals of these efforts rest in the personal self-awareness and self-realization that God intends for the individual. Teaching focuses on nurture and growth, as educators view life in a continuum rather than as discrete events along the life course. Christian educators often describe life as a journey or pilgrimage, and personal development emphasizes student participation (with the teacher a colearner, guide, or facilitator). Strategies include:

1. Expressive assignments (art, song, creative writing, media, etc.) that stress personal activities.
2. Awareness training exercises (blindfold "trust walk," journaling, self-portraits, silent retreats) that focus both on interpersonal and intrapersonal relationships.
3. Students often employ forms of self-directed learning contracts, mentoring, or spiritual direction in one-to-one encounters with Christian educators who may not have prescribed learning tasks but respond to personal concerns.
4. Educators may employ metaphorical thinking (analogies) to unlock human creativity. A simple opening exercise in a class might include the following phrase: "The gospel is like _____ because it is _____."

This family of methods may employ artistic events for developing self-awareness as well as a sense accomplishment and esteem, but rarely do educators anticipate unexpected encounters. While these strategies include intentional attempts to connect feeling and thinking creatively, they also risk the danger of superficial thinking (and feeling) when disconnected from specific content or discipline.

ACTION/REFLECTION

The final learning family, action/reflection, begins with the assumption that discipleship entails doing the truth (i.e., learning by doing). Christian educators assume that awareness follows experience (we tend to lend meaning to behavior). However, personal awareness alone proves insufficient. The personal meaning behind what one believes must relate to what one does, or our convictions become empty ideology without commitment ("faith without works is dead" [James 2:20, KJV]). The operative term in this learning family is the concept of praxis, or reflection in action. Educators employ teaching metaphors where reflective practice arises naturally, such as worship, stewardship, and daily discipleship. Educational opportunities surface in active settings: mission education, compassionate ministry, discipleship groups, Christian action groups, accountability teams, church ministry groups, and field education/internships. The key ingredients always include a regular process of active participation and reflection. Perhaps the best-known methodology within this family rests with the work of David Kolb (1984). Kolb emphasizes a cycle of experiential learning that (1) begins in daily activity/experience, (2) moves to reflection, (3) incorporates building concepts (based on the reflection but also in conversation with abstract concepts of the past, what Dewey calls the "funded experience of the past" (Dewey 1963, 42), and (4) concludes with practical application of knowledge to create new experiences so that people can begin the learning cycle again.

Intentional action/reflection strategies offer value wherever people are engaged and challenged to reflect on the meaning of that engagement:

1. Debriefing certain special events
2. Small-group ministry times of reflection
3. Special classes that immerse students in a new environment (urban plunge)
4. Board meetings in which church leadership reflects on policies and ministry
5. Personal strategies that encourage people to reflect on vocation
6. Opportunities to engage in and reflect on Christian witness/outreach

One prominent educational strategy, the AAAR method, employs a four-stage process to ensure both preparation and reflection during times of ministry engagement.

1. *Awareness.* Students select a specific challenge and ask, "What does the gospel say about this problem or challenge?"
2. *Analysis.* Students engage in a careful and thorough assessment of all the factors influencing this issue.
3. *Action.* Students develop and implement a plan of action to address the challenge.
4. *Reflection.* Students engage in careful observation of the outcomes of their ministry and discuss their implications, while in the midst of ministry and particularly following the activity.

The action/reflection approach reveals a traditional problem with many ministry efforts: the lack of debriefing after a ministry event. William Myers recounts a true story of suburban youth leaders who planned urban plunges for affluent, competitive youth. Following one such event (intended to raise compassion for the poor), Myers asked one girl about her experience. The girl remarked that she learned she needed to work harder in life so she did not end up like "those people" (1991, 77-79). Reflective engagement during and following ministry allows educators to help people check attitudes and outcomes in time to assist student practice in faithful discipleship.

TEACHING THE "FAMILIES"

Instructional strategies interact with the curriculum plan, often influencing both the design and delivery. Christian educators generally prefer one or two teaching families based on personal learning preferences and comfort level. Teachers should feel encouraged to develop these teaching strengths while also stretching occasionally with other methods and strategies. Educators will sometimes attempt to blend the different families for a more holistic curricular design. Be aware, however, that each strategy is designed to accomplish different goals, so the teacher needs to develop a rhythm in lesson planning that respects the intent of the methods used.

▶ CONCLUSION

Faithful discipleship occurs when we use the journalist questions to envision and prepare a sound curricular design and engage in the approach, delivery, or educational strategies that meet the specific needs of our congregation and community. One might wonder if there are general principles that guide both the design and delivery considerations of Christian education. Do certain teaching strategies serve the church more faithfully than others? Are there specific design guidelines? While prescribing a set curriculum is dangerous (there is no one-size-fits-all strategy to Christian education), one might discover some clues from previous chapters.

For instance, if we know that scripture primarily serves a narrative role, then we should understand that our efforts to relate experience and learning begin with attending to the narrative world of our students. Such an understanding encourages providing particular, formative experiences for children that are anchored in the biblical story (Pritchard 1992); encouraging redemptively relational connections between youth and the Christian story (Root 2007); and raising questions with adults that challenge their assumptions about life, so adults can reflectively reorient their lives within the biblical narrative (Groome 1980). If we take seriously the relational role of God in our Wesleyan theology, our method of education will be interactive, not only between teacher and student but also with the relational guidance of the Holy Spirit throughout life as we engage in the pilgrimage of learning.

When we raise issues concerning macro curriculum, we discover from the biblical narrative and from church history that the entire life of the congregation, including its engagement with society, constitutes the learning environment. Like Maria Harris (1989) and Robert Pazmiño (2008, 46), we begin to contemplate the life of the church in worship, fellowship, teaching, service, and witness as each of these domains of the congregation serves our macro curricular design. In addition, when developing micro curricular resources, we recognize God's call to teach not only the whole of scripture (the canon) but also the historical life and thought of God's people, as well as engaging our current efforts to live Christian lives. Our scope includes teaching Bible, church history, core theological doctrines, and issues in Christian living. Our sequence often emerges from the rhythms of the church, including its worship life and seasons (Advent to Pentecost, Christmas to Easter), which combine to tell the gospel story of Jesus as the church lives its life together.

Finally, when we seek particular goals or intended outcomes, our core conviction of holiness of heart and life should push us to lead people to discover what it means to know, live, and embrace (head, hands, and heart) the love of God in Christ. We pray with Paul that we "may have power, together with all the saints, to grasp how wide and long and high and deep is the love of Christ, and to know this love that surpasses knowledge—that you may be filled to the measure of all the fullness of God" (Ephesians 3:18-19).

As we engage the different educational strategies, we have to ask how each might serve as a means of grace in the way the Holy Spirit uses these practices to convey God's grace and lead us toward Christlikeness. In all of them, we can organize our curricular strategy around the three large categories of formation, discernment, and transformation within the life of a given congregation or community. Our goal remains: to participate in the means of grace in order to become a means of grace for God.

▶ REFERENCES

Bloom, Benjamin S., ed. 1956. *Taxonomy of Educational Objectives: Handbook 1: Cognitive Domain.* New York: David McKay.

Bruner, Jerome. 1963. *The Process of Education.* New York: Random House/Vintage Books.

_____. 1970. *On Knowing: Essays for the Left Hand.* New York: Atheneum Press.

Dewey, John. 1938, reprint 1963. *Experience and Education.* New York: Collier Books.

Dudley, Carl S. 1988. Using church images for commitment, conflict, and renewal. In *Congregations: Their Power to Form and Transform,* 89-113. Ed. C. Elis Nelson. Louisville, KY: John Knox Press.

Eisner, Elliot W. 1985. *Learning and Teaching the Ways of Knowing.* Chicago: Univ. of Chicago Press.

_____. 2002. *The Educational Imagination: On the Design and Evaluation of School Programs.* 3rd ed. Upper Saddle River, NJ: Merrill Prentice Hall.

Groome, Thomas H. 1980. *Christian Religious Education: Sharing Our Story and Vision.* San Francisco: Harper and Row.

Harris, Maria. 1989. *Fashion Me a People: Curriculum in the Church.* Louisville, KY: Westminster/John Knox Press.

Hestenes, Roberta. 1983. *Using the Bible in Groups.* Philadelphia: Westminster Press.

Kolb, David A. 1984. *Experiential Learning: Experience as the Source of Learning and Development.* Englewood Cliffs, NJ: Prentice Hall.

Little, Sara. 1983. *To Set One's Heart: Belief and Teaching in the Church.* Louisville, KY: John Knox Press.

Myers, William. 1991. *Black and White Styles of Youth Ministry.* New York: Pilgrim Press.

Neill, A. S. 1960, 1995. *Summerhill School: A New View of Childhood.* New York: St. Martins Griffin.

Pazmiño, Robert W. 2008. *Foundational Issues in Christian Education: An Introduction in Evangelical Perspective.* 3rd ed. Grand Rapids: Baker Books.

Pritchard, Gretchen Wolff. 1992. *Offering the Gospel to Children.* Lanham, MD: Cowley Publications.

Root, Andrew. 2007. *Revisiting Relational Youth Ministry: From Strategy of Influence to a Theology of Incarnation.* Downers Grove, IL: InterVarsity Press Books.

Tyler, Ralph W. 1949. *Basic Principles of Curriculum and Instruction.* Chicago: Univ. of Chicago Press.

Yount, William R. 1996. *Created to Learn: A Christian Teacher's Guide to Educational Psychology.* Nashville: Broadman and Holman.

PART 3

DESIGNING FAITHFUL DISCIPLESHIP IN THE CONGREGATION

We have considered the concepts and contexts of Christian education; how do we begin to envision the practice of faithful discipleship in congregations and other ministry contexts? This third section revisits our three domains of discipleship—formation, discernment, and transformation—from a congregational perspective.

Each of the previous chapters opened with scenarios of imagination to help you explore your own assumptions and practices. This exercise suggests that we begin with the challenges of ministry, reflect on our understanding, and then bring this knowledge into conversation with the resources presented in the text to envision a more faithful way of responding. The next three chapters will take a slightly different approach, asking first where you see formation, discernment, or transformation occurring in your congregation and then suggesting possible expressions of these domains for faithful discipleship in the local church.

Of course, the observations presented are suggestions for the general church that need to be fleshed out for local congregations and ministry contexts. In addition, we recognize that the three approaches to faithful discipleship, while discrete, often intersect as Christian education practices, programs, and strategies reach more than one goal. We envision faithful discipleship as overlapping concentric circles; every setting should have overlapping activities that inform and reinforce our collective attempt to use the means of grace.

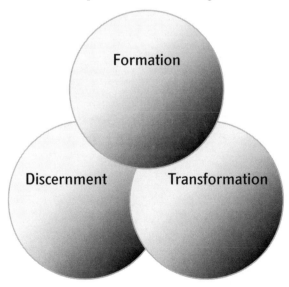

TWELVE

CONGREGATIONAL FORMATION

▶ INTRODUCTION

Take a moment to reflect on what you have already learned about formation. Where do you see this process occurring in your local congregation or ministry context? How could you develop formation strategies that might help move people toward faithful discipleship?

If you are not currently in a ministry context, consider the following scenarios:

- *Imagine you are a pastor and you are asked by a new Christian, "What are some of the most significant ways to grow spiritually?" You respond by saying that the most significant forms of spiritual growth takes place through congregational formation. The new Christians ask, "What aspects of congregational formation do you suggest?" What aspects of congregational formation would you identify to the new Christian as most important?*
- *Imagine your best Christian friend believes it is not necessary to participate in worship to grow as a Christian. She believes you can watch church on television and read the Bible privately to grow spiritually. Would you agree or disagree with her? If you disagree, what would you tell her is central to Christian formation?*
- *Imagine you are attending a congregation that celebrates the Eucharist each week. One of your friends who attends worship with you says, "I don't like having Communion each week because it becomes a ritual and loses meaning." Would you agree or disagree? Why?*

Congregational formation is an essential component of Christian discipleship that includes all aspects of the community's life that fosters faith formation. It is primarily concerned with how the practices of the community of faith shape, form, and transform persons. Congregations serve a distinct mission, providing a sacred place where God's Spirit promises to dwell among believers. Congregational formation's function is to build up, to shape communities of faith that serve God and love neighbors for the sake of transforming the world. It describes the corporate educational effort that nurtures and forms faith within the church and where the witness of the community occurs in the world (Foster 1994, 13).

All of the intentional activities within the faith community, including worship, education, service, and mission in the world, are essential aspects of Christian discipleship and settings for congregational formation. Discipleship includes passing on the traditions of the Christian faith through corporate memory (Nelson 1988), nurturing formation and education (Westerhoff 1978), and shaping identity and vocation (Seymour 1982). Congregational formation includes the total life of the congregation. Faithful discipleship includes not only understanding the primary purposes of congregational formation but also engaging specific formative processes that regularly shape Christian life.

▶ PURPOSES OF CONGREGATIONAL FORMATION

Each local congregation possesses a unique personality and history that shapes how people believe and practice their faith. This congregational identity stems from its link with one of the diverse groups of faith traditions and denominations, each of which reflects a particular aspect of the vision and mission of the church.

Congregational formation, therefore, first provides *corporate memory*. Each person is shaped and formed by the biblical and theological traditions passed on to him or her. Congregations are the primary avenues to transmit significant beliefs and practices—"who we are" and "what we believe"—to the next generation. Congregational memory includes the recognition of our place in the faith tradition and how that tradition will be carried to the next generation. Charles Foster expresses concern that congregations continue to lose corporate memory, especially with the loss of connectedness across generations and diminishing loyalty to particular faith traditions (1994, 23-24). Congregations also lose their memory with large increases in new people attending church. Recognizing, preserving, and developing memory is one of the primary purposes and tasks of congregational formation.

Congregational formation also creates *community*. This has become more difficult in societies shaped or influenced by a Western, individualistic mindset, which has an impact on the way Christians view faith. Many Christians maintain a privatized faith, believing they have no need for or responsibility to other people or the church. Part of the reason for this view is the continual fragmentation of lives busy with work, school, family, and church (Bettsworth 1990, 81-84; Putnam 2001). Congregations can speak to these challenges by creating community. Authentic community breaks through fragmentation and individualism and provides a place of acceptance. Communities share a common heritage that originates in God's love and grace and binds all ages and diverse groups together. The Christian community hears the story of God found in scripture and lives in a manner that is faithful to that story. Three important functions of Christian formation help shape community: *sharing stories of faith, nurturing intergenerational relationships,* and *practicing a communal lifestyle* (Foster 1994, 70-76).

- *The sharing of stories is an integral part of the church's vocabulary.* Telling stories helps people connect in ways that form and shape their faith. Formal approaches to congregational education often negate the importance of stories, but faithful discipleship includes the telling of individual and collective faith stories as a means of formation.

- *Nurturing intergenerational relationships offers each generation the opportunity to learn from others.* Congregational life fosters activities for all age-groups, providing opportunities for intergenerational formation. Adults nurture children and youth and provide models of faithful discipleship; younger generations bring fresh perspectives and new energy to adults who listen and learn. Congregational formation includes opportunities for all ages to worship, learn, and serve together. This may be a challenge to some congregations who have separated age-level ministries, but faithful discipleship includes finding creative avenues to integrate all generations.

- *Congregational formation includes practicing a communal lifestyle.* As faith is practiced within the context of the church, specific habits, beliefs, and behaviors develop. Congregational formation includes engaging in the practices of the church as a community. These include acts of social justice and service, care for the homeless, and Sunday school. The practice of participating in the instituted means of grace is central to faith formation and Christian community. Our participation in the body of Christ shapes and forms our faith.

Finally, congregational formation encourages *theological inquiry.* Parishioners often view theology as an abstract discipline for biblical scholars and theologians. However, theology is quite practical and finds its true home with the people of God. Congregational formation is the context in which people make meaning of life and faith as they struggle with deep theological issues and questions. People experience theology through faithful service to God and neighbor. Faithful discipleship calls educators to provide safe places for theological reflection, so that people can make sense out of the deep questions and struggles of their faith.

Christian educators serving in congregations need to give particular attention to developing corporate memory, creating authentic community, and encouraging theological inquiry, the formative aspects of congregational life.

▶ SCRIPTURE AS FORMATION

Christians believe that the Bible is authoritative for Christian faith and practice. In reading the Bible, Christians find guidance, inspiration, and knowledge for living out their faith. Christians believe that scripture provides God's specific revelation given through divine inspiration. They also believe the Bible to be central to Christian formation. Christians have often read the Bible merely to master a body of information. The Bible has been used as a way only to instruct, teach, and give information. Robert Mulholland states, "We are more often seeking some tidbits of information that will enhance our understanding of the Christian faith without challenging or confronting the way we live in the world" (2001, 52). In recent centuries, the interpretive practices of biblical scholarship have tended to focus on what the text meant, since these texts were written in and for particular historical contexts. These approaches to the Bible have often left the church wondering what, if anything, the Bible might say in contemporary settings. Historical interpretation offers an abundant feast of ways to read and understand the biblical texts in their original contexts but starving for a fresh message that engages the present. Passionate affirmations regarding the Bible's authority often ring hollow to contemporary audiences (Thompson 2008, 1-3).

More recently, Bible scholars have gained renewed interest in interpreting and reading scripture as a means of transformation instead of information. The Bible does much more than inform; through the mastery of materials, supremely scripture, it forms and transforms (Stevens and Green 2003, x). The Bible was written for the church, the people of God in all ages. Stephen Fowl writes, "Christian communities are formed through word and sacrament to read Scripture in light of their proper end in Christ" (2006, 127). The church is the place where Christians are formed as they interpret scripture in ways that enhance the goal of being Christlike. Any person, regardless of his or her level of biblical expertise, can read the Bible and encounter God. The movement from a historical (text-centered) approach to a narrative (reader-centered) approach to interpretation is based on the assumption that the inspired scriptures can be interpreted within the context of Christian community.

Formational reading includes opening to the text. In reading the Bible we seek to allow scripture to intrude into our lives, to address us, and to encounter us. Instead of mastering the text through study, formational reading invites the text to master and form us. We come to the text open to hear, to receive, to respond, and to serve the scripture. Sandra Schneiders asserts that biblical spirituality indicates a transformative process of the individual and communal engagement with the biblical text. The nonspecialist can approach the text, not merely as a historical record or even as a literary medium, but as the Word of God (2002, 136). Historical and critical analysis does not always lead to transformation, but the subjective reader is always transformed by the Word of God, by the work of the Holy Spirit.

Christians who read the Bible for transformation will find new excitement and energy. Formational reading calls the Christian educator to help develop practices and approaches for Christians to encounter scripture in new ways. We do not read scripture to retrieve facts or to gain information, but to be formed. Scripture does not present us with passages to be mastered but with the God's Word, which masters and shapes our lives. Certainly, scripture is read privately, but reading and studying scripture with other believers provides accountability for effective interpretation and application to life. Personal Bible reading is balanced when the community of faith reads scripture in corporate worship and studies in Bible study and small groups. It is essential for believers to read, study, and interpret scripture in the context of Christian community.

LECTIO DIVINA: EXPERIENCING SCRIPTURE

One approach to reading the Bible for transformation is the ancient practice of *lectio divina,* meaning "sacred reading" of scripture. Its roots are with the Benedictines, a religious order founded by Benedict of Nursia in the sixth century. *Lectio divina* is a process of scriptural encounter that includes a series of prayer dynamics, which move the reader to a deep level of engagement with the chosen text and with the Spirit that enlivens the text (see Hardy 2009, 39-41; Vest 1998):

- *Silencio* (Silence): First, approach the passage in open, receptive listening, reading silently.
- *Lectio* (Reading): Read the text aloud, slowly and deliberately, to evoke imagination. Hearing the text read reminds us of the spoken word of God. Follow the reading with a time of meditation. To meditate is to think about or mentally chew on what you have read. Take time to relax and mull over what you have read.
- *Ortio* (Praying): Talk to God as you would to one you are in a close relationship with. Speak to God, preferably out loud, or write your prayer in a journal.
- *Contemplatio* (Contemplation): Stop and rest silently before God. Receive whatever the Spirit gives.
- *Compassio* (Compassion): The fruit of the contemplation of God is love—love of God and neighbor. Whatever insight, feeling, or commitment emerges from time with scripture is to be shared as grace with others.

Encountering scripture through *lectio divina* is a new/old way of reading the Bible for transformation instead of information. Congregational formation includes providing opportunities for corporate expressions of sacred reading as well as helping persons develop personal skills in reading for transformation. While *lectio divina* can be pursued alone, small-group sharing of insights and inspiration offer an additional dimension to the practice.

▸ WORSHIP AS FORMATION

Worship is central to congregational formation. In worship, the people of God gather to give praise and thanksgiving to the Triune God. Believers respond to God's grace as the Word is proclaimed and the Eucharist is received. Many Christian educators believe worship anchors formation. Debra Dean Murphy believes Christians are formed and transformed through worship, praise, and doxology: "All efforts at forming and discipling Christians should presume the centrality of worship" (2004, 10). She argues that worship and Christian education appear as two separate enterprises because Christian education has been influenced by modern and liberal models of education that divide worship from education. Murphy calls for a catechesis that provides a rich theological heritage to unite Christian education and worship, discipleship and doxology. For Murphy, *catechesis* more fully captures the goal of Christian education as formation and transformation. Any formalized teaching about creed or doctrine must concede the primacy of worship for shaping people to be able to receive and understand such doctrinal instruction (105).

Catechesis is a journey of transformation that culminates in the praise and adoration of God. It begins and ends with liturgy, giving praise and worship to God. Thus worship confers and nurtures Christian identity. Through preaching, prayer, and the sacraments, corporate worship provides a robust form of Christian formation. Congregational formation through worship also includes significant events within the worshipping community. Charles Foster identifies four events that order congregational formation and nurture faith: *paradigmatic events, seasonal events, occasional events,* and *unexpected events.*

Paradigmatic, or community defining, events establish a pattern for Christian life and community that have origins in ancient traditions and rituals. For example, in the Wesleyan tradition the expectations for congregational life are shaped by patterns of piety, the means of grace related to prayer and the Lord's Supper. The influence of the rule of Benedict and the spiritual disciplines of John and Charles Wesley help renew and sustain congregational identity (Foster 1994, 44-45).

Seasonal events are rhythmical patterns of congregational formation that include the Christian calendar. The ritual processes that structure these events carry the congregation through the liturgical seasons from Advent through Christmas, Epiphany, Lent, Easter, Pentecost, and Saints' Day (45). Many seasons actually help Christians relive Jesus' birth, ministry, death, resurrection, and ongoing ministry through the church. James White notes that God's self is revealed through actual events in historical time: "God chooses to make the divine nature and will known through events that take place within the same calendar that measures the daily lives of ordinary women and men" (2000, 47). According to White, the Christian calendar provides the basic structure of Christian worship (ibid.). Congregations focused on formation express a renewed interest in following the Christian calendar and lectionary readings in worship. The *lectionary* is a list of Bible passages for reading, study, or preaching, that covers the majority of scripture in a three-year pattern. The lectionary readings usually include passages from the Old Testament, Psalms, Gospels, and Epistles. Some denominations, like the Catholic Church or the Lutheran Church, have their own lectionaries, while other denominations follow a common set of reading, such as the *Revised Common Lectionary*. Following the lectionary provides an educational curriculum that tells the complete story of scripture. In worship, the lectionary is used to guide scripture reading and preaching themes. The people of God make scripture central in the worshipping community as they read, experience, and interpret the Word of God. Following the lectionary as a curriculum for worship allows people to participate in the Christian story each year. It also provides the clearest and most consistent structure for congregational formation and education.

Congregations also use various forms of media to incorporate ancient images and icons as avenues for telling the story of scripture. Imagery includes appropriate vestments and colors that illustrate the seasons of the Christian calendar. For example, during the Lenten season ministers use the color purple or dark violet to symbolize Jesus' pain and suffering leading to the crucifixion as well as the suffering of humanity and the world under sin. Purple also symbolizes royalty, thus anticipating, through Christ's suffering and death, the coming of resurrection hope and new life.

Occasional events intensify community identity and mission by providing meaning and shared history. These events include weddings, funerals, baptisms, anniversaries, mission trips, homecomings, and church building dedications (Foster 1994, 45). A community's identity is heightened when a young couple brings a child to be dedicated or baptized. Homecoming ceremonies provide a time to retell the heritage of a congregation for new generations. Through these significant church events, faith formation takes place in the context of congregational practice and life.

Unexpected events interrupt the rhythmic patterns and structures that give order to the worshipping community. These unexpected events bring joy and sorrow, blessing and suffering. A tragic loss of life, the loss of employment, the birth of a child with disease, and natural disasters are examples of unexpected events that interrupt the normal flow of congregational life and worship (Foster 1994, 46). These events provide new meaning and understanding as the community responds to them.

Each of these movements or events form and shape faith as the people of God worship and live together. Worship is formative and transformative as people gather to praise and adore God, hear the scripture read and preached, tell and retell the gospel story, and share the burdens and joys of life.

▶ PARTICIPATION IN THE EUCHARIST

Most evangelical congregations identify with the proclamation of the gospel through preaching. These congregations, along with many Wesleyan congregations, see scripture as central to formation and proclamation. This reflects the influence of the Protestant Reformation, which placed a high value on scripture and proclamation. Many of these congregations are less likely to participate in Holy Communion, or the Eucharist ("giving thanks"), on a weekly basis. One of the primary reasons is that many Evangelical and Wesleyan congregations consider themselves "low" church, with a diminished view of liturgy, lectionary, and sacramental theology. But participation in the Eucharist, or table, on a regular basis doesn't replace the role of the Word in worship; rather Eucharist provides balance in worship. The table expands our understanding and discourse about God's grace by including a living sign of the gospel in tangible and visible form (Ruth 2002, 138).

Modern worship often emphasizes ideas and propositional truth more than encounter and experience. Recently, through an increased interest in ancient and historical practices in worship, evangelical and Wesleyan congregations are rediscovering the formative power of the Eucharist. Postmodern forms of worship place a great emphasis on experience, community, and mystery and have critiqued modern approaches that focus on more cognitive, transmitted forms of worship.

The Wesleyan tradition, based on the ministry and teachings of John Wesley, places a high value on the Eucharist in worship. John Wesley, an Anglican pastor, exhorted Methodists to practice "constant communion." Wesley generally took Communion every four or five days. He believed it was the highest point of Methodist worship; participation in the Eucharist was an opportunity to experience and commune with Christ. Through Communion persons experience the very presence of Christ. Wesley taught that Christ was present in the elements, though he did not hold the Roman Catholic view of *transubstantiation* (the bread and wine actually become the body and blood of Christ). For Wesley, since Christ was present, everyone was invited to participate, believers and nonbelievers. Christ was present spiritually, immediately, and independently, interacting with the recipient to convey grace. Wesley's view of the Eucharist as a sacrament reflects his belief that a person can receive forgiveness and reconciliation through obedient response to God's grace, including participation in the Eucharist. He believed that something divine takes place when a person comes with an open heart to receive the life-giving gift of bread and wine. In this respect, Wesley believed that the Eucharist was a converting element for those who confessed and believed *during* the Lord's Supper. Wesley's desire to see Methodist followers take Communion regularly was based on both obedience to Christ and the hope that blessing and holiness would follow the use of this essential means of grace.

THE EUCHARIST AS CHRISTIAN FORMATION

The Eucharist, according to Wesley, served as a channel of grace that formed and transformed the believer. Wesley's sermon "The Duty of Constant Communion" asks why Christians should participate in Communion on a regular basis and then provides a response. We are to participate in Communion as much as possible because Christ commanded us to "do this in remembrance of me" (Luke 22:19). The enormous benefits of Communion for all who participate in obedience to Christ include the forgiveness of past sins and the present strengthening and refreshing of our souls: "The grace of God given herein confirms to us the pardon of our sins, by enabling us to leave them. As our bodies are strengthened by bread and wine, so are our souls by these tokens of the body and blood of Christ. This is the food of our souls: This gives strength to perform our duty, and leads us on to perfection" (1872).

Communion, as a means of grace, is formative for those who are being drawn toward holiness and those who have been sanctified. For those desiring to grow in God's grace, which is a deepening of love for God and neighbor, Communion is the ordinary means of such growth. The sacrament serves not only to preserve and sustain but also to further progress and growth in faith and holiness. Wesley saw Communion as a significant means of grace, and he argued against those who feared that its frequency would diminish its impact ("If we do it too often, it will lose its meaning"). Should we pray less frequently because we fear it will lose its meaning? Should we read our Bibles less, go to church less, or minister to others less? No, of course not. Then why fear that celebrating Communion often will make it less meaningful? (See appendix 12.1.)

The Eucharist nourishes the soul. The act, which involves our personal and communal memory of Christ's suffering love, as well as the direct activity of the Holy Spirit, provides an immediate way of participating in the ongoing, transforming grace of God.

IMPLICATIONS FOR CONGREGATIONAL FORMATION

What are the implications of Wesley's view of Communion for congregational formation? First, Communion is the central act of the church in the ongoing growth of Christians. Participation in Communion is not simply a command to be obeyed, for Communion signifies the very meal that sustains and heals the church. Second, Communion offers sanctifying grace. Healing and formation occur in this encounter with God and others, symbolic of the future healing that will occur. Being present to God and one another describes an eschatological event, providing not only a vision of what will be but also an event that transforms the present into that future hope. Therefore, Christ's presence and the presence of others at the table are critically important. Third, through its offer of sanctifying grace, Communion provides for the renewal and reunification of the church, with Christ as the Head and each member as the body of Christ. Communion signifies the continuing transformation of the entire church, not simply an individual expression of personal piety. Fourth, Communion offers transformation and the renewal of persons in the image of God, which in turn yields hearts and lives where God's love flourishes. Participation in the means of grace is void if the love of God is not then welcomed into one's heart. Transformation and healing aim toward perfect love. Participation in Communion cannot be reduced to a simple act of piety; continual participation in Communion reflects both love and duty—with love as the primary goal. Living a life of love results in works of mercy (caring for the poor, etc.). Communion is not an end in itself but a means to share the love of Christ with others.

Congregations that include the Eucharist in worship provide congregants with food for their souls. Communion serves as one of the primary means of grace by which people experience the grace of God through participation in the presence of Christ. The Eucharist is another expression of the gospel of Jesus Christ in tangible form. It shapes, forms, and transforms each person who participates with an obedient heart. The Eucharist as a means of grace is one of the most powerful and formative aspects of Christian worship. The Eucharist and the preaching of the Word proclaim the gospel of Jesus Christ in tangible ways. One of the primary tasks of Christian discipleship is to provide both theological and practical education in the meaning and practice of the Eucharist. If people understand both experientially and theologically that the table forms and transforms them spiritually, then they will value regular participation in this essential means of grace.

▶ CONCLUSION

Congregational formation is an essential component of Christian discipleship, which includes all aspects of the community life that fosters faith formation. Christians are shaped individually and corporately through the formative aspects of scripture reading and worship, including Communion. Participation in the seasonal events of the church and following the lectionary provide avenues for congregations to tell and retell the gospel story. Through these formative events Christians are shaped and made as they live together in community. Faithful discipleship gives attention to intentional practices that shape and form corporate memory, develop community, and provide safe contexts for theological inquiry.

▶ REFERENCES

Bettsworth, Roger G. 1990. *Social Ethics: An Examination of American Moral Traditions.* Louisville, KY: Westminster/John Knox Press.

Foster, Charles. 1994. *Educating Congregations: The Future of Christian Education.* Nashville: Abingdon.

Fowl, Stephen E. 2006. Further thoughts on theological interpretation. In *Reading Scripture with the Church: Toward a Hermeneutic for Theological Interpretation,* 125-30. By A. K. M. Adam, Stephen E. Fowl, Kevin J. Vanhoozer, and Francis Watson. Grand Rapids: Baker Academic.

Hardy, Doug. 2009. Lectio divina: A practice for reconnecting to God's word. In *Preacher's Magazine: A Preaching Resource in the Wesleyan Tradition,* 38-41.

Mulholland, M. Robert, Jr. 2001. *Shaped by the Word: The Power of Scripture in Spiritual Formation.* Nashville: Upper Room Books.

Murphy, Debra Dean. 2004. *Teaching That Transforms: Worship as the Heart of Christian Education.* Grand Rapids: Brazos Press.

Nelson, C. Ellis, ed. 1988. *Congregations: Their Power to Form and Transform.* Atlanta: John Knox Press.

Putnam, Robert D. 2001. *Bowling Alone: The Collapse and Revival of American Community.* New York: Simon and Schuster.

Ruth, Lester. 2002. Word and table: A Wesleyan model for balanced worship. In *The Wesleyan Tradition: A Paradigm for Renewal,* 136-47. Ed. Paul W. Chilcote. Nashville: Abingdon.

Schneiders, Sandra. 2002. Biblical spirituality. In *Interpretation: A Journal of Bible and Theology* 56 (2): 133-42.

Seymour, Jack L. 1982. Approaches to Christian education. In *Contemporary Approaches to Christian Education,* 11-34. Ed. Jack L. Seymour and Donald Miller. Nashville: Abingdon.

Stevens, Paul R., and Michael Green. 2003. *Living the Story: Biblical Spirituality for Everyday Christians.* Grand Rapids: William B. Eerdmans.

Thompson, Richard P. 2008. Reading scripture as the church: Canon, authority, and Wesleyans. In *Catalyst* 34:4 (April), 1-3.

Vest, Norvene. 1998. *Gathered in the Word: Praying the Scripture in Small Groups.* Nashville: Upper Room.

Wesley, John. 1872. The duty of constant communion. In *The Works of John Wesley.* 3rd ed. 14 vols. Ed. Thomas Jackson. London: Wesleyan Methodist Book Room. See also http://wesley.nnu.edu.

Westerhoff, John. 1978. *Learning Through Liturgy.* New York: Seabury Press.

_____. 1979. A discipline in crisis. In *Religious Education* 74: 1 (January-February), 7-15.

White, James F. 2000. *Introduction to Christian Worship.* 3rd ed. Nashville: Abingdon.

Appendix 12.1

Summary of John Wesley's Sermon 101— "The Duty of Constant Communion"

The following discourse was written above five-and-fifty years ago, for the use of my pupils at Oxford. I have added very little, but retrenched much; as I then used more words than I do now. But, I thank God, I have not yet seen cause to alter my sentiments in any point which is therein delivered. 1788 J. W. "Do this in remembrance of me." Luke xxii. 19.

Why we are supposed to take Communion as often as possible.

1. **The First reason why it is the duty of every Christian so to do is, because it is a plain command of Christ.** *That this is his command, appears from the words of the text, "Do this in remembrance of me:" By which, as the Apostles were obliged to bless, break, and give the bread to all that joined with them in holy things; so were all Christians obliged to receive those signs of Christ's body and blood. Here, therefore, the bread and wine are commanded to be received, in remembrance of his death, to the end of the world.*

2. **The Second reason is the benefits of doing it are so great to all that do it in obedience to Christ:** *the forgiveness of our past sins, the present strengthening and refreshing of our souls.* So Communion is (1) a command by God and (2) a mercy (grace) to humans.

Wesley anticipated five objections:

1. *"I am unworthy."* Wesley replies, "Who is?" The original Pauline challenge (eating and drinking unworthy) actually addressed people who did not share their meal and who got drunk off the wine. Practices had changed to eliminate this possibility. Beyond this people feared they could not "live up" to the holiness implied in the sacrament. Wesley replied we come to the table and live our lives like all other Christians, in need of God's continuing grace and under God's command to live Christlike lives.

2. *Not enough time to prepare to receive Communion.* Wesley replied that all we need to prepare is to repent our sins and have faith in Christ (i.e., what any Christian should do). The same preparation we need for the Lord's Supper is what we need to remain Christian.

3. *Frequent Communion trivializes the sacredness of the event.* So, does obeying God's commandments trivialize them or is it the other way around?

4. *I no longer get anything out of it.* So what? Is taking the Lord's Supper about you getting anything out of it or is it about obedience to God? And whose fault is it that you do not "get anything" out of Communion, yours or God's? Perhaps you are receiving a benefit but at a level you cannot sense or understand. Hang in there and benefit will return.

5. *The church requires it only three times a year* (Anglican practice in Wesley's day). So, do you go by the church or by God's command? After all, the church provides Communion weekly (or daily) but has conceded that the minimum to even claim to be a Christian is three times a year. So do you walk in the center of the bridge or on the handrail when you cross a river?

Adapted from John Wesley, "The Duty of Constant Communion," in *The Works of John Wesley*. 3rd ed. Ed. Thomas Jackson. 14 vols. London: Wesleyan Methodist Book Room, 1872. Also see http://wesley.nnu.edu.

THIRTEEN

PERSONAL AND CONGREGATIONAL DISCERNMENT

Take a moment to reflect on what you have already learned about discernment. Where do you see this process occurring in your local congregation or ministry context? How can you develop discernment strategies that might assist people toward faithful discipleship?

If you are not currently in a ministry context, consider the following scenarios:

- *A person comes to you and asks: "I really want to get 'into' scripture to get past simplistic 'Sunday school' answers. Can you help me?" What would you say?*

- *A person walks up to you and a friend and says, "God really spoke to me last night! I have been learning this new formula for praying, one that really reaches up to God and can just change your spiritual life. If you ever had a powerful experience like I just had, you would know what I mean." As that person walks away, your friend comments, "I have never had God speak that way to me, but I have been as faithful as I know how, and I sense God quietly at work around me. Am I spiritual enough?" What would you say?*

- *A new couple joins your congregation. Soon you begin to hear from them how this church is different from their last experience. They ask why your congregation doesn't do more in particular areas of evangelism or care or service. After all, they claim, shouldn't every church do everything the same way? How would you respond?*

▶ TEXTS AND CONTEXTS

Discernment involves a gracious, challenging, imaginative inquiry into texts and contexts. Throughout the history of the church faithful disciples have inquired about the nature of God and the implications of the Christian life for communities and persons. As noted earlier, discernment often begins with an awareness of God at work in our lives through Christ, moves to inquiry about how to live a more faithful life as a result of God's grace, and arrives at perception of the Holy Spirit's activity in communities and throughout the world. Often discernment begins with texts, particularly scripture, and the church's accounts of God's work through doctrinal formulations. In addition, Christian educators find themselves called to discern God's work in specific contexts, either through the lives of individuals or in the midst of the detailed and dynamic complexity that shapes congregational life.

▶ SCRIPTURAL STUDY AND THEOLOGICAL REFLECTION

We have traditionally understood discernment in the role of special revelation, the Holy Spirit at work as scriptures were shaped and formed by the original writers. But the Holy Spirit continues to work in the community and persons who struggle to understand the meaning of scripture for today. We have discussed scripture reading as a formative process (see chapter 12), but the Bible also invites readers to discern the deep meaning of the text and its implications for daily life. Bible study serves more than a devotional role. The practice of digging out (exegesis) is also a means of grace as we learn specific word meanings, the genre of literature represented in a given passage, the historical setting of the original account and the community that first heard it as sacred text, and the relationship of a passage to other biblical texts. Each of these study tasks involve etymological, literary, historical, and canonical questions that culminate in a deeper discernment of the Bible. Congregations that see the Bible in active dialogue with the church (Maas 1982, 22-30) seek to discern not only the questions they raise about the text but also the questions the scripture raises about the life of the church! Learning to discern the deep meaning of the text does not give us control of the Bible; it prepares us to hear fully what scripture has to say to challenge the church and our Christian walk. Faithful discipleship includes the willingness to engage in sound study of scripture, to be a student of the Bible, and to give oneself to the difficult, yet rewarding task of disciplined Bible study.

Discernment also means applying the same set of critical and creative questions to other texts that guide the church, such as the Apostles' Creed and other doctrinal affirmations of faith. Exploring and working out the implications of our theological convictions is an important task of discernment. *Theology,* the active reflection on the nature of God and the work of God in the world, is the classic model of discernment. Charles Wood notes that cultivating theological imagination is essential for effective ministry. Wood and Ellen Blue note that our attentiveness to God often involves a range of theological resources, what they call the Wesleyan quartet (instead of *quadrilateral*)— scripture, tradition, reason, and experience—employed for the sake of our sustained, systematic, and practical engagement in theological reflection shaped deeply by a formative engagement with scripture (2008, 10, 13-14). Wood and Blue offer three primary questions that undergird theological reflection as a form of discernment (22):

What is going on in this situation?

How is God involved in what is going on?

What is a fitting response to what is going on?

These questions reflect an approach to theological study known as practical theology, which we will discuss more fully at the end of the chapter. For now, it is important to say that no form of theological reflection, or discernment, can occur without serious attention to the resources (the texts) of the Christian faith that have emerged across the centuries and from within Christian communities.

▶ SPIRITUAL DIRECTION AND CONGREGATIONAL ASSESSMENT

While discernment involves a close reading and understanding of *texts,* it also commands a close reading of *contexts.* This includes understanding people in the midst of their spiritual journey (Cunningham 2004) and also understanding the nature and role of the church as any congregation seeks to be a steward of God's work in the world. Individual spiritual guidance may be offered through various discernment processes, such as spiritual direction (Thompson 1995/2005, 107-24). Personal discernment may also occur through group processes, such as small groups that practice accountable discipleship (Watson 1984), or in the presence of a caring family (Thompson 1997). John Wesley employed specific questions that assisted small groups in seeking to know and live a holy life. Groups gathered to give personal testimony and then to ask one another difficult questions about personal challenges, devotional practices, public character, and even sinful struggles. In every circumstance, these questions were to be handled with pastoral care by an appointed group leader and all group members were to keep a covenant of mutual discretion and mutual accountability.

DISCERNING SPIRITUAL EXPERIENCE: TWO ROADS AND LOVE

The traditional practice of spiritual direction, the naming of God's gracious activity in the life of a believer, is a form of discernment. Spiritual direction may mean the employ of an individual director, guide, or faith mentor in a one-to-one relationship. It may also be the gentle presence of a spiritual friend, one who travels with us as a co-pilgrim rather than wise guide. The primary role of this form of direction is to understand and nurture the depth of one's faith journey with God. Such a journey may be quite different from one person to the next.

For instance, think about the biblical accounts of personal encounters with the resurrected Jesus. In Luke 24:13-35, two travelers journey to Emmaus. The risen Christ joins them on the way, but they do not recognize him.

As they travel, the travelers recount the gospel to Christ and receive instruction in scripture from him. They do not recognize Christ until, through a simple act of hospitality in the breaking of bread, Jesus becomes known to them, and then immediately disappears! The Emmaus travelers must return to Jerusalem, with warmed hearts, before they encounter Christ again.

For some people, the journey with Christ may be like that of the travelers to Emmaus. Their lives are connected to the presence of Christ through Christian community, steeped in the message, and yet they are unaware of the meaning. Perhaps through a small act of hospitality, they momentarily recognize the presence of Jesus, only to have him disappear in such a way that they must continue their journey to encounter him again. These believers have been transformed, but their journey is focused forward. They appreciate and share what they learned in that definitive moment of awakening and continue the journey in anticipation of another encounter.

In contrast, review the encounter of Saul (later Paul) with the resurrected Christ on a different road, the road to Damascus (Acts 9:1-31). Saul represents a passionate yet deadly enemy of "the way" of Jesus. Self-assured, Pharisee of the Pharisees, this antagonist heads to Damascus with murder on his mind. During the journey Saul finds himself slammed to the ground by the resurrected, blinding presence of Jesus. Saul's transformation is frightening to his companions as Christ confronts Saul, challenges his mission in life, and leaves him literally blind, stumbling, and broken. Only after Ananias explains the full implications of the encounter do the "scales" fall from Saul's eyes. Paul emerges an equally passionate advocate, but now for the message of salvation through Jesus Christ. This one-hundred-eighty-degree represents a fundamental change in Paul, from a man driven by hate to a man driven by love. Paul looks to this powerful moment of transformation (Paul testifies to his past three times in Acts!) as the motivation to move into the future, to press on toward the goal established in Christ.

For Damascus-road people, transformation is radical, often singular, and all-consuming. Often the conversion includes specificity (you are not likely to forget getting slammed to the road!), and their sense of Christian vocation uses the event from the past as a beacon for the future. Often these people (and the Ananiases of our world) spend considerable time interpreting and verifying for others what happened to them, seeking both a sense of congruence with their past ("I was . . . now I am . . .") and a sense of correspondence or relationship with people who have experienced the same type of transformation (Loder 1989, 4-5). Emmaus-road people do not see transformation as Damascus-road people do, and vice versa. Nevertheless, people on both of these roads can attest to the presence of the resurrected Christ in their lives. The challenge rests with Christian educators to help people discern how to appreciate what God has done in their lives while valuing how the Holy Spirit might work differently in the life of someone else.

▶ DISCERNMENT AND TRANSFORMATION

While truly transformative experience may appear differently among people, not all claims to spiritual insight prove equally valid. James Loder notes that people may succumb to self-deception, claiming insight based on human efforts and asserting a special, mystical knowledge that seems more like self-promotion than gracious love. Loder offers several criteria based on theological and psychological understandings to help us discern authentic transformation (1989, 183-210):

- Convictional experiences are initiated by God/Christ/Holy Spirit and not by human efforts.
- Experiences will result in a sacrificial love in the one transformed.
- People who undergo transformation will search for objective points of reference concerning God, whether through scripture, worship, or theological writings.
- People who experience transformation will see this as a breakthrough that cannot be reduced to something in their personal history alone.
- Transformed people will seek a social context that embraces and confirms what has happened to them but will not allow the event to be reduced to the actions of a specific guru rather than God.
- People tend to see their transformation as a complex event (no simple formula) that results in personal inner acceptance, positive valuing of change, recognition and acceptance of personal difference, embrace of community for the sake of ongoing growth, and a desire to take some emergent action, to do something positive as a result of the experience.

Loder's guidelines provide Christian educators with a set of criteria to employ in discerning the efficacy of personal transformation. One might say that transformed people live open lives marked by a search for truth *and* an expression of love. These particular traits marked John and Charles Wesley's desires long ago to bring knowledge and spirituality, learning and holiness, truth and love together as faithful disciples become living sacrifices for the sake of the kingdom of God (1763/1983, 7:643-44).

Unite the pair so long disjoin'd,
Knowledge and vital Piety:
Learning and Holiness combined,
And Truth and Love, let all men see,
In those who up to Thee we give,
Thine, wholly thine, to die and live.

▶ CONGREGATIONAL STUDIES:
DETAILED AND DYNAMIC COMPLEXITY

While discernment often involves personal contexts, delving deeply into experiences and commitments of individual Christians, the practice also describes larger undertakings such as understanding the nature of Christian communities for the sake of leadership and pastoral oversight. Pastors and other congregational leaders often employ discernment to guide their understanding of the detailed complexity of a community as well as the complex dynamics of the day-to-day decisions that influence the community. Recent research in congregational studies often includes exploring the overall working of a congregation based on the community's structure, the resources the church possesses, the social context that influences it, the processes that give the community a sense of identity, and the values that shape the character of the church.

Congregational studies provide more information about a church or ministry context than intuitive awareness or random investigation, forcing ministers to see beyond hunches and age-level statistics. The process of discernment tests our powers of observation and helps us to be more systematic in comprehending local congregations. This form of disciplined study confers a sense of balance and proportion often absent from spontaneous self-descriptions. The approach helps congregations unravel multiple, seemingly unrelated problems by uncovering structures or patterns in the apparent confusion. Congregational study can also help a congregation articulate its mission and ministry, therefore providing a deeper sense of purpose. Many churches suffer from one-line, simplistic descriptions, whether they come from the severest critic or the most enthusiastic promoter. The detailed complexity of a congregation is God's living organism, the church, and cannot be reduced to simplistic definitions.

Acknowledging complexity does not mean submitting to confusion. Serious, discerning study may reveal a history of patterns of conflict or renewal that a congregation needs to understand in order to move into the future with integrity. A church that gains a clear sense of identity evokes excitement in the members who know both who they are and where they are headed. A heightened sense of purpose encourages corporate participation. Leadership is more effective and more pastoral in a church that knows its identity, even if change is necessary. One caution: congregational studies can reveal what a congregation does not want to see. Sensitive leaders will approach this material carefully.

Engaging congregational contexts, as a form of corporate discernment, involves a number of assumptions. First, the church exists as both a theological/spiritual reality and a historical/cultural reality. Congregations represent the body of Christ based on what God is doing; however, those bodies also reflect or react to the culture and historical settings that shape them. Second, ministers must see the congregation as a whole as well as a collection of parts. One of the key strengths of a good leader is the ability to attend to the day-to-day relationships and tasks while maintaining a broader view of where the church is headed.

One final assumption rests with the assertion that congregations contain more than individuals. Congregations are people and their interactions: with one another, in smaller units (groups), with the history of the church, and with the vision of the church. The body that is the congregation organizes and coordinates its activities (usually under the leadership of the pastor). As complex social groups, congregations include those who need and those who give. Dynamic systems interact and change as new people arrive and new ideas are tried, but congregations also operate within particular denominational systems with particular forms of worship and governance.

A social system is actually a complex interrelationship of subsystems within an organization. A church is more than the sum of its people, groups, and the interactions that occur. Ministers must see the church both in the particular (age-level ministries, small groups, committee meetings, staff, individuals, etc.) and as a whole. Some basic premises govern the life of social systems, including:

- Anytime you change something in the system, everything else must adjust. No decision operates by itself; other decisions will follow that may change the outcome of the original act.
- Whatever goes into a system must come out, but it is changed by the system.
- All systems are unique, but there may be a number of common points among systems (e.g., churches are unique yet similar). As you review any church system, you should always ask one key question: "What is the one, unique thing that connects people and groups to this church?"
- Systems require care (money, attention, nurture, etc.).
- All systems have both function and structure.
  - *Function* describes what brought the system (church) into being in the first place. Why does it exist?
  - *Structure* describes what the system (church) does to accomplish its function (this reveals where the power is).
- Systems have connections and boundaries.
  - What holds people together in this system (congregation)?
  - How do people enter and exit the system? How do they know they belong?

Congregational studies use quantitative analysis (demographics and statistics). They also use qualitative analysis, or *ethnography,* which begins in observation and results in definitions. Ethnography is similar to the process used by anthropologists, who live in a culture and create descriptions about it from their observations. Ministers employ a number of strategies that provide a systematic view of the congregation; an ethnographic approach, however, reinforces connection with the people.

Through discerning study, ministry leaders develop acute attention to the systemic nature of decision making. Through the work of Peter Senge (1990) and other theorists (Hawkins 1997), leaders now understand that decisions rarely follow a simple line from initiation to completion. Decisions set into motion other dynamic actions that may resist, reinforce, or subvert leadership efforts. Careful discernment of the nature of relational systems, often using case-study methods and other reflective tools (Mahan et al. 1993), helps leaders learn how previous relationships within a congregation (some long past) may still influence the expectations and judgment (Cosgrove and Hatfield 1994; Friedman 1985; Richardson 1996). In addition, careful attention to the flow of outcomes within a congregation in the midst of change often calls leadership to work as a learning community with discernment helping to anticipate the need for future actions (Hawkins 1997, 58-75).

INSIDE OUT/OUTSIDE IN

Finally, one can understand a church inductively, from the inside out, using various categories to explore the inner life of a congregation. Just as human bodies have internal organs, basic descriptive categories help us understand the body of Christ from the inside out, moving from the internal workings of a congregation to a general, more holistic, description. An example of this approach appears in the text *Studying Congregations* (Ammerman et al. 1998), which organizes the life of a congregation around a number of sociocultural domains.

- *Ecology* (which includes the scope of the social contexts)
  - Social layers in the congregation (based on global, national, local influences)
  - Demographic picture and intrasocial networks at the church
  - Congregational history (how the church came into existence and important historical events)
- *Culture* (the processes that give the church a particular character or ethos)
  - Activities (rituals and other meaningful engagements)
  - Artifacts (important symbols, the arrangement of space, key narratives)

○ Accounts (the general worldview of church members, the specific heritage congregants draw upon in explaining the history of the congregation)

- *Processes* (methods for planning, community building, and resolving conflict)
- *Resources* (the programs, finances, people, etc., that sustain the congregation)

Ammerman and others believe that one can gain a fairly adequate understanding of a given congregation by using these categories to discern the nature of the church from the inside out.

Similarly, one may explore churches analogically from the outside in, using models or images for comparison. Regardless of our uniqueness as individuals, many of us bear a family resemblance to other family members, obvious even in those we barely know. Churches also bear family resemblances that allow us to compare them for aspects of commonality and difference. This allows us to work outside in, acknowledging the commonalities so we can also discover the differences that make a congregation unique. There are a number of ways to characterize a church beyond denominational affiliation. Size (megachurch, small church, etc.), social context (urban, suburban, rural), and economic status (affluent, working-class, impoverished) all imply something about the "family resemblances" among congregations (Dudley 1988, 90-96). One might even take the characteristics of Damascus-road and Emmaus-road people mentioned above and use them to envision congregations whose actions and activities resemble Damascus or Emmaus tendencies. Sometimes specific models are used that provide ideal representations of churches for the sake of comparison and contrast. Avery Dulles (1974/1991) provides five theological categories based on his understanding of Roman Catholic congregations, but their general depictions prove interesting for comparison.

- *Institutional:* The church focuses on structure as the agent for God's activity; entrance to and participation in the community are primary goals.
- *Mystical Communion:* Congregations are seen as interpersonal and organic, yet dependent on the movement of the Holy Spirit to empower and direct ministry.
- *Sacrament:* This model attempts to synthesize external and internal aspects of the church while incarnating Christ in the world.
- *Herald:* The church emphasizes faith and response over interpersonal relationships as congregants gather for the event of proclamation.
- *Servant:* The congregation exists to serve the world by fostering the fellowship of all persons and offering reconciling love.

In contrast, Carl Dudley and Sally Johnson (1993) use images of the church to suggest how different congregations might relate to one another. These authors believe communities form their lives around stories, symbols, and images in order to make meaning for their internal lives (identity) and their reason for being in society (ministry). They offer a typology through which to compare congregations:

- *Pillar:* The church is the center of local community life, engaging citizenship and discipleship in the same manner.
- *Pilgrim:* Congregations comprise a particular people, fellow pilgrims are often determined by social and cultural heritage; focus is on fostering a community identity.
- *Survivor:* Congregations shaped by tough challenges and a tenacious strength in the midst of difficult times.
- *Prophet:* Churches that seek to offer a visionary hope and passionate service to the world, often taking stances that challenge the social and cultural expectations.
- *Servant/Shepherd:* Congregations that provide compassionate fellowship both within and beyond the church as a natural expression of loving care.

Obviously no congregation neatly fits any general description. Using models and typologies often exposes novelties within a congregation that tell us more about the faith community than all of the general descriptions. More than simple stereotypes, however, these larger categories of family resemblance provide congregants with an opportunity to understand and appreciate the activities of their local congregation, their preferences for certain leaders, and their focus for ministry, while still seeing value in the ministry and service of other churches.

Regardless of general resemblances, the assumptions that drive congregational analysis remain rooted in acknowledging the complexity and uniqueness of each congregation. Ministers may fail in a given setting without fully understanding why. These failures are seldom caused simply by inadequate ministry skills on the part of the pastor. Sometimes ministers just fail to discern their church context and tailor their ministry for that setting. Congregational analysis offers ministers and parishioners an opportunity for discernment that can result in vibrant congregational ministry.

▶ Practical Theology:
An Approach to Discernment

Practical theology, a particular discernment approach, incorporates critical and creative practice that brings together texts and contexts in a model of theological reflection and ministry practice. According to editors James Woodward and Stephen Pattison, the term *practical theology* describes both a domain within the broad field of theology and a particular method of theological reflection (2000, 1-18). When ministers use the term *theology*, they primarily describe the discipline of exploring and talking about the nature and actions of God in the world.

In a practical theological method, ministers also engage daily living and their pastoral responsibilities in the life of church. This method has been a powerful resource for Christian educators in all age-level ministries, including youth ministry (Dean 2001, 27-36; White 2005, 89-199). While taking full advantage of the resources available within the life of faith, including God's revealed will found in scripture and Christian doctrine, ministers focus on everyday life and ministry practice. Experience, while not the final teacher, defines the context to shape our questions for learning (Kolb 1984).

First, practical theologians start by naming the concrete experiences influencing either individual lives or community settings, seeking to *connect* these experiences in order to ensure a real understanding of their true meaning. Ministers then *reflect* on those experiences, probing their own assumptions and revealing what they think are the most important parts of the activities. Practical theologians then consider knowledge gained from diligent study of the texts (Bible and doctrine) that shape Christian thought and practice. In this phase ministers attempt to *detect and evaluate* people's daily practice within the Christian faith, allowing their core Christian convictions to shape a more faithful ministry. Finally ministers attempt to *project* what new ministry will look like, ministry that is more faithful to the nature of God and what God is doing in the world, and ultimately seek to implement this ministry. Obviously these new, more faithful approaches to ministry create even newer experiences that begin the process of connecting, reflecting, detecting, and projecting once more in a cycle of discerning and developing a deeper and more mature approach to ministry (see figure 13.1):

- *Connect:* Naming and connecting everyday experiences that are part of our ministry. (How well do we see what is really happening?)
- *Reflect:* Taking a step back to probe our assumptions, selecting those aspects of the experience that prove to be most important. (How well do we understand the various influences that shape our experiences and what we value about them?)
- *Detect and Evaluate:* Bringing the big ideas that surface from our reflection into direct dialogue with scripture, Christian doctrine, and the history of the church. (How do the contents of the Christian faith critique or affirm our ministry actions?)

- *Project:* Beginning to imagine and implement new ministry strategies based on a more faithful vision of ministry. (How well do we learn from our experience as we plan the next ministry activities?)

Figure 13.1: Practical Theology as a Process of Discernment

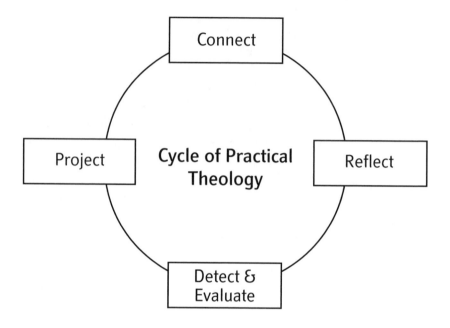

The process of practical theology provides one more example of discernment that shapes our theological awareness and directs us to more faithful discipleship. Our challenge remains to identify and engage different practices of scripture study, theological reflection, personal direction, and congregational decision making as modes of Christian education, means of grace that result in faithful discipleship.

▶ CONCLUSION

Discernment functions at both the individual and congregational level for Christian educators. Frankly, the very process of discernment often serves as a form of ministry in itself (Crain and Seymour 1996) as we learn to remain attentive, to distinguish the various means of grace, and to guide people and congregations to serve in faithful discipleship.

▶ REFERENCES

Ammerman, Nancy Tatom, Jackson W. Carroll, Carl S. Dudley, and William McKinney. 1998. *Studying Congregations: A New Handbook*. Nashville: Abingdon Press.

Cosgrove, Charles H., and Dennis D. Hatfield. 1994. *Church Conflict: The Hidden Systems Behind the Fights.* Nashville: Abingdon.

Crain, Margaret Ann, and Jack L. Seymour. 1996. The ethnographer as minister: Ethnographic research in ministry. In *Religious Education* 91, no. 3: 299-315.

Cunningham, Lawrence. 2004. Spiritual direction as Christian pedagogy. In *Educating People of Faith,* 330-49. Ed. John Van Engen. Grand Rapids: William B. Eerdmans.

Dean, Kenda Creasy. 2001. Fessing up: Owning our theological commitments. In *Starting Right: Thinking Theologically About Youth Ministry.* Ed. Kenda Creasy Dean, Chap Clark, and Dave Rahn. Grand Rapids: Zondervan.

Dudley, Carl S. 1988. Using church images for commitment, conflict, and renewal. In *Congregations: Their Power to Form and Transform.* Ed. C. E. Nelson. Louisville, KY: Westminster/John Knox Press.

Dudley, Carl S., and Sally A. Johnson. 1993. *Energizing the Congregation: Images That Shape Your Church's Ministry.* Louisville, KY: Westminster/John Knox Press.

Dulles, Avery. 1974/1991. *Models of the Church.* Garden City, NY: Doubleday; REI 2nd ed., Random House.

Friedman, Edwin H. 1985. *Generation to Generation: Family Process in Church and Synagogue.* New York: Guilford Press.

Hawkins, Thomas R. 1997. *The Learning Congregation: A New Vision of Leadership.* Louisville, KY: Westminster/John Knox Press.

Kolb, David A. 1984. *Experiential Learning.* Englewood Cliffs, NJ: Prentice Hall.

Loder, James E. 1989. *The Transforming Moment,* 2nd ed. Colorado Springs: Helmers and Howard.

Maas, Robin. 1982. *Church Bible Study Handbook.* Nashville: Abingdon Press.

Mahan, Jeffry H., Barbara B. Troxell, Carol J. Allen. 1993. *Shared Wisdom: A Guide to Case Study Reflection in Ministry.* Nashville: Abingdon Press.

Richardson, Ronald W. 1996. *Creating a Healthier Church: Family Systems Theory, Leadership and Congregational Life.* Minneapolis: Fortress Press.

Senge, Peter M. 1990. *The Fifth Discipline: The Art and Practice of the Learning Organization.* New York: Doubleday Currency.

Thompson, Marjorie J. 1995/2005. *Soul Feast: An Invitation to the Christian Spiritual Life.* Louisville, KY: Westminster/John Knox Press.

_____. 1997. *Family the Forming Center: A Vision of the Role of Family in Spiritual Formation.* Rev. and exp. Nashville: Upper Room Books.

Watson, David Lowes. 1984. *Accountable Discipleship.* Nashville: Discipleship Resources.

Wesley, Charles. 1763/1983/reprint. Hymn 461, For Children. In John Wesley, *The Works of John Wesley,* Vol. 7: *A Collection of Hymns for the Use of the People Called Methodists,* 643-44. Ed. Franz Hildebrandt and Oliver A. Beckerlegge. New York: Oxford Univ. Press; Nashville: Abingdon Press.

White, David F. 2005. *Practicing Discernment with Youth: A Transformative Youth Ministry Approach.* Cleveland, OH: Pilgrim Press.

Wood, Charles M., and Ellen Blue. 2008. *Attentive to God: Thinking Theologically in Ministry.* Nashville: Abingdon Press.

Woodward, James, and Stephen Pattison, eds. 2000. *The Blackwell Reader in Pastoral and Practical Theology.* Oxford: Blackwell Publishers.

FOURTEEN

CONGREGATIONAL
TRANSFORMATION

▶ INTRODUCTION

Take a moment to reflect on what you have already learned about trans-
formation. Where do you see this process occurring in your local congregation or
ministry context? How could you develop transformation strategies that might as-
sist people toward faithful discipleship?

If you are not currently in a ministry context, consider the following sce-
narios:

- *You attend a Sunday school rally where the guest presenter extols the vir-*
  tues of evangelism through Sunday school. The workshops presented all
  address outreach methods and new strategies for growing classes. Finally a
  member from your church complains that all of these efforts leave a church
  with a membership "a mile wide but only six inches deep" when it comes
  to spiritual maturity. How would you respond?

- *You strategize a youth trip to an impoverished region to practice compas-*
  sionate ministry. A parent stops you and asks, "I thought your job was
  Christian education, not compassionate ministry. Why travel all that way
  to a help a bunch of people when our youth need to be focused on Bible
  study, prayer, and learning about our church?" How would you reply?

- *You start a Bible study in a local coffee shop. Soon your group fills up*
  with neighborhood people who have no interest in coming to worship on
  Sunday, much less join the church. A board member stops and asks why
  you continue to meet at the coffee shop since "it does not help the church."
  What do you say?

As we have seen, transformation may describe both a process and an outcome . . . which leads back to the process. In short, transformational discipleship utilizes practices of congregational engagement (ministry acts of evangelism, service, compassion, advocacy, community education, etc.) whereby
practitioners grow and learn as they minister to others. The personal growth
that results from these actions leads to personal transformation best described
as holiness, which empowers the same people to manifest even stronger expres-

sions of holy love toward others. Faithful discipleship not only includes compassionate practice but also results in compassionate practice when we learn from our efforts. As we *practice* the means of grace, including works of mercy, we *become* means of grace for others and the world.

▶ DISCIPLESHIP: EVANGELISM OR EDUCATION?

Christian education has historically focused on efforts of engagement and formation. Did Sunday school begin as a strategy for evangelism or education? Did Augustine understand catechesis for the uninstructed as a means of outreach? Should children's ministries focus on reaching children, nurturing children, or serving as advocates for the sake of children? The desire to shape and nurture at each age level (formation) always lives in tension with the desire to reach out to new people (transformation).

The modern wedge driven between evangelism and education forced Christian educators to choose one approach over the other when defining discipleship, a move that often left churches confused and diminished in one of the dimensions of engagement and removed from the deeper task of Christian witness in a changing world (Stone 2007). Christian education has always been about evangelism, an evangelism of the ages, seeking not only to reach the current generation but also to prepare people to reach out to future generations. Without the support of educational ministry, congregational efforts at evangelism run the risk of lasting no more than one generation. This reality reflects the view that local communities (at least local congregations) are always one generation short of extinction without education (Brelsford 2001, 314-15; Brueggemann 1982, 1). Yet the Holy Spirit provides each generation with the resources to preserve the church through powerful evangelism. In a sense, Christian education also serves evangelism by conserving new converts as they enter the church. One observation by George Whitefield, the famous field preacher of the eighteenth-century evangelical revival, provides testimony to this need. Whitefield considered his ministry a "rope of sand" because he did not follow John Wesley's strategy of accountable discipleship in support of evangelism (Ayling 1979, 2001).

Of course, discipleship incorporates and supports more than evangelistic efforts. Every effort of the local church to serve as a witness to the grace of God through Jesus Christ by the power of the Holy Spirit is an act of transformation. As congregations participate in activities designed to engage local and global contexts, they also share witness of the love and power of God in acts of compassion, care, peace, and justice. In fact, the very act of teaching is a powerful mode of direct engagement with people and communities needing care and compassionate guidance. How can Christian educators organize their efforts at transformation so that members both practice and learn faithful discipleship? Two old-yet-new metaphors help to guide our actions.

▶ Parish Mind-set and Missional Engagement

Every generation must envision modes of engagement for the practice of faithful discipleship. Two terms from the church's history, *parish mind-set* and *missional engagement,* have reemerged with new energy to help describe these efforts. The first refers to life within the church but extends to include responsibilities to the community, or *parish,* that surrounds the congregation. The second term employs a view of God as a missionary God, who calls us to follow his mission and ministry in the world. Together, these terms shift the concept of Christian education from an invitational activity of the local congregation to an outwardly focused endeavor of transformation.

PARISH MIND-SET

Through the second half of the twentieth century, the church described evangelism primarily through the language of invitation. Efforts designed to evangelize the local community provided a number of programs—all located within the church—to draw people (believers and nonbelievers) through the doors and hopefully into saving faith. Programming could be elaborate, with entertaining and resourceful classes that dealt with daily living. When these efforts proclaimed the gospel and made a difference in people's lives, they served faithful discipleship. The unforeseen consequences emerged as churches became disconnected from their communities, some serving only drive-in members rather than connecting with their immediate neighbors.

Christian educators seem to be restoring an approach to evangelism that takes ministry within the community seriously. Norma Cook Everist notes, "No congregation is an island unto itself. Each community of faith resides in a parish, a place, a context. The congregation has at its doorstep, and needs to see and utilize, the community, the people, and the institutions, including those beliefs, values, and practices, of the entire parish" (2002, 21).

Everist envisions Christian education as an ongoing spiral, with moments of ministry leading to times of reflection and learning (262-64) reminiscent of David Kolb's cycle of experiential learning (see chapter 11). Engagement includes service, witness, compassionate care, outreach, ministry in everyday life, leadership for justice, and mission beyond borders. Each of these modes of engagement presents opportunities for learning, and the gathered knowledge leads back to continued ministry. "Learning leads to mission now—not just someday, but this very week" (263). Community action and congregational learning combine when the parish serves as the primary arena for Christian education. Local congregational programs still exist, but they serve not only to invite people into the church but also to prepare them to live and work within their parish community.

This approach is reminiscent of other eras of Christian discipleship when teaching was part of missions. Rather than merely empowering people for transformative acts, Christian education specifically served as a means of transformation. The initial efforts of the American Sunday School Union used educational strategies that combined literacy and devotion, often in communities that did not yet possess a church! Education as a means of ministry beyond church walls surfaces in community awareness programs, after-school mentoring, and life-skill training, as well as vocational resource education. Congregants bring the best of their gifts and training into the community where the Holy Spirit can use personal relationships as opportunities for transformation for everyone involved. What happens when congregations realize, like Wesley, that their parish may well be the world? How do transformative acts incorporate not only community but also regional, national, and global settings? Another old/new metaphor will help answer the question.

MISSIONAL ENGAGEMENT

Does the local church *possess* a mission strategy or does it *express* a mission strategy? In other words, does a congregation embrace missions as a program or engage the world as a missional church? One answer to these questions reveals a movement that takes transformation as normative for the life of the church. Traditionally, ministers study and discuss the nature and mission of the church. The missional-church perspective asserts that the church's nature *is* mission, primarily because God's nature *is* missional. The nature of the church, therefore, is seeking and following where God is already active in the world. This view sees the church in a new light, dedicated to engaging every context, particularly local culture, with a mission-shaped heart. The movement has sparked the development of organizations like the Gospel and Our Culture Network (2009) and Allelon: A Movement of Missional Leaders (2009).

Darrell Guder asserts that missional congregations embody five basic qualities: they remain biblically framed, historically grounded, contextually minded, eschatologically focused, and practiced (1998, 11-12). Each of these qualities serves an ongoing, passionate attempt to engage local and global culture. Missions may still be understood as a type of saltwater ministry, with missionaries crossing into strange and different cultures, employing cross-cultural creativity for the sake of transformation. However, missional ministers may also cross cultural boundaries just down the street, employing many of the same strategies to understand the marketplace culture of city streets

and popular technology. Local ministries often surface in quite nontraditional settings, reflecting new and renewed congregational strategies engaged in
transformational mission wherever God leads, in local or global settings. Sur-
prisingly, older, diminished congregations are finding new vitality and a new
reason for being through this approach.

Missional discipleship often begins with simple acts of hospitality, inviting people to gather and engage in service as well as discuss broader social and cultural concerns. Practice often precedes belief. People share meals,
serve others, discuss cultural issues in relation to Christian conviction, and
pray without specific invitations to accept the gospel. Moments of Emmaus
awareness do occur in the midst of these missional practices. While traditional evangelism stressed belief before belonging (one must accept the gospel
and then become assimilated into the church), missional engagement reverses
the trend, stressing belonging first (often tempered by Christian practices),
trusting that belief will follow. At times missionally minded members challenge larger social concerns, taking on projects that merge global and local, or
"glocal" concerns, such as child abuse, modern slavery, ethnic reconciliation,
advocacy for the homeless, and creation care. Such activities, often associated
with the term *peace and justice,* reflect a mind-set that action against social ills
follows a God who seeks to redeem all of creation, from the social policies that
shape human communities to the very fabric of the environment (Frost 2006,
203-72). Missionally minded discipleship invites people into these struggles,
recognizing that believer and nonbeliever can be changed as they see Christlikeness reflected in their efforts.

Youth and young adult ministers often enter into the lives of subgroups,
sometimes marginal groups, to understand and provide incarnational ministry (Ward 1999). These relationships do not serve coercive goals; simply being
present with people serves as a means for the Holy Spirit to act redemptively
within the situation as it unfolds (Root 2007, 62-80, 104-23). Moments of
service and times of thoughtful discussion open the door for deeper Christian
understanding; the service and discussion acting as means of grace, not means
to an end of inviting people into an established congregation. The church
finds itself born again in the midst of compassionate service and hospitable
conversation, particularly as Kingdom values surface and people awaken to
Christ's presence in their midst. Christian education occurs both within these
groups and in resourcing the ongoing expansion and collaboration of missional communities across local and global cultural settings.

Congregations within a Wesleyan tradition may find several points of
agreement with this movement (Blevins 2007). A missional church perspective resonates with the famous John Wesley dictum, "the world is my parish,"

and its efforts are consistent with the Wesleyan/Methodist movement. Christian historian David Hempton notes that Wesley's passion and subsequent Methodist practice were shaped by three theological themes: (1) the character of God and the nature of human responsibility; (2) the path to true spirituality containing practices (means of grace), including those of benevolence and charity; and (3) the possibility of true holiness as a scriptural injunction (2005, 57-58). In North America, the flexibility of Methodist practices and methods ensured Westward expansion through "conferences, districts, circuits, stations, and classes" (153). For all of the practices and methods, Wesleyan emphasis on expansion and mission was a grassroots effort. Hempton notes that Methodism possessed a mobile laity before the denomination had missionaries, and missionaries before it possessed mission organization. Methodism proved uniquely suited to work within rapid, international people movements fueled by trade and (British) empire building during the eighteenth and nineteenth centuries, establishing societies in the margins of the shifting social order (21).

Education served the missional heart of this ongoing movement. Russell E. Richey asserts that education provided the heart of Methodist connectionalism: the interrelated, cooperative practice of connecting different Methodist congregations and institutions together for mission and ministry. Richey notes that education, particularly colleges and seminaries, nurtured connectional relationships before the establishment of bureaucratic structures, a tendency that reflected John Wesley's proclivity for educational practices. Wesley employed a number of systems, from direct instruction for preachers to publications, book rooms, Sunday schools, and conferences, which turned Methodism into a giant classroom (2000, 57-58). Richey writes, "The activities and structures connected Methodists to Wesley and to one another. Therefore education in Methodism was connectional, and the connection was educational—and at the heart of both was Mr. Wesley" (59).

The movement often employed educational strategies as part of its missional efforts to Christianize indigenous natives in regions like West Africa. Hempton writes, "Schools supplied new generations of native preachers and teachers to continue work that white missionaries with their health frailties and cultural chauvinisms could not begin to accomplish on their own" (2005, 157). Education served mission by connecting Methodist efforts, extended mission to the next generation of indigenous ministers, and contributed to the comprehensive vision of Wesley, particularly the desire for the transformation of persons and communities into holiness. Methodist historian Richard Heitzenrater writes, "Education can thus be seen as one means of grace by which the original perfection of creation (a creature of wisdom and holiness), lost in the Fall, could be restored. The goals of this transformation in the believer is

nothing less than a recovery of the image of God, the 'one thing necessary'"
(2000, 11).

Education, like other practices, serves the larger Methodist pursuit of
holiness, a comprehensive description of Wesley's project of total transformation. Missional engagement occurs in local settings and across a global stage,
often with people on the margins of society, and education served a vital role.

The missional perspective reveals a discipleship strategy that begins and
ends in engagement. For the missional church, God's nature is God's mission.
However, the quality of missional engagement involves more than just outreach and service. Practitioners within this movement surveyed a number of
churches they identified as missionally minded to discern the core characteristics (Barrett 2004, 159-72). According to their findings, the missional church:

1. Proclaims the gospel
2. Is a community where all members are involved in learning to become disciples of Jesus
3. Accepts the Bible as normative for this church's life
4. Understands itself as different from the world because of its participation in the life, death, and resurrection of its Lord
5. Seeks to discern God's specific missional vocation for the entire
   community and for all of its members
6. Is known by how Christians behave toward one another
7. Practices reconciliation
8. Holds one another accountable in love
9. Practices hospitality
10. Accepts worship as the central act by which the community cel-
    ebrates with joy and thanksgiving God's presence and promised fu-
    ture
11. Possesses a vital public witness
12. Recognizes the church itself is an incomplete expression of the reign
    of God

A review of these core characteristics reveals a startling conclusion. Even
as missional churches raise the role of transformative engagement as the central act of God and the church, they continue to advocate for basic practices
that result in formation and discernment. In the midst of specific acts of proclamation, reconciliation, hospitality, and witness, churches are called to worship, accountability, engagement with scripture, and discernment for mission.
The missional church perspective reveals that even the most powerful expressions of transformation still live within an ecology that takes formation and
discernment seriously. Ultimately all three expressions of the congregational
life—formation, discernment, and transformation—remain interwoven in the

life of the church. Faithful discipleship acknowledges this reality. No matter where one begins—shaping Christians, seeking God's will, or advancing the kingdom of God—one must attend to all three domains for the sake of Christian education, for the sake of ministry, and for the sake of faithful discipleship.

▶ REFERENCES

Allelon: A Movement of Missional Leaders. 2009. Available online at http://allelon.org/ (accessed April 10, 2009).

Ayling, Stanley. 1979. *John Wesley.* Nashville: Abingdon Press.

Barrett, Lois Y., ed. 2004. *Treasure in Clay Jars: Patterns of Missional Faithfulness.* Grand Rapids: William B. Eerdmans.

Blevins, Dean. Between Athens and Berlin . . . and MySpace: Wesleyan reflections on theological education in a digital era. 2007. *Allelon Publishing* (February), available online at http://archives.allelon.org/articles/article.cfm?id=327 (accessed April 10, 2009).

Brelsford, Theodore. 2001. Educating for formative participation in communities of faith. In *Religious Education* 96, no. 3: 310-25.

Brueggemann, Walter. 1982. *The Creative Word: Canon as a Model for Biblical Education.* Minneapolis: Fortress Press.

Everist, Norma Cook. 2002. *The Church as Learning Community: A Comprehensive Guide to Christian Education.* Nashville: Abingdon Press.

Frost, Michael. 2006. *Exiles: Living Missionally in a Post-Christian Culture.* Peabody, MA: Hendrickson.

Gospel and Our Culture Network. 2009. Available online at http://www.gocn.org/ (accessed April 10, 2009).

Guder, Darrell L. 1998. Missional church: from sending to being sent. In *Missional Church: A Vision for the Sending of the Church in North America.* Ed. Darrell L. Guder. Grand Rapids: William B. Eerdmans.

Heitzenrater, Richard P. 1995. *Wesley and the People Called Methodists.* Nashville: Abingdon Press.

_____. 2000. Wesley and education. In *Methodism and Education: From Roots to Fulfillment,* 1-14. Ed. Sharon J. Hels. Nashville: General Board of Higher Education, United Methodist Church.

Hempton, David. 2005. *Methodism: Empire of the Spirit.* New Haven, CT: Yale Univ. Press.

Richey, Russell E. 2000. Connectionalism and college. In *Methodism and Education: From Roots to Fulfillment,* 57-76. Ed. Sharon J. Hels. Nashville: General Board of Higher Education, United Methodist Church.

Root, Andrew. 2007. *Revisiting Relational Youth Ministry: From Strategy of Influence to a Theology of Incarnation.* Downers Grove, IL: IVP Books.

Stone, Bryan. 2007. *Evangelism After Christendom: The Theology and Practice of Christian Witness.* Grand Rapids: Brazos Press.

Ward, Pete. 1999. *God at the Mall.* Peabody, MA: Hendrickson.

PART 4

PRACTICING FAITHFUL
DISCIPLESHIP

Faithful discipleship must inhabit ministries and congregations as a living theory of Christian education practice. By *practice* we suggest that Christian education—like medicine, music, or sports—is an art form that includes both sound fundamentals and daily innovation. Christian educators practice educational ministry within communities for sustained periods of time; the practice contains standards of excellence and calls for engagement with God in the midst of daily life both within and beyond the local church (Bass 1997, 6-8). As this final section unfolds, we will introduce the reader to a number of principles that shape faithful discipleship in the day-to-day life of Christian education. Many of the strategies we suggest stem from sound, current theories of Christian education. Some recommendations reflect a general understanding of discipleship in our current historical context. Think of these as best practices for the larger practice of faithful discipleship. *Part 4: Practicing Faithful Discipleship* divides into three subsections consistent with Christian education practice.

First, Christian educators approach their craft from the standpoint of the congregation as a whole, the various environments and larger structures that shape faithful discipleship. This broad view often understands Christian education as a programmatic venture with a number of responsibilities framed through large structures like the Sunday school (Haystead 1995) or small groups (Gorman 2002). This subsection focuses on how the learning environment shapes faithful teaching with specific emphasis on curriculum, both written and hidden (chapter 15). It also explores the primary contexts of faithful discipleship, Sunday school, and small groups (chapter 16).

A second, dominant strategy approaches discipleship as either a developmental/age-level issue or affecting the family at large (Burns and DeVries 2008/2001; Garland 1999; May et al. 2005; Wickett 1991). While a bit restrictive, this developmental approach allows Christian educators to frame discipleship within the specific contexts and challenges of children, youth, adults, or the family in general. This second section focuses on how practicing shapes understanding of age-level (children, youth, adult) and family ministries (chapters 17—20).

A final approach begins with the Christian educator as a professional minister and shepherd (Stubblefield 1993). This approach allows for more in-depth exploration of the roles and responsibilities of leaders in discipleship formation and growth. The section addresses how good practice involves Christian educators in specific areas of leadership: administration, legal considerations, and leadership (chapters 21—23).

▶ REFERENCES

Bass, Dorothy, ed. 1998. *Practicing Our Faith: A Way of Life for a Searching People*. San Francisco: Jossey-Bass.

Burns, Jim, with Mark DeVries. 2008. *Uncommon Youth Ministry: Your Onramp to Launching an Extraordinary Youth Ministry*. Ventura, CA: Regal/Gospel Light. Originally published, Jim Burns and Mark DeVries. 2002. *The Youth Builder*. Ventura, CA: Gospel Light.

Garland, Diana R. 1999. *Family Ministry: A Comprehensive Guide*. Downers Grove, IL: InterVarsity Press.

Gorman, Julie A. 2002. *Community That Is Christian*. 2nd ed. Grand Rapids: Baker Books.

Haystead, Wes. 1995. *21st Century Sunday School: Strategies for Today and Tomorrow*. Cincinnati: Standard Publishing.

May, Scottie, Beth Posterski, Catherine Stonehouse, and Linda Cannell. 2005. *Children Matter: Celebrating Their Place in the Church, Family, and Community*. Grand Rapids: William B. Eerdmans.

Stubblefield, Jerry. 1993. *The Effective Minister of Education*. Nashville: B&H Academic.

Wickett, R. E. Y. 1991. *Models of Adult Religious Education Practice*. Birmingham, AL: Religious Education Press.

ENVIRONMENTS OF FAITHFUL DISCIPLESHIP
Chapters 15—16

These chapters review the major contexts where faithful discipleship practice takes place. Chapter 15 explores the physical, relational, and even technological environments that shape effective teaching and learning. The organization of safe and secure educational space is critical to effective teaching. In addition, alternative learning environments allow for discipleship beyond the walls of the local congregation. Well-designed learning environments demonstrate God's care through rituals of care and community building. Technology also raises new opportunities for faithful discipleship in an online, virtual learning environment.

Chapter 16 explores the organization of Sunday schools and small groups. Historically, Sunday schools have provided one of the primary contexts for practicing faithful discipleship. Today Sunday schools still play a significant educational function, but teaching centers now focus on relationship and community building. Small groups play a significant role in faithful discipleship as people gather to deepen relationships and to shape faith. These groups have a wide variety of functions and purposes. Given our Wesleyan theological lens, this chapter also focuses on Wesley's group formation process and how it can inform faithful discipleship today.

FIFTEEN

LEARNING ENVIRONMENTS

▶ INTRODUCTION

Imagine you are asked to evaluate the children's ministry wing of a local church. What would you look for to ensure a safe environment and sound educational space?

Imagine that a young adult class approaches you about meeting at an alternative time for their Sunday school class, in a setting other than the church building. What guidelines might you give them?

When church leaders discuss the quality of their learning environments, evaluation often focuses on the availability of space and the quality of furnishings. Such considerations may serve as a beginning point, but a quality educational environment, one conducive to discipleship, must take into consideration both physical and relational concerns. Norma Cook Everist notes "effective teaching depends upon creating a setting in which we can be present—really present—with one another in safe, healthy, trustworthy ways" (2002, 61). Our responsibility involves not only the availability of space but also the availability of people during a learning experience. Mike King argues that one of our primary responsibilities rests with cultivating learning environments where creativity and relational empowerment allows the Holy Spirit to empower teachers and learners for faithful discipleship (2006, 86-97). Learning occurs best in an environment that communicates a sense of hospitality, safety, and comfort.

▶ PHYSICAL SPACE

Christian educators traditionally have addressed physical space requirements within the church building. While discipleship may occur in a number of settings, churches often set aside specific facilities to enable learning at a developmental level. Many of these endeavors have followed public school recommendations, often a helpful starting point. In almost any period of modern Christian education one will find administrative handbooks that provide recommendations for room size, age-appropriate furnishings and equipment, decorations, resources, technology, and storage or resource space (Blazier and Isham 1993; Haystead and Haystead 2000; Krau 1989; Whited and Whitworth 2003). Many of the recommendations include space for activities and the number of teachers needed in each setting. For instance, Wes and Sheryl Haystead offer basic guidelines for room size and occupancy based on the following formulas (2000, 201-3; see figure 15.1).

Figure 15.1

Room Specifications

Age-Group	Space Per Person	Maximum Attendance	Room Size	Teacher: Learner Ratio
Early Childhood				
Ages 0 through 12 mo.	30 to 35 sq. ft.	12 to 15	900 sq. ft.	1:3 or 4
Ages 1 through 3	30 to 35 sq. ft.	16 to 20	700 to 900 sq. ft.	1:5
Ages 4 through 5	30 to 35 sq. ft.	20 to 24	800 to 900 sq. ft.	1:6
Children				
Grades 1 to 5 (ages 6 through 11)	25 to 30 sq. ft.	24 to 30	800 to 900 sq. ft.	1:6 to 8
Youth				
Grades 6 to 12 (ages 12 through 18)	20 to 25 sq. ft.	30 to 40	900 sq. ft.	1:8
Adults				
Ages 18+	10 to 15 sq. ft.	30 to 40	450 sq. ft.	1:8

Often such resources suggest arrangements based on teaching goals, including the arrangement of tables, location of shelving, strategies for subdividing a room into learning centers, and so forth. Such suggestions might seem ideal or idealized (depending on the size and resources of the local congregation), and they are often geared to Western cultural assumptions. However, these guidelines serve as helpful reference points when conceptualizing educational usage.

Instead of specific room arrangements, Christian educators do well to incorporate several operating principles when considering the physical quality of the learning environment. For instance, Evelyn Johnson and Bobbie Bower developed a simple phrase, SCANR, that they believe helps guide children's space design: Safe, Clean, Attractive, and Neat so that they will Return (1992, 68-81). While such memory devices may seem helpful only for administrative oversight, several key concerns surface through this simple formula.

SAFETY

One of the key concerns in any physical setting, the church building or other settings, rests with the issue of safety. This often includes the quality of the building, its cleanliness, and security measures. Children and parents need assurance that the learning environment includes durable, age-level-appropriate furnishings. They need to know that harmful resources are kept out of reach of children or youth. Children need to be kept safe from infection and disease as much as possible through cleaning toys and rooms between uses. Today similar concerns relate to children's snacks and food allergies and the cleanliness of bathrooms. Christian educators need simple but effective guidelines that address how to act during dangerous weather, fire, or other disaster. Ministers are habitually vigilant with designated children's areas, but they often overlook the same concerns in other parts of the building where children go with their parents. The safety measures needed in the children's section should govern other public spaces: fellowship halls, church foyers, and church buses. These same considerations need to be given to the use of homes, businesses, and other public spaces where church activities may occur.

Security for children and youth is a primary issue. Careful discernment of those who work with children and youth represents a growing concern in church polity, in light of the ongoing struggle with child abuse (as will be discussed in relation to legal issues; see chapter 22). General principles need to be in place to assist child screening and reporting guidelines. Churches may feel overwhelmed when implementing a prepackaged child security program, though a number of corrections may be made through a simple security audit. One model for evaluating your church's security environment involves five questions (Blevins 2006):

1. *Name five times a child might be unsupervised in your church.* What you are looking for are those places where children are released long enough to disappear from parental (or supervisory) view. Often these include moments when children depart from the main foyer for church school, go to a bathroom unattended, wait for a parent who is in a meeting, and so forth. One church discovered that parents releasing children from the sanctuary during worship for a bathroom break assumed the ushers would supervise them. Follow-up questions revealed that the ushers did not even stay in the hallways.

2. *Name five blind spots, or places children might be kept from sight.* All churches provide unmonitored, out of the way places (empty offices, corners in hallways, prayer rooms, libraries, etc.) where a child might be trapped, even unintentionally. A simple walk-through often reveals a number of surprising closets, classrooms, and even kitchens left unlocked and unattended during part of the church day.

3. *How many doors do you have through which an adult could remove a child in five steps?* One church I know coupled their sanctuary with an existing manufacturing building (renovated as educational space). In one hallway, adjacent to the children's rooms, there were five doors that led directly outside the building. In that circumstance the church had at least three doors an adult could reach in less than five steps. This was quite a shock to the auditors. Often we think such doors remain guarded, if only casually, by greeters. However, they are often left unattended at various times of the day. Backdoors to kitchens, side doors to the sanctuary, and basement emergency exits often qualify.

4. *Name five potential flash points where children often mingle informally with youth or adults.* Many churches provide nurseries on major hallways, which become jammed with people before and after worship. In one setting the youth group used the children's church space for Sunday school, so senior high youth and children roamed through the same door during transitions. Fellowship dinners might not seem to qualify, but kids often engage strangers at these events, assuming everyone must be a part of the church.

5. *Name five new faces in the congregation that you cannot identify after checking with three people.* Actually, many people in a church are known by someone active in the congregation. Greeters might know that the person came in the door with a relative. People at an information desk might know that a newcomer attended a particular Sunday school class, and you can check with the teacher. Can a person arrive and leave, formally or informally, without being known?

Impromptu audits during a walk-through of the facility by a group can identify potential trouble areas. Resolving these issues before problems occur provides an environment that frees Christian educators from troubling distractions like lawsuits (Crabtree 2008, 27-39). More important, such interventions demonstrate stewardship of our concern for the well-being of all God's people.

LEARNER FRIENDLY

In addition to providing a safe and secure setting, physical spaces need to be learner friendly. Often, Christian educators either struggle with out-of-date facilities or contend with new construction that resists rigorous use. Churches do not always consider educational issues when conceiving new facilities, even when children or youth are the focus of the development. Architects and building committees focus on presentation, not functionality. I (Dean) remember a church that renovated the educational wing of the church. The building committee remarked how modern the rooms appeared, like a convention center. However, the walls were painted a muted maroon tone that smudged easily, new facility guidelines prohibited placing personal artwork or posters on the walls, and resources were reduced to offset renovation costs. Rather than creating a vibrant space for children with bright colors, posters, and developmentally appropriate resources, toddlers to elementary kids became strangers in the very rooms they had previously occupied.

Spaces must be developed with the learner in mind. Too often, artwork or shelving is placed at adult height, even in children's classrooms. I often ask adult teachers to navigate their classrooms on their knees to see the room from the perspective of the child. The placement of artwork and resources at a child's height indicates that adults intend the space to serve children. Sufficient space must be given for different learning activities. Rooms may require carpets to reduce noise and protect children when they fall. Materials need to be organized and accessible when needed. Children's rooms need to be located close to adequate restrooms and incorporate access to resources like running water and storage. Christian educators often divide a room into learning centers that children can begin using when they first arrive, rather than sitting and waiting for a large class activity. Centers can be created for different learning styles or interests: artwork, reading, music, storytelling, and games that reinforce the story of God.

For youth and adults, chairs need to be arranged to match the style of teaching. Chairs arranged in a circle, V-shape, or elongated U allow students to see and speak to one another and the teacher. Rooms for senior adults should accommodate losses in mobility, hearing, and eyesight. Small churches sometimes hold senior adult classes in the sanctuary, which is large and often dimly lit—the most counterproductive location in the building for the learning process. Physical space must serve educational needs whenever possible.

SPECIAL POPULATIONS

In addition to traditional settings for learning, congregations now recognize their responsibility to make facilities open to special populations with disabilities or exceptional needs. Many congregations appear loving but are unprepared for these challenges, whether the issues surface through birth, as a result of a tragic accident, or emerge late in life. Churches would do well to conduct accessibility reviews on a regular basis. Physical concerns include points of access to the building, worship and educational settings, bathrooms throughout the facility, parking, ramps, signage, and water fountains.

In large churches the responsibility for facility review may fall to maintenance or housekeeping staff. In other settings lay leadership through the church board or subcommittee may have oversight. Nevertheless, Christian educators should accept responsibility for occasional review of facilities in order to ensure a reasonable learning environment. Maintaining a checklist like the one offered below helps to avoid overlooking a key area of responsibility.

Figure 15.2

Facility Review Checklist						
Room Number or Designated Area	Educational Ministry (Age-Level or Other)	Adequate and Accessible Space	Appropriate Furnishings and Storage	Equipment Needed and Working	Proximity Issues (Bathrooms, etc.)	Safety or Security Issues

ALTERNATIVE LOCATIONS

Efforts are now being made to provide evangelism and discipleship in nontraditional locations, known in North American settings as third places (Frost 2006, 56-63), which include popular gathering spaces other than home or work. These locations are distinctive yet informal, with diverse contacts yet a sense of being at home. Following the work of Ray Oldenburg, missiologist Michael Frost suggests that these places create a sense of community and companionship as people relax, feel connected to one another, and enjoy a deep sense of place (2006).

Such gatherings are crucial in North American settings where many people feel isolated. Robert Putnam offers a provocative and disturbing observation here. Drawing from a wide array of research studies (including over 500,000 interviews from the last quarter century), Putnam notes:

> For the first two-thirds of the twentieth century a powerful tide bore Americans into ever deeper engagement in the life of their communities, but a few decades ago—silently, without warning—that tide reversed and we were overtaken by a treacherous rip current. Without at

first noticing, we have been pulled apart from one another and from our communities over the last third of the [twentieth] century. (2000, 27)

Putnam calls this a loss of "social capital" in civic groups or more informal gatherings of friends and families. We are more isolated and less inclined to socialize in almost all settings other than work. However, Putnam's follow-up research finds new settings for community in branch libraries, neighborhood initiatives, school clubs, professional settings, on the Internet, and, yes, in churches (2003).

While these are diverse settings, Frost asserts that several common features characterize third places. Regardless of interpersonal issues, Christian educators may find it striking that physical location and amenities are important characteristics for such settings:

- They must be free or quite inexpensive.
- Food and drink, though not absolutely essential, are important factors.
- They must be highly accessible to neighborhoods so that people find it easy to make the place a regular part of their routine.
- A lot of people should be able to comfortably walk to the place from their home.
- They should be places where a number of people regularly go on a daily basis.
- They should be places where a person feels welcome and comfortable and where it is easy to enter into conversation.
- A person should expect to find both old and new friends on each trip to the place. (2006, 57-58)

Several concerns should be addressed when preparing for educational ministry in such settings. Ministers cannot overlook issues of safety, security, and accessibility. Permission should be secured from the third place for group meetings, particularly those with a specific agenda (Bible study, accountability, ministry preparation) where group dynamics might close participation to others in the third place. Certain choices may also exclude church members who might not attend because of the setting. Christian educators need to be attentive to the overall purpose of the third place, whether to serve food or engage in paid recreation and attempt to adapt to the culture of the location as much as possible by Christian standards. They must demonstrate respect and consideration if they hope that faithful discipleship will occur in such settings.

Third places illustrate faithful discipleship that occurs beyond the church walls. Christian educators need to maintain a parish mind-set, seeing the entire neighborhood as part of the learning environment (Everist 2002, 74-75; see chapter 14). Ministers should seek to ensure the safety and security of the neighborhood, provide resources, engage community concerns, and work to provide a hospitable learning environment for people who live near the church, the parish. If the church understands that classrooms, families, and communities all provide places for learning, similar strategies may guide faithful discipleship. Expanding our horizon of learning environments allows us to ask broader questions about work among churches, communities, nations, and around the globe (76-81).

▶ RELATIONAL SPACE

Alternative locations like third places also remind Christian educators that the relational environment is just as important as physical conditions when securing a sound learning environment. Christian educators use a number of factors when discussing relationships: respect for time, authority, emotional awareness, intellectual challenge, interpersonal boundaries, and social/cultural challenges (Everist 2002, 81-91). How we receive people, motivate them to learn and grow, and release them for ministry frame our efforts as much as the walls and ceilings of our physical locations. More important, they remind us of basic human practices that shape community in any setting, from the traditional classroom to the Acacia tree.

MAKING GOD'S CARE VISIBLE

Charles Foster notes that volunteer teachers often face the task of ensuring they not only teach but also create an environment of care that "makes God's care visible" even before the lesson begins (1986, 34). While concerned to some degree with the physical environment, Foster considers the relational environment central to resolving this issue, and offers a series of key indicators:

People know they are expected: The learning environment is prepared for those who come (similar to SCANR, rooms are ready for learners). People are greeted as they arrive through physical gestures and attentive listening. In short, we pay attention to people as they enter the learning environment.

People feel at home: Foster recommends that the physical environment include indicators of belonging through personalized objects such as photos, posters, or other small additions. Offer opportunities to express personal issues of importance, perhaps in preparation for prayer, and to socialize over special outings, class meals, or other social gatherings.

Activities respect people's interest and abilities: The educational content varies to accommodate different learning tendencies and specific issues. The teacher provides content that addresses differing needs among the class, if only at strategic moments. Educators should give specific attention to time constraints and other issues that inhibit learning.

We let students know what we expect of them: Clear ground rules help a class know the expectation of their time together. Often shaped in the language of explicit or implicit covenants, clear expectations free students to know how to respond when creativity or conflict may challenge the learning environment. (36-43)

Foster notes that environments that make God's care visible extend through caring actions, both within community and by the teacher. Learning environments demonstrate a relational richness as communities extend care to one another. Often this care comes through simple rituals that bind people together and intensify their relationships (47). Ritual actions do not require ornate activities but point to basic practices that embody meaning. Ritual interactions occur throughout nature and often, among humans, fuse meaningful action with narratives of life and belonging (Anderson and Foley 1998, 20-32). Foster suggests a simple sequence that typically occurs as groups interact over significant events (pleasurable or painful):

1. A situation or event is announced (so everyone has the same information).
2. The group responds to the announcement (giving congratulations or condolences).
3. A "blessing" is given (often by a designated or impromptu leader, recognizing God's presence in celebration, for healing, for strength).
4. Those involved in the situation are given opportunity to respond (so that those directly affected by the event and attention have opportunity to respond to the grace extended by others). (1986, 48)

Simple actions like celebrating birthdays or mourning the loss of loved ones take on special meaning when people employ ritual actions. Such practices celebrate passages and help people cope with crisis; they also reinforce group identity and organize the corporate life of the group. When a class or group engages in regular activities that incorporate special meaning, they grow together. Foster encourages actions by teachers that extend God's care through prayer and discernment, as well as by preparing oneself spirituality (53-58). God's care extends through Christian educators as they relinquish themselves to God's guidance in order to be means of grace for their communities. Developing such openness also allows the Christian educator to facilitate relationships within the learning environment as relationships change over time, guiding groups to remain open to other persons.

FACILITATING RELATIONSHIPS WITHIN AND BEYOND COMMUNITY

When people sing together, laugh and cry together, pray together, and even suffer through conflict together, they grow pretty comfortable with one another. These experiences reflect a normal part of a social-psychological process associated with just about any class or group. Most small-group experts chart at least four phases of transition in community development.

- *Tentative or pseudo-community:* This first phase (the honeymoon phase) exists in small groups when people want to have community but do not know one another very well. The phase includes people intent on being nice, even if they have not sorted out their expectations. Christian educators often focus on facilitating clarity and depth communication at this stage to encourage people to move past simple attachments.

- *Storming community:* The second phase is one of the most difficult as people sort out individual roles. Certain people try to control group processes, or at least impose their assumptions and expectations on the group. While this is a time of conflict, confrontations should be honest, not hostile, as the group sorts out the type of community they truly want to be. Christian educators should remain patient during this phase, avoid personal allegiances, and focus the group on their covenant purpose for gathering (see chapter 14). Often the most difficult phase, some groups disband during the storming phase because of the church's discomfort with conflict.

- *Norming community:* If the group reaches this level, it includes a kind of letting go of personal agendas and really listening to other people in the group. Group members do not identify particular winners and losers but accept a mutual meeting of minds and hearts over the group's identity. Christian educators often focus on the vision of the community, reminding people of specific gifts and graces each possess to accomplish their shared goals.

- *Performing community:* At this phase the group is in sync as they work together for the kingdom of God. Never a static phase, groups need ongoing renewal and challenge to keep them vibrant and open to the future. Christian educators balance celebration with challenge, often helping groups negotiate their future and often anticipate their ending.

As noted, not all groups progress through all four phases, particularly in church cultures that do not know how to deal with constructive conflict (see chapter 23). Relationships fragment and dissolve if group members cannot let go of personal agendas.

However, there is an even greater danger for groups that survive but fail to thrive. A small group can develop into a *clique* rather than a community. The term *clique* normally defines an informal group, often formed by mutual social interests but exclusive of other people. Some groups at the first phase become cliques to avoid conflict. Other groups may survive all four stages but still develop cliquish attitudes and behaviors. When a small group closes its boundaries, new people have a difficult, if not impossible, time connecting with the group. These petrified communities are networks of frozen and brittle relationships. How do Christian educators avoid isolation in group formation? How can groups that survive the four phases of community formation thrive and embrace new people and new possibilities?

No matter how tight-knit a small group might be, true Christian community is willing to receive others, including those with social or cultural differences, because of God's missional nature. Christian educators must include rituals of hospitality commensurate with their settings that help groups invite new people. Inclusiveness, however, means more than mere invitation. Community members must also be willing to seek out new people and extend table fellowship or other forms of hospitality. The early church recognized that we must be willing to cross the borders of social, economic, and cultural boundaries to ensure that everyone who desires it experiences the quality of fellowship Christ has to offer (see Acts 6:1-7). Authentic community occurs when relationships extend outward as means of grace to the larger world. Such movement opens the relational space for new learning from others who may be perceived as strangers by the existing group. In the same way that people explore new physical locations, third places, as potential learning environments, they must also accept new relationships as means of grace in the learning process.

▶ "VIRTUAL" SPACE: LEANING ENVIRONMENTS IN A TECHNOLOGICAL WORLD

Relatively recent developments, particularly in communication technology, open new learning environments that pose new challenges to current understandings of physical and relational space. The Internet and social networking strategies through computers-based Web sites, online gaming, and even cell phones need further exploration as new learning environments (Blevins 2008). Technologies that rarely existed in North American homes just a few years ago now dominate most households (Digital Future 2004, 97). People are discovering multiple intersections between the Internet and religion (Last 2005, 34-40). Developmental psychologists explore online issues of identity, self-worth, sexuality, and health behaviors (Greenfield and Yan 2006, 391). Blogging involves identity building more than previous media (like television), which approached viewers as passive consumers. Adolescents online "are basically co-constructing their own environments" (392).

Christian educators tend to approach these new environments cautiously, often concerned with technology's ability to impede rather than extend faithful discipleship. Thomas de Zengotita argues that our understanding of humanity begins to blur between reality and media construction (2005, 270-72). Children and youth are subjected to a delusional form of self-flattery and niceness through media that robs their sense of true competence and diverts their desire to engage the complex, fluid world as adults (73-110). This form of mediated flattery (which avoids hard assessments) results in "adultolescence" where people prefer a mediated, constructed personhood (an avatar) to facing the daily conditions of the world and their own lives, refusing to "get a life" (181-90). Richard Gaillardetz questions whether technology risks distracting us from the ordinary yet essential engagements in our lives that lead to spiritual growth and become "meditations of grace and occasions of divine blessing" (2000, 27). Marva Dawn links technology with consumer preoccupation (2003, 1-60; 1995). Both authors invoke social theorist Albert Borgmann's technological paradigm in which technological devices serve as "focal things" around which people order their practices (Gaillardetz 2000, 23) and their lives rather than cultivating "focal concerns" of love of God and love of neighbor (Dawn 2003, 41-60, 79).

Quentin Schultze offers an equally measured but more cautionary treatment of the spiritual life in an otherwise high-tech world (2002). Schultze suggests that technology presents a moral challenge. He encourages practitioners to engage technology through a series of virtues—moderation, wisdom, humility, and authenticity—in order to raise the moral issues behind technological technique, while staying supported by a community that gives life to these virtues. While acknowledging the potential for technology, Schultze sees more challenge than support in the digital universe. In advocating a heart-felt life, Schultze suggests that technology needs to be held lightly at best:

> After we first *admit the lightness of our digital being,* we should *distrust the prevailing techno-magic* that promises us unrealistic benefits from cyber-technologies. We should also *de-technologize our religious traditions* by ridding them of excessive technique and renewing their virtue-nurturing practices. Thankfully accepting our inheritance of the created world, we should *responsibly serve God and neighbor. Inviting friendship* is one of the most fitting means of cultivating moral relationships. Finally, we should *sojourn with heart* through life. (2002, 190, italics original)

Each italicized phrase represents either prohibitive or proactive practices for Schultze, who urges a deeply moral engagement with technology that will avoid a surface, or tourist, understanding of it. For Schultze, the challenge rests with the individual to strenuously hold technology at a respectful distance lest our preoccupations transform us into "mere thieves and beggars" (206).

With these cautions in mind, developing technology has the potential to offer vital and vibrant learning environments. Online resources allow youth to collect and distribute health information globally for the sake of marginal communities (Greenfield and Yan 2006, 393). Some youth use social networking to fight other forms of injustice, such as slavery, or to promote creation care (Rymer 2007). Blog sites allow for alternative modes of identity construction, reminiscent of earlier forms of journaling, but with unique elements of immediate feedback that potentially offset self-deception (Blevins 2007b).

Continuing research is revealing positive outcomes through distance learning when it is offered in a way that respects the strengths of this learning environment. Original suspicions seem to be giving way to the potential for constructive educational practices. The use of Internet technology may offer new opportunities to empower transformative ministry at the very margins of society, reminiscent of the early Wesleyan movement (Blevins 2007a).

The advent of new, technologically shaped, learning environments presents both challenges and opportunities, but technology should always serve deeper issues of Christian practice and Christian virtues. Christian educators engaging this environment may want to keep three basic principles in mind (Blevins 2008).

1. Technology should be an extension of, rather than a replacement for, human activity. Technology must foster a deeper sense of *relationality*, both within and among human beings. Technology that opens people to self-awareness and to an interpersonal appreciation of others provides a faithful form of technological practice.

2. New technology that replaces older versions should always be viewed with a sense of *contextuality* that includes both history and context (Hipps 2005, 41-43). Christian educators need to explore potential social consequences (both positive contributions and unexpected outcomes). In short, technological practice should resist any sense of decontextualization or commodification that separates it from history, heritage, and social implications. Vincent Miller argues that consumers need to recognize the historical and cultural context behind each consumable product (2003). Similarly, Christian educators need to ask key questions: How does the technology provide a sense of historical continuity? What is the quality of the social setting around the technological practice?

3. Technology should foster a deeper sense of *complexity* (at least complex practice) that invites empowerment through practice. Christian educators should avoid technology that prohibits participation through intimidation (requiring a level of necessary mastery) or results in passive consumption that subverts any sense of developmental growth and empowerment. While not a universal mandate, technology that

encourages human production rather than passive consumption may prove to be faithful technological practice.

With these guidelines in place, Christian educators may be able to enjoy the benefits of engaging this learning environment as much as the physical and relational spaces that shape other settings.

▶ CONCLUSION

Christian educators need to consider how faithful discipleship takes place within different learning environments shaped by physical, relational, and technological influences. Providing safety and security for learners, including the special people God graciously entrusts to congregations, ensures that physical environments will enhance the learning process, whether inside or beyond the church building. Shaping learning that communicates God's care and binds people together relationally while helping them stay open to new opportunities ensures a healthy relational environment that also stimulates learning. Recognizing the strengths and limits of technology ensures wise use of virtual learning environments. Collectively these environments open the possibility for faithful discipleship both within and beyond the life of the congregation or local ministry.

▶ REFERENCES

Anderson, Herbert, and Edward Foley. 1998. *Mighty Stories, Dangerous Rituals: Weaving Together the Human and the Divine.* San Francisco: Jossey-Bass.

Blazier, Kenneth D., and Linda R. Isham, eds. 1993. *The Teaching Church at Work: A Manual for the Board of Christian Education.* Rev. ed. Valley Forge, PA: Judson Press.

Blevins, Dean G. 2006. Take five: Jumpstarting your child safety program. In *Children's Teacher* 14, no. 1 (fall): 33-34.

———. 2007a. Between Athens and Berlin . . . and MySpace: Wesleyan reflections on theological education in a digital era. *Allelon Publishing* (February). Available online at http://archives.allelon.org/missional_journey/?p=33 (accessed April 22, 2009).

———. 2007b. Story telling or storied telling? Media's pedagogical ability to shape narrative as a form of "knowing." In *Religious Education* 102, no. 3 (summer): 250-63.

———. 2008. Technology and the transformation of persons. In *Christian Education Journal,* Series 3, vol. 5, no. 1 (spring): 138-53.

Bower, Bobbie, and Evelyn M. Johnson. 1992. *Building a Great Children's Ministry.* Nashville: Abingdon Press.

Crabtree, Jack. 2008. *Better Safe than Sued: Keeping Your Students and Ministry Alive.* Grand Rapids: Zondervan Youth Specialties.

Dawn, Marva J. 1995. *Reaching Out Without Dumbing Down: A Theology of Worship for This Urgent Time*. Grand Rapids: William B. Eerdmans.

―――. 2003. *Unfettered Hope: A Call to Faithful Living in an Affluent Society*. Louisville, KY: Westminster/John Knox Press.

de Zengotita, Thomas. 2005. *Mediated: How the Media Shapes Your World and the Way You Live in It*. London: Bloomsbury.

The Digital Future Report, Surveying the Digital Future, Year Four, Ten Years Ten Trends. 2004. USC Annenburg School for the Digital Future. Available online at http://www.digitalcenter.org/downloads/DigitalFutureReport-Year4-2004.pdf (accessed April 22, 2009).

Everist, Norma Cook. 2002. *The Church as Learning Community: A Comprehensive Guide to Christian Education*. Nashville: Abingdon Press.

Frost, Michael. 2006. *Exiles: Living Missionally in a Post-Christian Culture*. Peabody, MA: Hendrickson.

Gaillardetz, Richard R. 2000. *Transforming Our Days: Spirituality, Community and Liturgy in a Technological Culture*. New York: Crossroads Books.

Greenfield, Patricia, and Zheng Yan. 2006. Children, adolescents, and the Internet: a new field of inquiry in developmental psychology. In *Developmental Psychology* 42, no. 3: 391-94.

Haystead, Wes, and Sheryl Haystead. 2000. *How to Have a Great Sunday School*. Ventura, CA: Gospel Light.

Hipps, Shane. 2005. *The Hidden Power of Electronic Culture: How Media Shapes Faith, the Gospel, and Church*. Grand Rapids: Zondervan.

King, Mike. 2006. *Presence-Centered Youth Ministry: Guiding Students into Spiritual Formation*. Downers Grove, IL: IVP Books.

Krau, Carol Fouts, ed. 1989. *Planning for Christian Education: A Practical Guide for Your Congregation*. Nashville: Discipleship Resources.

Last, Jonathan V. 2005. God on the Internet. In *First Things* 158 (December): 34-40.

Miller, Vincent J. 2003. *Consuming Religion: Christian Faith and Practice in Consumer Culture*. New York: Continuum.

Putnam, Robert. 2000. *Bowling Alone: The Collapse and Revival of American Community*. New York: Simon and Schuster.

Putnam, Robert, and Lewis M. Feldstein. 2003. *Better Together: Restoring the American Community*. New York: Simon and Schuster.

Rymer, Sally. 2007. Clapham sect phase II. Available online at http://csp2justiceseekers.com/8.html (accessed April 17, 2009).

Schultze, Quentin J. 2002. *Habits of the High-Tech Heart: Living Virtuously in the Information Age*. Grand Rapids: Baker Academic.

Whited, Linda R., and David Whitworth. 2003. *The Ministry of Christian Education and Formation: A Practical Guide for Your Congregation*. Nashville: Discipleship Resources.

Wuthnow, Robert. 1996. *Sharing the Journey: Support Groups and the Quest for a New Community*. New York: Free Press.

―――. 2001. *I Come Away Stronger: How Small Groups Are Shaping American Religion*. Grand Rapids: William B. Eerdmans.

SIXTEEN

CONGREGATIONAL CONTEXT AND SMALL GROUPS

▶ INTRODUCTION

Imagine you are serving as a Christian education director and have been asked to develop a small-group ministry for your church. You have some experience in small groups, but you are not sure what kinds of groups would be best in your context. Where would you begin in assessing need? What would be their primary purposes?

Imagine you are in charge of the Sunday school ministries of your local church. Classes during the traditional Sunday morning hour are declining in membership. Most of the adult classes are in master teacher format, which focuses on lecture and instruction and does not meet relational needs. How can you repurpose Sunday school to address these concerns and needs?

Imagine you participate in a small group on a weekly basis. The group has existed for several months and includes some of your close friends. The central content of the group is Bible study, fellowship, and prayer. The group seems to be working well, but frustration is growing because the group lacks a clear purpose and covenant to guide process. What is the purpose of your group? What aspects of covenant need to be established for the group to function more efficiently? How will you help the group explore these questions?

Faithful discipleship takes place in all aspects of congregational life. As people participate in the worship, teaching, service, and mission of a local church, lives are formed and transformed. Congregations have a wide range of contexts for faith and spiritual formation, and many congregations organize and plan their discipleship programs around age-level categories of children, youth, and adult ministries. Each of these discipleship programs has unique qualities that address the developmental needs and challenges of each group. The next several chapters will explore these important ministry areas, but it is important to see these individual ministry areas as part of the broader discipleship ministries of the church.

Discipleship, organized around these three age-level ministries, often takes place on Sunday morning through traditional Sunday school ministries and programs, providing the primary avenue for education and formation. Other discipleship ministries take place in more nontraditional times, such as

Sunday or Wednesday evenings or during the week in Bible study and other small groups. Faithful discipleship includes planning, organizing, and implementing both traditional and nontraditional ministries.

▶ SUNDAY SCHOOL

The Sunday school served as the primary context of discipleship for more than two hundred years and remains the major teaching arm of many evangelical churches. Sunday schools exist to communicate a divinely given message and to pass on the Christian faith (Borchert 1990, 623). It includes opportunity for evangelism as well as community development. Sunday school continues to develop disciples, deepen faith, build character, and provide awareness of the role of the church in the world. It is the longest-lasting vital religious movement in American protestant history (624). As Sunday schools declined in recent years, evangelical congregations responded with a variety of ministries to meet educational needs. Vacation Bible school, small groups, Christian camping, retreats, and conferences serve as alternatives in Christian discipleship.

Age-level departments (children, youth, and adult Sunday school) provide the overarching framework for congregational discipleship that is designed to plan, organize, promote, and conduct the ministry of teaching. Ministries for each age level may include Sunday morning classes and specific programming and activities (e.g., Caravan ministry, vacation Bible school, youth activities, and Bible study) that encompass aspects of leadership development, continuing education, and Bible study. Along with the preaching ministry of the local church, Sunday school ministries provide the core of the church's education in scripture, faith development, and theology. Whether classes meet on Sunday morning at the church or other times in other settings, Sunday schools still provide one of the primary contexts for the teaching ministry of the church.

THEOLOGY OF SUNDAY SCHOOL

A theology of Sunday school starts with viewing classes as communities of grace. Through sharing community together, class members live and share grace. These communities of grace provide four primary aspects of Christian discipleship: learning, fellowship, service, and evangelism.

First, people engage scripture for contemporary life (learning). Sunday school provides a safe environment where people can read, interpret, and apply scripture. Sunday school, in this regard, serves as the primary teaching office of the local church. People meet on a regular basis to interpret the ancient truths of scripture and apply them to contemporary life. Faithful discipleship includes using appropriate teaching methods to make the Bible pertinent for everyday life, especially in a postmodern, changing culture.

Second, people develop relationships with Christ and others (fellowship). Sunday schools as communities of grace provide a context for developing connection and friendships with other believers. People share personal needs and prayer requests. Sunday school may include activities and times of fellowship outside of the formal classroom setting where community develops. People grow in their relationship with God as they study the Bible and pray together. Sunday school provides spiritual accountability for people to bear one another's burdens and celebrate God's grace.

Third, people participate in service and ministry to others (service). As communities of grace, Sunday schools, care for one another and minister to people in the community. Sunday school classes practice social holiness through helping the needy, serving on mission trips, and addressing the social and justice issues of society. In this regard, Sunday school classes become missional, engaged in God's redemptive work in the world.

Fourth, transformation takes place as people encounter the living Word of God (evangelism). Sunday school communities of grace create space to invite people to accept the saving grace of Jesus Christ. Sunday school, especially for children and youth, can be a context in which people make a decision to be a follower of Jesus Christ. Sunday school is a place where seekers can explore and encounter the reality of the gospel message (Haystead and Haystead 2000, 16).

Faithful discipleship takes place through Sunday school classes where people feel welcomed, accepted, and experience the grace of God. Sunday schools as communities of grace provide a context for learning from scripture, building significant relationships with others and God, participating in service to the community, and providing opportunities for evangelism. These primary aspects of Sunday school provide the Christian educator with a balanced approach to faithful discipleship.

BIBLE STRATEGIES FOR EFFECTIVE SUNDAY SCHOOL

Congregations must develop strategies and plans for effective Sunday school programs. These strategies, while not inclusive, provide Christian educators with a framework to revitalize and maintain healthy Sunday schools.

First, congregations should cultivate a relationship between Sunday school and congregational life. Congregational life is primarily concerned with how the community, as a whole, forms and shapes faith. The teaching ministry of the church provides an important link to congregational formation, including worship (Hemphill 1996, 26). It should be viewed as an integral part of worship, preaching, and service. The pastor's commitment to Sunday school is critical to its success. A pastor who participates in, supports, and celebrates Sunday school increases its effectiveness.

Second, understand the distinct needs of learners and provide appropriate teaching methodologies. Teachers and leaders need to understand the unique needs of their students and provide teaching methodologies that engage the learner.

Third, recognize the distinct purposes of Sunday school classes. Classes may be more teacher-centered or student-centered. Some focus more on teaching and learning while others focus more on community and building relationships. Christian educators need to determine the primary purpose of each class for each age-group.

Fourth, create a context for affirmation and assimilation. Making God's care visible creates an environment in which people feel loved and accepted. Caring Sunday schools also provide a context for new people to connect to the church. The assimilation of new attendees is an important function of Sunday school classes. It may include sending a card of appreciation for attending or an invitation to share a meal.

Fifth, the personal and spiritual life of the teacher is critical for effective teaching and mentoring. Teachers model Christlikeness and a holy life. As Parker Palmer states, "Good teaching cannot be reduced to techniques; good teaching comes from the identity and integrity of the teacher" (1998, 10). Teachers teach out of who they are. The teachers' love and care for the students is made evident as they invest their lives in their students. This is why congregations must invest in the training and preparation of teachers.

Sixth, teachers partner with God in the transformation of the human person. Sunday school teachers do not change lives, but through their faithful service the Holy Spirit works through them to change and transform people. Sunday school ministries should be immersed in prayer and the power of the Holy Spirit.

These strategies and others enhance faithful discipleship by giving attention to the functional impact of Sunday school. Sunday school programs can be vibrant avenues of grace as people gather to study scripture, to fellowship, and to grow in their relationship with God. Congregations should be intentional in finding appropriate avenues to develop Sunday school classes that are connected to congregational life. Sunday school is still one of the most significant contexts for faithful discipleship.

▶ SMALL GROUPS

While small groups are often considered just one aspect of educational ministry, they provide one of the most formative aspects of faithful discipleship in the local church. The small group movement that began in the 1960s and 1970s changed the church's understanding of community and helped redefine spirituality (Gorman 2002; Wuthnow 1994). Christians find small groups significant because they provide a means for developing community and relationships with other Christians. In many respects small groups mirror the early church model of community as reflected in Acts 2:42, "They devoted themselves to the apostles' teaching and to the fellowship, to the breaking of bread and to prayer." The early followers of Jesus met regularly in homes to learn about the life, death, and resurrection of Jesus; to receive and give support through fellowship; and to spend time in prayer for one another. Assailed by persecution and suffering, these early groups understood the importance of developing community and significant relationships. Struggling with the challenges of contemporary life, the body of believers still gathers in small groups for support and encouragement, to study the scriptures, and to pray.

Small groups also provide a context for deepening relationships and connectedness. Reflecting the very nature of the Triune God, humans are created as relational beings in need of acceptance, love, and care. As John Wesley said, "There is no personal holiness without social holiness." Spiritual formation and growth always take place within a social context. The Christian life is not a solitary journey, but a pilgrimage made in the company of other believers (Hestenes 1983, 11). Participation in a small group offers believers a sense of well-being, connectedness, and ownership of their life and faith formation. In the field of psychology, attachment theory focuses on the need of a child to have secure relationships with adult caregivers. In the same way, adults need attachment to other adults through significant interpersonal relationships. Small groups provide a context for this through the development of authentic Christian community, which is at the heart of Christian identity and reflects the relational nature of the Triune God.

The significant growth of small groups in congregations makes it difficult to cover here the variety of communities available. Depending on the group's purpose, communities may be open for people to come and go or closed with defined expectations. Small groups serve various functions and purposes. The list below includes some representative types of the small groups offered in Christian discipleship.

Covenant or Discipleship Groups (three to five people): Covenant groups vary in focus, but the primary emphasis of these groups is mutual accountability. These intimate gatherings of three or four people provide personal and spiritual accountability (Halverson 2000, 64). Some covenant groups include men only or women only to focus on issues that pertain to distinct gender needs and challenges. The primary focus of these groups is to foster spiritual growth and active discipleship in the world.

Life Groups (eight to fifteen people): Life groups focus on building relationship and developing community. Life groups often use a particular topic or book as a framework for discussion. Most life groups meet in homes during the week or during scheduled times at the church. Many Sunday school classes function as life groups. This is probably the most popular small group in the local church.

Bible Study Groups (eight to fifteen people): Bible study groups meet primarily to focus on reading and interpreting scripture. They may include times of fellowship, but the purpose of the group is to receive teaching and instruction from scripture.

Affinity Groups (eight to fifteen people): Affinity groups gather around a common interest or goal (e.g., basketball, exercise, biking, golfing, camping, and sewing) for encouragement and growth. The possibilities are endless, but affinity groups offer popular avenues to connect with fellow Christians who share common interests and needs. Because group activities often occur outside the church building, affinity groups can offer a powerful witness to the community.

Support/Recovery Groups (size varies): Support groups provide a safe environment in which people can share their life journeys with others. Support and recovery groups employ proven methods to help people develop new, healthy patterns of behavior. The encouragement and support of others who face the same difficult challenges can help people move to new levels of trust and obedience. Support and recovery groups focus on areas of addiction (substance, sexual, food), domestic and sexual abuse, divorce, and grief. These groups assist congregations to meet the diverse needs and issues people face both inside and outside of the faith community.

BENEFITS OF SMALL GROUPS

The benefits of small groups include developing community and growing in the grace of God, needs central to life and faith. Robert Hestenes says small groups fulfill many needs (1983, 10):

- The need for spiritual growth and development
- The need for friendship, support, and encouragement
- The need for strength in the face of temptations and trials
- The need to give and receive love
- The need to serve others

Other benefits include the development of lay leadership. Small groups provide a context for people to learn, use, and develop their spiritual gifts and graces for ministry. For example, leaders with the gift of hospitality provide a warm and inviting context for people. Leaders who are gifted at pastoral care have the opportunity to shepherd others. Small groups give the church an important avenue to develop leaders for the church and aid the pastor in shepherding and caring for the broader needs of the faith community. Small groups also help people engage in service and ministry to others, both inside and outside the group context. Small-group members participate in ministry to the needy and in acts of social justice. Finally, small groups can provide an avenue for building relationships with nonbelievers. People seeking faith may be more likely to visit a small group hosted at a home than to attend a church service. Small groups can bridge to neighbors interested in talking about matters of faith and seeking a place for love and acceptance.

DESIGNING, PLANNING, AND FACILITATING SMALL GROUPS

Faithful discipleship includes designing small groups that address the distinct needs of the congregation's context. It is very important to develop a balanced approach to Christian discipleship in small-group design. Adding groups just for the sake of having more defeats the purpose of small groups. Each group must address a specific need within the life of the church. Julie Gorman provides seven of the most essential elements of small group design: purpose, commitment, size, configuration, timing, leadership, and climate (Gorman 2001, 178).

- First, groups need to develop a shared purpose from the beginning.
- Second, expectations and responsibilities within the group need to be shared upfront. Is this an open or closed group? Who participates, men or women, or both? When will the group meet? What are the requirements to participate? The level of commitment of the participants should be clarified.
- Third, the size of the group will influence its purpose and intent. Does the group focus on deeper forms of accountability or address broader topics of interest? The size of the group influences the intimacy a group can develop. A group larger than eight members increases the likelihood that some members will remain silent and not contribute. Larger groups tend to inhibit intimacy and close relationships.
- Fourth, group configuration has an impact on the success of a group. Physical space, seating, and eye contact with other members can inhibit or enhance group dynamics.
- Fifth, meeting frequency is important to the development of the group. More frequent group meetings create greater trust and openness among group members. The length of meetings also influences group dynamics. Obviously groups that spend more time together, sharing meals, retreat, study, and play, develop closer relationships. Also, the longevity of a group is a factor in group dynamics. Groups

often need to be together for several months or even years to develop close relationship.

- Sixth, the leader's role, style, personality, and experience influence the effectiveness of the group. A controlling group leader results in a breakdown of trust, but lack of direction from a laissez-faire leader can cause frustration. Effective leaders are good facilitators, flexible in their leadership style as the group grows and develops.

- Seventh, leaders and group members determine group identity by establishing spoken or unspoken standards of behavior. Do they create a context of acceptance for one another and new attendees, or do they create insecurity and defensiveness? (2001, 178-79).

Once the criteria of the small group are decided, it is important to establish an explicit, shared covenant among the members. While each covenant will be unique to the group, Roberta Hestenes provides a list of characteristics essential to all covenants:

- *The Covenant of Affirmation (unconditional love).* There is nothing you have done or will do that will make me stop loving you.

- *The Covenant of Availability.* I am available to you both during the group session and outside of the group session. My time, energy, and resources are available to you.

- *The Covenant of Prayer.* I will pray for you on a regular basis, asking God's blessing on you.

- *The Covenant of Openness.* I promise to strive to become a more open person, disclosing my feelings, struggles, joys, and hurts with you and other members of the group.

- *The Covenant of Honesty.* I will try to mirror back to you what I am hearing you say and feel. I will trust our relationship enough to take risks by "speaking the truth in love" (Ephesians 4:15).

- *The Covenant of Sensitivity.* I will be sensitive to you and to your needs to the best of my ability. I will hear you, see you, and feel where you are and provide encouragement.

- *The Covenant of Confidentiality.* I promise to keep whatever is shared in this group in confidence in order to promote trust and openness.

- *The Covenant of Accountability.* I will be accountable for my behavior, and if there are any areas of my life that should be liberated, I will communicate them to the group. (1983, 20-21).

Facilitators manage the small-group process. They need to know how to balance the content and process of the group discussions. An effective facilitator understands how to ask good questions, which can be used to gain information, demonstrate or promote interest, clarify, make conversation, express emotion, motivate, and restate understanding. Good questions are simple, clear, and uncluttered. Open-ended questions facilitate discussion. Avoid leading questions, which tell the members where you want them to go. These discourage participation and can lead to mistrust and suspicion. Be considerate and encourage others in the group to ask good questions as well.

How do you manage silence in a small group? What do you do if no one answers your question? It may be that you have not given enough time for people to respond, or people may be thinking deeply about your question. In some cases, the question may not be clear and you will need to redirect or restate it in another way. Discomfort with silence can make a group feel rushed and edgy. It is important to be comfortable with silence and allow it to occur naturally, when necessary.

How do you respond to someone who has given a blatantly wrong answer (not simply one with which you disagree)? One approach is to confess miscommunication in the question. You can then clarify by giving another example or restating your question. Other group members will sometimes correct the wrong response by giving the right answer. You can also ask the person to support the answer with clarification or an example. It is important to create an environment in which people feel free to respond openly.

How do you respond to inappropriate questions? Try redirecting the question back to the group by asking, "What do all of you think about this question?" If a question is irrelevant to the current task or topic, acknowledge it and suggest an alternative time to pursue the answer. In some cases, invite the group to decide whether or not to deal with the question now. It is important to acknowledge any question posed, to foster an open, accepting environment.

BIBLE STUDY IN SMALL GROUPS

Although small groups have a wide range of purposes and approaches, one of the primary resources for shaping the life of the church emerges from Bible study in small groups (Hestenes 1983, 15). Scripture forms and shapes people's lives. Formational reading includes opening to the text, allowing the text to master the student instead of the student attempting to master the text (see chapter 12). Formational reading invites people to come to the text open to hear, to receive, to respond, and to serve the Word of God. Sandra Schneiders indicates that biblical spirituality represents a transformative process of person and communal engagement with the biblical text. The nonspecialist approaches the text, not as a historical record or even as a literary medium, but as the Word of God (2002, 136).

For people with a limited knowledge of the Bible, reading and studying the Bible in the context of an intimate group gives opportunities for learning and spiritual growth. People who will not read the Bible on their own at home will read it in the context of a small group (Hestenes 1983, 16). Studying the Bible in a small group helps people broaden and deepen their understanding of a given passage, while guarding against misleading, individual interpretations of scripture. Scripture should always be interpreted and understood in the context of community. Studying the Bible in a group also helps people make meaning of their faith by verbalizing what the Bible means and how it applies to a life of faith. On their own, people easily ignore the relationship of biblical truth to their own lives. In a group setting, people talk about scripture together, which helps them apply what they are learning to their lives (17).

Faithful discipleship includes studying the Bible in small groups. Bible study is especially important as biblical literacy declines and people with little or no background with the Bible or the church come into our congregations. Bible studies in small groups provide congregations with a significant context for faithful discipleship.

▶ WESLEY'S GROUP FORMATION

A discussion of small-group formats and systems would not be complete without observing John Wesley's small-group system. Wesley provides a model of a holistic approach to Christian discipleship. Even though Wesley's groups were developed more than three hundred years ago, they are relevant today and can be adapted for contemporary discipleship ministries. Wesley has been called the "father" of the modern small-group concept (Hunsicker 1996, 210). Wesley employed a methodical approach to spiritual formation through group formation. For Wesley, interlocking groups provided the primary avenue to foster holiness of heart and life. D. Michael Henderson argues that Wesley's interlocking groups include a hierarchy of instruction for each group, tailored to a specific function. Henderson distinguishes each group—societies, classes, and bands—with a specific educational mode (1997, 83).

Societies—the Cognitive Mode: The term *society* is synonymous in size to a *congregation.* This group includes all official members plus any adherents who attended open functions of the fellowship. The Methodist society was the focal point of group identification. It was the hub of the organization. The primary function of the society was cognitive instruction. The tenets of Methodism were delivered through this teaching or educational channel. These tenets were primarily conveyed through lecture, preaching, public reading, hymn singing, and exhorting. A large group (fifty or more) sat in rows and listened to a speaker give a prepared talk. Little provision was given for personal response or feedback (84). The learning environment for this cognitive process was the Methodist chapel, a plain, austere building with no musical instruments and separate areas for men and women. All segments of society were represented, from the refined to the working class. John and Charles Wesley led the societies, but as the movement later expanded, they delegated oversight to lay assistants in the absence of ordained clergymen. Everything about the society mode—setting, officers, special occasions, and so forth—facilitated its concentration on cognitive function. Naturally, considering the impassioned preaching and fervent singing, there was an affective dimension of instruction. The major aim, however, was to present scriptural truth so it could be clearly understood.

Class Meeting—the Behavioral Mode: The class meeting was the most influential instructional unit in Methodism and probably Wesley's greatest contribution to group experience. Its success centered on behavioral change. Every Methodist became a member of a class and attended regularly, or else he or she was no longer a member of the society. The class comprised ten or twelve people who met weekly for personal supervision of spiritual growth. The *Rules for the United Societies* provided the primary framework for class meetings (Watson 1998, 45), specifying the basic process of "inquiry" and the subject matter as "how their souls prospered." There was no room for lecture or preaching; led by a fellow seeker, not a professional trainer, the emphasis rested clearly on present and personal growth (Henderson 1997, 96). The *Rules* provided a sort of constitution for the class meetings. There were three specified categories of behavior: (1) Prohibitions, or things not to do; (2) Exhortations, or positive behaviors; (3) Helpful practices to be maintained, which were known as the "means of grace." The only requirement for attending the classes was "a desire to flee the wrath to come, to be saved from their sin" (Henderson 1997, 97).

The class meeting served as an exception to Wesley's segregation of men and women. The leadership was open to women. Class meetings were coeducational experiences in small-group development. Groups were also heterogeneous in terms of age, social standing, and spiritual readiness. Wesley wanted the classes to represent a cross-section of Methodism. Some members were at very different points in their spiritual maturity, and the classes accepted people from a variety of social backgrounds, helping to break up the rigid class system of eighteenth-century England.

The class meetings were held in homes, shops, schoolrooms, attics, and even coal-bins—wherever there was room for ten or twelve people to assemble. As Methodist chapels were built, small rooms were provided for class meetings (Henderson 1997, 98-99). The format of a class meeting never varied. It began with a short hymn, followed by the leader stating the condition of his or her spiritual life, sharing honestly about failures, sins, temptations, or inner battles. The leader was the role model for the group. The subject matter of the class meetings was personal experience, not doctrinal ideology or biblical information, and the collective goal was personal holiness or perfect love lived out in daily life. The leader was a fellow struggler who started the meeting, provided spiritual oversight or pastoral care to others—a subpastor in the Methodist organizational hierarchy—and carried the concerns of the class through the week. This position was the first rung in the ladder of leadership in Methodism. The leader created a context of acceptance and commitment, which included an atmosphere of trust to "bear all things."

Bands—the Affective Mode: The bands facilitated emotional change. Unlike the classes, bands required homogenous grouping by sex, age, and marital status. They were voluntary cells of people who professed a clear Christian commitment and who desired to grow in love, holiness, and purity of intention. The group environment was one of ruthless honesty and frank openness, in which members sought to improve their attitudes, emotions, feelings, intentions, and affections. One might say the society aimed for the head, the class meeting for the hands, and the band for the heart. The central function of the band included what Wesley termed "close conversation," by which he meant soul-searching examination, not so much of behavior and ideas, but of motive and heartfelt impressions.

During both band and class meetings, the following questions were asked:
- What known sins have you committed since our last meeting?
- What temptations have you met with?
- How were you delivered?
- What have you thought, said, or done of which you doubt whether it to be sin or not?
- Have you nothing you desire to keep secret? (Henderson 1997, 117-18)

The bands, as voluntary associations, had limited success in Methodism. They were Wesley's favorite, however, perhaps because of his own appreciation for the help he had received from "close conversation" in similar gatherings of leaders. He respected his peers who cared enough about him to ask hard questions.

IMPLICATIONS OF WESLEY'S GROUP FORMATION

Some specific aspects of Wesley's small-group approach are not applicable to the church today, but his holistic approach to spiritual formation that develops the mind (cognitive), the hand (behavioral), and the heart (affective) provides a model of intentional development through small groups. Each group has a specific purpose and function. The groups develop community through which spiritual formation and growth can take place. Small groups can give support and hold people accountable for their growing relationship with Christ. Since being a Christian includes relationship with others and relationship with God, small-group formation helps people live and serve more faithfully as they participate on a regular basis. Wesley's innovative use of laity, men and women, was a radical shift for his day. His structural approach provides stepping-stones upon which Christian educators can build models of discipleship that reach Christians today. Wesley's focus on discipling Christians and reaching the lost and dying world provide the church with a helpful example of faithful discipleship (Hunsicker 1996, 210).

▶ SUNDAY SCHOOL AND SMALL GROUPS

Historically, Sunday school classes primarily focused on teaching the Bible. Now, however, Sunday school classes engage current topics or issues that people face in life. They can be organized around similar interests or age-group affiliation. Increased interest in developing relationships and building community has prompted these changes. People are more likely to engage in dialogue and conversation about scripture and matters of faith in a safe learning context where their views are valued. Smaller Sunday school classes, usually eight to fifteen people, are designed to build community and develop significant relationships.

Newly planted congregations meet in small groups before gathering for worship. Missional and emergent congregations elect to move away from traditional times or worship on Sunday to include cell groups and service opportunities during the week. More traditional congregations maintain Sunday school classes and add small groups during the week, but must decide which is most important. Some experts say that congregations cannot have successful small groups and Sunday school classes at the same time because of busy schedules and too much variety. Each congregation must evaluate what kinds of groups work best in its ministry context. Here are some questions to ask when determining and evaluating the value and effectiveness of small groups and Sunday school classes:

- What are the primary purposes of small groups or Sunday school classes?
- Are Sunday school classes designed to be small groups that foster community or larger teaching classes?
- Can traditional Sunday school classes and small groups coexist and be successful?
- Are adult classes organized by adult stages of development, or do they include all adult ages?
- If your congregation has an effective Sunday school ministry program, do you need to hold small groups or Bible studies during the week?

- Should traditional Sunday school classes be replaced with small groups and Bible studies during the week?

▶ CONCLUSION

Faithful discipleship takes place through a wide variety of congregational contexts such as worship, teaching, service, and mission. It takes all of congregational life to shape and form persons into faithful disciples. In most contexts, Christian education is organized and developed for specific age levels of children, youth, and adults. Organizing and planning discipleship includes incorporating these age-level ministries in the broader scope of congregational life and formation. When the people of God gather in Sunday school classes or small groups to study the scripture, fellowship, and pray, lives are formed and transformed by the power of the Holy Spirit. In these intimate gatherings people are open to one another and to the inspiration of scripture. Sunday school classes and small groups are a means of grace that help people grow in holiness of heart and life because spiritual growth and faith formation take place in the context of community. Our personal spiritual growth includes the social dimension of faith that occurs as people share life together in the context of Christian community.

Congregations should give specific attention to developing groups that reflect John Wesley's holistic system formation that fosters development of mind, heart, and hand. A Wesleyan approach to Christian discipleship couples personal holiness and social holiness, a helpful reminder to congregations that Christian faith is always lived in community. Faithful discipleship includes both the individual's relationship with God and active participation in the lives of other people. By the grace of God, as we meet in classes and groups, we become the people God has called us to be, a people growing in the knowledge and grace of Jesus Christ.

▶ REFERENCES

Borchert, Doris Cox. 1990. Sunday school. In *Harper's Encyclopedia of Religious Education*, 623-24. Ed. Iris V. Cully and Kendig Brubaker Cully. San Francisco: Harper and Row.

Gorman, Julie. 2001. Small groups in the local church. In *Introduction to Christian Education: Foundations for the Twenty-first Century*, 176-84. Ed. Michael Anthony. Grand Rapids: Zondervan.

_____. 2002. *Community That Is Christian*. 2nd ed. Grand Rapids: Baker Books.

Halverson, Delia. 2000. *Nuts and Bolts of Christian Education*. Nashville: Abingdon Press.

Haystead, Wes, and Sheryl Haystead. 2000. *How to Have a Great Sunday School*. Ventura, CA: Gospel Light.

Hemphill, Kenneth. 1996. *Revitalizing the Sunday Morning Dinosaur: A Sunday School Growth Strategy for the 21st Century.* Nashville: Broadman and Holman.

Henderson, David Michael. 1997. *John Wesley's Class Meeting: A Model of Making Disciples.* Nappanee, IN: Evangel.

Hestenes, Roberta. 1983. *Using the Bible in Groups.* Philadelphia: Westminster Press.

Hunsicker, David. 1996. John Wesley: Father of today's small groups. In *Wesleyan Theological Journal* 31:1 (spring): 192-211.

Palmer, Parker. 1998. *The Courage to Teach.* San Francisco: Jossey-Bass.

Schneiders, Sandra. 2002. Biblical spirituality. In *Interpretation: A Journal of Bible and Theology* 56 (2): 133-42.

Watson, David Lowes. 1998. *Covenant Discipleship: Christian Formation Through Mutual Accountability.* Eugene, OR: Wipf and Stock.

Wuthnow, Robert, ed. 1994. *I Come Away Stronger: How Small Groups Are Shaping American Religion.* Grand Rapids: William B. Eerdmans.

DEVELOPMENTAL FAITHFUL DISCIPLESHIP
Chapters 17—20

The following chapters focus on practicing faithful discipleship through our understanding of age-level (children, youth, and adult) and family-based ministries within defined, dynamic, and practical frameworks. Chapter 17 provides biblical, theological, and developmental foundations for understanding the lives of children. The chapter reviews existing and emerging strategies of children's ministry with implications for how congregations provide ministry *to, for,* and *with* children. Chapter 18 provides an overview of the theological, developmental, and historical aspects that shape our understanding of youth. Current theories and approaches to youth ministry offer guidance for faithful practices in youth ministry. Chapter 19 gives an overview of biblical, theoretical, and developmental aspects of faithful discipleship in adults. The chapter develops practical approaches to adult ministry along with examples of faithful adult discipleship. Chapter 20 provides biblical and theoretical foundations for understanding families. The chapter explores the definition of *family,* traditional approaches to family ministry, and concludes with a congregational approach to family ministry. Each chapter includes suggestions for congregations to practice faithful discipleship through age-level and family-based ministries.

SEVENTEEN

CHILDREN'S MINISTRY

▶ INTRODUCTION

Imagine you are attending a Sunday school training seminar with a group of teachers from your church. The presenter argues that, since children remain inherently sinful, the most important things teachers do involve discipline. The presenter makes an impassioned plea for corporal punishment in children's classes, arguing that until children make a decision for Christ as young adults, they do not have the capacity to understand right from wrong, much less make positive decisions in church. After the session, one of your teachers asks, "So, do kids have anything good to offer?" How do you answer?

In a church board meeting you hear a proposal to keep children in the ministry wing of the church so that they go directly from Sunday school to children's church every week. The presenter argues that children can then receive age-appropriate instruction freeing adults to worship. Another person says that they don't mind kids in the service, and children's church needs to be more than babysitting. How do you respond to these issues?

Without a doubt, children's ministry is one of the most important arenas of Christian education and inspires passionate opinions. Few ministries in the church attract as many participants, not only because of the large age range involved (newborn to teen years) but also because of the number of parents and adult volunteers involved in various aspects of the ministry. As an emerging field, children's ministry in the United States and other regions took shape against the backdrop of public schooling, both a blessing and a problem in some settings. Faithful discipleship challenges us to take seriously our responsibility to children but calls us to advocate for the role of children in the entire life of the church.

▶ DEFINITIONS: MINISTRY TO, BY, OR WITH?

It's Sunday morning and time for the toddler choir to sing to a congregation that, judging from the facial expressions, holds mixed emotions about the event. Parents line the front pews (perhaps the closest some have ever gotten to the altar rail), sitting behind the blinking red lights of video cameras that are ready to capture the young virtuosos during their five minutes of fame. The toddler choir director sits directly in front of the children, alternately pointing to the lyrics and making "smile" motions as she sings at the top of her voice to provide some harmony. The child closest to the microphone holds a peculiar musical perspective, reasoning that as the notes go up the scale, one should get louder while maintaining an astringent G-flat, especially during the chorus (only children can redefine the musical scale and receive applause for it). The choir assistant stays busy chasing down stragglers who use the worship platform as a launching pad into the congregation. Do you call this children's ministry?

BIBLICAL PERSPECTIVES OF CHRISTIAN DISCIPLESHIP WITH CHILDREN

Faithful discipleship begins with providing a formative community where children can learn, grow, and ultimately embrace the faith of Christ as previous generations have done. We often find children at the center of God's covenant relationship with God's people: Isaac (Genesis 15—22) establishing Abraham's hope and faith before God or Jesus placing a child in the midst of the disciples and announcing the kingdom of God for children like these (Matthew 18:2-5; Mark 10:13-16; Luke 9:47-48). By their simple presence within the biblical narrative, children signal the presence of God's covenant love and Kingdom power, based not on the inherent goodness of children but on their marginality as people desperately in need of grace. A number of biblical passages gesture toward adult responsibility to nurture children in the faith:

> Hear, O Israel: The LORD our God, the LORD is one. Love the LORD your God with all your heart and with all your soul and with all your strength. These commandments that I give you today are to be upon your hearts. Impress them on your children. Talk about them when you sit at home and when you walk along the road, when you lie down and when you get up. Tie them as symbols on your hands and bind them on your foreheads. Write them on the doorframes of your houses and on your gates. (Deuteronomy 6:4-9)

> In the paths of the wicked are snares and pitfalls, but those who would preserve their life stay far from them. Start children off on the way they should go, and even when they are old they will not turn from it. (Proverbs 22:5-6, TNIV)

Passages such as Deuteronomy 11 or selections from Proverbs (2:9-11; 3:1, 5-6, 11-12; 4:10; 6:20, 23) indicate the Old Testament concern to raise, form, and shape children in religious life, cultivating their appreciation for God, family, community, and the world.

By the New Testament era, the approach to children took on a new tone when Jesus radically situated children as central to the kingdom of God: "He called a little child, whom he placed among them. And he said: 'Truly I tell you, unless you change and become like little children, you will never enter the kingdom of heaven. Therefore, whoever takes a humble place—becoming like this child—is the greatest in the kingdom of heaven. And whoever welcomes one such child in my name welcomes me'" (Matthew 18:2-5, TNIV).

Jesus' admonition, replicated in all three synoptic Gospels, reveals a startling fact that the role of children (often through the advocacy of children's ministry) is to disclose the nature of the kingdom of God. Judy Gundry-Volf suggests that welcoming children "is to welcome Jesus himself in the sense that he humbled himself like a little child and endured the worst lot of the little child in carrying out his God-given mission" (2001, 45). Gundry-Volf offers a range of children's realities that resemble the nature of God's kingdom: (1) the Kingdom is invested in those without power or prestige; (2) children model an understanding and appreciation of Jesus; and (3) children serve as recipients and expressions of the power of holiness in and through the lives of parents who are consecrated to God (45, 46-48, 52; see 1 Corinthians 7:14). In short, children reveal the power of the Kingdom by both receiving and expressing Christlikeness among families and within the family of God, the church.

THEOLOGICAL PERSPECTIVES

The power of children to reveal the Kingdom apparently prevailed in the early church. However, issues soon surfaced that created real theological differences over ministerial approaches toward children. O. M. Bakke asserts that early church fathers viewed children as innocent, or at least morally neutral, until the fifth century, when a battle with Pelagianism (which denied the existence of original sin) forced a doctrine of original sin that portrayed children as sinful and deserving of judgment (2005, 105). To be sure, the early church acknowledged children as moral subjects who bore responsibility for their actions, but a child's capacity for moral action might culminate in Christian virtue rather than sin, even though the possibility of sin continued as the child grew older (106-7). Augustine's vision, however, cast children as bearers of original sin and thus recipients of a judgment of eternal damnation unless baptized (Storz 2001, 78-102). Wesley, who often began from Augustinian assumptions, nevertheless overturned this view with his deep confidence in prevenient grace and the power of the Holy Spirit to work in and through children (Stonehouse 2004, 135-36).

This tension—children as neutral but capable moral agents versus children as necessarily evil, even in the womb—influenced the church's teaching from the fifth century forward in Western Christianity. Eastern Orthodox theologians and other world Christians avoided much of the tension, viewing human mortality rather than sinful action as the primary consequence of the Fall (Guroian 2001, 67). Nevertheless the Augustinian view prevailed in the

West, particularly through the Reformers and in Puritan child-rearing principles (Sisemore 2004, 222-26).

Shifts toward revivalism and strong emphasis on personal faith statements generated other issues, still drawing from the Augustinian view. One issue concerned the emphasis placed on the child's responsibility, and ability, to make a faith statement at a particular "age of accountability." With many churches rejecting infant baptism, ministers had to suggest a type of intermediate state where children could remain within God's grace until they were morally culpable for their sin or responded to God. Identifying the timing of this move fluctuates with different theorists and proves increasingly difficult as the popularity of "faith decisions" decreases and the sense of children's culpability lessens (Sparkman 1983). Historically, this tension manifested in different understandings of infant baptism. Under the Augustinian model, baptism deteriorated into serving either a perfunctory role of insuring salvation (Stookey 1982, 119-23) or a superficial but public role of lending witness to an adult faith decision. Many churches rejected infant baptism because of their struggle with individual accountability. As we have already noted, Wesley believed that infant baptism, though beneficial and effective, could be lost over time (as any faith decision might). Commitment and accountability remained interdependent, yet infant baptism reflecting God's prevenient grace was always the first movement in any approach to responsive faith (Stonehouse 2004, 137-40).

An alternative approach, anchored in Wesleyan sensibilities, understands infant baptism within covenantal language that expresses God's prevenient grace through the church and the elevation of children as a vital part of the community of faith (Staples 1991, 161-200). In this approach, infant baptism serves as a means of grace that binds the church, the family, and the child under a bond of God's grace. Everyone benefits through this sacramental act, anticipating the child's personal commitment and God's justifying grace (Stookey 1982, 44-50). Many churches still publicly dedicate children to God and acknowledge responsibility as congregations and families to raise children "in the nurture and admonition of the Lord" (Ephesians 6:4, KJV). While lacking the theological strength of baptism, infant dedication may serve as a means of grace in many settings (Staples 1991, 199-200).

A second concern arose in the nature of child-rearing methods. Some theorists suggest that revivalism, as an extension of Puritanism, provided a particular socialization of children (Bendroth 2001, 352-54; Greven 1977, 87-99). This socialization produces adults (those past the age of accountability) who accept a need to be *broken*, that is, "to subdue the self, and to obey the word and will of God" (Greven 1977, 99). In contrast, other ministers, notably Horace Bushnell, argued that "the child is to grow up a Christian and never know himself as being otherwise" (1908/2000, 10). Bushnell's approach, often associated with efforts in family ministry, advocated a nurturing or formational approach where family life shaped the child in Christian living. Reminiscent of an Eastern Orthodox view of the godly family as an image of the church (Guroian 2001, 64), Bushnell envisioned family life in play, prayer, government, interpersonal relationships, and even physical exercise as a means of grace (1908/2000, 271-93).

Christian educators and children's ministers struggle to reconcile contemporary interpretations of John Wesley's approach to child rearing practices with his writings (Heitzenrater 2001, 279). Wesley's own words and actions send mixed signals (at best), and ministers are wise to recognize and name the problems inherent in some aspects of Wesley's philosophy. As noted earlier (see chapter 5), Wesley was a disciplinarian who believed in bending or breaking the will of children to make them pliable to their parents and educators, and therefore, to God. Wesley's educational approach must be understood in the context of traditional views of child rearing, including his mother's, and the eighteenth-century educational structure whose curriculum influenced Wesley's strategies for schooling. Ministers today can appreciate Wesley's spiritual admonitions to both immerse children in Christian practices and assert that children's spiritual lives serve as a means of grace to others through testimonies and written accounts. Wesley's employ of the means of grace, as well as his appreciation for the spiritual presence of children in the ecology of Methodism, provide a strong framework for the spiritual nurture of and expressions by children (Blevins 2007).

Children's ministers must acknowledge that a primary challenge to nurturing and empowering children rests with adults. As Bonnie Miller-McLemore notes that the first concern to address when it comes to faithful discipleship is adult conceptions of children (2003, xxv). Theorists have changed their view of children through historical shifts in intellectual understanding. Early attempts portrayed children within certain extremes that either promoted children or restricted them. These now seem to give way to Miller-McLemore's observation that "a rich moral and religious complexity has returned along with the honesty and real ambiguity of children and parenting" (21-22). A balanced view that projects neither an idyllic view of children as unblemished romantics nor a demonic view of children as willful sinners probably serves a Wesleyan perspective best. With Miller-McLemore, Christian educators can see children as a "labor of love" (105-36) that requires attention yet also serves as a means of grace to adults.

▶ DYNAMIC CONSIDERATIONS

A number of contexts shape any contemporary understanding of children, including sociological placement and political influence over the care and welfare of a child's growth. Theorists increasingly seek to discover the implications of genetics and social context in the shaping of the quality of children's lives (Cook and Cook 2005, 40-169, 460-553). As important as both concerns are for faithful discipleship, Christian educators focus on the general development of children and their capacity for learning to help shape curriculum design and delivery for the majority of children. One must acknowledge that such general descriptions do not preclude the church's role in caring for children with exceptional developmental needs or socially at-risk behaviors (Cook and Cook, 554-92). Ministry design, however, deals with the basic tendencies of everyday childhood and then proposes special approaches to incorporate exceptional children in the mainstream of Christian education.

CHILD DEVELOPMENT THEORY

Developmental considerations arose in the modern era with romantic views like those of Rousseau and experiential efforts of Pestalozzi and Froebel. The establishment of psychology as a discipline, however, in conjunction with the North American emphasis on public schooling, led to many of the classifications used today. Parents, educators, and ministers often divide children along the basic categories of infants and toddlers, preschool, and school-age children (May et al. 2005, 73-83). Drawing from Piaget, Erikson, and other developmental theorists, this approach acknowledges that childhood appears to be bracketed by two periods of rapid growth in either basic biological development (newborns) or cognitive capacities (emerging adolescence).

Following the work of Jean Piaget (Cook and Cook 2005, 178-92), children may also be grouped into four large age-levels. Departing from Piaget, however, these age-level eras incorporate more than cognitive development as children move outward from primary social attachments to more extended relational networks. In a sense cognitive ability mirrors social capability as children learn to develop through their relationships with both the world of ideas and the world of people.

Birth to two years of age: known as the *sensorimotor* stage during which children primarily know the world through the senses and their physical or motor activities. This stage includes phenomenal physical growth (one reason physical ability is central) as well as the basic development of eyesight, walking, language, and preliminary social engagement—much of which occurs by the end of the first year. Babies engage in an intense differentiation of self and *other,* including a sense of separation from their environment (the range of their world literally changes with perception since newborns lack a sense of object permanence), an identification with caregivers (and the emotional tasks of attachment and anxiety when caregivers leave), and learning to express basic emotions through relationships (Balswick et al. 2005, 120-37).

Two to seven years of age: known as the *preoperational* stage when children are just beginning to employ mental operations (concrete symbols, images, ideas) and nascent logic (knowledge primarily comes through direct, though imperfect, association with the real world). Symbols, concepts, and ideas often operate minimally as children learn simple tasks through play and a rudimentary logic that often cannot be reversed. Children struggle with the relationships between objects of different sizes, number, and weight. They also develop a relational understanding between themselves and an expanding world of significant others, including not only family members but also peer relations via friends. Children learn basic relationships, including separation from primary caregivers and engagement with friends through cooperative play and appropriate demonstrations of aggression. Deemed the "play years" by some theorists, as relational and emotional skills help children differentiate their life from other primary relationships, they learn a social and linguistic "grammar" of living within a social world (Balswick et al., 143-47). In addition, basic issues of gender identity and expectations begin to develop.

Seven to twelve years of age: known as the *concrete-operational* stage, children develop a stronger logical base for handling multiple concepts that is still grounded in everyday reality. Following schooling models, educators often divide this group into early and late elementary age levels. While younger elementary children deal with basic issues of concept formation, many children move quickly to more complex mental activities that require memory and metaphoric thinking. These "little professors" begin to engage and manipulate ideas (numbers, letters, volume, etc.) as long as they have direct relationship with concrete expression. In a sense, children learn to think *about* objects as means and methods for manipulating reality. Children also learn to live and survive within multiple relationships and communities. These school years include basic tasks of self-esteem, competency, and other social challenges that help children understand their place in the larger social matrices that shape their extended lives (Balswick et al. 2005, 148-60). They seek a sense of personal accomplishment, undergo multiple roles that require perspective and empathy with others, and engage in moral decisions based on tangible consequences they might face.

Twelve years and beyond: children begin to transition from childhood to adolescence in this stage (sometimes designated as "preteen"). Known as the *formal operational* stage, children begin to develop a logical base for thinking about concepts as concepts without the requisite grounding in everyday experience. In a sense, they learn to think about thinking through greater use of abstract reasoning. Socially, children begin to engage a larger context than either immediate or extended social networks. They begin to situate themselves within the larger, extended world that shapes their lives. By this stage, children are capable of exploring and evaluating the cultural influences that form the last of the ecological systems that Urie Bronfenbrenner proposes shape children's lives: the micro-system of parents/siblings/friends, the meso-system of home/school/neighborhood, the exo-system of extended family/parental workplace/government regulations, and the macro-system of customs/laws/values/resources that constitute their social world across time (Cook and Cook 2005, 17-19).

While there are a number of other important developmental theories, Piaget, adding the relational lens of Erik Erikson and the ecological view of Bronfenbrenner, provides the basics for a general charting of children's lives. Admittedly, cultural differences shape the nature and quality of these interactions; however, this overall view of the intellectual and social capacity of children influences our understanding of their ability to learn and model faithful discipleship.

IMPLICATIONS FOR DISCIPLESHIP WITH CHILDREN

Parents and children's ministers often benefit from general descriptions of children when planning and responding to larger issues. For instance, recognizing that children are innately egocentric between ages one and three helps ministers explain to anxious adults why children engage in parallel play or often talk *at* adults rather than engage *with* them (Cook and Cook 2005, 183-84). Rather than dismissing such action as sinful, a developmental view explains this behavior through the stages of cognitive and social development.

At the same time, developmental categories should serve as *descriptive* tendencies, not *prescriptive* frameworks that limit the child's participation in the church. Child psychologist David Elkind notes that developmentalism assumes a modernist perspective that accentuates regularity and progress across universal categories. Postmodern perspectives elevate particular and cultural experiences that also include personality differences and the irregular tendencies that specific children may express (1998, 1-43).

Karen Marie Yust and others caution that cognitive categories can lead Christian educators to assume that children cannot express faith until later in life. Such an assumption rests in a limited view of childhood and a definition of faith restricted to primarily cognitive terms (2004, 10-13). Instead, Yust and others offer a relational and behavioral expression of faith as an active verb that involves not only *head* but also *heart* and *hands* as active categories. Faith expresses itself across the developmental categories (following James Fowler, John Westerhoff, and others; Stonehouse 1998, 145-68).

LEARNING THEORY AND CHILDREN

Traditional approaches to learning often struggled over the child's ability to participate in the learning process, stressing either an active or passive view

(May et al. 2005, 8-12). Modern educational theories, including John Dewey's, tend to portray an interactive engagement between teacher and child. Nevertheless, one of the primary learning theories that undergirds childhood education is learning by association. Following the work of Friedrich Herbart (1776-1841), the approach assumes that new knowledge is gained by associating new concepts or ideas with previous experience and understanding (Reed and Prevost 1993, 248-51), following a predictable pattern:

- *Preparation:* the student is prepared for learning by recalling past experiences and concepts.
- *Presentation:* the new body of information is made available and explained to the student.
- *Association:* the student explores the relationship between the new information and past experiences.
- *Generalization:* the student discerns a principle from what was learned in the previous step.
- *Application:* the student experiments with the principle through application in real life and simulations.

This approach involves the teacher as the primary supplier of concepts and ideas, even in interactive teaching methods tailored to the experiential world of children. Studies of children's learning tend to blend the traditional learning domains—behavioral (psychomotor or hands), cognitive (intellectual or head), and affective (social or heart)—at age-appropriate levels. In graded curriculum, educators focus on designing activities and addressing concepts that engage children according to their developmental capabilities. These traditional approaches to learning occasionally acknowledged the formative role of experience and imaginative play in the lives of young children as part of the educational journey.

An alternative learning theory, anchored in the work of John Amos Comenius and Johann Pestalozzi but popularized by Maria Montessori and Sofia Cavalletti, argues that learning in children occurs through sensory engagement, narrative, and imaginative wonder (Berryman 1991; May 2006). This approach stresses the use of "manipulatives," personal learning processes that open children outward to the world and inward to their own imaginative life. From a cognitive perspective, the approach focuses on the intake of experience and its ability to expand horizons and deepen personal identity. Karen Marie Yust offers a modified approach that incorporates multisensory learning methods and basic Christian practices (2004, 7-10, 21). She offers a series of categories that she believes condition but also lend expression to a child's spiritual life (13-19). Consider their implications in the life of the church:

- *Belonging:* being embraced by God and a community of faith as beloved and accepted. Where do kids feel connected in your church?
- *Thanksgiving:* living with a sense of gratitude for the gift of faith and God's provision for one's daily needs. Where do kids see gracious actions in your church?
- *Giftedness:* knowing that each person is wondrously and uniquely made, with gifts and abilities to contribute to the community. Where do kids display their gifts? Where do they get a chance to express purpose or vocation in the church?
- *Hospitality:* sharing one's gifts and welcoming the gifts of others so that God's vision of a just and peaceful world can be realized. Where do kids practice hospitality or display an open spirit in your church?
- *Understanding:* reflecting on one's spiritual experiences in order to become aware of how they shape one's life and commitments. When are kids encouraged to be reflective? In what settings are they asked to discern the different choices they must make in their life?
- *Hope:* expecting that there is something more of human existence than what we presently see or know. Where are kids encouraged to display optimism?

Yust's approach resembles other strategies (Berryman 1995) that seek to integrate emotion, imagination, spirituality, and basic Christian practices into an alternative approach to age-level learning. This narrative approach to child learning combines formative practices with a broader understanding of participation in the story of God (Pritchard 1992, 1-14). Based on an alternative view of childhood that respects narrative identity, ritualistic play, and imagination, these learning theories stress both wonder and participation (Berryman 1991, 17-19) as children engage in the life of the church.

▶ FAITHFUL DISCIPLESHIP FOR CHILDREN

Christian educators may explore traditional approaches to children's ministry through the use of the proverbial object lesson. This widespread practice uses image-based learning (flannel-graphs, work sheets, puppetry, or the well-known children's sermon), where specific items serve to connect everyday life with a biblical or moral principle. Learning by association undergirds this approach through a simple formula: *relate abstract concept* (Bible/doctrinal propositions) *to concrete experience* (children's experiences or activities) *by association* ("this is that").

The majority of children's ministry methods are indebted to the approach that separated cognition from experience (concepts from activity), though theorists on either side of the equation assert themselves through particular emphases. Christian educators who value the *source* of knowledge (*concepts*) tend to emphasize information-processing methods, while ministers who appreciate *experience* focus on active learning methods.

When approaching children's ministry from the conceptual side of the learning equation, theorists stress developmental readiness (graded curriculum). The focus is on recognition and recall of key Bible passages (Ten Commandments, Beatitudes, Great Commission) or doctrinal information (via catechisms) by certain ages. Often associated with an instructional approach (Carlson and Crupper 2006), educators motivate children with mental puzzles or direct reward (gold stars) to use cognitive skills for memorization and recall (May et al. 2005, 12-15). These cognitive efforts include suggestions or direct guidelines for application, but ministers often assume that the cognitive content has intrinsic worth; assent to the claims in the Bible or basic statements of faith will lead to salvation.

Theorists emphasizing the experiential side of the educational divide tend to focus on activities (behavior) that motivate students, reducing resistance through entertainment and pleasurable experiences. Engagement and application of principles reinforce learning. These approaches can be rather demonstrative, resembling a carnival atmosphere (May et al. 2005, 15-16). With direct emphasis on activity, these ministries may employ application (Graves 2006) or media saturation (Ellis et al. 2006) to create an alternative and incredibly active world. Ultimately, application and activity must associate biblical or theological concepts with the children's understanding of the world at their developmental level.

Regardless of approach, traditional ministry *for* children is organized around several key domains. First, ministries follow *age-level education* based on developmental abilities and the availability of children. These divisions begin with nursery through preschool classes, then follow with grade levels one to three and four to six respectively. Children's church and alternative evening programming (clubs, sports activities, etc.) often reflect some age-level classification. The second large domain is *event-centered ministry,* special activities such as vacation Bible school, camps, and holiday events. Events may recur every year, but rarely last more than a week at a time. A third domain is *parent support and family training,* which includes basic child-care support for adult activities, regular or occasional times of parent education, and pastoral care of families and children through in-home visits.

In addition to these key domains, children's ministers may select and evaluate curriculum as well as locate and store resources for volunteer teachers (resource center and/or closets). Christian educators develop classroom learning centers to enhance learning, diversify learning styles, and enable class management. Children's pastors often lead children's church or develop resources, such as brochures, for regular worship events. Children's ministers may coordinate children's service projects and special efforts in child evangelism in reaching out to the local community. In addition, children's pastors need to develop adequate policies of child safety and security and establish guidelines for discipline in various ministry settings. These activities cover most ministries organized and directed on behalf of children. However, new approaches attempt to incorporate the gifts and graces of children in the church and family—ministry *with* children.

▶ FAITHFUL DISCIPLESHIP WITH CHILDREN

New strategies that embrace ministry *with* children begin with a renewed recognition of the role of the child within the church. We find clues to this approach within larger conversations on the role of family in relation to the church and growing literature best described as children's spirituality. Theorists within this movement validate the spiritual experiences of children (Hay and Nye 2006; Ratcliff 2008, 21-57).

Educational methods within this approach draw from the work of Maria Montessori and Sofia Cavalletti, who emphasized the worth of the child in the world of the church (May 2006, 54-56). If the object lesson serves as the symbol of traditional children's ministry, the sanctuary may well define the role of children in the life of the church under this new approach as children enter a world of biblical narrative and Christian practice (Stewart and Berryman 1989).

Rather than learning by association, formation begins by nurturing children in the larger, narrative life of scripture rather than applying biblical principles from the text (Pritchard 1992, 18). Simple stories include *manipulatives* (small objects) or specific, deliberate actions. Teachers invite students to engage their imaginations and join the search for meaning. Jerome Berryman writes, "The sacred story, parable, liturgical action, or profound silence is entered into by the storyteller in an authentic way, but the meaning gained by the storyteller is not what is shown to the children. It is the act of making meaning that is shown. The storyteller invites the student into the language of the Christian tradition by example, and shows how to be involved" (1995, 34).

This existential approach, which emphasizes imagination and wonder, is conditioned by congregational practices of worship and ministry. Characterized by contemplative-reflective aspects (May 2006), the approach includes dynamic participation in formative environments (rituals, festivals, community gatherings) throughout the church, resulting in a comprehensive socialization into the Christian world, with children and adults as co-pilgrims in a search for discernment (Westerhoff 2006). Scottie May characterizes this as an ongoing circular movement: Encounters with God *lead to* developing a sense of awe and wonder, which *leads to* knowing God's character and actions, which *leads to* knowing and being formed in the character of God's people, which *leads to* owning an identity as part of the people of God, which *leads to* engaging in service and mission. May assumes that children may enter at any point of the cycle. Each movement indicates ongoing transformation via the Holy Spirit, with adults providing guidance and participating with children in the journey (2006, 68-69; see figure 17.1).

Figure 17.1

Cycle of Encounter and Discernment

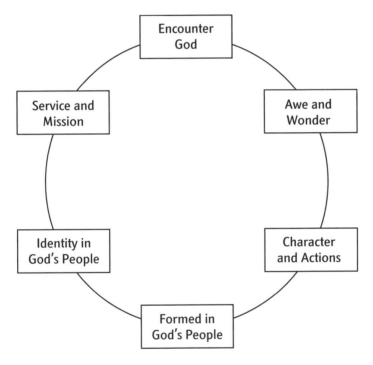

This cycle includes aspects of formation and discernment as well as moments of transformative ministry. Christian educators often take on the role of advocate for children as participants in church life. Adults condition their teaching to balance cognition with imagination so that worship (even children's church) serves as an entrance into God's mystery as well as behavioral training or entertainment. Formative practices include learning the Christian language and story through experience (e.g., Christian calendar festivals and storytelling), engaging in redemptive community relationships, and participating in prayer and service. Discernment includes taking in knowledge to stretch the mind and shape character, testing limits and imagining new possibilities through constructive activities. The result is students living out transformed spirituality for their own sake and for the sake of others. Children engaged in service and compassionate action, within the church and beyond, reflect the ministry of the church as they act out their faith.

▶ CONCLUSION

Churches may envision faithful discipleship as both *for* and *with* children. Some churches organize their ministry around a larger theme that expands some aspect of Christian education with children:

- *Program-Centered:* maintains a comprehensive series of programs, with one or two signature programs (clubs, children's church) that define the ministry
- *Child Outreach:* often includes large events or entertainment to attract children in a carnival-like atmosphere
- *Instructional Discipleship:* framed primarily through educational activities like quizzing or other Bible applications
- *Mission/Service:* dedicated to empowering children to engage the world through ministry
- *Family:* anchored in family life and resources (either family-focused or just family-friendly)
- *Worship-Centered:* anchored in specific child-focused worship celebration
- *Christian Practices:* reframes personal and congregational spiritual formation practices with children in mind

When considering how to organize the ministry, several key questions might be asked:

- How does the approach form children into Christians?
- How does the approach teach children to discern what is authentically Christian?
- Where and how does transformation occur with children so that they can authentically engage the world as a means of grace?

Think again about the toddler choir scenario that opened the chapter. In spite of the chaos, the children on the platform represented two realities that Sunday morning. They mirrored the desire of people in the congregation to offer uninhibited praise to God for the grace that we have received (whether or not we are on key). The children also represented hope, affirming that children have a right to be there and that God's redemptive activity will continue into the future. For congregations going through difficult times, such hope is essential for survival.

Children's ministers were active in directing children's efforts; adults responded and encouraged movements, even from behind cameras. Yet the ministry *to* children was no more important than the ministry *by* children and the children's ministry *with* adults, sharing in worship and discipleship. Those children, along with their dedicated children's workers, were a means of grace to an entire congregation.

▶ RESOURCES

Bakke, O. M. 2005. *When Children Became People: The Birth of Childhood in Early Christianity.* Minneapolis: Fortress Press.

Balswick, Jack O., Pamela Ebstyne King, and Kevin S. Reimer. 2005. *The Reciprocating Self: Human Development in Theological Perspective.* Downers Grove, IL: InterVarsity Press.

Bendroth, Margaret. 2001. Horace Bushnell's *Christian nurture.* In *The Child in Christian Thought*, 350-65. Ed. Marcia J. Bunge. Grand Rapids: William B. Eerdmans.

Berryman, Jerome W. 1991. *Godly Play: An Imaginative Approach to Religious Education.* Minneapolis: Augsburg Press.

_____. 1995. *Teaching Godly Play: The Sunday Morning Handbook.* Nashville: Abingdon Press.

Blevins, Dean. 2005. Faithful discipleship: A conjoined catechesis of truth and love. In *Considering the Great Commission: Explorations for a Wesleyan Praxis of Mission and Evangelism.* Ed. W. Stephen Gunter and Elaine A. Robinson. Nashville: Abingdon Press.

Bushnell, Horace. 2000/1908 Reprint. *Christian Nurture.* New York: Charles Scribner's/Eugene, OR: Wipf and Stock.

Carlson, Greg, and John K. Crupper. 2006. Instructional-analytic model. In *Perspectives on Children's Spiritual Formation*, 103-64. Ed. Michael J. Anthony. Nashville: B&H Academic.

Cook, Joan Littlefield, and Greg Cook. 2005. *Child Development: Principles and Perspectives.* SOS ed. Boston: Pearson.

Elkind, David. 1998. *Reinventing Childhood: Raising and Educating Children in a Changing World.* Rosemont, NJ: Modern Learning Press.

Ellis, Tim, Bill Baumgart, and Greg Carper. 2006. Media-driven active-engagement model. In *Perspectives on Children's Spiritual Formation*, 225-78. Ed. Michael J. Anthony. Nashville: B&H Academic.

Graves, Trisha. 2006. Pragmatic-participatory model. In *Perspectives on Children's Spiritual Formation*, 165-224. Ed. Michael J. Anthony. Nashville: B&H Academic.

Greven, Phillip. 1977. *The Protestant Temperament: Patterns of Child-Rearing, Religious Experience, and the Self in Early America.* Chicago: Chicago Univ. Press.

Gundry-Volf, Judith M. 2001. The least and the greatest: Children in the New Testament. In *The Child in Christian Thought*, 29-60. Ed. Marcia J. Bunge. Grand Rapids: William B. Eerdmans.

Guroian, Vigen. 2001. The ecclesial family: John Chrysostom on parenthood and children. In *The Child in Christian Thought*, 61-77. Ed. Marcia J. Bunge. Grand Rapids: William B. Eerdmans.

Hay, David, and Rebecca Nye. 2006. *The Spirit of the Child*. Rev. ed. London: Jessica Kingsley.

Heitzenrater, Richard P. 2001. John Wesley and children. In *The Child in Christian Thought*, 279-99. Ed. Marcia J. Bunge. Grand Rapids: William B. Eerdmans.

May, Scottie, Beth Posterski, Catherine Stonehouse, and Linda Cannell. 2005. *Children Matter: Celebrating Their Place in the Church, Family, and Community*. Grand Rapids: William B. Eerdmans.

May, Scottie. 2006. The contemplative-reflective model. In *Perspectives on Children's Spiritual Formation*, 45-102. Ed. Michael J. Anthony. Nashville: B&H Academic.

Miller-McLemore, Bonnie. 2003. *Let the Children Come: Reimagining Childhood from a Christian Perspective*. San Francisco: Jossey-Bass.

Pritchard, Gretchen Wolff. 1992. *Offering the Gospel to Children*. Cambridge, MA: Cowley Publications.

Ratcliff, Donald. 2008. "The spirit of children past": A century of child spirituality research. In *Nurturing Children's Spirituality: Christian Perspectives and Best Practices*, 21-57. Ed. Holly Catterton Allen. Eugene, OR: Cascade Books.

Reed, James, and Ronnie Prevost. 1993. *A History of Christian Education*. Nashville: Broadman and Holman.

Sisemore, Timothy A. 2004. From doctrine to practice: The influence of the doctrine of original sin on Puritan child-rearing. In *Children's Spirituality: Christian Perspectives, Research, and Applications*. Ed. Donald Ratcliff. Eugene, OR: Cascade Books.

Sparkman, G. Temp. 1983. *The Salvation and Nurture of the Child of God: The Story of Emma*. Valley Forge, PA: Judson Press.

Staples, Rob. 1991. *Outward Sign and Inward Grace: The Place of the Sacraments in Wesleyan Spirituality*. Kansas City: Beacon Hill Press of Kansas City.

Stewart, Sonja M., and Jerome Berryman. 1989. *Young Children and Worship*. Philadelphia: Westminster Press.

Stonehouse, Catherine. 1998. *Joining Children on the Spiritual Journey*. Grand Rapids: Baker Books.

_____. Children in Wesleyan thought. 2004. In *Children's Spirituality: Christian Perspectives, Research, and Applications*, 133-48. Ed. Donald Ratcliff. Eugene, OR: Cascade Books.

Stookey, Lawrence Hull. 1982. *Baptism: Christ's Act in the Church*. Nashville: Abingdon Press.

Stortz, Martha Elen. 2001. "When or where was your servant innocent?": Augustine on Childhood. In *The Child in Christian Thought*, 78-99. Ed. Marcia J. Bunge. Grand Rapids: William B. Eerdmans.

Wesley, John. 1988-1995. On the education of children. *Sermons* 3:354. In *The Works of John Wesley,* bicentennial ed. Ed. Albert Outler. Nashville: Abingdon Press.

Westerhoff, John H. 2006. *Will Our Children Have Faith?* Rev. ed. Harrisburg, PA: Moorehouse Publishing.

Yust, Karen Marie. 2004. *Real Kids Real Faith: Practices for Nurturing Children's Spiritual Lives.* San Francisco: Jossey-Bass.

EIGHTEEN

YOUTH MINISTRY

▶ INTRODUCTION

Imagine you are leading a Bible discussion when a junior high boy blurts out, "Look at the acne on her face!" A young girl blushes and runs out of the room. The young man and his friends break out laughing, knowing they have touched a nerve. How would you respond?

Imagine you are in senior high Sunday school when one of the youth announces, "Everyone in this church is a hypocrite! If we really followed what Jesus commanded, we would sell everything we have and hit the streets proclaiming the gospel." How would you respond?

Imagine you serve as a college chaplain when a young woman asks for an appointment. She admits that her philosophy class has challenged her faith. She has decided that "people are entitled to believe what they want because everything is relative." How would you respond?

Entering into faithful discipleship with youth brings us into the very heart of the church. Young people represent not only the future but also the congregation's present heartbeat. Kenda Creasy Dean notes that youth often supply the kind of passion that gives life to the congregation, fresh visions of what the church can accomplish for the kingdom of God and compassionate care for people that often challenge the limits of other church members (2004). Youth represent emerging independence, the ability to be both weak and strong at any given moment. They can be fragile, like children, needing extreme protection and guidance. But young people can also demonstrate seasoned maturity and resilience that allows them to meet challenges more mature adults struggle to overcome. No longer fully dependent on adults but not completely independent of adult guidance and support, the "semi-dependence" (Kett 1977, 14-37) of youth allows them to exercise their gifts while relying on the guidance of others. Youth embody the term *relational* (Balswick et al. 2005, 180-83). In their most independent moments they still recognize the need to be in relationship with others. In weaker times, they recognize that relationships support their lives during tough moments.

▶ DEFINITIONS: FAITHFUL YOUTH

Faithful discipleship, both for and with youth, seeks to help them define the quality of their relationships through the gospel, so relationships may be understood as holiness or Christlikeness. Christian education and youth ministry support youth in areas where they still depend on adult guidance and empower youth to live out their Christian lives to the fullness of their potential, in witness, love, faith, and purity. Following the Apostle Paul's advice to Timothy, we confidently say to youth, "Don't let anyone look down on you because you are young, but set an example for the believers in speech, in life, in love, in faith and in purity" (1 Timothy 4:12).

BIBLICAL PERSPECTIVES

Young people need opportunities to hear and respond to the good news of Jesus and to learn to live within the Christian story, so they can manifest holiness of heart and life. What role do young people play in the Bible that relates directly to young lives today? Youth ministers often turn to 1 Timothy 4:12; however, the passage has less relevance when we read commentaries that argue that Timothy must have been between thirty and thirty-five years of age when he received the letter, based on when he joined Paul and when Paul wrote the letter (Fee 1988, 106-7, 111). In some cultures and historical periods, thirty-five may be considered young, particularly for leadership. But many Christian educators work with adolescents half this age. Other youth ministers turn to the "young" Jesus of Luke 2:52, who "increased in wisdom and in years, and in divine and human favor" (NRSV). Luke also tells us, however, that Jesus' active ministry began much later, when he was about thirty years of age (Luke 3:23).

So where does one turn to validate the role of youth in scripture? Kenda Creasy Dean and Ron Foster argue that we might begin with Mary, the mother of Jesus, as the "God bearer" (1998, 43-53). Based on marriage customs in Jesus' day, Mary may have been about sixteen years old, yet she was given the special role of bearing the Son of God (Brown 1977, 123-24). We might also read about Samuel's anointing of David. In a culture that valued the number seven, David was not only the youngest but also the eighth son (see 1 Samuel 16). Samuel anoints David, the marginal son, who will change the destiny of Israel (Brueggemann 1990, 121-23). David, Joseph (see Genesis 30—37), Jeremiah (Varughese 2008, 40), and even Samuel as a child are unlikely candidates to be called so early in life. David and Mary represent younger people on the edges of the social order, not those we expect God to use as leaders. Paul embraced an even younger Timothy as part of his ministry and, as Dean and Foster note, Paul also saw Timothy as an agent (not object) of God's mission:

"a young man transformed by the Gospel who can convey this transforming good news to others" (1998, 26).

THEOLOGICAL PERSPECTIVES

The biblical witness reminds us that God is vitally involved with people that society might not consider mature enough or ready to represent the kingdom of God. Adults tend to view youth as in between childhood and adulthood, unable to take responsibility or not quite ready. Yet God reaches into the lives of these young people and calls them forward, like David, Mary, and Timothy. Christian educators and youth ministers must prepare youth not only to accept the gospel but also to embrace God's call on their lives, even when society says they might not be ready. Our responsibility is to understand the marvelous ways God is at work in the lives of youth and to guide, empower, and serve as advocates for young people as they awaken to what God might do through them.

Providing Christian education with youth requires a series of theological convictions that shape our efforts (Dean 2001, 27-36). Young people are a key component of the ministry of faithful discipleship that calls the church to model holiness of heart and life and pursue God's mission to redeem creation. Youth ministry finds its identity in God's redemptive activity through Jesus Christ and incarnated in the world as the Holy Spirit works through communities of faith. No youth ministry (parish or parachurch) may be separated from the church universal. Therefore, faithful discipleship with youth should function cooperatively with other congregational ministries and be held accountable to biblical standards. Youth serve not only as recipients of ministry but also as agents of God's missional efforts both within and through the life of the congregation.

Christian education with youth primarily occurs through relational bonds, a particular strength and need among young people in most cultural settings, but youth programs and ministers do not save youth; only Christ does that (Dean 1998). God calls people working with youth to witness to the biblical story of Jesus Christ and allow the Holy Spirit to work through their actions to communicate grace. Relationships between adults (Christian educators, youth ministers, adult volunteers) and youth are important models of the relational love of the Father, the Son, and the Holy Spirit. Such love never manipulates or coerces youth for a goal that serves the youth minister but not young people (Root 2007). Instead, youth ministers allow God's love to flow through them to teaching the basics of the faith, nurture devotional practices, and empower youth for God's mission to the world.

Faith discipleship must learn to address people throughout their developmental lives, including the period commonly known as youth or adolescence. Christian educators seek to redemptively address the contextual issues of youth, while encouraging them to continue to grow in grace and thus "come to the unity of the faith and of the knowledge of the Son of God, to maturity, to the measure of the full stature of Christ" (Ephesians 4:13, NRSV).

▶ DYNAMIC CONSIDERATIONS

While biblical studies of children and the family have increased in recent years (Bakke 2005; Balch and Osiek 2003; Osiek and Balch 1997; Perdue et al. 1997), specific studies of youth or young adults remain limited. Perhaps for good reason, since one of the earliest biblical accounts of youth or young adults is Deuteronomy 21:18-21, which gives parents permission to punish disobedient sons by stoning them to death (Blenkinsopp 1997, 70-71). Nevertheless, one does find evidence of youth and youth culture in history. In preindustrial Europe, poor youth did not qualify to inherit family farms and were forced to wander the countryside or move to towns. These young people (mainly boys) banded together in apprenticeships or other loosely fraternal arrangements in Britain, Germany, and France until they reached professional competence or economic independence (Gillis 1974, 8-35).

The concept of *youth* seems to be transcultural and transhistorical, but it is always related to social/cultural descriptions that anticipate, and to some degree find definition in, adulthood. Educators will find the North American norms and expectations for youth ministry in a global youth culture that has been communicated through Western media and merchandizing. Recognizing this prevalent view of youth and youth ministry, Christian educators may find it instructive to explore how these concepts emerged in addition to the psychological perspectives of this age level.

YOUTH DEVELOPMENT THEORY

When discussing the developmental characteristics of youth, theorists must resolve a key question. Is adolescence a transitory stage or a stage with transitions? Young people live in a world neither fully dependent on adults nor fully independent as contributors to society (Kett's "semi-dependence"). Historically and culturally, the term *youth* described a marginal or transitional phase (transitory stage) between childhood and adulthood (Grimes 2002, 121-25; Koteskey 1991, 42-69). Adolescence has not always been considered on its own in historical studies. Until the end of the nineteenth century, *childhood* included some of the teenage years. The time for transition to adulthood was generally quite short, though recognized, if for less than desirable reasons. For instance, beginning in the early 1800s, many U.S. founding "fathers" blamed young people for spiritual and moral decline in the United States (Wallach

1997, 1-54), and young people were the primary target of many revival campaigns of the eighteenth and nineteenth centuries (Schultze et al. 1991, 24-27).

The primary shift to viewing youth as adolescents (a stage with transitions) occurred around the turn of the twentieth century. Many social factors influenced this development: the rise of the industrial era when fewer young people needed to work, the creation of mandatory public school systems that provided new social settings, and the increased wealth that turned young people into consumers (Hine 1999). Social scientists like G. Stanley Hall provided primary motivation for the category. Heavily influenced by the ideas of Darwin, Hall applied the scientific and biological aspects of Darwin's views to the study of adolescent development. A 1904 two-volume work, *Adolescence,* affirmed Hall's belief that heredity interacts with environmental influences to determine development. Hall defined *adolescence* as a time of "storm and stress," during which conflict abounds (Santrock 2007, 6). Hall's definition combined with social influences to create a view of the distinct age-level or youth subculture that we recognize today (White 2005, 19-41). The post-World War II concept of *teenager* surfaced in a 1941 issue of *Popular Science* magazine (Hine 1999, 9; Savage 2007, xv); the idea of young people struggling to make the now-longer transition from childhood to adulthood became part of the social fabric of Western society.

Globally, the ages of *youth* vary between age ten and age twenty, though some cultures extend this upward, including some U.S. social theorists who now posit a provisional or emergent adulthood associated with late adolescence (Arnett 2004; Sheehy 1996, 8). Transitioning through youth includes moderating levels of dependence and rites of passage. Regardless of social indicators, several biological changes and psychosocial challenges occur during this period of transition (Santrock 2007, 70-82, 97-101, 239-57):

- *Rapid Physical Growth:* particularly spurts that occur at strategic points in early adolescence
- *Sexual Maturation:* often associated with puberty/menarche
- *Secondary Sexual Characteristics:* the onset of body sculpting that enhances masculine and feminine traits
- *Motivational and Emotional Changes:* including hormonal changes and surges in the limbic brain pathways
- *Cognitive Development:* particularly in formal operational thinking
- *Maturation of Judgment, Self-Regulation Skills:* resulting in different levels of moral decision making and risk taking among youth (also see Galvan et al. 2006; Holmes 1978)
- *Brain Changes:* linked to each dynamic mentioned as the brain sculpts neurons and synaptic pathways based on experiences, though specific ar-

eas within the brain appear to mature at different times, creating some disconnect between basal and higher brain level function (also Giedd 2009)

Theorists divide young people roughly into three cohorts drawn from American public school approaches, beginning with early adolescence related to middle school or junior high school age. The range may begin as early as ten years of age, though the transition traditionally occurs as one becomes a teenager at thirteen.

Historically, preteen children were not considered early adolescents, but two important social changes now cause theorists to include these young people with teenagers. First, a rise in global healthcare has lowered the age for the onset of puberty, particularly the advent of the menstrual cycle, or menarche. In 1850, the average onset of menarche was 17+ years; by 1975, the age had dropped to 13.5 years and now may occur as early as 10 years of age (Santrock 2007, 73). The inclusion of younger people also comes from studies of at-risk behavior that threatens children's lives (Carnegie Foundation 1995). Often forced into social puberty, acting beyond their level of cognitive decision making, preteens face adolescent problems in childlike bodies (Mowry and Robinson 1993). Relationally friendly, these youth discover an interpersonal perspective ("I see you seeing me . . . seeing the person I think you see") that betrays a new quality of self-awareness based on assumptions of how other people see them. Socially aware, these early adolescents can experience insecurities because of rapid changes in body type, hormonal imbalances including acne, or other uncomfortable traits. Youth of this age often identify with groups, trends, and fads to offset the chaos of heightened personal decision making and the scrutiny of others. Nevertheless, younger adolescents exhibit promising developmental characteristics, revealing a sense of optimism and hope even as their bodies undergo physical adjustments.

Mid-adolescence, now defined as the high school level, marked the final stage of adolescent behavior in Western industrial society through the 1950s (Schneider and Stevenson 1999). Physically, the stage includes the final maturation of secondary sexual characteristics. Masculine and feminine characteristics may change a bit in later adolescence, but the qualities of body type appear established. Cognitively, this stage marks the height of Piaget's formal operations, often leading to youthful idealism. Youth at this stage engage in alternating tasks of intrapersonal identification (the search for personal identity by differentiating from others) and interpersonal intimacy (engaging others with the depth and closeness often associated with family members). Peer relations take on new meaning as primary communities. For some social theorists, these subcultures of youth emerge out of abandonment by adults. Patricia Hersch and Chap Clark argue that North American culture tends to isolate youth into cultural subclusters (Clark 2004, 75-86) as a "tribe apart" (Hersch 1999, 17-22, 30) in desperate need of adults to engage their personal-relational world. Whether socially conditioned by the absence of adults or socially formed through intense peer relationships, young people seem to resonate with both peer groups and close-knit family relationships. Relational identity incorporates both personal integrity and interpersonal intimacy.

Late adolescence or emerging adulthood includes a number of younger people from college age to the late twenties. Defined by social expectations, many of these youth represent a new cultural phenomenon of delayed decisions concerning typically adult markers: starting a family, entering a permanent vocation, serving community leadership roles, and so forth. Jeffrey Arnett notes five characteristics of emerging adults: identity exploration (trying out various vocational and romantic possibilities), instability, self-preoccupation, feeling in between or in transition (neither adolescent nor adult), and yet hopeful because of multiple opportunities to transform one's life (2004, 8). Sharon Parks notes that passage through this age represents the critical years of negotiating the final stages of cognition, dependence, and community that are crucial for adult life (1986). Many of the descriptors offered with this final group demonstrate the relative nature of developmental categories. While the stage of late adolescence is present in many Western industrial settings, youth this age in other cultures do move into standard adult roles of work, family, and child-rearing; they also take on adult aspects of interdependence with people of different generations. Such indicators should remind us of the psychosocial implications of any descriptive category. Youth remain youth (particularly in late adolescence) due in part to adult expectations and empowerment.

IMPLICATIONS FOR DISCIPLESHIP WITH YOUTH

As much as childhood is determined by biological change in relation to cultural influence, adolescence seems even more deeply shaped by social and cultural interpretations of biological and psychological growth. While elusive, there does seem to be a relationship between a social view of young people who are no longer children but not quite adults, and the culture they live in. Rather than fixing a strict age level to this category, one must pay attention to the specific historical and cultural expectations and then ask how the church can best minister with a group of people who live in the transition between childhood and adulthood. The elongation of adolescence renders several social and cultural problems. For instance, the time between sexual maturity and formalizing a relationship was relatively short in the Western world of the 1950s (Schneider and Stevenson 1999, 15-30). Youth reached puberty around age fourteen, and often married four to five years later upon leaving high school. By the twenty-first century, the same period of abstinence, in a sexually charged media culture, might easily extend to fifteen years or more. Developing modes for encouraging Christian behavior is a crucial challenge when social customs break down. In addition, social commentary sometimes portrays young people as dangerous or delinquent in nature, when the adult commentators prove to be the greater culprits in antisocial behavior (Males 1999). When adults portray youth as wounded or dangerous, Christian educators must intercede to lift up the positive traits of youth. Regardless of age, youth crave relationships that both validate and empower their lives.

LEARNING THEORY AND YOUTH

The deeply relational nature of this age informs a large portion of our understanding of youth learning theory. Many youth enter this stage operating within a concrete framework but soon exercise formal operational thought focused on concept formation and ideas (see Piaget). Idealization often shapes the cognitive framework, though students may not always be consistent in matching beliefs to lifestyle. Youth often desire to engage with learning in a way that allows them to co-construct knowledge through moments of shared meaning and interpersonal growth (i.e., *constructivism;* see chapter 10). In addition, Albert Bandura's theory of learning via modeling undergirds a number of efforts to use relationships as a source for behavioral change (Yount 1996, 179-85). Bandura argues that youth learn by observation (through media, fashion, social groups, or local celebrities) and adjust their lifestyle to coincide with people they wish to emulate (Davies 1991, 22-32).

Motivation for new learning can be deeply tied to identity and commitment (Santrock 2007). James Marcia notes that adolescent identity formation often revolves around moments of meaningful crisis and the challenge to make a commitment to a particular role and path in these moments. Marcia defines the various combinations of crisis and commitment, and he offers a typology that describes how well a young person negotiates openness to these new experiences and responds with new commitments. (1) A young person who is open to transition (crisis) but has not yet made a commitment is in "Identity Moratorium." This perspective is normal and healthy for the majority of young people during a portion of adolescence. (2) A young person who resists transitions but maintains specific commitment is "Identity Foreclosed." (3) Youth who both resist transitions (crises) and possess no commitments appear as "Identity Diffused." (4) Young people who can engage transitions and maintain commitments have reached a perspective that Marcia terms "Identity Achieved" (see Santrock 2007, 154-56). Young people often bring these predispositions to the learning process, which deeply shapes the cognitive and relational framework of their learning.

Sharon Parks (1986), building on Marcia and the work of William Perry (1968/1970), notes that middle and late adolescence also undergo similar intellectual and relational changes as they approach adulthood. Anchored in her understanding of faith development, Parks' approach helps Christian educators understand the learning processes (cognitive and relational) as older adolescents encounter new ways of thinking. When confronted by new knowledge and experience, particularly in authoritative settings where they feel compelled to address the presented material, young people transition through various stages. Cognitively, youth move from a conventional viewpoint with an accepted knowledge base (authorities provide information) to a probing exploration of knowledge (often idealistically) before settling with a set of commitments they have tested and believe true for their lives. Similarly, youth move from an early sense of relational dependence to a time of fragile inner-dependence (learning to trust themselves in the midst of relationships), as they move to a healthy interdependence that is shaped by mutual respect. Early communities that shape these youth are quite conventional and reflect the cultural heritage. Over time, youth seek groups that match their ideological commitments (often subgroups at school) before finding specific communities that both reflect their lives and future goals and encourage them to remain open to people who are unlike them. In each circumstance, young people move from an embedded, unreflective life to a reflective but deeply relational position (82-110). Parks observes that unqualified relativism or the absence of community connection does not reflect maturity. The unexamined believe that "my community possesses all truth and other people are wrong" is no different from the assumption that everything is relative; the absolutism of both positions serves the same ends. Until youth can hold to certain truths while conceding the possibility of different viewpoints, they lack cognitive and relational maturity.

Parks also asserts that imagination plays a large role in the adolescent capacity to construct knowledge and in energizing faith through intuiting and responding to transformative visions of the future. Imagination is a third primary resource for understanding how youth learn and grow in faith. Kenda Dean notes that youth bring passion to the learning process, so the term *imagination* describes not only cognitive ability but also emotional desire and relational hope that the future can be changed. Harnessing these abilities to dream dreams and envision the kingdom of God provides an incredibly important resource in the learning process.

▶ APPROACHES TO YOUTH MINISTRY

A logical beginning point to describe a consistent approach to faithful discipleship with youth, at least in Western culture, might be Robert Raikes' creation of the Sunday school in eighteenth-century England. While normally associated with ministry to younger children, there is evidence that Raikes' ministry included older children that today would be considered young adolescents. The rise of Sunday school ministries marked the beginning of a parachurch ministry marked by special emphasis on providing Christian education to children and youth, which spread throughout North America. The early efforts of Robert Raikes (circa 1780-86) in England provide the impetus for just one of many historical expressions of youth ministry in North America. Similarly, the Christian Endeavor Societies (circa 1881) serve as forerunners of the modern youth group (Senter and Kesler 1992, 85-106). These societies, initiated and supervised by adults, invited young people to meet independently in groups that were often run by the youth and based on basic rules of mutual accountability, called the pledge. The societies were so popular, they were adopted by many churches and denominations, including the Luther League and (Methodist) Epworth League, as church-related youth groups.

These groups changed dramatically as modern ideas of youth shifted during the twentieth century and innovative parachurch ministries like Youth for Christ (YFC) and Young Life dominated programming ideas. However, the concept of youth groups as a primary vehicle for discipleship seemed settled. Most current thinking about the need for youth to gather together formally in the church for the purpose of developing Christian principles and leadership owe their origins to Christian Endeavor; while most youth ministry strategies dedicated to connecting and relating to youth find their source in YFC movements. Each of these discipleship innovations are indebted to innovative Christian leaders who responded to social and cultural forces (Senter and Kesler 1992, 107-52). These historical frameworks reflect forms of ministry that are similar to those covered in the chapter on Christian education with children.

▶ FAITHFUL DISCIPLESHIP *FOR* YOUTH

The early endeavors of Sunday school and the YMCA/YWCA provided ministry for youth who were dislocated, on the margins of society because of relocation or urban anonymity, often looking for work. By the middle of the twentieth century, the public high school became the social milieu for youth. Ministry reflected a need to support youth in their settings by providing programming that resonated with their interests and connected youth to caring adults through nurturing relationships. Often couched in evangelistic terminology, the relationships served as a means for introducing the gospel and guiding youth in their Christian growth.

As Jim Burns and Mike DeVries note, ministry with youth requires entering their world, demonstrating unconditional love, engaging in relationships where adults provided nurture and modeled Christian values and practices (2008/2001, 18-26). This approach, anchored in the life of the youth leader and other caring adults, incorporated a variety of other practical strategies including evangelistic outreach, small-group development, worship leadership, youthful ministry and mission, camping and retreat opportunities, experiential teaching, and leadership development. Instructional approaches varied with the youth leaders' understanding of scripture (see chapter 2). At the core of these efforts were caring adults who explicitly trusted in their ability to relate to youth through activities and programs while providing grounded instruction, accountability, Christian modeling, and often large doses of pastoral care (78-149, 242-308).

Relational youth ministers employed programming to open doors and create space for relationships with youth. Historically, relationships tended to center on the youth leaders; however, the role of the family emerged as another significant relational center (DeVries 1994). Youth ministers began to acknowledge that their ministries were removed from the life of families and the general church, creating "one-eared" Mickey Mouse ministries that isolated youth from intergenerational influence.

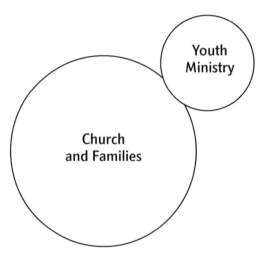

Recognizing the power of families to shape mature faith (or create hostile environments), Christian educators sought to resource families and employ family-like relationships within youth ministries. Family-oriented youth ministry took several forms, including family-focused (the family as the primary locus of ministry) or family-friendly (youth ministry alert to family needs), often including formational and relational skills to be used within the family (Justice 1998, 31). While such efforts provided a powerful corrective, considerable attention must be given to the overall spiritual depth within the family. For instance, in North America, many adults struggle (as do their children) with a social-religious environment that supports a view characterized by Christian Smith as "Moral Therapeutic Deism," which portrays God as one who makes people happy, supplies needs, and calls persons to act nicely toward others (2005, 162-71). Smith notes that teenage religion largely reflects adult religion, so faithful discipleship must include both parents and youth (170).

The introduction of family-based youth ministry expanded the relational model, but it still envisions relationships flowing in one direction, resourcing youth through education, nurture, guidance, even pastoral care for young people within the local community or isolated in youth subcultures on the margins of society. These strategies use large entertainment events, afterschool gatherings, or one-to-one encounters to bring youth into the relationship. The outcomes often rest on the interpersonal and spiritual wisdom of adults, so careful screening is necessary, and clear boundaries must be maintained. Powerful, relational, and directive, this approach assumes that youth need direct guidance because of dangerous cultural influences in media or popular culture (Mueller 2006). Relationships provide the means of grace to introduce vital teaching, mentoring, and care.

▸ FAITHFUL DISCIPLESHIP *WITH* YOUTH

Beginning with Christian Endeavor, a number of discipleship strategies also envisioned youth at the center of ministry. While under some level of adult supervision, youth possess a range of abilities that empower them to directly engage in the life of the church. Recently, ministers have begun to reject the preponderance of youth programming. Superficial relationships in which adults see youth as a means to fulfill evangelistic or programming goals are giving way to a view of relationships with youth as a valuable goal. The emergence of postmodern culture reemphasizes the need for communal participation alongside individual relationships (Folmsbee 2007; Jones 2001). Charting each creative response and development may be difficult unless they are organized under some general guide. Following the overall intent of this text, we will use the Wesleyan categories of formation, discernment, and transformation. In response to some of the limitations of standard relational youth ministry, youth ministers now argue for an emphasis on formative Christian practices that youth can engage for personal transformation, for greater discernment in the quality of their relationships, and for a transformative engagement in changing and shaping the world.

Christian educators who take seriously spiritual formation practices see youth as co-pilgrims and participants in their own formative processes (King 2006; Yaconelli 2006). This approach reframes relationship so neither the developmental needs of youth nor the personal goals of adults set the agenda. Instead, through Christian practice, God sets the agenda by shaping the lives of youth and adults together (Dean and Foster 1998, 26-29).

Formative discipleship notes the importance of grounded adult leadership and participation with the entire congregation. Youth need to engage in formation practices communally, with adults in the congregation as well as among themselves. Kenda Dean, responding to concerns about isolated youth groups, notes that some congregations have attempted to disband youth groups (often for economic reasons) without understanding the symbiotic relationship between the larger adult community and the subcultural needs of youth (1998, 211-12). Youth gather to support and empower one another. Formation occurs with a deep understanding that scripture provides a narrative world of story and ritual to shape both daily practice and in-depth encounter (Blevins 2001; Green 2001; Middendorf 2000). Practices may vary, such as youth using different forms of prayer (King 2006, 112-38), but young people maintain consistency through a rule of life that guides their ongoing encounter with God (151-82). When Christian educators frame these gatherings with Christian practices, youth encounter deep moments of formation and transformation. Developing a balanced youth group while also serving as an advocate in the larger congregation ensures that youth have opportunities to participate on an equal level. They can become a means of grace to the local congregation while being shaped by formative practices within the faith community.

Concerns with relational approaches have prompted theorists to envision a means of relationship that empowers rather than manipulates youth. As noted, some youth ministers raise concerns that relational youth ministry serves the desires of adults more than the needs of youth (Root 2007, 62-80). Similar to critiques of youth programming devolving into meaningless events, this concern argues that lack of discernment reduces a youth minister's true attention toward youth. A complementary, yet reductionist definition of relationship with God (the "Jesus is my boyfriend" syndrome) also risks reducing young people's theological understanding of the magnitude of God, the depths of Christ's suffering, and the cost of the call to true discipleship. In response, youth theorists now call for a disciplined attentiveness to the lives of youth, including the world they live within (142-65). This approach seeks to assist youth to discern the nature of their relationships as a form of spiritual practice (White 2005, 63-85), thus helping them resist viewing the world and Christianity as consumable products of personal choice.

In North America, where youth refuse to believe in the influence of out-side cultural forces, adults often initiate the discernment process (Smith 2005, 234). Youth eventually embrace the approach and accept the call to discern-ment as their task. This begins to empower youth to name their world, raise critical and creative questions in light of their understanding of the gospel, and to imagine an alternative way of life shaped by the gospel (White 2005, 88-200). Often framed in efforts to resist consumer culture (Mahan, Warren, and White 2008), this approach also guides youth toward transformational practices of peace, justice, and care of the earth.

A third approach intentionally engages youth in the life of the church and the world through redemption ministries. Many of these efforts involve compassionate activities related to short-term missions, urban encounters, and various service projects within and beyond the church (Dean and Foster 1998, 149-58), missional engagements from within youth ministry itself (Folmsbee 2007, 85-97). However, youth are now addressing larger issues of justice, such as child labor (Kielburger and Major 1999) and modern slavery (Rymer 2007). Working with Internet resources, local networks in schools and neighbor-hoods, and traditional youth groups, young people engage the world creatively and critically. Youth identify with marginalized groups, serving as advocates artistry, raising funds and community awareness, and direct protest with adult authorities. These strategies extend relationality to a global context, refram-ing relationships through moral and ethical lenses that involve communities, nations, and the world. Christian educators are developing strategies to both nurture and perpetuate such movements. Not all such efforts will develop into long-term ministries, but the youth involved in them are empowered and transformed.

▶ CONCLUSION

Just as God used young people strategically in the biblical story (David, Mary, Timothy) and through the history of the church, the Holy Spirit con-tinues to empower and guide young people to follow God's mission to passion-ately engage the world and build up the body of Christ. For all their perceived frailties and limitations, young people possess vibrant desire and imagination that equip them to live out the kingdom of God, modeling holiness of heart and life. This ability blossoms when the church guides and empowers youth as coparticipants in the kingdom of God.

▶ RESOURCES

Arnett, Jeffrey Jensen. 2004. *Emerging Adulthood: The Winding Road from the Late Teens Through the Twenties.* New York: Oxford Univ. Press.

Bakke, O. M. 2005. *When Children Became People: The Birth of Childhood in Early Christianity.* Minneapolis: Fortress Press.

Balch, David L., and Carole Osiek, eds. 2003. *Early Christian Families in Context: An Interdisciplinary Dialog.* Grand Rapids: William B. Eerdmans.

Balswick, Jack O., Pamela Ebstyne King, and Kevin S. Reimer. 2005. *The Reciprocating Self: Human Development in Theological Perspective.* Downers Grove, IL: InterVarsity Press.

Blenkinsopp, Joseph. 1997. The family in first temple Israel. In *Families in Ancient Israel: Family, Religion, and Culture,* 48-103. Ed. Leo G. Perdue, Joseph Blenkinsopp, John J. Collins, and Carol Meyers. Louisville, KY: Westminster/John Knox Press.

Blevins, Dean. 2001. Narrative teaching: Learning how to teach the story of God. In *Worship-Centered Teaching: Guiding Youth to Discover Their Identity in Christ,* 63-80. Ed. James Hampton and Rick Edwards. Kansas City: Beacon Hill Press of Kansas City.

Brown, Raymond E. 1977. *The Birth of the Messiah: A Commentary on the Infancy Narratives in Matthew and Luke.* Garden City, NY: Doubleday.

Brueggemann, Walter. 1990. *First and Second Samuel.* In *Interpretation: A Bible Commentary for Teaching Preaching.* Ed. James Luther Mays. Louisville, KY: John Knox Preaching.

Burns, Jim, with Mark DeVries. 2008. *Uncommon Youth Ministry: Your Onramp to Launching an Extraordinary Youth Ministry.* Ventura, CA: Regal/Gospel Light. Originally published in 2001 as *The Youth Builder.* Ventura, CA: Gospel Light.

Carnegie Foundation of New York. 1995. *Great Transitions: Preparing Adolescents for a New Generation.* Available online at http://carnegie.org/sub/pubs/reports/great_transitions/gr_intro.html (accessed April 13, 2009).

Clark, Chap. 2004. *Hurt: Inside the World of Today's Teenagers.* Grand Rapids: Baker Book House.

Davies, James A. 1991. Adolescent subculture. In *Handbook of Youth Ministry,* 7-41. Ed. Donald Ratcliff and James A. Davies. Birmingham, AL: Religious Education Press.

Dean, Kenda Creasy. 2001. Fessing up: Owning our theological commitments. In *Starting Right: Thinking Theologically About Youth Ministry,* 27-36. Ed. Kenda Creasy Dean, Chap Clark, and Dave Rahn. Grand Rapids: Zondervan.

———. 2004. *Practicing Passion: Youth and the Quest for a Passionate Church,* 1-69. Grand Rapids: William B. Eerdmans.

Dean, Kenda Creasy, and Ron Foster. 1998. *The Godbearing Life: The Art of Soul Tending for Youth Ministry.* Nashville: Upper Room Books.

DeVries, Mark. 1994. *Family-Based Youth Ministry: Reaching the Been-There, Done-That Generation.* Downers Grove, IL: InterVarsity Press.

Fee, Gordon D. *1 and 2 Timothy, Titus.* 1988. In *New International Biblical Commentary.* Ed. W. Ward Gasque. Peabody, MA: Hendrickson.

Folmsbee, Chris. 2007. *A New Kind of Youth Ministry.* Grand Rapids: Zondervan/Youth Specialties.

Galvan, Adriana, Todd A. Hare, Cindy E. Parra, Jackie Penn, Henning Voss, Gary Glover, and B. J. Casey. 2006. Earlier development of the accumbens relative to orbitofrontal cortex might underlie risk-taking behavior in adolescents. In *Journal of Neuroscience* 26, no. 25 (June 21): 6885-92.

Giedd, Jay N. 2009. The teen brain: Primed to learn, primed to take risks. In *Cerebrum Journal*, The Dana Foundation (February). Accessed online at http://www.dana.org/news/cerebrum/ (April 2, 2009).

Gillis, John R. 1974. *Youth and History: Tradition and Change in European Age Relations 1770-Present.* New York: Academic Press.

Green, Tim. 2001. Participating in the story of God. In *Worship-Centered Teaching: Guiding Youth to Discover Their Identity in Christ,* 23-34. Ed. James Hampton and Rick Edwards. Kansas City: Beacon Hill Press of Kansas City.

Grimes, Ronald L. 2002. *Deeply into the Bone: Re-Inventing Rites of Passage.* Berkeley, CA: Univ. of California Press.

Hampton, James, and Rick Edwards, eds. 2001. *Worship-Centered Teaching: Guiding Youth to Discover Their Identity in Christ.* Kansas City: Beacon Hill Press of Kansas City.

Hersch, Patricia. 1999. *A Tribe Apart: A Journey into the Heart of American Adolescence.* New York: Ballantine Books.

Hine, Thomas. 1999. *The Rise and Fall of the American Teenager: A New History of the American Adolescent Experience.* New York: Avon Books.

Holmes, D. S. 1978. Projection as a defense mechanism. In *Psychological Bulletin* 83:677-88.

Jones, Tony. 1991. *Postmodern Youth Ministry.* Grand Rapids: Zondervan/Youth Specialties.

Justice, Mike. 1998. *It Takes a Family to Raise a Youth Ministry: Developing an Effective Strategy for Serving Families.* Kansas City: Beacon Hill Press of Kansas City.

Keilburger, Craig, and Kevin Major. 1999. *Free the Children: A Young Man Fights Against Child Labor and Proves That Children Can Change the World.* New York: Harper Perennial.

Kett, Joseph. 1977. *Rites of Passage: Adolescence in America, 1790 to the Present.* New York: Basic Books.

King, Mike. 2006. *Presence-centered Youth Ministry: Guiding Students into Spiritual Formation.* Downers Grove, IL: InterVarsity Press.

Koteskey, Ronald L. 1991. Adolescence as a cultural invention. In *Handbook of Youth Ministry.* Ed. Donald Ratcliff and James A. Davies. Birmingham, AL: Religious Education Press.

Mahan, Brian J., Michael Warren, and David F. White. 2008. *Awakening Youth Discipleship: Christian Resistance in a Consumer Culture.* Eugene, OR: Cascade Books.

Males, Mike A. 1999. *Framing Youth: 10 Myths About the Next Generation.* Monroe, MA: Common Courage Press.

Middendorf, Jon. 2000. *Worship-Centered Youth Ministry: A Compass for Guiding Youth into God's Story.* Kansas City: Beacon Hill Press of Kansas City.

Mowry, Kathy Lewis, and Ed Robinson. 1993. *Preteen Ministry: Between a Rock and a Hard Place.* Kansas City: Beacon Hill Press of Kansas City.

Mueller, Walt. 2006. *Engaging the Soul of Youth Culture: Bridging Teen Worldviews and Christian Truth*. Downers Grove, IL: InterVarsity Press.

Osiek, Carolyn, and David L. Balch. 1997. *Families in the New Testament World: Households and House Churches*. Louisville, KY: Westminster/John Knox Press.

Parks, Sharon. 1986. *The Critical Years: The Young Adult Search for a Faith to Live By.* San Francisco: Harper and Row.

Perdue, Leo G., Joseph Blenkinsopp, John J. Collins, and Carol Meyers. 1997. *Families in Ancient Israel: Family, Religion, and Culture*. Louisville, KY: Westminster/John Knox Press.

Perry, Willam G., Jr. 1968/1970. *Forms of Intellectual and Ethical Development in the College Years: A Scheme*. Fort Worth: Harcourt Brace Jovanovich College.

Root, Andrew. 2007. *Revisiting Relational Youth Ministry: From a Strategy of Influence to a Theology of Incarnation*. Downers Grove, IL: IVP Books.

Rymer, Sally. 2007. Clapham sect phase II. Available online at http://csp2justiceseekers.com/8.html (accessed April 17, 2009).

Santrock, John W. 2007. *Adolescence*. 11th ed. Boston: McGraw Hill.

Savage, John. 2007. *Teenage: The Creation of Youth Culture*. New York: Viking Press.

Schneider, Barbara, and David Stevenson. 1999. *The Ambitious Generation: America's Teenagers Motivated but Directionless*. New Haven, CT: Yale Univ. Press.

Schultze, Quentin J., Roy M. Anker, James D. Bratt, William D. Romanowski, John W. Worst, and Lambert Zuidervaart. 1991. *Dancing in the Dark: Youth, Popular Culture, and the Electronic Media*. Grand Rapids: William B. Eerdmans.

Senter, Mark, III, and Jay Kesler. 1992. *The Coming Revolution in Youth Ministry: And Its Radical Impact on the Church*. Wheaton, IL: Victor Books.

Sheehy, Gail. 1996. *New Passages*. New York: Ballantine Books.

Smith, Christian, with Melinda Lundquist Denton. 2005. *Soul Searching: The Religious and Spiritual Lives of American Teenagers*. Oxford: Oxford Univ. Press.

Stafford, Tim, and Tom Albin. 2003. Finding God in small groups. *Christianity Today* 47 (August): 42-44.

Steele, Les L. 1990. *On the Way: A Practical Theology of Christian Formation*. Grand Rapids: Baker Books.

Strauss, William, and Neil Howe. 1998. *The Fourth Turning*. New York: Broadway Books.

Taylor, Mendell. 1948. *Nazarene Youth in Conquest for Christ*. Kansas City: Beacon Hill Press.

Varughese, Alex. 2008. *Jeremiah 1-25: A Commentary in the Wesleyan Tradition*. Kansas City: Beacon Hill Press of Kansas City.

Wallach, Glenn. 1997. *Obedient Sons: The Discourse of Youth and Generations in American Culture, 1630-1860*. Boston: Univ. of Massachusetts Press.

White, David F. 2005. *Practicing Discernment with Youth: A Transformative Youth Ministry Approach*. Cleveland: Pilgrim Press.

Yaconelli, Mark. 2006. *Contemplative Youth Ministry: Practicing the Presence of Jesus*. Grand Rapids: Zondervan/Youth Specialties.

Yount, William R. 1996. *Created to Learn: A Christian Teacher's Introduction to Educational Psychology*. Nashville: B&H Academic.

NINETEEN

CHRISTIAN DISCIPLESHIP
WITH ADULTS

▶ INTRODUCTION

Imagine you are teaching an adult Sunday school class that includes young, middle, and senior aged adults. You are struggling to connect with each of these distinct age-groups. When you adjust your teaching approach to reach one group, the other groups disconnect. What does this tell you about how adults process information at different stages of their development?

Imagine you are asked to lead a Bible study for a middle-aged adult group. You are in your twenties and realize that these adults are at a different stage of life. As you prepare for the study, you try to understand more fully the issues facing adults at this age. What do you need to know about middle adult age development in order to understand their context?

Imagine you are in your early twenties and are asked to serve on a committee to help develop a new, intergenerational worship service with a contemporary focus. At the first committee meeting, you realize you are the youngest member of the group, and the other members of the committee have very different ideas about life and worship. You ask your pastor for some guidance on dealing with the differences. What advice can your pastor give you that is helpful in dealing with older adults?

Adults provide the backbone of the local church because they lead in teaching, mentoring, service, and stewardship. Adults provide financial support, make significant decisions about the future of the church, give spiritual direction to children and youth, and engage in service to the community. Discipleship ministry with adults includes understanding how to minister at different stages of their development. Discipleship also includes understanding how life transitions provide an avenue of spiritual growth and transformation, preparing and equipping adults to be followers of Christ.

Regardless of their stage of development, all adults face stresses and life challenges that find their way into the life of faith. The church, and more specifically, Christian educators provide appropriate approaches for continued learning and spiritual development as adults make sense out of life. The great responsibilities of family, work, church, and life are often difficult to balance. Discipleship ministries provide resources and tools to help adults grow and develop personally and spiritually, as they adjust to the demanding challenges of life.

▶ DEFINITIONS: CHRISTIAN DISCIPLESHIP WITH ADULTS

Adults search for approaches that make meaning in their lives. Spiritual or faith formation is central to that process. Adult Christian discipleship focuses on the transformation of the human person into the image and likeness of Christ Jesus.

BIBLICAL CONSIDERATIONS

Paul offers a metaphor for the process of transformation and spiritual formation in Galatians 4:19, "My dear children, for whom I am again in the pains of childbirth until Christ is formed in you." In Greek, the word for "form" is *morphoo'*, closely related to *metamorphoo* ("transform")—and it refers to the essential nature, not merely the outward form. Paul prays that the inward nature of the Galatian believers would become so like Christ that one could say that Christ has been formed in them. They would be more human, not divine or a Savior themselves, but they would have real Christlike character and behavior (Tracy et al. 1994, 9). Thus, *spiritual formation* can be defined as "the whole person in relationship with God, within the community of believers, growing in Christlikeness, reflected in a Spirit-directed, disciplined lifestyle, and demonstrated in redemptive action in our world" (12). Spiritual formation is the work of the grace of God in the hearts and actions of human beings. Robert Mulholland says, "Spiritual formation is a process of *being conformed* to the image of Christ, a journey into becoming persons of compassion, persons who forgive, persons who care deeply for others and the world" (1993, 25). We cannot conform ourselves to the image of Christ, but God conforms and transforms us by the power of the Spirit. Dallas Willard states that "spiritual formation, without regard to any specifically religious context or tradition, is the process by which the human spirit or will is given a definite 'form' or character" (2002, 19). Spiritual formation refers to the process of shaping our spirits, giving them definite character in conformity with the Spirit of Christ.

Adult Christian discipleship is best lived in community through shared worship, fellowship, small groups, and service. Spiritual formation takes place in and through the faith community. The metaphor of *journey* is used to describe faith formation of adults (Fowler 1995; Mullholland 1993; Hagberg and Guelich 2005), a lifelong journey through the stages of development: "A journey involves process, action, movement, change, experience, stops and starts, variety, humdrum and surprises. Whereas a trip focuses on a destination, a journey has significance when seen as a whole" (Hagberg and Guelich 2005, 5). Our journey of faith connotes the process and passages in our response to God's overture to us. Hagberg and Guelich, along with James Fowler, use stages of faith as a way to view our faith journeys. For Fowler, these are predictable life stages; Hagberg and Guelich develop phases from the life of faith as recorded in the history of the church (6).

The idea of faith formation as a continuous process that requires patience and endurance contrasts with our society's focus on instant gratification. The path to spiritual formation includes joy and success as well as struggle and disappointment. Much of the history of Christianity reflects struggle and suffering, based on the suffering of Christ, as a necessary aspect of growth and maturity. Robert Mulholland says that "life itself is a process of spiritual development. The only choice we have is whether that growth moves us toward wholeness in Christ or toward an increasingly dehumanized and destructive mode of being" (1993, 24).

The Christian journey, therefore, describes an intentional and continual commitment to a lifelong process of growth toward wholeness in Christ. It includes the process of "grow[ing] up in every way into him who is the head, into Christ" (Ephesians 4:15, NRSV), "until we all attain to . . . mature person[hood], to the measure of the stature of the fullness of Christ" (v. 13, ESV). God remains present and active in every moment of our lives for this purpose (Mulholland 1993, 24).

Christian discipleship of adults includes providing educational opportunities that foster faith formation and the inner transformation of the human person into the likeness of Jesus Christ. This transformation takes place as humans participate in avenues of God's grace such as worship, prayer, Bible study, Communion, and acts of service. These intentional practices are means of grace that provide a channel for participation and communion with the Triune God.

THEOLOGICAL FOUNDATIONS

The purposes of adult Christian discipleship may be delineated by three New Testament terms that identify the mission of the church. The church exists to make meaning available, to assist people in exploring and expanding meaning structures and to facilitate the expression of meaning through actions that result in human transformation. The church accomplishes these through *kergymatic, diakonic,* and *koinonia* functions (McKenzie 1986, 16).

The *kergymatic* function (*kergyma* means "proclamation" or "message") includes the proclamation of the gospel as expressed in the life, death, and resurrection of Jesus. Christian faith and meaning find expression in the life and teachings of Jesus (McKenzie 1986, 16). Proclamation refers to teaching and preaching the gospel and includes the need for human response. Adults are not educated into God's kingdom, but adult ministries are opportunities for adults to explore the dimensions of faith in response to the gospel (Pazmiño 1997,

45). Thus, Christian education for adults addresses biblical and theological reflection that engages the reality of the life of Jesus. Through this process adults make meaning out of life and faith.

Through the *diakonic* function (*diakonia* means "service"), the church serves as the instrument by which the gospel of Jesus Christ attends to the spiritual needs of adults. Adult ministry equips adults for service to others in and through the church. Christians are called to be salt and light to the world, to work for justice and the dignity of humanity (47). The servant church provides a healing presence that reaches out to anyone who is in need. Adult Christian discipleship includes providing education opportunities that aim at serving the needs of adults (McKenzie 1986, 17). For example, church may serve a critical role for the single adult mother who needs child care while she balances work and life.

The *koinonia* function (*koinonia* means "fellowship") describes the church as a community that fosters fellowship with God and with other Christians. The church as a community supports and sustains the exploration and expression of faith through relational learning. Adults grow in faith as they engage in significant relationship with others in the context of Christian community.

These three functions are central to the mission of adult Christian discipleship. Focus on studying the Bible and engaging theological inquiry remains important; however, adult ministry also brings people together in the context of the church, addresses the everyday needs of adults, and equips them for service and ministry in the world.

▶ ADULT DYNAMICS

DANIEL LEVINSON'S ADULT DEVELOPMENT THEORY

Christian educators need to understand how adults grow and develop throughout life. Daniel Levinson (1978, 1996) remains one of the most influential scholars on adult development. Levinson, a colleague of Erik Erikson, builds his theory on Erikson's psychosocial stages of development by tracing the course of adult development through three primary life eras: young, middle, and late adulthood. Each is a developmental period marked by a distinct biopsychosocial character. A major transition occurs between each era; minor transitions occur within each era (Pullman 2001, 67).

Levinson says that adults experience life structure changes. Life structures represent the "underlying pattern or design of a person's life at any given time" (Levinson 1978, 6) and the boundaries that mediate and govern the relationship between the individual and the environment. Life structures divide into internal and external aspects. The external aspect focuses on one's relationship to society through social and cultural roles affecting work, marriage, family, and religious faith. The internal meaning of these roles evolves as if attached to a time clock announcing that one's perceptions are due for a change at each era in the life cycle.

A transition period serves to terminate an existing life structure and create the possibility for a new one to be formed. Each of these structures has three major roles: (1) to evaluate the existing life structure; (2) to explore potential areas of change in self and how one deals with the world; and (3) to commit to making significant choices that assist in the formation of a new or transformed life structure in the new era (Levinson 1978, 55-59). As a person moves through these transitional periods, growth and development take place. A brief overview of Levinson's eras and transitions follows here (also see the table at appendix 19.1). Eras and transitions are presented as age ranges that will overlap; progression will vary among individuals. While Levinson's work was specifically related to men's lives, his life structure approach is equally valid for women's lives.

Early Adult Transition (seventeen to forty): The first phase of development is the *early adult transition.* During this preadulthood transition, persons start a new period of individualism, modifying relationships with family and society in order to transition into the adult world. The primary task of the early adult transition is to leave the preadult world by establishing identity and a life separate from one's family. Levinson calls this new period "Entering the Adult World" (1978, 78). He goes on to say that this process includes "exploration of self and world, making and testing provisional choices, searching the alternatives, increasing one's commitments and constructing a more integrated life structure" (79). This early adult transition includes developing financial and psychological independence and the formulation of dreams for future life and work.

Early Adulthood Era (seventeen to forty): The early adult transition disappears into the *early adulthood era.* A time of great energy and excitement, the era also includes great contradictions and stress. The twenties and thirties mark the peak of biological strength and performance. The primary task is still forming an adult identity, including making choices about career, marriage, children, and lifestyle. Long-term romantic relationships often begin here. Adults at this stage can experience stressful competition in the workplace, and career mentors may be extremely significant.

Age Thirty Transition (twenty-eight to thirty-three): Levinson argues that this transition is more stressful for men because most men feel "time is running out" and change must be made soon if the transition requires new commitments (1978, 58). As cultural changes have influenced lifestyles, these changes may now apply more equally to men and women. Individuals may decide to either have children or begin a career, depending on their decisions during the twenties. It is a time to reevaluate and rediscover feelings, interests, talents, and goals that have been ignored because they interfered with goals formed in their twenties. Levinson states, "The shift from the end of the thirty transition to the start of the next period is one of the crucial steps in adult development. At this time men [and women] may make important new choices, or they may reaffirm old choices" (59).

Midlife Transition (forty to forty-five): The next major adult transition is the *midlife transition.* This is the vehicle for the culmination of the early adulthood era (Levinson 1978, 59). The two primary tasks of this transition are: (1) establishing a niche in society (anchoring life more firmly, developing competence in a chosen craft, and becoming a valued member of a valued world); and (2) striving to advance or progress on a timetable (Levinson 1978, 59). An adult uses this time to measure success in obtaining self-selected goals that indicate he or she has become "one's own man or woman." Adults feel successful when they see work flourish, obtain a certain position or career influence, and have seniority in terms of rewards and responsibilities.

Many people understand this transition as a midlife crisis. It is traditionally (and certainly by Levinson) associated with a man's strong feeling that he will not achieve his "culminating event" to mark the accomplishment of his dream. His dreams may have been blocked, and the realization that they are not going to be achieved results in a diminished view of himself and the world. The midlife transition does not have to be a time of crisis, however, and occurs in women as well as men. It is an opportunity to revisit dreams of career, family, marriage, and work. In essence, this is a period of evaluation: "What have I done with my life?" and "What shall I change to make my life better in the future?" It is an intense time of making meaning out of life and looking to the future. Adults may also begin mentoring others, helping to prepare the next generation of young adults.

Middle Adulthood Era (forty to sixty-five): In the *middle adult era* adults become senior members of their worlds. The primary task involves making significant choices about life and constructing a life structure around these choices. These choices can have either positive or negative implications. On the positive side, adults filled with satisfaction and meaning find this era to be the most creative and productive time of their adult lives (Levinson 1978, 61). On the negative side, adults can face the pain and detachment of job changes, marital separation, termination of significant relationships, or relocation.

Late Adult Transition and Late Adulthood (sixty and older): The *late adulthood era* is initiated with the *late adult transition* from age sixty to sixty-five. Late adulthood is marked by physical, biological, psychological, and social changes. Adults become aware of bodily decline and limitations. Society sees them as senior citizens. With retirement and a change of social status, responsibilities decrease but financial concerns may limit their choices, unless they have planned well for this time. The primary task of this era is to accept new realities and come to terms with the reality of death.

Levinson's ages for transition may require rethinking. Gail Sheehy notes that many contemporary adults resist transitions to midlife and late adulthood (1995, 2-56). Nevertheless, Levinson's approach to structures and transitions bear close attention.

IMPLICATIONS FOR ADULT CHRISTIAN DISCIPLESHIP

Why are these life structures and transitions important for Christian discipleship? First, they remind us that humans continually wrestle with the existential questions: "What is my life like now?" or "What are the most important areas of my life and how are they related?" and "Where do I invest most of my time and energy?" Second, they raise the possibility that adults are open and receptive to change. Particularly during transitions, guided by the work of the Holy Spirit, the Christian educators can minister to adults through presence and support. Third, they remind us of the importance of relationships to adults. The church can be a safe environment where adults in groups can examine life structure in light of the scripture, as guided by the Holy Spirit (Wilson 1995, 174).

Levinson's adult development theory, based on life transitions and eras, provides the Christian educator with an overview of the dynamics of adult life. Christian educators provide ministry opportunities for transformation and change within the context of Christian community. As adults transition from one era to the next, they are vulnerable; these are important times of discernment and spiritual formation. Issues of relationship, work, marriage, family, and meaning find their way into the life of faith. Christian educators minister more effectively through the power of the Holy Spirit when they understand the predictable life events, transition periods, and adult crises of development.

ADULT LEARNING

Christian discipleship with adults includes understanding the societal shifts that impact their lives. Faith formation is never divorced from the realities of life, which makes it important for the Christian educator to understand the shifting tides of the culture. One of these shifts includes growing numbers of adults returning to school to retool for their next job or career change. Patricia Cross states, "The changing demographics, economical, and technological advances of society has forced adults to continue to learn. The change in demographics since World War II and the baby boomers have contributed to a population bulge in the middle adult years. This increasing population coupled with advanced technology has forced more people to become adult learners" (1991, 6-7). As the career ladder becomes congested, adults experience the economic squeeze that forces them to look at possible alternatives, all of which have ramifications for adult education (Thomas 1991, 22; Cross 1991, 6). Downsizing corporations result in adults retiring early or seeking new skills for employment.

Second, adult Christian discipleship requires understanding of the unique characteristics of adult learners. Adults learn different from children and adolescents. Rosemary Caffarella provides five characteristics of adult learners (Caffarella and Barnett 1994, 29-34):

1. *Adults bring prior knowledge and experience into the learning context.* The adult learner is able to call upon past experiences and prior knowledge in formulating learning activities as well as serving as a resource for other learners (see Knowles 1980). In reflecting on past experiences and prior knowledge, adults want and need to modify their values and beliefs and reintegrate what these experiences mean in terms of their values and beliefs.

2. *Adults bring different processes of learning to the learning context.* Adults have different learning styles, and teachers should not focus on one mode of learning. Adults tend to be more reflective and dialectical in their thinking. They appear to be more tolerant of contradictions and ambiguity, and they engage more often in problem solving.

3. *Adults are active learners.* Adults prefer to be actively involved in the learning process rather than passive recipients of knowledge. They want to be empowered to engage in the process of learning.

4. *Adults are collaborative learners.* Adult learners prefer to set their own learning goals, such as contractual learning agreements, and they enjoy being involved in the learning process.

5. *The adult context for learning is different.* Adults, depending on their stage of development, are at different stations of life. It is important to identify and adapt to these.

These characteristics and needs of adult learners provide the Christian educator with an understanding of how to effectively minister to them. Unfortunately, many traditional Christian education programs do not consider the needs of adult learners. Ted Ward notes that educators often place all learners on the same level instead of providing varied learning experiences that reflect the needs of the adult learner. He calls this the "herding method" of education (1997).

ANDRAGOGY

Malcolm Knowles developed the adult theory of andragogy, arguing that adults learn different from children. He defines *andragogy* as "the art and science of helping adults learn in contrast to pedagogy as the art and science of teaching children" (1980, 42). Knowles suggests that differences between children and adult learners rest with four critical assumptions: self-concept, experience, readiness to learn, and orientation to learning. Each concept expands progressively and developmentally as the individual matures (see appendix 19.2). Knowles asserts that pedagogy, a teacher-centered approach to learning, makes the student dependent on the teacher. He asserts that effective adult teaching includes the student's independence from the teacher and that adults become more self-directed in their learning as they mature. Self-directed learning is the process by which adults develop and formulate their own learning based on life situation and circumstances.

Faithful discipleship with adults includes a movement from pedagogical to andragogical teaching. The teacher serves as a facilitator of learning by including discussion and dialogue. The teacher seeks to empower the students to take ownership of their learning.

LIFELONG LEARNING

Christian educators assume that adults continue to learn and grow throughout life. Patricia Cross notes several aspects of lifelong learning: "formal, informal, and non-formal education; lifelong learning begins in the home and continues throughout the life span; and community plays a vital role in learning. Lifelong learning is characterized by flexibility and diversity in content, time, and techniques with the ultimate goal of improving the quality of life" (1991, 261).

Horace Reed and Elizabeth Lee Loughran substantiate Cross's claim: "One of the hallmarks of society is that learning occurs throughout the lifespan; that learning occurs in informal, non-formal, and informal settings; that learning is aimed at improving the quality of life" (1984, 5).

Adult Christian discipleship provides educational opportunities that foster continual learning. Christian educators are reminded that learning and growth take place not only in Sunday school classes and Bible studies but also in homes, in communities, and in society. Christian discipleship with adults needs to be holistic, including discipleship ministries of the local church but not limited to church context. Learning takes place in all of life, and effective adult Christian discipleship recognizes the importance of these diverse learning opportunities.

▶ ADULT MINISTRY APPROACHES

Christian discipleship for and with adults includes a variety of approaches and methods, depending on how the Christian educator organizes and plans the adult ministry program. Congregations may organize and plan adult ministry programs around one or more of the following approaches:

- *First, Christian educators can design adult curriculum around affinity groups.* As with youth, affinity groups incorporate similar interests or commonality of life and can meet within the church or in nontraditional formats. Adult ministries designed around affinity groups are more likely to take place in larger congregations. These groups are beneficial because the common life interests of the members helps bond them together. Affinity groups risk becoming cliques that exclude diverse views and ideas (see chapter 15).

- *Second, Christian educators can develop adult programs based on the proximity of the adult learners.* Some adult ministries may not include formal Sunday school classes or church-based programs but meet in homes for Bible study or small-group gatherings. This is particularly true in larger metropolitan areas where people are separated geographically and travel to the church requires extended time. Curriculum for these home groups may look different from traditional pedagogical formats. The benefits of organizing adult ministries based on proximity include faith formation and spiritual growth contextualized for the local setting. However, proximity groups risk isolation, limiting exposure and connection to the broader church community.

- *Third, Christian educators can organize and develop adult ministries by the life stage of adults.* Many adult ministry programs are organized according to Levinson's stages of adult development. These can include young adults, single adults, married adults, middle-aged adults, and senior adults. The benefit of life-stage development is the focus on the specific needs and challenges of the particular stage. Adults typically enjoy being in groups and programs where they can identify with others who have similar life concerns and issues. Age-level programming can, however, inhibit learning from adults at other stages of development. For example, newly married couples can learn from couples who have been married for several years.

- *Fourth, adult ministries can be organized around specific needs or support groups.* A growing number of congregations are developing adult ministries that address specific emotional or behavior problems. These include support groups for single parents, divorce recovery, substance abuse, sexual abuse, and grieving. These support or need-based groups provide adults with encouragement, counsel, and prayer during some of the most difficult times of life. The benefits include holistic support for adults who are experiencing pain and hurt in their lives. The church can become a safe place for redemption and recovery for these adults. Support or need-based programs enhance existing adult ministry programs by addressing distinct needs. Participation in support groups may stigmatize church members or cause them to withdraw from the larger congregation. Church collaborations are helpful here, as church members attend support groups at different congregations to maintain some anonymity.

- *Fifth, adult ministries can be organized around intergenerational adult groupings.* There is renewed interest in intergenerational forms of Christian education that include the whole family (White 1988). Adult ministries could incorporate programs and groups on special topics or shared themes of interest. For example, an adult Bible study group on the book of Genesis could be attended by all adults, regardless of their developmental stage. The benefits emerge as young adults learn from more mature adults and vice versa in a dynamic context for growth and development. Intergenerational studies must be carefully facilitated, however, to avoid flattening learning differences.

- *Sixth, adult ministries can be organized around segregated groups.* Also, many adult ministries are designed and organized around segment groups. For example, some small groups or Sunday school classes consist of married couples, while others focus on single adults. The primary reason for these segregated groups rests with the distinct life needs of singles as compared to married couples. Also, with the increased ethnic and racial diversity of our world, congregations should be more inclusive of all peoples, but some find it hard to minister to some ethic groups. In addition, ethnic groups in the minority often need times to gather for mutual affirmation and empowerment to preserve their ethnic heritage. For example, one congregation has several different ethnic groups that meet in one building. They provide a specific service for Koreans, another for Chinese. The benefits of these groups are that they provide these ethnic groups the opportunity to learn and grow in their own cultural context. Negatively, total isolation fragments diverse perspectives and expressions of the body of Christ, often to the detriment of the dominant ethnic group who could learn and grow from these encounters.

Christian educators must discern the approach that works best in organizing and planning adult ministry in the local church, balancing the benefits and weaknesses of each approach. Consider the size of the church, its social and demographic setting, and the overall vision and mission of the local church in choosing the most effective method for adult Christian discipleship. The old adage, "one size fits all," does not work when choosing an adult ministry approach. Also, the Christian educator will have to resist the temptation to impose forms of adult ministry that may work in one setting on a new context. Each congregation is unique and requires fresh discernment for effective ministry.

▶ FAITHFUL DISCIPLESHIP WITH ADULTS

Faithful discipleship with adults is a broad field, which cannot be fully covered here. The following, however, are some key considerations.

First, create safe places for learning and critical thinking. Adults learn when they are in supportive environments. These safe places allow adults to explore the difficult questions of faith and theology without being judged or criticized. Adults typically accept other people's ideas and views in an atmosphere of mutual respect and trust. Studies show that adults prefer to be in small groups and Sunday school classes that challenge their thinking (Schuller 1993, 10-12). As lifelong learners, adults want to engage in learning experiences that connect to their life and faith journeys.

Second, develop groups or programs that foster significant relationships. Adults look for friendships to provide encouragement and affirmation. They want to know that individuals or groups of people care about them, will pray for them, and wish to join them in learning. The establishment of authentic Christian communities in which people can share their lives together is critical for faithful discipleship.

Third, empower adults for ministry and service. Adults are willing and interested in ministering in the local church and serving in the community. Adult ministry teaches and promotes the "priesthood of all believers," that everyone ministers and fills a significant role within the body of Christ. Adults possess distinct gifts and abilities with which to serve local congregations (see Ephesians 4:11-13). Faithful discipleship empowers adults to use their gifts and graces for ministry in the church and for the Kingdom.

Fourth, develop and mentor the next generation of leaders. Adults want to invest in the lives of others through mentoring and leadership development, to pass on the faith tradition to the next generation. They provide exemplary models for children and youth. Adults can share their faith journey with the next generation as a testimony to God's grace in their lives. Adults can also engage in developing future leaders in ministry through teaching and serving together.

▶ CONCLUSION

Adult Christian discipleship is critical to the ministry of the local church. Adults provide leadership in a wide variety of ministries and engage in ministry and service on several levels. Faithful discipleship with adults includes understanding how they learn, grow, and develop throughout life. Recognizing and understanding these changes and transitions provides the Christian educator with opportunities to foster transformation through the power of the Holy Spirit. Eager to learn and grow spiritually, adults want to make meaning of the complexity of life. Faithful discipleship includes the development of adult ministries that address their diverse needs and concerns and provide the means to help them grow to maturity in faith.

▶ RESOURCES

Caffarella, Rosemary, and Bruce Barnett. 1994. Characteristics of adult learners and foundations of experimental learning. In *New Directions for Adult and Continuing Education* 62 (summer): 29-42.

Cross, K. Patricia. 1991. *Adults as Learners: Increasing Participation and Facilitating Learning.* San Francisco: Jossey-Bass.

Erikson, Erik H. 1982. *The Life Cycle Completed: A Review.* New York: Norton.

Foltz, Nancy T. 1986. Basic principles of adult religious education. In *Handbook of Adult Religious Education,* 25-58. Ed. Nancy T. Foltz. Birmingham, AL: Religious Education Press.

Fowler, James. 1995. *Stages of Faith: The Psychology of Human Development and the Quest for Meaning.* San Francisco: HarperOne.

Hagberg, Janet O., and Robert A. Guelich. 2005. *The Critical Journey: Stages in the Life of Faith.* 2nd ed. Salem, WI: Sheffield.

Knowles, Malcolm. 1980. *The Modern Practice of Adult Education.* Englewood Cliffs, NJ: Prentice Hall.

Levinson, Daniel J., et al. 1978. *The Seasons of a Man's Life.* New York: Ballantine Books.

_____. 1996. *The Seasons of a Woman's Life.* New York: Ballantine Books.

McKenzie, Leon. 1986. The purposes and scope of adult religious education. In *Handbook of Adult Religious Education,* 7-23. Ed. Nancy T. Foltz. Birmingham, AL: Religious Education Press.

Mulholland, M. Robert, Jr. 1993. *Invitation to a Journey: A Road Map for Spiritual Formation.* Downers Grove, IL: InterVarsity.

Pullman, Ellery. 2001. Life span development. In *Introducing Christian Education: Foundations for the Twenty-first Century,* 63-72. Ed. Michael Anthony. Grand Rapids: Zondervan.

Reed, Horace B., and Elizabeth Lee Loughran, eds. 1984. *Beyond Schools: Education for Economic, Social, and Personal Development.* Amherst, MA: School of Education, Univ. of Massachusetts.

Schuller, David S., ed. 1993. *Rethinking Christian Education.* Atlanta: Chalice Press.

Sheehy, Gail. 1995. *The New Passages: Mapping Your Life Across Time.* New York: Random House.

Thomas, Allen M. 1991. *Beyond Education: A New Perspective on Society's Management of Learning.* San Francisco: Jossey-Bass.

Tracy, Wesley E., et al. 1993. *The Upward Call: Spiritual Formation and Holy Living.* Kansas City: Beacon Hill Press of Kansas City.

Ward, Ted. 1997. Non-Formal Education Lectures. Trinity Evangelical Divinity School (summer).

White, James W. 1988. *Intergenerational Religious Education.* Birmingham, AL: Religious Education Press.

Wickett, R. E. Y. 1991. *Models of Adult Religious Education Practice.* Birmingham, AL: Religious Education Press.

Willard, Dallas. 2002. *Renovation of the Heart: Putting on the Character of Christ.* Colorado Springs: NavPress.

Wilson, Fred. 1995. Adult development. In *Nurture That Is Christian.* Ed. James C. Wilhoit and John M. Dettoni. Wheaton, IL: Victor Books.

Appendix 19.1
Daniel Levinson's Adult Development Theory*

Stage	Age	Description
Early Adult Transition	17-22	Leave the family and adolescent groups and make preliminary choices for adult life
Entering the Adult World	22-28	Initial choices in love, occupation, friendship, values, and lifestyle: conflict between desire to explore and desire to commit
Age 30 Transition	28-33	Period of reworking, modifying life structure; smooth transition for some, disruptive crisis for others; growing sense of need for change before becoming locked in because of commitment
Settling Down	33-40	Establish a niche in society; progress on a timetable in both family and career
Midlife Transition	40-45	Life structure comes into question, usually at a time of crisis, in the meaning, direction, and value of each person's life; neglected parts of the self such as talents, desires, and aspirations seek expression
Entering Middle Adulthood	45-50	End of appraisal; time of choices forming a new life structure in relation to occupation, marriage, locale; wide variation in satisfaction and extent of fulfillment
Age 50 Transition	50-55	Work further on the tasks of midlife transition and modification of structure formed in the mid-40s; crisis if there was not enough challenge during the midlife transition
Culmination of Adulthood	55-60	Build a new life structure; time of great fulfillment for middle adults who can rejuvenate and enrich their lives
Late Adult Transition	60-65	Reappraisal of life; moments of pride in achievement are interspersed with periods of despair
Late Adulthood	65-80	Confrontation with self and the need to make peace with the world; fewer illusions, broader perspective on life
Late-Late Adulthood	80+	Final transition; period of further psychosocial development; preparation for death

*Adapted from Ellery Pullman, "Life Span Development," in *Introduction to Christian Education: Foundations for the Twenty-first Century,* ed. Michael Anthony (Grand Rapids: Zondervan, 2001), 68.

Appendix 19.2

Malcolm Knowles'
Four Critical Assumptions of Andragogy*

ASSUMPTIONS	CHILD	ADULT
1. Self-Concept	From dependent	To interdependent
	Few decisions	To many decisions
	From other-directed	To self-directed
2. Experience	From limited experience	To wealth of experience
3. Readiness to Learn	From readiness to learn the developmental tasks	To readiness to learn the developmental tasks involving social roles
4. Orientation Toward Learning	From postponed application of knowledge	To immediate application of knowledge
	From subject-centeredness	To problem-centeredness

*Adapted from Nancy Foltz, "Basic Principles of Adult Religious Education," in *Handbook of Adult Religious Education* (Birmingham, AL: Religious Education Press, 1984), 31.

TWENTY

FAMILY MINISTRY

▶ INTRODUCTION

Imagine you are asked to speak at a family ministry retreat for your local church. As you prepare, you decide to include family activities after your presentation. These activities are designed to help families talk about life stories and their faith. However, you realize some people attending will not have a family. You struggle with how to include them in family units. In what way does this reflect your view of the family; does it extend beyond the nuclear (traditional) family?

Imagine you are engaged and plan to marry next year. As part of your preparation, you and your fiance participate in premarital counseling sessions with your pastor. In your first session the pastor says that the spiritual direction of the family is the responsibility of the husband. As the woman in this relationship, you disagree with the pastor and believe that there are equal roles in the family. You decide to talk with the pastor about this at the next session. What are the biblical bases for your position?

Imagine you are a teenager attending a group gathering. The youth pastor offers a devotional about what it means to be a disciple and follower of Jesus. He challenges teenagers to minister not only at school but also in their families. What does it mean for a teenager to minister to the family?

Christian educators need to have an understanding of what constitutes the family and its relationship to the church in order for faithful discipleship to take place. Why are they important to each other?

▶ DEFINITIONS: CHURCH AND FAMILY

Family ministry has grown tremendously since the late 1980s. Congregations hire family-life ministers to address the growing demands that families face in a complex and changing society. Congregations are beginning to understand the potential power and influence of families for discipleship and formation. Studies indicate that the family is the primary positive agent in faith formation (Roehlkepartain 1993, 25). However, we do not idolize the family; we recognize the church as the primary agent of God's reconciliation, the primary vehicle of God's grace to the world (Clapp 1993, 68). Families and churches serve as part of God's incarnational power on earth in a symbiotic relationship. The whole church (the people of God) needs to understand and empower the domestic church (the local family). The family, living authentically in relationships and roles, serves as a means of grace.

BIBLICAL CONSIDERATIONS

Developing a definition of family ministry from scripture can be challenging. On the one hand, a biblical view of the family includes the nuclear family. Scripture teaches that a family consists of a man and woman who are united together in marriage (Genesis 2:24). On the other hand, scripture teaches that *family* extends beyond the reach of kinship and marriage to embrace others. Jesus worked to transform our understanding of family in Matthew 12:46-50: "Whoever does the will of my Father in heaven is my brother and sister and mother" (v. 50). This adoptive view of family is a reminder that anyone who decides to be a follower of Jesus is a member of the Christian family. Thus, the church bears responsibility to ensure that no one in the family is left outside of its nurture. In the community of faith, labels of "single" or "married" or "divorced" are less significant than that of "believer," as the community of faith creates and reinforces bonds of mutual commitment and love as real as any legal or biological bond recognized by society.

The New Testament view of households and household roles (see Romans 12:13; Ephesians 2:19) provides a rationale for the function of family. In ancient times, survival depended on membership in a household. Those without such membership—widows, orphans, sojourners—were in a desperate situation. Paul's letters suggest that the household of God should include these persons, including freed slaves, as family members. He echoes the Old Testament view of incorporating the hopeless into the family/household (e.g., Zechariah 7:9-10; see Garland 1999, 331).

The family was created for partnership (Genesis 1:26-28), companions in God's work. God created the partnership of family so that the work of caring for creation would not be done in isolation. The first man and woman were created not simply to be together, but to be companions in work. Families have a purpose, a calling from God, to be in mission together. The church serves families so that families, the domestic church, can model faithful discipleship with one another and for the world. Families are the channel through which ministry takes place in the name of Christ. They provide a graphic portrayal of what God is like, and they will be held accountable: "The family must be subject to the rule of the kingdom of God and finally measured by its contribution to the realization of the kingdom of God" (Browning 2007, 88).

BIBLICAL ROLES IN MARRIAGE

While the term *family* can represent many different groups and relationships, the role of husbands and wives in marriage is foundational to any discussion of family ministry. Interpretations of the roles of husbands and wives as portrayed in the Bible have varied widely. The church's traditional (though not always historical) view was hierarchical, with the husband providing leadership over wife and family. This view of the father as breadwinner and the wife as homemaker has certainly been challenged, in part by the influence of women's studies and feminist theology. These movements provide a needed corrective to views of women as submissive, liberating and redefining the role of women, particularly in American culture. Biblical scholars also argue for equality of roles for men and women based on Genesis 1:26-31. The Hebrew words for *man* (*ish*) and *woman* (*isha*) both come from the same root word. Genesis 2:20, which refers to the woman as a "helper" may be translated as "partner" or as someone who "corresponds to him." As Walter Brueggemann suggests, "In God's garden, as God wills it, there is mutuality and equality" (1982, 51). The Genesis passage does not establish a hierarchy but shows that both husband and wife enjoy equal roles in the family.

Another often misunderstood passage, Ephesians 5:22-33, instructs wives to "submit to your husbands" (v. 22). When read in context, we find that husbands are also to love their wives as Christ loved the church; and verse 21 reads, "Submit to one another out of reverence for Christ." Paul suggests that the principle governing Christian marriage must include mutuality and partnership under the lordship of Christ. These were radical statements in a culture that viewed women as inferior to men.

Even though scripture clearly advocates for equal partnership in marriage, the church's hierarchical view of the family, reflected in and influenced by the culture, persisted for centuries. Even today, women spend at least twice as much time on household chores and caring for domestic concerns as do men. Culture is slow to change. Husbands and wives can decide how they want to share responsibility in the family, but scripture does not provide guidance on the specific roles they should take (African-American families, for example, hold a more egalitarian view of marriage than most Caucasian marriages). Christians have also taken the Ephesians passage to mean that the husband should be the spiritual head of the family. Again, scripture does not support this view. The spiritual leadership and growth of the family include the love and nurture of both husband and wife, but Christ is the spiritual head of all Christian families. Paul's admonition was a breath of fresh air in the first-century church and in our own time as well. Husbands are to love their wives in the same way that Christ demonstrates love for the family of God. Wives are to be viewed as equals and honored as "co-heirs" of God's grace. The principle that governs the Christian marriage relationship is mutuality and partnership under the lordship of Christ (Garland 1999, 195).

Faithful discipleship to families provides forums for exploring the biblical roles of the family, beginning with marriage. Discussions on this topic can be difficult because of the culturally embedded views of many families, but they are needed to provide a corrective to long-held misunderstandings about the roles of husbands and wives. This foundational relationship has significant implications for ministry *to* families and *with* families.

MARRIAGE AND DIVORCE

Marriage as an institution has suffered significant decline in recent years. More than 50 percent of marriages, both Christian and non-Christian, end in divorce (Garland 1999, 543). Debates about same-sex marriages have raised concerns about what constitutes marriage. Despite these challenges, marriage is still the primary institutional relationship between a man and woman, bound in a public ritual that reminds the couple of their mutual covenant and obligation and confirms it in community. Christian marriage includes covenant with God, friends, and family that echoes the biblical command: "A man will leave his father and mother and be united to his wife, and they will become one flesh" (Genesis 2:24). Two distinct people now share life as one unit. The covenantal relationship is a lifetime commitment that includes friendship, love, and sexual fidelity. Christian marriage is also a partnership of mutual submission to God and a call to faithful discipleship. Married couples participate in God's creative and redemptive work in the world. One crucial role of family ministry is to build, equip, and strengthen marriages. More than workshops, seminars, and retreats, family ministry helps couples have more fulfilling marriages. It must also communicate that marriage is not the most important relationship in our lives—our most important relationship is with God.

Faithful discipleship to families is faced with the challenge of upholding the sanctity of marriage while providing healing and restoration to people whose marriages have ended in divorce. Since this represents over half of all marriages (and half of recent weddings are remarriage for at least one partner), the church has a significant role in ministering to these families. Divorce has a negative impact on both children and parents. It is clear from the biblical witness that God did not intend divorce to take place (Deuteronomy 24:1-4; Malachi 2:16). When Jesus was questioned about divorce, he quoted Genesis 2:24 in his response (Matthew 19:3-11; Mark 10:2-12). God intends marriage to be an irreversible bond between a man and a woman, but situations of neglect, abuse, unfaithfulness, and irreconcilable differences occur that cannot be overcome.

What about divorce and remarriage? Jesus names divorce as sin but provides for remarriage as an extension of grace (see, e.g., the Samaritan woman at the well [John 4:16-42]). Jesus provides a message of redemption. No matter what the laws do or do not allow, relationships between persons cannot be formed or destroyed by legal categories; everyone falls short of God's intention in relationships. Past sins can be forgiven and persons can be reconciled to God and begin again.

Family ministry should strengthen families by providing resources to prepare, enrich, and equip couples for more fulfilling marriages. The church should uphold the sanctity of marriage by developing avenues for conversation and dialogue about the joys, struggles, and challenges that married couples face. Faithful discipleship to families also includes providing space for healing, restoration, and forgiveness for those who have experienced or who consider divorce. Many people carry unresolved pain and guilt because of broken relationships. Children often believe they are the cause of divorce. Congregations also need to teach about family transitions of integrity for people who feel stuck in unfaithful or unhappy marriages and have deep questions concerning God's forgiveness if they decide to get a divorce.

THEOLOGICAL CONSIDERATIONS

Human beings are created by a relational Triune God to be in significant and fulfilling relationships, which can mirror the relational power of the Triune God for redemptive purposes. Relationship is the primary way in which human beings reflect the image of God (see Genesis 1:26-27). A Trinitarian view of the family includes interdependence and the uniqueness of each person. The complex nature of rationality (distinction and unity) is the central theme in understanding family relationship (Balswick and Balswick 2007, 18). Families are particularly powerful when they reflect the challenge of loving the other equally; parents and children seek to offer authentic love to more than one person. The ability to give oneself over to another, to enter into deep communion as a spouse yet also express generative love and desire with children, reflects the ongoing, outward focus of God's love (Thatcher 2007, 78-111). As Adrian Thatcher notes, a "social-personalist" view may argue that we exist as persons in relation, "but it says nothing about the quality of those relations that, without much virtue or resolve, will lack love" (109). Families not only reveal the relational nature of human beings but also indicate the quality and character of those relationships in loving and generous terms.

According to Garland, the church has a responsibility to nurture the growth of "faith-families," which can include persons who are alone because they have no family or because their biological/legal family is not Christian (1999, 374). The church enriches the life of all families by nurturing the development of ties to faith-family members; it is an extended family in support of faith-families. Faithful discipleship to families includes helping congregations provide community and support for everyone in the church. The size of some congregations, the individualism of Western culture, and the exclusivity of some biological families combine to make this challenging. Christian educators overcome these barriers by intentionally creating avenues and programs that include all of God's family.

Families also need the church as God's primary agent to model re-deemed relationships. Historically, the church has had an amazing influence over families, often determining how they are formed, nurtured, dissolved, and perpetuated over multiple generations. On their own, families struggle to locate the resources they need to endure and grow in faith. The church is uniquely positioned to help families through extended relationships that offer the kinship networks often lacking in our transient world.

We must acknowledge, however, that the quality of those relationships often limits the effectiveness of churches as family models. Charles Sell reminds us that churches may be "family like" but often run short of being fully family in the way they "do church business" day-to-day (1995, 14). Churches can also take on family-like struggles. One of the greatest gifts that has emerged from family-systems studies is the way many of those forms of relationships often appear in the church.

▶ DYNAMIC CONSIDERATIONS

STRUCTURAL AND FUNCTIONAL FAMILIES

The family is one of the most powerful moral and political symbols in today's culture. Everyone is pro family, though there is sharp disagreement about what constitutes *family*. In American culture, much of the debate centers on the definition of a nuclear or traditional family. The *nuclear* family, in sociological terms, consists of a married heterosexual couple and their children, people related to each other by marriage, birth, or adoption. It is iconically reflected in the 1950s television show *Leave It to Beaver:* the husband is the primary breadwinner and head of the household, the wife is a homemaker who cooks meals and cares for the home and the children. Definitions of the *traditional* family have extended to include blended families, couples in second or later marriages with children from previous unions. Another television example, *The Brady Bunch* of the 1960s, includes widowed, single parents with children who marry and create a combined household. The husband is still the head of the household who works while his wife stays at home. These traditional views of the family may represent an ideal, but at the end of the twentieth-century, they made up less than 27 percent of the households in America. Married couples with children made up 30 percent of the population and 25 percent of families were led by single parents (Garland 1999, 23). The traditional family actually represents a small portion of American culture. Some people are concerned that decreases in the number of nuclear families indicate that this form of family is being replaced, that society and culture are stripping away the traditional view of family.

Nuclear and traditional family definitions base relationships on structures and how persons are related by blood lineage or legal bonds of adoption and marriage (Garland 1999, 35). The defining features in this *structural* definition are marriage and parenthood. The patterns created by marriage, adoption, and parenthood define what a family is and provide clear-cut, often rigid, boundaries between the home and workplace and between parents and children (Elkind 1994, 1). Women, in the traditional family, have a defined role and place, submissive and controlled by the husband.

Diana Garland provides a more inclusive view of the family that is based on the ways persons behave toward one another, a *functional* view of family (1999, 38); how people relate to one another in family-like ways determines family membership, not the formal and biological status they hold. This view makes room for blended and stepfamilies. The functions that the family plays in persons' lives are distinct from other interpersonal relationships. Garland defines the functional family as "the organization of relationships that endure over time and contexts through which persons attempt to meet their needs for belonging and attachment and to share life purposes, help and resources" (39). David Elkind (1994) refers to the functional family as the *permeable* family; the lines between responsibilities blur and are difficult to discern. According to Elkind this describes the *postmodern* family: more fluid, flexible, and vulnerable to outside pressures (1994, 3). This postmodern, permeable family incorporates a variety of relationships: both parents working, single mothers or fathers and children, or surrogate-parent families (31).

IMPLICATIONS FOR DISCIPLESHIP WITH FAMILIES

What are the implications of structural and functional views of family for faithful family discipleship? The functional view of families is more encompassing and can include nonbiological family members. For example, a child who has been abandoned by his parents might find love, support, and security with a close friend or mentor who becomes the child's new family. The structural view can run the danger of excluding those who might fulfill the functions of a family but do not have the required status. While the nuclear family is still the structure used to develop many family ministries in the local church, it limits the broader opportunities for ministry offered by the functional definition. The functional view of families represents the ideal; it is closer to Jesus' teaching about family. Followers of Christ are not to be bound by the structures of legally recognized or biologically based relationships; families are defined by relational processes—loving one another, being faithful to the same Lord, and adopting one another as brothers and sisters in the household of faith (Garland 1999, 50).

Family ministry that includes both the nuclear family and the functional view of family gets closer to the biblical witness. Faithful discipleship with families celebrates and provides resources for the nuclear family while developing a broader functional view that addresses the changing social reality. Both understandings are critical for faithful discipleship to families. Some congregations will have to adapt their ministry and approach to families. Others will have to educate the congregation on how to be inclusive of nontraditional families and functional views of family.

Before Christian educators can provide ministry to families, they must deal with their own perceptions, which are embedded in personal family histories. Our understanding of families is governed by our experience. We may not all be fathers or mothers, but we are all sons or daughters, and ministry to families can be either blessed or cursed by our assumptions and experiences. Family identity influences how we relate interpersonally at every level. An individual's identity may not represent a biblical view and can be an impediment to understanding God, grace, and relationships. The church requires a more comprehensive look at the definitions of family, marriage, and child-rearing. Faithful discipleship to families includes knowing how our perceptions influence our ministry of helping others redeem their kinship networks and so redeem the church and the community. Churches can make a difference in families, and families can make a difference in churches. This symbiotic relationship reveals itself in the ministry strategies used to implement family ministry.

Family ministry includes any activity of church or church representatives that (1) develops faith-families in the congregational community, (2) increases the Christlikeness of the family relationships of Christians, and (3) equips and supports Christians who use their families as channels of ministry to others (Garland 1999, 374). According to this definition, family ministry is not a set of programs that address family issues; rather, family ministry includes all aspects of congregational life, intentionally or unintentionally. Families are formed and shaped through worship, education, service, and ministry as they live together in the context of the church.

FAMILY AS THE FORMING CENTER: LEARNING WITHIN THE FAMILY

Scripture offers no perfect models of families. God works through all kinds of families. The goal of Christian families is to live righteously within their given state of family relationships (see 1 Corinthians 7:10-24). Families have the potential to teach what it means to love and to love in ways that form others in the ways of Christ as God speaks through the ordinary daily routines of our lives. Families are the "forming center" for spiritual formation (Thompson 1996, 19). Faith is nurtured first in the domestic church, the family. Families communicate values and a vision of faith through daily life together and through intentional spiritual practices. One of these intentional practices is table spirituality. Families gathering to share a meal offer a prayer of thanksgiving, a sacramental act that invites God's blessing on the meal and the table conversation. Families can share other spiritual formation practices: praying for one another, family devotions, attending worship together, keeping the Sabbath, and reading scripture. Families can practice together the spiritual disciplines of prayer and reflection. Families can also participate in God's redemptive work in the world by serving together at a soup kitchen, on a mission trip, or in addressing ecological concerns (recycling or waste management). And finally, families can provide hospitality by welcoming guests and strangers. The family models a life of discipleship for one another, neighbors, and the world.

Thompson's thesis of the family as the forming center is not new to Christian discipleship. Horace Bushnell states, "A child is to grow up a Christian, and never know himself as being otherwise" (1871, 10). Reacting to the revivalist movement of the mid-1800s, Bushnell suggested that families give more attention to nurturing and teaching children about matters of faith. The family serves as the primary avenue of spiritual growth for children. Christian families should take seriously their role to shape the faith of their children, nurturing them into faith. Ministers criticized Bushnell for his views, but his focus on nurture provided a helpful response to the rigid revivalism of his time. He reminds Christian educators that the Christian home serves as the most powerful forming center for faith. Christian educators have a responsibility to encourage, resource, and equip families to provide spiritual formation in the home. Often Christian discipleship focuses on what happens at the church, but faithful discipleship with families includes empowering the domestic church, the family, to nurture faith through a life of discipleship.

Diana Garland offers similar observations from her research that incorporates more than one hundred different accounts of faith and families (2003, xv-xvi). Garland observes families nurture and shape faith through everyday rituals and storytelling. She notes that family stories may address beginning or new beginnings in family life—loss, heroes or ancestors, survival, caution, or just humor—revealing the sacred dimensions of encounter with God and deepening of faith (19-28). Families also construct meaningful rituals that bind them together and provide the context for shaping goals and dreams (57-86). These processes expand the myriad means by which families learn and nurture faith.

▶ WHAT IS FAMILY MINISTRY?

Congregations use the term *family ministry* to encompass a broad range of meanings. For some congregations family ministry describes all of the activities outside of the local church that relate to the daily lives of church members, including exercise and fitness, stress management, support groups, parenting classes, seminars, counseling, and marriage enrichment. For other congregations, family ministry refers to strategies used to strengthen and support church families. These programs focus on marriage enrichment, family-life education, strengthening families through shared activities (camping, retreats, and sports) and counseling (Garland 1999, 371). Some congregations use family ministry as a form of evangelism in the community. They believe that people who will not attend a worship service will attend a course on parenting issues. Ministers assume that these practical resources provide a bridge to the gospel message.

According to Diana Garland, the major reason congregations give attention to family ministry is concern about the state of families. Since the 1940s, church leaders have worried that families are falling apart, with families in congregations as much at risk as those outside the church. The increasing number of divorces is one example. Congregations provide marriage enrichment workshops to address such concerns (1999, 374). Garland also addresses family ministries that adopt the mental health model of the 1960s and 1970s from the social service professions. The primary goal of this model is to prevent problems through education, and when that fails, provide crisis services to limit the damage. Some family ministry programs resemble these programs of social service agencies, while others include in-house counseling services for families in crisis (373).

These programs can prove helpful, but congregations should be cautious in embracing these approaches and models. Congregations need to develop family ministries based on mission and purpose. Is the primary purpose of the church to strengthen families through education or counseling, or is the crumbling of families a symptom of societal problems that require a more systematic response in which churches can participate? Is the primary purpose of the church to uphold a nuclear view of the family, or is *family* defined more broadly in scripture? What constitutes a family? How churches answer these questions determines the congregational approach to family ministry.

▶ TRADITIONAL APPROACHES TO FAMILY MINISTRY

Faithful disciples with families includes more than offering programs, it includes the whole activity of the church in shaping and forming families. Faithful discipleship to families encompasses a wide range of approaches. We will briefly cover some of the major models:

INTERGENERATIONAL RELIGIOUS EDUCATION (IGRE)

James White defines intergenerational ministry as "two or more different age groups of people in a religious community together learning/growing/ living in faith through in-common-experiences, parallel-learning, contributive-occasions, and interactive sharing" (1988, 18). White's intergenerational ministry approach has the potential to bridge all sectors of the church family in organizing family ministry. Intergenerational activities include family groups, Bible studies, worship services, and family retreats. These activities can keep family units together while fostering intergenerational relationships. The benefit of organizing family ministry around intergenerational groups is that it helps build strong community while nurturing all aspects of the faith community.

FAMILY MINISTRY INCLUDES "FIVE ROOMS"

Charles Sell uses the metaphor of five rooms in a house to describe his family ministry approach. The first room explains how to make the whole congregation more family-like through small groups and intergenerational activities. The second room focuses on providing the content and methodology of marriage enrichment. The third room gives attention to training and preparing parents. The fourth room focuses on specialized ministries such as dysfunctional families, families in transition, support groups, and ministry to single adults. The fifth room involves administration, describing the practical steps a church can take to implement family ministry in its organization and life (1995, 173-332).

LIFE SPAN APPROACH

The developmental stage or life span approach to family ministry remains very popular in many congregations. Ministries organize around the ages and stages of family development, centered on the growth of children. Duvall and Miller (1984) provide the following stages of family development.

- Stage 1: Beginning families (married with no children)
- Stage 2: Childbearing families
- Stage 3: Families with preschool children
- Stage 4: Families with school-age children
- Stage 5: Families with adolescents
- Stage 6: Families as launching centers
- Stage 7: Families in the middle years
- Stage 8: Aging families

The benefits of organizing family ministry around developmental stages include providing specific programs that meet the needs of families at each stage. However, this approach favors the nuclear family over a functional view of families, and stages are less clearly defined as family life spans grow longer in a postmodern world (Schweitzer 2004, 5).

FAMILY DEVELOPMENT PHASES

Diana Garland suggests that family development takes place through phases that resemble a spiral more than a circle or linear path. Each time the family enters a phase of family life, it does so in a different way, bringing with it all of its history and changing culture. Although the themes of the phase seem similar, the family finds itself in a different place. A cycle implies returning to the same place. But the movement of revisiting a development phase does not mean the family is regressing. Families move forward as they revisit previous phases in new ways (1999, 126).

- *Phase 1—Courtship:* Individuals go through a period of courting as they either choose or feel compelled to form a family unit. This is a prefamily phase of contractual relating.
- *Phase 2—Formation:* As persons decide or commit to becoming a family, they enter the formation phase. The movement from contract to covenant begins, forming the foundation for intimacy, cohesion, entitlement, and permanence.
- *Phase 3—Partnership:* Families collaborate by becoming partners in their work. This phase corresponds to Erik Erikson's stage of generativity (see chapter 8).
- *Phase 4—Consolidation:* This phase is characterized by processes of closure and completion of life tasks and commitments that were central during the partnership phase. This can include the empty-nest syndrome as couples redefine their roles without children at home. It can also include retirement and career changes.
- *Phase 5—Transformation:* At this phase, the core family relationships end and the remaining members no longer constitute a family. This can include the death of a spouse or lifelong roommate. Transformation can also include courtship for a new or altered family system (Garland 1999, 126-38).

IMPLICATIONS FOR FAITHFUL DISCIPLESHIP

Christian educators should decide which approach or combination of approaches work best in their ministry context. The following questions are helpful in discerning the appropriate family ministry approach:

- What kind of families are in your congregation (blended, nuclear, singles, etc.)?
- What are the processes of family life in these families (communication, conflict, etc.)?

- What kinds of stresses are they experiencing?
- What are their felt and apparent strengths, needs, and challenges?
- How are they experiencing and growing in faith together?
- How do they define family roles and functions?
- What do they hope or expect the church can do to help them?

Congregations can assess the effectiveness of their family ministry approach by exploring the following questions (see Carroll et al. 1986):

- In what ways does the church support (or not support) the family?
- Do some families dominate church life, and are some families ignored?
- In what ways does the programming create stress for the family?
- In what ways does the congregation support and challenge family life?
- In what ways does the congregation support spiritual formation in the family?
- What programs are offered that provide direct and indirect discipleship for the family?
- What kinds of programs are available for specific family ministries (single parents, marriage, parenting, etc.)?

▶ CONGREGATIONAL LIFE AS FAMILY MINISTRY

Faithful discipleship with families includes the entire faith community. Regardless of the definition applied, structural or functional, the church plays an important role in nurturing and ministering to families.

First, family ministry includes participation in intergenerational forms of worship that include children. Worship should include all age-groups. The stories, rituals, and symbols of worship help the congregation remember the story of the biblical families of faith, while encouraging them to tell the story to others. Family ministry includes education about the sacraments of baptism and the Eucharist as central aspects of the worshipping community. Congregational participation in infant baptism rituals provides a means of grace that fosters faith formation in individuals and the entire faith family.

Second, congregational life as family ministry includes faithful discipleship. Families gather for Bible studies, small groups, and "family clusters" (Sawin 1979) to develop the faith of families, not just that of individuals. Congregations offer unified lessons for all age-groups to study the same Bible lesson or theme. One of the benefits of this approach is a shared topic for table conversation after church. Congregations include life span education, focusing on the needs of families at different stages of development. All of these avenues help foster faith in families within the context of congregational life.

Third, congregational life as family ministry includes ministry and service. Congregations provide opportunities for families to serve together in ministry through volunteer service projects or community efforts. Service should be a shared ministry, including all ages of the church family. Congregations often provide mission and service projects for particular age-groups (e.g., youth), but faithful discipleship to families includes opportunities for everyone to share in service. Congregational life can support, encourage, and empower families to serve in ministry together in the local church, community, and around the world.

Fourth, congregational life as family ministry provides encouragement and supports strong families. Congregations should give priority and time to family ministries. It is one thing to say families are important; it is another to create space for family ministries to be developed and provide the necessary resources. Congregations can make an intentional commitment to develop significant relationships among families to deepen connection and offer support in times of need. Churches that give priority to families will invest time in meeting family needs, working together, and enjoying shared recreation.

Fifth, congregational life as family ministry includes support groups and counseling services for families. As families face crises and hardship, the church can provide resources through a wide range of networks and support-group structures. For example, churches can offer Christian support groups for the divorced or grieving. Professional counseling services can be provided at a reduced rate to church families or made available through a professional referral service. Edwin Friedman's approach, based on family-systems theory, suggests that the study of family systems can help families understand how their experiences are constructing the "self" (1985). Christian educators can learn to use this theory to help families understand the "web of relationships" that continue cycles of pain and dysfunction. The church should be a safe place of care for hurting families. In some settings, the church can advocate for families with specific needs and concerns in the church and community.

Sixth, congregational life as family ministry fosters a wide range of specialized ministries. The diverse landscape of families includes individuals that are often overlooked: singles and single parents, the widowed and widower, and the divorced. Family ministry should include singles-based ministries that address their needs and concerns. Patricia Fosarelli addresses the increased physical and emotional load that single parents carry: "A single parent is likely to be tired because she is doing the work of two parents" (2003, 32). The church family can provide support and resources to single parents. Singles ministries will vary in different contexts; congregations will have to be creative in developing new avenues of ministry that address these and other special needs.

▶ CONCLUSION

Faithful discipleship with families includes the symbiotic relationship between the church and the family, or domestic church, where faith is modeled, nurtured, and developed. The church's role is to equip, encourage, and empower the family through educational ministries. Scripture teaches that family households include members outside the biological family. Defining families must embrace a broader, functional view than the traditional, structural view of the nuclear family. The church embraces all members of the family, ensuring that no person is left outside the family of faith. Congregational family ministry includes worship, education, and service. Families serve as God's creative and redemptive agents in the world and provide a glimpse of the very nature of the Triune God. When congregations give time, energy, and intention to family ministry, they are helping fulfill God's mission and purpose for families as faithful disciples who display love toward one another, neighbors, and the world.

▶ RESOURCES

Balswick, Jack O., and Judith K. Balswick. 2007. *The Family: A Christian Perspective on the Contemporary Home.* 3rd ed. Grand Rapids: Baker Books.

Browning, Don S. 2007. *Equality and the Family: A Fundamental, Practical Theology of Children, Mothers, and Fathers in Modern Societies.* Grand Rapids: Eerdmans.

Brueggemann, Walter G. 1982. *Genesis.* Atlanta: John Knox.

Bushnell, Horace. 1871. *Christian Nurture.* New York: Charles Scribner.

Carroll, Jackson, Carl Dudley, and William McKinney, eds. 1986. *Handbook of Congregational Studies.* Nashville: Abingdon.

Clapp, Rodney. 1993. *Families at the Crossroads: Beyond Traditional and Modern Options.* Downers Grove, IL: InterVarsity Press.

Duvall, E., and Brent C. Miller. 1984. *Marriage and Family Development.* 6th ed. New York: Harper and Row.

Elkind, David. 1994. *Ties That Stress: The New Family Imbalance.* Cambridge, MA: Harvard Univ. Press.

Fosarelli, Patricia D. 2003. *Family Ministry Desk Reference: Holistic Responses to Contemporary Challenges.* Louisville, KY: Westminster/John Knox Press.

Friedman, Edwin H. 1985. *Generations to Generations: Family Process in Church and Synagogue.* New York: Guilford Press.

Garland, Diana R. 1999. *Family Ministry: A Comprehensive Guide.* Downers Grove, IL: InterVarsity Press.

———. 2003. *Sacred Stories of Ordinary Families.* San Francisco: Jossey-Bass.

Roehlkepartain, Eugene C. 1993. *The Teaching Church: Moving Christian Education to Center Stage.* Nashville: Abingdon Press.

Sawin, Margaret. 1979. *Family Enrichment with Family Clusters.* Valley Forge, PA: Judson Press.

Schweitzer, Friedrich L. 2004. *The Postmodern Life Cycle: Challenges for Church and Theology.* St. Louis: Chalice Press.

Sell, Charles M. 1995. *Family Ministry.* 2nd ed. Grand Rapids: Zondervan.

Thatcher, Adrian. 2007. *Theology and Families.* Malden, MA: Blackwell.

Thompson, Marjorie J. 1996. *Family the Forming Center: A Vision of the Role of Family in Spiritual Formation.* Nashville: Upper Room Books.

White, James W. 1988. *Intergenerational Religious Education.* Birmingham, AL: Religious Education Press.

SHEPHERDING FAITHFUL DISCIPLESHIP
Chapters 21—23

The final chapters address the administration, legal considerations, and leadership of faithful discipleship. Faithful discipleship begins as Christian educators conceive and organize their ministries for their context. Chapter 21 focuses on administration, the development, planning, and facilitation of Christian education programs, including issues of budgeting and promotion. Chapter 22 covers legal issues and provides both a theological and theoretical foundation for legal considerations in faithful discipleship. Christian discipleship programs that minister to children and youth require that educators understand the need to create safe environments to protect students. These include developing screening and reporting processes for issues of neglect or abuse and information on the liability insurance that must be provided to protect ministers, teachers, volunteers, and the church. Faithful discipleship includes defining and fostering leadership through the exercise of authority and calling people to covenant ministry. Chapter 23 reviews the meaning of leadership, the development of volunteer leaders, and the establishment of leadership covenants. Good leaders play a key role in the success of faithful discipleship ministries, particularly in engaging others and resolving conflict.

TWENTY-ONE

ADMINISTERING FAITHFUL DISCIPLESHIP

▶ INTRODUCTION

Imagine that the church board asks you to restructure the age-level ministries of your church. How would you begin?

Imagine that you have to plan a year of Christian education activities. Where would you start? How much money would you need? How would you publicize key events?

Imagine that you are asked to lead a meeting of the Children's Council? How would you plan the meeting? What would people need to know in advance? How would you make decisions?

One of the core responsibilities of faithful discipleship centers on the daily tasks of planning and administering Christian education (Stubblefield 1993). Often seen as one of the least important ministry tasks, planning and decision making shape the ministry and set the stage for failure or success.

▶ ORGANIZING FAITHFUL DISCIPLESHIP

While Christian educators may bring particular plans to a new ministry, the context often influences the shape of the final structure. As we have seen, congregations embody formative practices, moments of discernment, and transformative efforts in very different ways, and yet remain faithful to the pursuit of holiness of heart and life. Faithful discipleship can be expressed through several different organizational strategies. The challenge is determining which approach works best within the present context.

The work of shaping any new ministry begins with building the framework. Answering several key questions helps choose the best approach, but remember that undue reliance upon any one may limit the overall ministry.

PEOPLE: WHAT TALENTS AND GIFTS DO WE HAVE?

Most ministries are indebted to the time, talent, and treasure that volunteer leaders bring to the setting. Christian educators recognize that they cannot conduct ministry alone. Children's pastors often shepherd more adult laity than any other ministry in the church. New youth pastors sometimes attempt to center ministry on their own personality and energy, and then they discover the need for grounded adult leaders, if only to avoid burnout. Adult and family ministers begin with the assumption that adults will contribute to the learning process. The challenge is discovering the available strengths and passions of adult students and teachers.

New opportunities surface when least expected. A new couple with musical ability wants to start a youth choir. A local counselor offers to conduct a family retreat. Many ministries begin with the passion of adult workers who recognize a need or sense a calling. Christian educators need to know and nurture available human resources, but undue reliance on talented, available people can create problems. In a highly mobile society people often relocate, taking their abilities with them. Many church closets contain resources (puppets, drama, and music) that bear witness to short-term ministries. Encourage leaders to develop teams that can continue the ministry beyond their availability. Sometimes the people do not move, but the ministry changes. Helping leaders move through change when they are committed to a specific vision of ministry may prove difficult, especially if they have invested a number of years in the effort. Ensuring (even insisting) that teachers are part of the larger Christian education organization helps them understand the broader picture. Nevertheless, ministries thrive under the strength of volunteer leadership, so teachers and leaders need to be recruited and nourished over time.

EVENTS AND PROGRAMS: WHAT HAPPENS HERE?

Christian educators rarely begin with a blank slate when organizing ministry. Existing programs and events give shape to the faithful discipleship of each congregation. Traditional events and programs lend a certain degree of stability and often tell the church's story of discipleship. Understanding and nurturing existing programs can help Christian educators recognize the strengths and needs of the community. A reasonable guideline is for ministers to keep programs and events in place until they have time to understand the history, heritage, and potential legacy of the activity.

Many denominations include basic structures and regional events that offer continuity and stability to church members who move from one church setting to another. Large churches can serve as either flagship partners with smaller churches in regional or district activities or feudal states that ignore the strengths small churches bring to shared efforts. Large churches may possess greater resources than the regional council of small churches; however, their participation may be crucial as a positive influence within these regional events.

Again, perpetuation of programs and events without considering other aspects of ministry may create problems. Without examining and understanding how events and classes contribute to discipleship, ministers may be stuck with mediocre and marginal programs that stagnate, lose focus, and actually work against the congregation's mission. Churches tend to be comfortable adding new ministries but are often reluctant to end outdated or counterproductive programs or events until the entire ministry system collapses under the weight of too many responsibilities. All programs and events need regular review to see if they still serve the educational needs and goals of that setting and to make sure that adequate resources are available.

NEEDS AND OBJECTIVES: WHAT DO WE WANT TO ACCOMPLISH?

Most church ministries operate with a basic sense of people's needs or specific objectives for programs to fulfill. Many Christian educators craft a mission or vision statement that guides the overall approach to ministry. Theorists have used terms like *mission, vision,* and *objectives* interchangeably. Reasonable definitions may help clear the confusion.

Mission is the most basic definition of a ministry. A mission statement expresses the implicit philosophy/theology of the minister in dialogue with the specific context of the ministry: needs, challenges, and opportunities. If one's theology is anchored in the kingdom of God, one's mission statement answers the question, "What constitutes faithful discipleship for living out the Kingdom in this setting?" In a sense, mission is the engine that gives energy and purpose to the ministry.

If mission is the engine, *vision* reveals the destination of a ministry over time. Without vision, we drive aimlessly, wasting the engine's energy. Christian educators must be able to see ministry's destination, what it might accomplish in time. A vision statement answers the question, "What will the kingdom of God look like in this context in one, two, or five years, if we practice faithful discipleship?"

Once Christian educators are prepared with the engine of mission and envision the destination, ministry *objectives* serve as map points that give more detailed directions for the journey. There are many routes we can take on a given journey. Determining the best route involves assessment of the possibilities and plotting points (intersections, rest stops) on a map. In organizing ministry, objectives are the plot points. Objectives should always be "SAM": Specific, Attainable, and Measurable. People need to know that an objective speaks directly to the context, can be accomplished, and provides some indicator of success once completed.

Christian educators need to ensure the alignment of mission, vision, and objectives. If the mission statement includes instilling in children the saving knowledge of Jesus (based on a theology that values children and a context that includes a number of unreached children), the vision statement might include: "incorporate a vibrant summer outreach ministry to children in the next two years." Some objectives might be: (1) conduct a community assessment in a one-mile radius and determine the best way to reach children within six months, (2) choose and implement a one-week pilot program the first summer, (3) gather community support and resources for a larger program the following summer, and (4) inaugurate a sustainable summer program by year two. As each objective is achieved, ministry leaders assess progress and adjust as needed. One might discover that summer programming will not reach children in this area, the pilot program does not draw in new children, changing resources will not support the chosen program, or the program does not lead to transformed lives. At each map point, leaders have a fresh opportunity to test the strategy and renew the vision without abandoning the mission of faithful discipleship.

Understanding mission and vision, and maintaining clear, reasonable objectives, assists Christian educators to serve as good stewards of their ministries. Discipleship becomes more intentional and less reactionary. Leaders may feel empowered to discard programs and events that do not align with the mission and begin new ones with a greater sense of focus and potential.

Again, this framework comes with limitations. Too often, new Christian educators feel compelled to create a new mission or vision statement as soon as they arrive. With the high turnover of ministers in some areas, such a strategy subjects churches and ministry organizations to brainstorming a new mission statement every year or so. Congregants become numb to the constant pursuit of the right mission or vision statement. Some ministers set numerical objectives: so many children available, a specific level of attendance in the pilot program, a specific amount of resources, or a particular number of lives transformed. Unless goals are truly attainable, quantitative assessments like these can become discouraging. Preoccupation with numbers is the primary weakness of undue emphasis on goals and objectives. Faithful ministry pays attention to people, not numbers. Leadership can also become a rigid, autocratic bureaucracy if ministers fail to implement a strong communication and feedback system. Leaders and volunteers may see themselves as interchangeable parts of a machine-like organization in which fulfilling the objectives becomes the mission. Leadership preoccupied with this approach may also overlook the more organic and unpredictable nature of congregations and the unexpected opportunities of grace that often occur in the messiness of ministry. Christian educators must remain vigilant that objectives serve the kingdom of God as articulated in mission and seen in vision. Nevertheless, this approach provides a basic map for ministry when used in tandem with other frameworks.

FUNCTIONS: WHAT SHOULD A CHURCH OR MINISTRY DO?

If a minister assesses mission and vision, current programs and people, does this ensure that the efforts will serve a larger purpose in the life of the church? To answer this question, Christian educators first ask how the church has functioned historically to embody the gospel, how its education ministry has organized the practices of formation, discernment, and transformation. Various theorists have sought to group the larger life of the church in ways that reveal basic categories for organizing ministry. Maria Harris explored the description of the New Testament church in Acts 2:42-47 and asserts that the basic tasks of discipleship should be organized around the domains of worship (*leitourgia*), service (*diakonia*), teaching (*didache*), fellowship (*koinonia*), and witness (*kerygma*) (1989). Robert Pazmiño, using some of the same language, argues that comprehensive Christian education occurs through an integrated model of: *koinonia* (education for and of community), *kerygma* (education for and of proclamation), *prophetia* (education for and of advocacy), *diakonia* (education for and of service), and *leitourgia* (education for and of worship) (2008, 46-53).

Other theorists following similar patterns (Williamson and Allen 1998). Rick Warren adapted the Great Commandment and Great Commission (Matthew 22:37-40; 28:19-20) to characterize the five purposes of the church in much the same way: worship (loving God with all your heart), ministry (loving neighbor), mission (go and make disciples), fellowship (baptizing), and discipleship (teaching to obey) (1995, 102-9). Using any of these outlines to review the overall structure of Christian education will reveal if each of the basic church functions appear. Christian educators often organize committees or subgroups based on one of these general outlines and then arrange programs and construct events to fit those large domains.

A variation of this approach begins with characterizing the people within a church and then designing ministry that serves their levels of attachment and commitment. Rick Warren's model uses basic levels of commitment for this task. The community represents the larger neighborhood. The crowd represents those with nominal engagement with the church, moderately affiliated members who attend general worship. The congregation represents members who engage in one or more activities on a regular basis (e.g., worship and Sunday school). The committed represent those who take some level of leadership, and the core are the most strongly invested members who regularly engage with and lead ministry (1995, 131-34). Arranged in concentric circles or levels (like a funnel), this approach designs programming to meet people at their current level of engagement with the intent of moving them deeper into the life of the church toward committed and core activities. Christian educators assess the church's ability to engage people at their current level and encourage them toward greater commitment, often by assigning a specific descriptor to the activities for each level: come, grow, disciple, develop, and multiply (Robbins 1990, 108).

Organizational schemes that take seriously the larger life of the church in ministry or specific populations within the church offer a comprehensive approach to educational ministry. As with other approaches, however, this framework carries certain limitations when used exclusively. Very few programs and events operate within just one domain. Would Sunday school be considered teaching or fellowship? Do summer programs serve as outreach or service? Many activities serve more than one function. In addition, age-level ministries risk separation from the larger congregation when they try to replicate every ministry function within their private domain. Age-level ministries must recognize that the larger life of the congregation also serves as a resource for ministry. Ministries organized for targeted populations can struggle with defining activities strictly for one group. Christian educators must guard against the assumption that greater activity equals greater commitment. Ministers spend time pressuring people to graduate to more structured programs and events, assuming that participants moving through the funnel reflect greater levels of discipleship and leadership. Such an approach often overlooks specific gifts of leadership or service by people deemed marginal. Much like the focus on objectives, leadership must recognize the organic nature of the church, seeing the functions serving less as departments of ministry and more as mutually informing domains of formation, discernment, and transformation. Nevertheless, the functional approach can help Christian educators recognize how their ministry fits into the larger life of the church.

WHICH APPROACH?

Each framework helps shape educational ministry. As presented, they move from specific concerns (available human and program resources) to larger perspectives (mission and ministry of the church), and each presents particular strengths and limitations. Attempting to integrate all may make organization tedious, while adopting just one framework risks blind spots. A good general rule is to first ascertain which framework (if any) governs an existing ministry and assess the quality of that approach. Next, determine which of the other frameworks complement identified theological convictions and the ministry context. Remember that frameworks serve the ministry; the key is staying as consistent as possible.

▶ ORGANIZING PRINCIPLES

The four frameworks (people, program, needs/objectives, and functions) provide large organizing perspectives. Christian educators must tailor these perspectives to specific ministries and contexts. When finalizing design of age-level ministry and larger Christian education programs ministers might apply these organizing principles.

- *Simple Design:* Keep the organization as simple as possible. Resist the temptation of elaborate structure; volunteers generally prefer simplicity and direct lines of communication. Church leaders now advocate for a simple structure that provides a greater sense of clarity, encourages better flow of communication, aligns people for given tasks, and keeps the ministry focused (Rainer and Geiger 2006, 70-78).

- *Owned by Group:* Key leadership of the group needs to embrace the organizational structure. Inviting key members to help conceive and implement the organizational structure does more than ensure cooperation; weak spots are often revealed through communal discernment.

- *Comprehensive:* This does not mean complicated. However, leadership should be able to identify key ways in which the ministry fulfills its purpose. If it addresses specific age-level students, does it also resource age-level oriented leadership? How does the ministry align with actions and goals of the church and denomination? What lines of communication and accountability exist among the general church leadership, parents or other supportive people, and parish-based community organizations?

- *Correlated and Coordinated:* Almost all ministries intersect with other congregational efforts. Identifying lines between ministries (correlation) and working cooperatively with them (coordinated) ensures faithful ministry for the broader church.

- *Feedback and Flexibility:* Faithful discipleship is never frozen. Organizations, like living organisms, need to breathe. Developing strategies that encourage feedback from coleaders and participants helps with evaluation and responsiveness. Maintaining flexibility also assists the organization to respond creatively and gracefully when necessary.

- *Defined Roles:* Whether these are stated explicitly or implicitly, the organizational structure needs to help participants know their role in the ministry: expectations on key issues like participation, responsibility, ministry definition, authority, and evaluation. Ministry profiles (often called job descriptions) help teachers or other volunteer leaders understand their place in the structure, as do behavioral covenants within groups.

Whether Christian educators use the language of councils, committees, or teams, the overall structure of ministry should respect these organizational principles. Whether an organization is shaped by an elaborate constitution or held together by informal relationships, these principles help both leaders and participants understand their roles and responsibilities, which leads to more effective ministry.

▶ ADMINISTERING CHRISTIAN EDUCATION

Once Christian educators and laity determine the best organizational plan for a ministry, leadership still faces the tasks of planning, facilitation, budgeting, and promotion. Often associated with administration, each task includes a number of key responsibilities that ensure the ongoing life of the ministry. Ministers avoid these responsibilities to the detriment of the ministry. Associate ministers and Christian educators who model strong vision and planning often influence others, including those they serve in ministry (Fisher and Sharp 1998). Learning how to plan, determining how to lead or facilitate basic meetings, developing a budget, and designing promotion strengthens relationships and keeps the missional goal of the ministry in front of participants, congregants, and leaders.

PLANNING

When planning for faithful discipleship, Christian educators need to recognize that certain plans emerge from the cyclical life of the ministry while others require particular attention as special events that do not follow the normal flow. Cyclical events include basic ministry activities such as worship, fellowship gatherings, teaching, and service. They follow a particular rhythm of the year whether through set curriculum, school events, or the church calendar. Planning also includes regularly scheduled meetings and the decisions made there, common times of transition (e.g., graduations, weddings, baptisms), maintaining communication and promotional media, and the other activities and events that populate a ministry calendar (youth gatherings, fund-raising, reviewing scholarship applications, etc.). Christian educators must be careful not to overlook other regular activities, such as scheduled maintenance of existing programs by nurturing the people who lead and participate in them.

Special events are those that may not occur every year or in the same form. These events are special because they are outside the expected flow of ministry, though they may recur periodically over the course of several years. Special events may include camping, retreats, or mission trips. Special emphases also incorporate strategic use of youth revivals, Christmas cantatas, or Easter events, depending on the context. Christian educators avoid returning to these activities too regularly as they place particular stress on the ministry. One general rule is that events or activities require three continuous years to establish a tradition of annual expectation. Recognizing that many ministers do not serve in one setting much longer than three years, ministers should remain cautious how often they repeat large events. Other special events may surface that ministers cannot plan for: pregnancy, drug abuse, death, equipment breakdown, even sudden growth in ministry challenges existing structures. While Christian educators cannot anticipate specific crises, they can rehearse with case studies and scenarios to test the responsiveness of the ministry to unexpected events and plan for contingencies.

One general suggestion might be to plan a year at a time (with other leaders at a planning retreat), but plan twice a year. For instance, your team may begin by planning January to January each year, yet also schedule a meeting in June to plan ministry to the following June. Each planning session maps out the general plan for the entire twelve months, focusing on the specific details of implementing ministry over the next six months. This provides a working twelve-month plan at any time so that educators do not run out of ideas, and allows new members of the ministry to assist in implementing existing plans while dreaming the future. Some large events require a longer timeline; other events may need constant renewal. Dream; don't just solve problems. Creatively look for opportunities and potential concerns by establishing and revisiting two-year and five-year goals.

Some educators supply notebooks or folders to team members to help keep and organize information. Detailed planning includes keeping a working calendar of the ministry that includes influences from church, school, national or regional holidays, sports events, and so forth. Accept that scheduling conflicts will occur, although you should try to avoid them. When a scheduling conflict occurs, telegraph it by letting people know far in advance, particularly when the conflict involves other church ministries. Remember, you are not alone in ministering to others. Keep an open-ended checklist of ideas and programs you have tried (even if they fail). Keep a resource sheet on each program or event, as well as a historical profile, short reports from leaders or participants detailing the steps of their particular project. These profiles often provide critical information for future planning (key contacts, resources, specific challenges), particularly if new leadership must oversee the event in the future.

Each program and planning event usually includes steps that must be addressed along the way. Camps, for instance, require visiting (promotional materials rarely give a true or full picture), securing the location, resources (both human and material), funding, promotions, medical releases, transportation, housing assignments, programming, and feedback. Design a method to address and track each intermediate step. Do not assume that tasks will take care of themselves. Effective ministry events and programs do not just happen, but many disasters just happen because of unanticipated consequences.

Remember that even at Pentecost the disciples were planning leadership development and, most important, praying for the ministry.

EVALUATION

Planning should always include evaluation. Identify and share goals and expectations early in the planning process; these provide the criteria for evaluation. The concept of evaluation often intimidates leadership because of negative connotations from school or work environments. A simple process for overcoming the "E" word includes seeking information around three key concepts.

- *Celebrate:* Invite first reflections on what went well. In what ways did the program achieve its stated goals? What was surprising?
- *Change:* Invite reflection on changes in leadership style or approach that might be helpful if the event is repeated.
- *Reconsider:* Invite suggestions for improvements to the program that will help it better fulfill expectations and meet stated goals. Using "reconsider" language allows reflection on the possibility of improvement without pressure to make immediate changes.

Responses in these categories help evaluate the success of an event in relation to the set goals. Sometimes unexpected outcomes occur, worth celebrating, that give the event new meaning and purpose. It can also identify areas for improvement in both leadership and implementation. This simple process helps leaders determine whether or not to repeat some events. Unfortunately, most evaluation occurs late in the process, following the event. When possible, incorporate at least one informal time of evaluation during an event or program so that leadership can make adjustments as necessary.

BUDGETING

The planning process includes budgeting for ministry. Ideally, budgeting should begin with the needs for ministry and then ascertain the necessary funding. A comprehensive budget submitted for approval (for instance, to a church finance committee) should identify general funding areas. In addition to the submitted budget, the Christian educator should have a carefully detailed plan available on how monies will be used. This demonstrates depth in planning and helps answer questions that may arise. Budgets include cyclical programming, special events, scholarships for deserving students, and long-term replacement of items like church vans or sound systems. If a church cannot fund the entire ministry, the finance committee should indicate the amount of funding available but should not suggest programs or events to eliminate; the Christian educator should make the final determination in consultation with the committee. Finance committees sometimes try to resolve budgeting concerns through selective approvals, often shaping the educational ministry by approving or rejecting specific funding. As professionals, Christian educators should resist this approach, retaining the right to determine the approach to ministry based on the funds available.

Many Christian educators inherit a budget with predetermined expenditures and resources. They should study the existing budget, exploring the history and rationale for each expenditure as well as implicit assumptions concerning how money will be raised for certain events. Ministers need to explore how much of the budget comes from outside funding sources—fund-raisers, sponsors, and general donations—and which events rely most on these sources. Budgets often contain some, if not all, of the minister's compensation. In some settings, ministers may designate part of their salary for professional development, which allows them to use pretax resources for professional reading and conferences. While considered part of the minister's overall compensation (along with salary, insurance, social security, and housing allowance in many North American settings), professional development may be listed as part of the ministry program. Recognizing idiosyncrasies in a budget may save future embarrassment.

In addition to assigned budgetary items, ministers should also investigate other revenue sources within and beyond the congregation. Sunday school resources can sometimes be used for weekday ministry as well; worship ministries may supplement age-level music programs, and building maintenance may have resources for updating technology or replacing a church bus. Locating such sources can help stretch a budget. Beyond these resources, Christian educators should be cautious in how they raise funds from within a congregation. When possible, ministers should focus fund-raising efforts on populations beyond the immediate church. Too often, fund-raising events place undue pressure on parents and parishioners, increasing their obligation to the local church.

Financial management of the budget demonstrates the Christian educator's ability as a steward of ministry. Ministers should carefully track ministry expenses, submitting receipts for purchases, documenting and tracking student fund-raising efforts, maintaining basic records of all monies that flow through the ministry. Whenever possible, a minister should avoid handling funds directly. In all circumstances, the minister should work diligently to provide a comprehensive account of all expenditures, which often raises confidence in the ministry and respect for budgets presented in the future.

PROMOTION

Developing technology has opened new avenues for promoting ministry programs and events. Sound promotion, though, relies less on the attractiveness of a brochure or Web site than on clear and tasteful communication, offered as regularly as possible to the people affected by the ministry. First, promotion requires consistent communication concerning the life of the ministry. Then simple updates through newsletters, Web sites, or other vehicles inform the church of the faithfulness of a ministry. News updates help members of a congregation or community appreciate and understand the importance of special initiative and events.

Christian educators need to understand that most problems associated with an event begin with poor communication. All promotional materials should include basic information that answers key questions:

- Who? (Who should attend, who needs to be involved, and who is in charge?)
- What? (What will happen?)
- When? (When will the event program take place [dates and times], and when do people need to commit or register?)
- Where? (Where will the event occur; where will people meet to travel, if necessary?)
- Why? (Why should I be involved? Why should I care?)
- How? (How do I participate?)
- How much? (How much will it cost me in time, money, and commitment?)

Obviously not every piece of promotional material will incorporate answers to all of these questions, which is one reason that more than one promotional effort is needed. However, each promotional material should include the means for gathering the rest of the information, such as a contact phone number, e-mail, Web site, or general location, such as a ministry bulletin board.

Promotional material should be tasteful and attractive, but Christian educators must balance cost with influence. Expensive brochures may limit production, an expensive video or Web site design may preclude creating other, low-tech materials for people who respond best to print resources. Promotional material serves to motivate, but its primary goal is to communicate the basics of the ministry, not to manipulate people by making promises that cannot be met.

Announce early, middle, and late. Christian educators need a plan or timeline for promoting special events. Preregistration due dates help ministers increase interest and often alert leadership to the potential impact of the event (though local culture may work against preregistration). The strategy may include promotional pieces that target the people most likely to attend the event as well as more general notices in church-wide or community publications. One approach is the *one-three-one* strategy. *One:* promote the event very early to people most likely to attend, often through direct mailing or some other specific announcement. This initial notice may not have all of the information but should contain enough to answer the basic questions listed above. *Three:* promote the event later using three more general means of notifying the congregation or community: newsletters, Sunday bulletins, posters, and so forth. These include less specific information but may offer updates or key points of interest. *One:* close to the deadline for event registration, send a second, specific invitation with detailed information to the original target population and to others who responded to the general announcements. The first and the final efforts may involve cost to the ministry, but the event or program receives comprehensive exposure. Whether using this approach or another strategy, the more a community hears of an event with accurate and pertinent information, the better the response will be.

MEETINGS

Planning, budgeting, and promotions all require decision making, often accomplished through committee or team meetings, perhaps the least favorite exercise for most ministers and Christian educators. However, these gatherings are crucial in the relational and decision-making life of the ministry. Not all meetings seek the same goals and not all decisions seek the same outcomes. Christian educators need to understand the role of each type of meeting and the process for effective decision making in a variety of circumstances.

Most organizations require up to five different forms of meeting, each designed to achieve certain goals. Some elements may be combined; however, one meeting rarely seeks to achieve all five goals.

1. *The Ritualistic Meeting:* These are regular, scheduled meetings that contribute to the flow of communication in an organization. They consist largely of receiving reports and updates that relate to maintaining the organization.

2. *The Briefing Meeting:* Briefings serve to provide members with information and updates on plans already underway. The leader provides instructions on individual roles and responsibilities: who is to do what, when, and where.

3. *The Training Meeting:* Training meetings (workshops, seminars) help members become proficient in their responsibilities. Often elective in nature in the world of ministry, many vocations require regular updates or in-service educational events as part of professional development.

4. *The Consultative Meeting:* A leader often consults with a group directly connected with the ministry in order to get their advice concerning

a decision. The leader may make the decision alone, incorporating feedback from the consultation and taking seriously the advice given during these meetings.

5. *The Decision-making Meeting:* At this meeting, the group bears responsibility for making decisions and owns (has responsibility for) the decisions it makes. Such meetings clearly identify moments of decision by either announcing the moment with language (e.g., action item) or framing the decision in a formal voting process that follows some modification of parliamentary procedure (*Robert's Rules of Order*).

As noted, meetings may include more than one function, moving from reports to action items or beginning with briefing and concluding with consultation. Developing a clear agenda helps participants understand the shifts within a meeting and anticipate when their responsibilities will change.

Decision making may seem the most important task of meetings, but not all decisions set new directions for ministry. Some decisions recur in predictable cycles; this allows participants to establish patterns for discernment. *Cyclical decision making* includes Sunday school curriculum review, worship planning, budgeting, and general administrative processes. Some decision making occurs because of confrontation, forced by circumstances or events beyond routine activity. A particular crisis (which can be negative or positive) may shape the decision-making process, often in the form of problem solving. *Confrontational decision making* involves conflict among leadership, the need for additional resources for an expanding Sunday school class, or as the result of a ministry vacancy. Finally, innovation may require decision making. These opportunities occur only when Christian educators seek them out. They do not often arise naturally, but may be intentionally cultivated. *Innovative decision making* comes from a desire to increase outreach, through long-range planning, or is the result of a deliberate review of a congregational survey.

When facilitating or leading a meeting, Christian educators must first answer one key question: "What kind of meeting do I need and what types of decisions will I seek?" Problems arise in meetings when participants are unsure of their role in the process. Parents arrive at a meeting expecting to participate in a decision-making process (perhaps only small decisions based on cyclical needs) only to be "briefed" on the decisions already made by the minister. A major confrontation surfaces late in a lengthy ritualistic meeting, requiring unexpected decision making. Teachers arrive for a training meeting and are asked to brainstorm innovative strategies without clear direction on how they benefit from the exercise. Mixed messages often undo the effectiveness of many meetings.

Leaders can overcome such problems by clearly communicating their expectations for the meeting, providing an agenda that details the major elements, developing clear guidelines for discernment and decision-making processes, and summarizing transitions from one type of engagement to another. Leaders may need to create intentional opportunities for innovation rather than problem solving, to look at long-range potential, listen to group members who may be considered difficult, and celebrate observations without drawing conclusions.

Boards, committees, and teams work best when they have a specific purpose beyond traditional decision making. Christian educators may use committee or team gatherings as times for discipleship and reflection (Olsen 1995). Ministers may introduce a team covenant that offers internal direction to the group. The covenant should include a preamble (brief statement of what God has done to bring these people together) as well as a purpose (the goal of the committee or team). After determining the introductory material, the covenant may include specific commitments the team will keep, including personal and ministry practices. The covenant may conclude with an opportunity for commitment. Leaders should always plan adequate time to orient new team members to the purpose of a group. Ministers should provide a consistent format for reports and responses and may use liturgies or simple rituals with prayer and scripture to begin and end meetings, which help reinforce the purpose of the group. Most teams need opportunities to celebrate God's grace, and leaders need to bless team efforts as meetings end.

▶ CONCLUSION

Christian education administration includes discerning the best structure for ministry, organizing the various elements into a coherent form, and shaping the ministry through regular processes of planning, budgeting, promotion, and facilitation. Rarely the most popular aspects of ministry, these basic tasks are crucial for faithful discipleship. Christian educators may sometimes sacrifice opportunities to be up front so that other leaders can learn the benefits of careful preparation and planning. Wes Haystead reminds educators that the term *administer* means "to minister alongside" people, "sharing the load, encouraging, supporting, and enabling them to develop their gifts and potential" (1995, 109). Providing a sound structure, working behind the scenes to ensure comprehensive plans, and preparing early for meetings and promotions to provide sound decisions and clear communication all serve the larger process of ministry. Faithful discipleship develops through these broad strategies in transformed lives and transforming ministry.

▶ REFERENCES

Fisher, Roger, and Alan Sharp. 1998. *Getting It Done: How to Lead When You're Not in Charge.* New York: HarperBusiness.

Harris, Maria. 1989. *Fashion Me a People: Curriculum in the Church.* Louisville, KY: Westminster/John Knox Press.

Haystead, Wes. 1995. *The 21st Century Sunday School: Strategies for Today and Tomorrow.* Cincinnati: Standard Publishing.

Olsen, Charles M. 1995. *Transforming Church Boards into Communities of Spiritual Leaders.* Herndon, VA: Alban Institute.

Pazmiño, Robert. 2008. *Foundational Issues in Christian Education.* 3rd ed. Grand Rapids: Baker Books.

Rainer, Thom S., and Eric Geiger. 2006. *Simple Church: Returning to God's Process for Making Disciples.* Nashville: Broadman and Holman.

Robbins, Duffy. 1990. *Youth Ministry Nuts and Bolts: Mastering the Ministry Behind the Scenes.* Grand Rapids: Zondervan.

Stubblefield, Jerry. 1993. *The Effective Minister of Education.* Nashville: B&H Academic.

Warren, Rick. 1995. *The Purpose-Driven Church: Growth Without Compromising Your Message and Mission.* Grand Rapids: Zondervan.

Williamson, Clark M., and Ronald J. Allen. 1998. *The Vital Church: Teaching, Worship, Community, Service.* St. Louis: Chalice Press.

TWENTY-TWO

LEGAL CONSIDERATIONS FOR CHRISTIAN DISCIPLESHIP

▶ INTRODUCTION

Imagine you, the youth pastor, receive a note from regional leadership requiring all sponsors, who work with children or youth under age 18, to complete a background check including fingerprinting from the local police department. Several adults ask you why, after a number of years of service, they suddenly have to go through this process. What would you say?

Imagine you are driving a group of children to a quiz competition. The van you are driving has enough space for eleven people, including you. You are told that the church insurance policy covers a total of eleven people on the van, and if you go over this amount you and the church could be held liable. When you go to the church to pick up the children, twelve children climb into the van. You realize you have too many children in the van. How do you resolve this problem?

Ministry in the twenty-first century has become more complicated. Sexual misconduct and child abuse charges against Roman Catholic priests have raised awareness of the legal implications of using positions of power in negative ways. Congregations begin to see the need for programs and policies to ensure safety for all involved parties. Christian educators acknowledge the impact of governmental policies and legal concerns on ministry. Pastors and Christian educators do not always value these safeguards as ways to protect them, the church, and the people they serve. Faithful discipleship, however, requires full understanding of the legal issues that affect ministry, including confidentiality and volunteer screening.

▶ THEOLOGICAL CONSIDERATIONS

When addressing administrative functions such as legal concerns, confidentiality, and volunteer screening, many pastors and Christian educators believe the primary rationale for these endeavors relates to legal obligations. While these are significant, Christian educators and ministers of the gospel must also understand the theological rationale: the intrinsic value of human persons created in the image and likeness of God. Faithful discipleship includes creating a safe place where all human persons are respected and valued. Human beings reflect the Triune God through their relationships with one another. When leaders use their positions of power to control, neglect, or abuse others, they violate the very nature of the Triune God. Holy living includes loving each person completely, regardless of race, age, gender, or nationality. Civil law provides protection from those who violate the very law of God—the love of neighbor.

The church, bound both by the law of love as recorded in scripture and the civil laws established by the government, provides guidelines to uphold the dignity and respect of all persons. When leaders violate the law of love, it harms the community of faith. Legal guidelines also protect leaders from those who intend harm. In both cases, guidelines reflect the biblical principle of love and care for each person as created in the "image and likeness" of God. When harm occurs, congregations must speak the truth; they must investigate and reveal the perpetrator. A congregation may choose to redemptively support a perpetrator, but not in secret and not at the victim's expense. The duty to report represents the truth spoken in love.

▶ CREATING SAFE SANCTUARIES

Creating a safe sanctuary for children is critical for faithful discipleship (Melton 1998). The church should be a safe place that fosters faith formation and development. Christian educators need to work proactively with local church leadership to create safe places for children and youth (Cobble et al. 2003). Any child-safety plan for the local church should include the following five basics (Blevins and Hart 2009):

1. *Church Awareness:* Start by sharing your vision with your pastor, then your leadership team. This group can recruit a task force to design a plan, with a timeline and an appropriate policy. They can share the tasks of research, communication, and support. This team will be especially valuable in communicating the need to the congregation. Be prepared with facts, statistics, and examples from other churches. Clearly state how this policy and plan will help the church more effectively accomplish its purpose and mission. Church leadership must both approve and fund the plan to ensure appropriate implementation. Involve your team when you meet with workers and parents. They can help field questions and share the process you have employed to develop the plan.

2. *Safety Audit (facility):* Evaluate your facility to identify potential trouble spots (see the section on Safety in chapter 15). Plan changes that will make these less accessible or attractive.

3. *Personnel/Policy Design:* The personnel policy should include: *(1) Prevention*—This is your primary goal. The existence of clear policies

and procedures for workers, including background checks, is the best deterrent to potential perpetrators. A well-designed plan protects children and also helps protect workers from unfair accusations. *(2) Reporting*—When an incident or accusation occurs, emotions run high and it is easy to forget what to do next. The personnel policy and plan must have clear and direct reporting procedures that include forms, timelines, and chain of authority (see considerations below).

4. *Responding:* The church's response is crucial. A prompt, honest, caring response may begin healing for the victim and family; a poor response will cause more damage. Responding proactively goes a long way to maintain caring relationships. Congregations should also remember to pray for the perpetrator while holding him or her accountable for his or her actions.

5. *Policy Implementation (who, what, when):* A great policy accomplishes nothing if you are not willing to implement the plan. Implementing the policy should include training, accountability, and clear procedures that are evaluated on a regular basis. Procedures must be clearly articulated in writing and in your training materials. Test your policy before you need it. Use case studies or hypothetical situations and take your workers/volunteers through each step. Provide drills to prepare people to respond appropriately before a problem occurs (see considerations below).

6. *Ongoing Education, Monitoring, and Assessment:* Church personnel often change, making continuing lay training essential. Plan to evaluate your procedures at least once a year. Survey workers, parents, and visitors. Invite educators from other churches to tour your facilities and arrange to visit theirs. Give each other safety report cards. Be open to new ideas and learn from mistakes and successes. Be aware of events or incidents in your community and keep communication open with the congregation.

The image of the church must be that of a safe sanctuary, free of barriers to the gospel. Several important considerations will contribute to the success of this mission as Christian educators apply the five basics of child safety (Blevins and Hart 2009).

Be Educated on the Issues. Provide continuing education on important aspects of child safety. Educate yourself, your pastor and board, your staff (volunteer and paid), and those you serve. Constant communication is the key to effective education. Legal issues vary from state to state. Be sure you have the latest updated information. Legal definitions of abuse and neglect should be clearly communicated and understood. As noted above, use scenarios and case studies to illustrate the need for a policy and to guide leadership in anticipating problems.

Develop Policies. As noted above, this should be done by a task force, which should include parents, workers, and educators. This provides ownership of the plan and will help ensure implementation. In addition to the general areas of prevention and reporting noted above, the policies should include:

- *Screening:* Both volunteer and paid work begins with an application, complete with references, and a signed release of background information with driver's license number. Check with other churches in your area, your insurance company, and the local police or Department of Human Services for companies that serve your area. There are a variety of fee structures, so persevere until you find what works for your church.

- *Training:* Workers who know how to follow proper procedures and guidelines will provide protection for the child and the worker. Communicate expectations to hold workers accountable. An important step is having a follow-up system in place to evaluate and assess the effectiveness of your procedures and to implement change as needed.

- *Reporting:* Reporting suspected abuse or knowledge of abuse is not as simple as you might think. Each state has different requirements, definitions, and time limits. Know what your state requirements are before establishing your procedures. All workers need this information. There should be a clearly communicated chain of authority to follow when reporting. For example, workers report to supervisors, supervisors to ministry leaders, ministry leaders to parents and attorneys, insurance company, authorities, and district leadership. Someone should also be prepared to talk to the media.

- *Responding:* Plan ahead to ensure appropriate and effective church response to allegations of abuse. This is never easy. Always take an accusation seriously and show immediate concern for the victim. Treat the accused with dignity and respect, but remove the accused from any responsibility for children until a thorough investigation is completed. When responding to the congregation and the media, it is best to have a written statement. Be sensitive and refrain from sharing unnecessary details or placing blame; maintain confidentiality where appropriate.

Document Policies and Procedures. To be credible, policies and procedures must be available in written form, and church board approval must be documented. A file on each worker, volunteer or paid, should include application, completed reference follow-up forms, signed release of background information, consent to screening form, and receipt for training on policies and procedures. Teachers should have access to incident-report forms and forms for suspected children. Files on children should include a signed medical release and parental consent for activities.

▶ Legal Considerations

Faithful discipleship requires careful management and administration in a contentious and constantly changing legal climate. Congregations can no longer operate independent of legal considerations and need to consult with legal professionals on current laws that affect them. The cultural tendency is to see law and religion as separate categories, which often prevents a ministry from effectively employing available protections and leading to great peril when laws are ignored (Henze 2005, 274).

Given the diverse scope of legal issues and laws, this chapter cannot cover every situation. We will review some of the most critical areas of legal liability for churches. Mark Henze identifies five primary areas (see 2005, 287-90):

1. *Negligent Hiring:* An employer may be liable for the intentional or criminal misconduct of an employee. Often this involves a claim that the employer was negligent in the selection and hiring of the wrongdoer. In other words, an employer has a duty to use reasonable care in investigating a prospect and evaluating his or her suitability for the position.

2. *Negligent Supervision:* Once hired, an organization has a duty to reasonably and properly supervise the actions of the employees. Many cases of negligent supervision involve incidents of child molestation and sexual misconduct. Christian educators need to keep attendance records, not allow children to be released to strangers, restrict restrooms in children's facilities, conduct counseling within the view of witnesses with open doors, and use multiple chaperones during offsite activities.

3. *Negligent Retention:* An organization may have acted responsibly in hiring and supervising employees. However, congregations may be found guilty of negligence if they unreasonably retain an employee after receiving information that the employee has developed a propensity, pattern, or disposition of placing others at risk of harm.

4. *Malpractice:* Malpractice consists of a professional person's deviation from the reasonable standards of care expected of those within that profession. Lawyers typically append claims for clergy malpractice to claims for intentional acts (such as criminal acts or sexual misconduct) or to claims for negligence in counseling. Most courts reject these claims based on the specific professional duties of a minister.

5. *Confidentiality of Communication and Clergy Privilege:* Confidentiality and privilege are two different concepts. Typically, there is no legal requirement that a minister's conversation with a parishioner remain confidential. In fact, unless a conversation occurs in private with no other parties present and with an expectation of confidentiality, ministers normally should not regard the conversation as confidential. In most cases, any duty of confidentiality remains moral in nature, not legal. However, confidentiality, or at least discretion, should be maintained in order to develop trust. Each church or denomination needs to have a written and established policy about the confidentiality of clergy communication. The concept of privilege deals only with the ability to legally compel a minister to disclose confidential communications in a court of law. The rationale for privilege revolves around protection of a person's right to religious confession (penitence) and a preservation of the confidence and therapeutic value of such communications. State law governs in defining privileged communication for a minister.

▶ RISK MANAGEMENT

Christian educators and ministers can help prevent lawsuits and liability through risk management. It helps protect the minister, the congregation, and the people they serve. In many ways, risk management is good stewardship of resources.

First, congregations must be sufficiently insured. Property insurance should include the church building, cars and vans, and machinery. Liability insurance deals with leadership, travel incidents, errors and omissions, directors and officers, and crime and dishonesty. Liability insurance will protect the church in the event that someone is injured or suffers some other form of damage on church property (Garland 2001, 186). Exclusion insurance covers such issues as sexual misconduct, contractual liability, personal property of staff, and libel and slander. It is essential for congregations to have enough insurance to cover the scope of the church's ministry. Pastors, Christian educators, and trustees should consult legal counsel to ensure that the church is significantly covered.

A second area of risk management is the use of waivers and medical release forms. It is important to educate parents and participants about inherent risk of injury whenever people gather in public spaces. Every time a Christian education worker conducts a ministry activity with children and youth under the age of eighteen, he or she is taking a significant risk (Garland 2001, 188). These forms also provide added protection for the church by creating a defense to a claim. Medical release forms must be included on children and youth activities, mission trips, and retreats. The child's release form should be signed by all parents of children who participate in church events (Haystead and Haystead 2000, 108). Some congregations keep a signed medical release on file for all church-related activities. This provides helpful protection to the church and the family. When students participate in international travel, they may need to include an insurance rider for travel outside the United States (Garland 2001, 188). Groups are also encouraged to provide additional group medical insurance (Pearsall and Russell 2008).

A third area of risk management is confidentiality. The question often arises, "When am I allowed to keep a confidence, and when could I be required by law to reveal what I have been told?" (Garland 2001, 189). As noted, confidentiality entails both lay and legal definitions. The lay definition involves the discretion of the individual receiving confidential information; it is a moral issue. The legal definition, as noted above, refers to privilege and arises in certain defined relationships of attorney-client, clergy-penitent, and counselor-client. Privilege may apply in settings where one can reasonably anticipate confidentiality, such as the pastor's office or counseling room. Information is not confidential when shared within a group or if there is a reasonable expectation of harm to a third party or client/penitent. Ministers must report reasonably suspected abuse of a minor. Christian educators or church leaders may want to talk to a senior pastor before reporting to state or local authorities, but the duty to report harmful acts remains.

Confidentiality also relates to respect of personal privacy, particularly in third-party conversations. Discretion remains incredibly important; however, churches are small worlds, and it is difficult to fully disguise someone's identity. Full confidentiality is never guaranteed and may become a legal issue if a person is a danger to self or others. It is helpful to set limits at the beginning of a confidential conversation: you cannot keep secrets that will harm the person, abuse others (particularly children, which you have a duty to report), or hurt the community of faith you represent. If you have not been able to set guidelines before you hear a confidence, you might need to make a judgment in the moment and suggest including others in the conversation. This a strong, loving, but firm way to respect the speaker and avoid misunderstanding or harm.

A fourth area of risk management is counseling. Christian educators and leaders must be aware of laws that govern the counseling process. Church settings are particularly complicated. Perhaps a person approaches you after church to share his or her story. In the midst of that conversation, the person shares confidential information, but in this context you are not in a privileged position. In other words, your confidential role as a minister is compromised.

Ministers must understand what it means to have privileged communication with others.

It is important to note that most ministers are not professional, licensed counselors. The role of the minister is to provide pastoral care and support through listening, praying, showing compassion, and providing practical advice. Clinical pathologies (e.g., chemical, emotional, biological, and psychological), however, call for extended and professional counseling. In these cases, it is very important to refer the individual to a professional, licensed counselor. Here are some practical guidelines and ideas to help govern your counseling experiences and protect you from possible liability concerns:

- Know your limitations as a counselor. As a minister or Christian educator you are not a trained, certified counselor.
- Identify and write down the boundaries for the counseling you will offer.
- Develop a referral list and make appropriate referrals. Refer when you realize that the situation is beyond your abilities. When you refer someone, you do not stop investing in care and support of the individual; you are broadening and sharing care in the best interest of the individual.
- Keep records of your counseling sessions. Record the date, time, and reason for the session along with good notes.
- Consult and study existing resources that govern counseling in your church (policies, manuals, ethical codes, etc.).
- Learn the extent of insurance coverage.
- Don't have any person under age 18 sleep at your house, particularly if you are single.
- Don't allow minors (or unreliable adults) to drive other minors anywhere on an officially sponsored church activity.
- When counseling, don't make promises you cannot keep.
- Make sure that any church vehicles and equipment you use are properly maintained.
- Volunteer staff (high school volunteers, nursery workers, etc.) should be appropriately trained and, if at all possible, screened for prior criminal record.
- Church policies and procedures need to be in place to protect the church from liability and from irresponsible workers/volunteers.
- Church boards need to be educated to eliminate potential risks.
- Someone should periodically perform an audit of state laws that might have impact on the church (a member of the church who is an attorney or church legal counsel can do this) (Pearsall and Russell 2008).

A fifth area of risk management is congregational safety. The church, including buildings and surroundings, must be a safe and secure place. Are the facilities accessible to all members of the congregation? Do children have appropriate furniture that is easily accessible to them? Are there enough emergency exits to get everyone out in case of a fire? Are adequate escape plans posted in every classroom? Has the congregation been trained in this escape plan in case of an emergency (Whited and Whitworth 1989, 43-44)? Is a first-aid kit available and updated on a regular basis?

Congregations should be informed about the specific aspects of risk management needed to protect the minister, the workers, and the congregation. Neglect of these areas can lead to painful and costly liability issues. Pastors and Christian educators need to be intentional about processes and policies that reduce and manage risk.

▶ SCREENING VOLUNTEERS

While serving as a youth pastor, I (Mark) made the screening process mandatory for all leaders, administered by a third party. One leader resisted, saying, "I have been working with children for over thirty years and I don't need to be screened." I responded by letting the gentleman know that times had changed, and we could no longer assume that all leaders are trustworthy. This didn't mean he was suspect, but we needed to implement the process to protect the church, us, and the people we serve. Today, most congregations and ecclesial bodies require anyone working with children or youth under age 18 to complete a background check. All church workers should provide references and agree in writing to a background check before they will be considered for ministry service. Christian educators need to contact all references. Personal interviews should also be documented and should include the person's Christian testimony, special interests, past teaching and volunteer experiences, and other related information. All information obtained during the interview and screening process remains confidential; files should be kept in a secure area (Purcell 2005, 253).

The primary reason for requiring screening of volunteers is to create a safe environment for children and youth. Parents are aware of the dangers that children face at school, and in the local community. The church is not exempt from this concern. Christian educators have to be proactive in developing a plan to ensure the protection of children and youth. A comprehensive screening process is one avenue to ensure parents that the church is serious about providing a safe place for their children. A second reason for screening of volunteers is today's litigious culture. Lawsuits are prevalent phenomena in our society. Parents sign waivers for their children to participate in school sporting events or recreational activities, and the church must do the same for its legal protection (ibid.). Since legal issues constantly change, congregations should have a lawyer available to provide legal counsel to the pastor and the leadership. As we have noted, congregations should also carry liability insurance.

The National Child Protection Act of 1993 was established to encourage states to improve the quality of their criminal-history and child-abuse records. This act establishes safeguards for children and agencies caring for children. As a result of this act, states now mandate that organizations, including churches, complete a nationwide criminal history background check on prospective employees and volunteers serving children, youth, the elderly, and individuals with disabilities. Churches should cooperate and embrace these measures for higher moral reasons as well (ibid.).

▶ CONCLUSION

Faithful discipleship includes providing a safe sanctuary for children and youth in order for them to learn and grow in their faith. Congregations need to be made aware of the legal considerations that have an impact on faithful discipleship. The development of policies and procedures that reflect legal recommendations is critical in protecting the Christian educator, the congregation, and the people being served. Christian educators need to be aware of how to manage risk through sufficient insurance, medical release forms, counseling, confidentiality, and safe facilities. Each congregation needs to consult the laws and regulations mandated by the state, especially as they change. Congregations should consult legal counsel (lawyers) who can help interpret laws appropriate to the church context. These safeguards are not only legal obligations but also theological mandates. The theological understanding of human persons as created in the image and likeness of God becomes the theological foundation for providing a safe sanctuary. Attention to these matters helps the church fulfill its mission of making faithful disciples. Lack of attention to legal concerns can prevent the church from being a means of grace to one another and to the world.

▶ RESOURCES

Blevins, Dean, and Leslie Hart. 2009. Safe sanctuaries, safe kids: Reaching out for safe places for children. Unpublished document.

Cobble, James F., Jr., Richard R. Hammar, and Steven W. Klipowicz. 2003. *Reducing the Risk II: Making Your Church Safe from Child Sexual Abuse.* Mathews, NC: Christian Ministry Resources.

Garland, Ken. 2001. Legal and ethical issues in ministry. In *Introduction to Christian Education: Foundations for the Twenty-first Century,* 185-91. Ed. Michael Anthony. Grand Rapids: Zondervan.

Haystead, Wes, and Sheryl Haystead. 2000. *How to Have a Great Sunday School.* Ventura, CA: Gospel Light.

Henze, Mark. 2005. Legal and ethical considerations in ministry. In *Management Essentials for Christian Ministries,* 274-92. Eds. Michael J. Anthony and James Estep Jr. Nashville: Broadman and Holman.

Justice, Mike. 1998. Working Document. "Children and Youth Ministry Screening: A Program to Help Prevent Child Abuse in the Local Church." Kansas City: Nazarene Youth Ministries, Church of the Nazarene.

Melton, Joy Thornburg. 1998. *Safe Sanctuaries: Reducing the Risk of Child Abuse in the Church.* Nashville: Discipleship Resources.

Pearsall, Joel, and Bill Russell. 2008. *Legal Toolbox.* Nampa, ID: Lectures in Pastoral Leadership, Northwest Nazarene University.

Purcell, Larry. 2005. Recruiting and screening volunteers. In *Management Essentials for Christian Ministries,* 244-57. Eds. Michael J. Anthony and James Estep Jr. Nashville: Broadman and Holman.

Whited, Linda R., and David Whitworth, eds. 1989. *The Ministry of Christian Education and Formation: A Practical Guide for Your Congregation.* Nashville: Discipleship Resources.

Appendix 22.1
Child Safety Process

Congregations are to adopt written policies for children's and youth ministries at the church board level. These policies are to become the official policies of the local church. These policies assist congregations in providing for safety and responsibilities of employees and those to whom they minister.

1. Require a criminal background check of all staff and volunteers who work with children and youth.
2. Develop a worker's application form that includes a place for the worker to sign, giving permission for a background check. No exceptions can be made.
3. Require that all child-care groups have a minimum of two workers present, no exceptions. One of the two must be an adult.
4. Require that a person be a member of the church for a minimum of six months before he or she can teach any class.
5. Provide regular orientation of all teachers and workers about the church's policies relating to child care and sexual abuse issues. Teach them how to recognize a child who may have been abused. Local police and social service agencies can offer suggestions.
6. Schedule and conduct an annual review of child-care policies, workers' personnel files, and so forth. Make updates as needed, informing all workers in writing.
7. Require that if any person acts questionably or fails to follow the policies, that person will be suspended immediately from working with children until the situation is investigated and resolved.

Determine who will serve as the media spokesperson for the church if a problem arises (Purcell 2005, 244-57).

Several agencies and denominations have developed working documents that serve as unofficial guidelines for a screening process for youth and children's workers. They encourage local churches to develop a strategy to prevent and respond to child abuse in the local church (Justice 1998).

Step 1: Definitions

The first step in this process involves understanding some basic terminology. These definitions will help you as you screen those who work and volunteer in your church:

- *Child:* any person, regardless of physical or mental condition, under age 18.
- *Child Abuse:* bringing harm to a child that occurs immediately or through accumulated effects over a period of time. There are four basic categories

of child abuse: emotional abuse, neglect, physical abuse, and sexual abuse (see definitions).

- *Emotional Abuse:* when children are consistently told they are of no worth and/or never will be of any worth. Name-calling and threatening harm or injury are forms of emotional abuse.
- *Ephibophilia:* an adult's exclusive sexual interest in adolescents usually of the same gender.
- *Liability:* the legal responsibility for one's conduct often results in monetary damages.
- *Neglect:* when harm is caused by withholding life's necessities (food, clothing, and shelter). The ability to provide life's necessities but failing to do so is the factor that separates neglect from poverty.
- *Negligence:* the failure to exercise reasonable care.
- *Negligent Selection:* the failure to exercise reasonable care in hiring employees or selecting volunteer workers.
- *Negligent Supervision:* the failure to exercise reasonable care in supervising either employees or volunteer workers.
- *Pedophilia:* an adult's exclusive sexual interest in children who are under the age of puberty.
- *Physical Abuse:* any kind of bodily injury to a person.
- *Program:* any class, organization, activity, group, event, and so forth.
- *Punitive Damages:* monetary penalties enforced by a court against a person or organization that engages in reckless behavior.
- *Reasonable Care:* the care that would be exercised by an ordinarily prudent person under the same or similar circumstances.
- *Respondent Superior:* a legal principle in which an employer is legally responsible for the negligence of its employees while within the scope of their employment.
- *Sexual Abuse:* any sexual activity between a child and an adult, or between children when there is an unequal distribution of power. This includes exposing children to sexual activity or pornography.
- *Training:* organized study programs that enhance skills. These programs may include: home study courses, workshops, seminars, conferences, and mentoring relationships (Justice 1998, 2-3).

Step 2: Develop a Strategy

The second step in the process is to develop a strategy. The strategy includes: screening, training, safeguards, swift action, and reporting.

Screening: Using an established procedure to screen workers will help minimize the risk of abuse in the church. The selection of adults to share in ministries to children and youth requires a moral and legal responsibility from each church. When abuse happens within the church, lifelong religious confusion and deep feelings of hatred toward God and church can occur. Therefore, all potential workers should go through a screening process before they begin ministry. An effective screening process involves checking references—including background and criminal records checks. The following information can be used at all levels of ministry (i.e., children's minister, VBS director, children's workers, youth minister, volunteer youth sponsors, camp staff, and Sunday school teachers).

Training: It is strongly recommended that workers and staff attend annual training classes through local or state social service agencies. Providing training opportunities for workers and staff will sensitize them to the issues of abuse—preventing, detecting, responding, and reporting. Training of workers and staff on the local church's child abuse policy and reporting procedures should also occur annually. A copy of the certificates for completing training should be kept on file in the church office.

Safeguards: Safeguards are key elements in a church's program to help prevent child abuse. A church can use reasonable care in selecting workers and still be liable for injuries sustained during church activities on the basis of negligent supervision. Negligent supervision refers to a failure to exercise reasonable care in the supervision of church workers and church activities. Some safeguards that can be helpful are as follows:

- *Two-Deep Leadership:* At least two workers should be present at all activities. One worker for every eight children or youth at any event is strongly recommended. Coed groups and activities should have coed leadership.
- *Visible One-on-one Contact:* All contacts between workers and children/youth should be in view of other adults and children/youth. Classrooms should have windows (preferably in the door) so all activities can be monitored.
- *Respect of Privacy:* Workers need to respect the privacy of children and youth in shared housing accommodations (i.e., retreats, camps), and they should protect their own privacy as well.
- *Appropriate Dress:* Proper clothing for activities is required. Dress codes should take into consideration the Christ-centered nature of ministry.
- *Constructive Discipline:* Discipline should be constructive and reflect Christian values. Corporal punishment should *never* be permitted. It is suggested that workers be made aware of acceptable discipline techniques to avoid any difficulties.
- *Appropriate Physical Contact:* Physical contact between children/youth and workers is an area where great wisdom must be exercised at all times. Physical contact should always be for the benefit of the child/youth (i.e., to give affirmation, to provide comfort when hurting, or to express joy).

Swift Action: Respond quickly to allegations of child abuse by removing the alleged offenders from contact with children and youth and reporting the situation to the proper authorities. Swift action in dealing with suspected abuse is essential. Having all staff and volunteer workers aware of the church's policy on child abuse will help to handle incidents efficiently.

Reporting: Churches need to encourage children and youth to report improper behavior directed toward them and to cooperate with church officials and local, state, and federal authorities when reporting child abuse. This can be done through giving the information to parents and having them educate their children. Educational programs on child abuse and training personnel are generally available from local social service agencies. Paid church staff and volunteer workers are obligated to understand their personal and legal responsibilities, as well as to follow the reporting procedures. All children and youth workers should be aware of the state laws that govern reporting child abuse. Abuse reports can be reported on forms like the "Abuse Report Form" and "Steps for Reporting Suspected Abuse" forms found in this appendix. By assuring these six principles are well known and followed by all, a church will enhance the quality and professionalism of ministry and provide protection of those involved (Justice 1998, 4-5).

Many states require that any church employee who comes into possession or knowledge of any evidence of abuse, whether or not it is conclusive, must report that to local law enforcement officials or a child protection agency immediately. Failure to do so constitutes a criminal offense and all church officials and employees who came to know of that evidence could be liable and prosecuted. This can be the hardest step in the process of reporting.

Step 3: Screening Process

At the heart of any ministry are adults who willingly give time, talent, and self to the church. Adults who view involvement with children and youth as a *ministry* are crucial for successful ministry. Books, videos, games, and activities are all-important, but these only have true value when used by dedicated, trained, and caring workers. Being a children's or youth worker is a privilege and a responsibility. Care must be given when granting this privilege and trusting this responsibility to others. The following screening process can help assure that your workers are worthy of that responsibility. Responsibility and protection needs to be established in a ministry program. The following definitions can aid in assuring responsibility and protection.

- *Guest Minister:* people who bring specialized ministry to a program on a short-term basis, such as a special speaker for camps, retreats, midweek program, afterglows, and so forth. They might be parents, pastors, or persons with a special skill that adds to the program. Guest ministers should be screened if they will be used for more than three days, or if they will be directing children or youth without an adult present.
- *Volunteer Workers:* a person who does not receive monetary compensation for working with children or youth. A volunteer worker ministers

independently or under the direction of a children's or youth minister, depending on whether the church has such paid staff.

- *Paid Church Staff:* all paid church employees. This includes clergy, secretarial workers, custodians, and so forth. Screening should take place as part of their application process (Justice 1998, 5-7).

When there is a need for a worker or when an individual asks to work with children or youth, the following process should be followed:

1. *Explain the purpose of the screening process to the prospective worker.* Parents have the right to expect that their children's and youth workers are of the highest caliber. The process helps assure the physical, emotional, and spiritual safety of those involved in your church's programs. To help ensure a safe, quality program, it is appropriate to ask persons to be screened even if they are not currently serving. This allows for substitutes or replacements without jeopardizing the ongoing safety of a program.

   It is important for those who are already working with children and youth to be screened. Criminal convictions that should disqualify an individual from working with children and youth in the church include: any offense of violence, assault/physical abuse of a minor, child abuse, child pornography, endangering children, gross sexual imposition, kidnapping, public indecency, incest, murder, pedophilic/ephibophilic behavior, rape, sexual imposition, sodomy, voyeurism, or any existing or former offense of any municipal corporation, any state, or any nation that is substantially equivalent to any of the above offenses. It does not matter how long ago these offenses occurred; it is in everyone's best interest to not use someone in your children's or youth ministry who has had such prior convictions (Justice 1998, 5-7).

   NOTE: If any current worker has been convicted of any of the listed criminal actions, that worker should be sensitively relieved of any duties in working with the children and youth without delay.

2. *Have the applicant complete the "Release of Information" and "Request for Criminal Records Check."* A sample of these forms is included in this appendix. Have your church's attorney review them to make sure they comply with your state laws. The prospective worker needs to answer all of the questions and sign both forms. These forms serve as releases of information and authorize the local police department to conduct a check of the applicant's criminal record. A copy of picture identification (driver's license) needs to be attached to the applicant's file.

3. *Check the references.* Copies of the signed *"Request for Criminal Records Check"* form will need to be sent or faxed to your local police department. Using the *"Record of Contact"* form supplied in this appendix, contact the personal references. Use the *"Screening Tracking Form,"* also found in this appendix, to help you track the screening process. *All information*

gathered must be kept confidential. Keep all original documentation for the registration process in a separate file in a secured file cabinet.

Several states require child-care providers to obtain criminal records checks on its workers. If your church operates a child-care program, be sure to confirm whether or not your state has such a law. Also, be aware that most criminal record checks will cost $5.00 to $25.00 (Justice 1998, 5-7).

▶ RESOURCES

Justice, Mike. 1998. Working Document. "Children and Youth Ministry Screening: A Program to Help Prevent Child Abuse in the Local Church." Kansas City: Nazarene Youth Ministries, Church of the Nazarene.

Purcell, Larry. 2005. Recruiting and screening volunteers. In *Management Essentials for Christian Ministries*, 244-57. Eds. Michael J. Anthony and James Estep Jr. Nashville: Broadman and Holman.

Appendix 22.2
Release of Information
(all information given will be confidential)

This release of information is to be completed by all persons wishing to serve in any position (volunteer or compensated) involving the supervision or custody of minors in the _____ Church. The intent of the reference and criminal records checks are to help ensure that the church provides a safe and secure environment for those who participate in any programs, classes, and/or activities.

Date _____

Full Name _____
Last/First/Middle Initial/Maiden/Former

Current Street Address _____

_____
City/State/Province/Zip

Home Telephone _____ Work Telephone _____
Identity must be confirmed with a state driver's license or other photographic identification.

List the name, city, and state/province of any other congregations you have attended regularly in the past five years: _____

_____

Have you ever been convicted of a crime, other than a minor traffic violation?

__ No __ Yes. If yes, please indicate the date, state, and nature of the offense:

_____

Are you currently under investigation, or have you ever been recorded by the Department of Social Services (or any equivalent department/agency) for child abuse and/or neglect or any criminal activity involving a minor? __ No __ Yes. If yes, please indicate the date and nature of the record: _____

_____

Appendix 22.3
Personal References *(No relatives)*

Name: _____

Address: _____

_____

Phone: _____

Name: _____

Address: _____

_____

Phone: _____

Name: _____

Address: _____

_____

Phone: _____

I authorize any references or churches listed in this release of information to give any information that is requested regarding my character and fitness for ministry. I release all such references from any and all liability for any damage that may result from furnishing such evaluations. I also waive any right that I might have to inspect information provided on my behalf.

I hereby attest and certify that I have never been convicted of nor pled guilty to any offense of violence, assault/physical abuse of a minor, child abuse, child pornography, endangering children, gross sexual imposition, incest, kidnapping, murder, pedophilic/ephibophilic behavior, public indecency, rape, sexual imposition, sodomy, voyeurism, or any existing or former offense of any municipal corporation, any state, or any nation that is substantially equivalent to any of the above offenses. (If you have been convicted of or pled guilty to any of the above offenses and wish to explain the circumstances thereof, please do so on a separate sheet of paper.) I further certify that I have never been discharged from employment or a volunteer position because of any activity covered by the aforementioned.

I hereby authorize any present or former employer, church employee, and firm, corporation, physician, or government agency to answer any and all questions and to release or provide any information within their knowledge or records.

I agree to hold the aforementioned free from any liability for releasing any truthful information that is within their knowledge and records.

I hereby attest and certify that the above information provided by me is true and correct to the best of my knowledge. I understand that any misrepresentations or omissions may disqualify me from or result in my immediate dismissal if I am already serving in a youth-related program.

_____   _____

Signature   Date

Appendix 22.4
Request for Criminal Records Check
Confidential Information

I hereby request the _____ Police Department to release any information that pertains to any record of convictions contained in its files or in any criminal file maintained on me whether local, state, or national (federal). I hereby release said police department from any and all liability resulting from such disclosure.

I further authorize _____ Church to conduct a check of my criminal records and agree that I will fully cooperate in providing all information and signing all documents necessary to conduct such a check.

_____   _____
Signature   Date

Print Name _____

Maiden Name (if applicable) _____

Print all aliases _____

_____

Date of Birth _____

Place of Birth _____

Social Security Number _____

Drivers License Number _____

Street Address _____

_____
City/County/State/Zip

For Office Use Only:

Record Sent to: _____

_____

Name/Title/Agency

_____

Address   Date

Appendix 22.5

Record of Contact
Confidential Information—For Office Use Only

Name of Prospective Worker: _____

First Reference

Person Contacted _____

Title _____ Date _____ Time _____

Method of Contact: __ telephone __ letter __ other: _____

Name of Person Making Contact: _____

Reference's Comments About Applicant Were: __ favorable __ guarded
__ unfavorable

Summary of Reference's Comments: _____

_____

Second Reference

Person Contacted _____

Title _____ Date _____ Time _____

Method of Contact: __ telephone __ letter __ other: _____

Name of Person Making Contact: _____

Reference's Comments About Applicant Were: __ favorable __ guarded
__ unfavorable

Summary of Reference's Comments: _____

_____

Pastor/Third Reference

Person Contacted _____

Title _____ Date _____ Time _____

Method of Contact: __ telephone __ letter __ other: _____

Name of Person Making Contact: _____

Reference's Comments About Applicant Were: __ favorable __ guarded
__ unfavorable

Summary of Reference's Comments: _____

_____

Signature of Person Filing This Report:

_____ Date: _____

Appendix 22.6
Screening Tracking Form

Name: _____

☐ References Contacted:

   1. _____ Date: _____

   2. _____ Date: _____

   3. _____ Date: _____

☐ Criminal Records Checked:

   __ yes

   __ no

   Area of Service: _____

Appendix 22.7
Indicators of Sexual Abuse

The indicators of abuse vary. No child or caretaker will exhibit all of the physical or behavioral indicators listed, neither will any one indicator show abuse. Indicators should be used as a guideline to raise awareness and to show a need for closer scrutiny. It should also be noted that physical indicators are present in only a small percentage of sexual abuse cases. Therefore, the absence of physical indicators should not be considered conclusive evidence that an allegation is unsubstantiated.

Behavioral Indicators of Sexual Abuse in Infants and Preschoolers
1. Being uncomfortable around previously trusted persons
2. Sexualized behavior (masturbation, sexually inserting objects, explicit sex play with other children, etc.)
3. Fear of restrooms, showers, or baths (common locations of abuse)
4. Fear of being alone with men or boys
5. Nightmares on a regular basis or about the same person
6. Abrupt personality changes
7. Uncharacteristic hyperactivity
8. Moodiness, excessive crying
9. Aggressive or violent behavior toward other children
10. Difficulty in sleeping or relaxing
11. Clinging behavior, which may take the form of separation anxiety
12. Passive or withdrawn behavior

Behavioral Indicators of Sexual Abuse in Older Children
1. Being uncomfortable around someone previously trusted
2. Specific knowledge of sexual facts and terminology beyond developmental age
3. Sexualized behavior (masturbation, sexual acting out with other children on a regular basis, seductive toward peers and adults, etc.)
4. Wearing multiple layers of clothing, especially to bed
5. Parent-like behavior (pseudomaturity, acts like a small parent)
6. Fear of being alone with men or boys
7. Fear of restrooms, showers, or baths
8. Constant unexplained anxiety, tension, or fear
9. Frequent tardiness or absence from school, especially if male caretakers write excuses
10. Attempts to make himself or herself ugly or undesirable (poor personal hygiene)
11. Eating disorders (obesity, bulimia, anorexia)
12. Self-conscious behavior, especially regarding body

13. Reluctance to go home after school
14. Abrupt personality changes
15. Child acquires toys or money with no explanation
16. Wetting of bed or clothing
17. Nightmares on a regular basis or about the same person
18. Change in sleeping habits (tries to stay up late or seems constantly tired)
19. Moodiness, inappropriate crying
20. Unusual need for assurance of love
21. Regressive behavior (fantasies and/or infantile behavior)
22. Uncharacteristic aggressive or violent behavior
23. Tendency to seek out or totally avoid adults

Behavior Indicators of Sexual Abuse in Adolescents

1. Sexualized behavior (promiscuity, prostitution, sexual abuse of younger children, etc.)
2. Running away, especially in a child normally not a behavioral problem
3. Drug and alcohol abuse
4. Talks about, gestures, or attempts suicide
5. Frequent illness
6. Unexplained aches and pains
7. Self-mutilation
8. Extreme hostility toward a parent or caretaker
9. Parent-like behavior (pseudomature, acts like a small parent)
10. Self-conscious behavior, especially regarding body
11. Wearing multiple layers of clothing, especially to bed
12. Eating disorders (usually obesity)
13. Nightmares or other sleeping problems (bed-wetting, sleep disturbances)
14. Constant fear or anxiety
15. Delinquent behavior
16. School problems (academic or behavioral)
17. Defiance or compliance to an extreme
18. Friends tend to be older
19. Withdrawal
20. Clinging behavior
21. Crying for no apparent reason

Physical Indicators of Sexual Abuse

1. Pain or itching in the genital areas
2. Difficulty in walking or sitting
3. Vaginal discharge
4. Bruises or bleeding of external genitalia, vaginal, or anal regions
5. Venereal disease

6. Swollen or red cervix, vulva, or perineum

7. Pregnancy when a child refuses to reveal any information about the father or there is a complete denial of pregnancy by the child or her parents

8. Torn, stained, or bloody underclothing

9. Unusual or offensive odors

Family Indicators of Child Sexual Abuse

1. Role reversal between mother and daughter

2. Extreme overprotection or jealousy toward a child by a parent (parent sharply restricts a child's contact with peers and adults outside the home)

3. Inappropriate sleeping arrangements (child sleeps with a parent on a regular basis or with both parents where she is exposed to sexual activity)

4. Prolonged absence of one parent from home (through death, divorce, etc.)

5. Mother who is often ill or is disabled

6. Extreme lack of communication between caretakers

7. Inordinate participation of father in family (father may interact little with family members or may insist on being in charge of all family activities)

8. Extreme paternal dominance of spouse (for instance, mother is not allowed to drive or to talk to school personnel, etc.)

9. Work or activity schedules that result in a caretaker (especially male), spending large amounts of time alone with a child or children

10. Extreme favoritism shown to a child (father may spend a lot of time and attention on one daughter)

11. Severe overreaction by a parent to any sex education offered to a child

12. Geographic isolation of family

13. Overcrowding in a home

14. Caretaker who has been sexually abused as a child

15. Family has no social or personal support systems

16. Alcohol or drug abuse within the family

Follow-up Responses After Abuse

When abuse occurs in the church, it is hard to objectively determine what the needs are for the church and the individuals closely associated with the abuse to recover from the trauma in effective ways. It is highly recommended that a team of leaders meet to discuss some intentional steps of how to respond after a possible case of abuse has occurred in the church. Having prepared a plan of action in case of abuse, assists the church to be intentional in the healing of this crisis.

Also, many states require that any church employee who comes into possession or knowledge of any evidence of abuse, whether or not it is conclusive, must report that to local law enforcement officials or a child protection agency immediately. Failure to do so constitutes a criminal offense, and all church officials and employees who came to know of that evidence could be liable and prosecuted. This can be the hardest step in the process of reporting.

Here are some areas the team needs to address:

- *The Care and Safety of the Victim.* This is a top priority. Therefore, be ready to offer a good resource person who is knowledgeable and capable of therapeutic and spiritual counseling for abusive situations within the teen context.
- *Intentional Care Toward the Church.* The church needs to be able to respond positively to this crisis. How will the crises be addressed to the congregation? From the pulpit, support groups, individual counseling, parent meetings? If the abuse involved a worker, the adults may be questioning safety. Help them learn how to respond to questions about the abuse.
- *Intentional Care Toward the Children and Youth in the Church.* This crisis can devastate a ministry if not handled appropriately. How will the need for counseling of people who may have been closely associated with the accused abuser be addressed? How will trust be rebuilt? How will questions be responded to?
- *Response to the Media.* By not talking to the media, some may infer that the church has something to hide. Should a local press conference be held? Should information be released to the news media before any misinformation gets into the public? Exercise caution in releasing information because that information may influence a court case. *Do not release any names!* The team should designate one person to be the spokesperson for the church to the media. This person should be the official voice of the church in dealing with the media.

▶ RESOURCES

Purcell, Larry. 2005. Recruiting and screening volunteers. In *Management Essentials for Christian Ministries,* 244-57. Eds. Michael J. Anthony and James Estep Jr. Nashville: Broadman and Holman.

TWENTY-THREE

EDUCATIONAL LEADERSHIP IN COMMUNITY

▶ INTRODUCTION

Imagine you are challenged by a senior minister to spend more time casting the vision of your age-level ministry than working relationally with volunteer teachers and leaders in your group. How would you respond?

Imagine you have the task of replacing three volunteer teachers in the children's ministry area. How do you proceed?

Imagine you need to resolve a conflict between two volunteer workers. What would you do first?

Christian educators seeking to develop learning environments in a church or local ministry must accept their role as a leader within those contexts. Often an elusive task, leadership (in church as in the rest of society) involves "a person, group or organization who shows the way in an area of life—whether in the short-term or the long-term—and in doing so both influences and empowers enough people to bring about change in that area" (Banks and Ledbetter 2004, 16-17). Leadership entails a number of challenges: setting vision, inspiring others in ministry, calling people to covenant relationship, and resolving conflicts as they occur. What constitutes a person who is capable of accomplishing these tasks—capable of leading—is a subject of ongoing study.

▶ THE HISTORY OF LEADERSHIP AND MANAGEMENT

Following periods of preoccupation with pastoral practices like evangelism and counseling, ministers are now inundated with leadership literature. Multiple reasons exist for this emphasis, including the expansion of business and management paradigms in church ministry. In the latter half of the nineteenth century, approaches to studying leadership focused on great men who affected the course of history (Bank and Ledbetter 2004, 50-53). During the first half of the twentieth century, the focus shifted to empirical study of leaders' character traits. Later studies focused on leadership behavior and style. All three of these approaches retain some popularity. Beginning in the 1970s, leadership studies took context into account, which led to approaches in situational leadership by Paul Hersey, Kenneth Blanchard, and Dewey Johnson. Their widely used, regularly revised text, *Management of Organizational Behavior: Leading Human Resources* (1969/2007), emphasizes the vision- and people-oriented approaches addressed in this chapter.

Parish leadership practice in the late twentieth century might be traced to at least one seminal text, *Why Leaders Can't Lead,* in which author Warren Bennis noted that many North American leaders often get bogged down with day-to-day micromanagement and forfeit their role as visionaries (1989, 59-66). Leaders needed a larger, more global perspective. In response, a number of texts surfaced on setting vision and mission. Of course, the leaders Bennis discussed possessed large administrative staffs assigned to take care of day-to-day tasks, resources few pastors can afford. Nevertheless, *leadership* books, articles, and gurus emerged and continue to dominate the market. *Management* seemed relegated to second-class status, a theme still evident in contemporary work (Godin 2008, 13-14). However, a view of management as an alternative but complementary task to leadership did enjoy some attention (Banks and Ledbetter 2004, 17-20). In another classic study, Thomas J. Peters and Robert Waterman argued that most successful companies in the United States included leaders who exercise "MBWA": Management By Wandering Around (1983/2004, 121-38). They acknowledge a relational component as leaders become familiar with workers' daily tasks. Subsequent texts explore less formal leadership in organizations of decentralized networks. Such settings view leadership primarily in catalytic and collaborative terms, with the occasional charismatic leader or hero to provide a public rallying point to organizational efforts (Brafman and Beckstrom 2006). These developments help avoid the danger of separating day-to-day relationships from visioning in definitions of leadership.

Many pastors of smaller churches and associate ministers in larger settings now accept a less hierarchical structure in relationships with other congregational leaders. Very few ministers can afford to operate in just one role, particularly since many of the tasks associated with management are the administrative duties discussed in chapter 21. Collectively, leadership and management need to be as effective and as efficient as possible. David Arthur Bickimer discusses tensions that permeate leadership concerns, both in the congregation as a whole and in individual relationships, which creates concerns for faithful leadership and management (1990, 61). Roles shift with need as emphasis changes vision to relationship. If the people need motivation and specific direction, ministers call on leadership skills to provide vision. When the need is for encouragement and gentle guidance to empower goals and desires for a ministry, ministers employ management skills to provide relational support. Adapting the work of Hersey and Blanchard, one might conceive of a grid where leader and follower readiness shape decisions based on attention to vision or the need to develop stronger relationships, calling in turn for a focus on management or leadership (see figure 23.1).

Figure 23.1: Relationship/Vision Grid
of Leadership and Management

High Relationship ↑ M a n a g e m e n t	Leaders provide catalytic leadership, working alongside followers and encouraging them. Followers seem capable but unwilling or insecure in fulfilling their role.	Leaders appear collaborative, providing needed expertise or talent. Followers not as capable but willing and/or confident they can succeed with help.
	Leaders delegate, willing to relinquish responsibility. Followers prove quite capable and confident in their roles and vision of ministry.	Leaders appear authoritative, confident, and quite directive to ensure outcomes. Followers lack capability or seem unwilling or insecure in their roles.
Low Relationship/ Low Vision		Leadership→
	High Vision	

Leaders in educational ministry may tailor their approach depending on the priority of vision or relationship or the capability or willingness of followers. However, leaders cannot abandon one aspect of ministry entirely for the sake of the other. Christian education leadership rests on a vision of the kingdom of God and focuses on helping people become Christlike in relationships. In a sense, relationships are a part of vision, and vision surfaces through relationships as the community seeks faithful discipleship together.

▶ Theological Reflections on Authority in Leadership

Faith traditions conceive of authority differently, relying on a particular theological understanding of the church (ecclesiology) and church order (polity) to undergird ministerial authority. Episcopal models situate authority with the historical leadership of the church. Pastoral authority is generally independent of the desires of the local congregation. It is validated by tradition and accountable by polity to leadership beyond the local church. Congregational models locate authority within a local church's call and validation of pastoral oversight, contingent on the support of local leaders. Each model includes sophisticated theological rationales consistent with their approach. A third model, more charismatic in nature, situates authority within the specific gifts and graces of the individual pastor, at times over and against either larger historical or immediate congregational oversight. This third view situates authority neither in the historic church nor in the local congregation but primarily in the personal connection between the minister and God.

The Wesleyan tradition poses particular difficulties when considering the historical context that shapes polity and authority for leadership. John and Charles Wesley served as Anglican priests within a modified episcopal vision of leadership (Richey and Frank 2004, 43-59). However, John Wesley also saw his assistants as ministers in their own right; they often served as itinerant preachers in Methodist preaching circuits (Heitzenrater 1995). Wesleyan denominations grew within North American revivalism, which led to both strong charismatic preaching and democratization of leadership, particularly in frontier settings where ministers maintained large circuits (Hempton 2005). These dynamic factors lead to a blended, if not chaotic, view of leadership authority (Richey and Frank 2004, 30, 90).

Perhaps the best understanding of authority in a Wesleyan context acknowledges leadership with both *conciliar* and *constitutive* influences. Church authority based on *conciliar* relationships begins with the church councils of the first century, perhaps even with the casting of lots in the Upper Room (Acts 1:12-26). Conciliar leadership is lived out in community, often through processes of discernment and mutual decision making (Osmer 1990, 78-79). Regardless of gifts and graces, even pastoral authority granted at ordination depends on extended periods of preparation and discipline as well as systems of accountability through local and regional oversight. Relying on communal authority rather than personal charisma does not always rest well with pastors. Ministers sometimes invoke an old joke: "For God so loved the world he sent his son . . . not a committee." Wesleyans, however, recognize that no one person stands in the place of Jesus; ministers are witnesses (apostles) and disciples of Christ, the Lord and true head of the church. Authority rests upon the grace of God, the power of the Holy Spirit, and calls the body of Christ, the church, to Christlike servant leadership.

The term *constitutive* reminds leaders that authority arises within a context and for a purpose. Ordination services that include the scriptural admonition "take thou authority" call the pastor to exercise that authority on behalf of the kingdom of God (the context) for the sake of the people of God (the purpose). Faithful disciples recognize that this authority empowers the pastor's gifts and graces, not personal desires. Leadership authority includes the responsibility to discern and engage God's call. The challenge is in discerning the Kingdom needs of the community and responding by channeling gifts and graces in response. Jackson Carroll argues that leaders must be theologically grounded but always bring their theological perspective into discussion with the social setting, drawing from experience and theoretical perspectives to see the complex narrative that informs the leadership process (1991). A leader's attention to people in their context is a ministry in itself.

Ministers require authority for the basic tasks of motivation and mediation. Leadership never occurs in a vacuum, always in community. Carroll reminds us that people *allow* leaders to lead; authority for leadership (both prophetic and priestly) comes from the relationship between parishioners and leaders as well as from the kingdom of God (83-87). When acting prophetically in the face of unfaithful congregational practices, ministers may sometimes need a larger vision of the community of faith, and call on the conciliar vision of the larger church (87-89). But even a prophetic stance does not absolve the minister from relationship in the community. The term *servant leader* remains important, particularly for Christian educators who serve a shared vision of the kingdom of God with the very people they are called to lead.

▶ CALLING MINISTERS

Charles Foster notes that people who work within the educational ministry of the church, particularly volunteer teachers, arrive with their own calling. Teachers may be recruited (or drafted when no one else is available), volunteer for the role, stumble into the opportunity to teach, or accept Christian education as part of their role and responsibility (1986, 14-15). Regardless of how people arrive, Foster asserts: "Most of us received the call to teach through some common and ordinary channel of God's grace" (16). Recognizing such a basic calling frees leaders to both understand the challenges and appreciate the gifts that teachers and other workers bring to faithful discipleship. Ministry is time-consuming, relentless, and often thankless for busy volunteers. Each week brings new challenges, and volunteer teachers are often lonely and unknown. Parishioners may not take teachers seriously or demean their teaching efforts, ridiculing their work and Sunday school answers. However, teachers are vital to the church. They give their ministry freely as volunteers, often sustaining the life, heritage, and meaning of the congregation. Volunteer teachers and ministers live in covenant faithfulness to their calling, which was given by Jesus. They are part of a special fellowship of other great church teachers in history . . . including Jesus himself. Cultivating a climate that both acknowledges the challenges and celebrates the contributions of these called ministers is a primary leadership responsibility.

RECRUITING LAITY

Congregations are primarily volunteer organizations, particularly so in America where membership and financial support are elective activities. But many members view service in the church as a reflection of one's faith. Ministry recruitment in today's church lives in the tension between effectiveness (helping people the best we can) and efficiency (helping so that the organization does not collapse) (Bickimer 1990). Historically, this tension has been resolved in various ways:

- Connecting service to salvation (a version of legalism)
- Connecting service to membership (establishing up-front expectations)
- Connecting service to fit (emphasizing spiritual gifts)
- Connecting service to fun (encouraging project-oriented service based on personal interests)
- Connecting service to fear (death of a particular ministry . . . or the church)
- Connecting service to grace (encouraging response to grace received)
- Connecting service to shared leadership (parishioners generate leadership when needs arise)

Most congregations live in the tension between elective service and faithful ministry obligation. Sound strategies may ensure a stronger base of called ministers.

Begin with Current Ministers: Christian educators need to attend to the treatment of existing teachers. You cannot recruit if you cannot nurture, and eventually you will burn out your resources. The first step in recruitment is to make your programming realistic, accessible, and functional through ministry teams where possible. People in ministry need information that explains their role. Churches usually call these job descriptions, but *ministry profiles* may be better language. Recognize the various levels of expertise of existing volunteers and develop a system of accountability for them as volunteers and leaders. Once leaders establish nurturing practices, volunteers often serve as the primary recruiters with leaders providing personal follow-up. Ministers need to be a part of the process but cannot do it all (a sure path to burnout). It is always better to ease new volunteers into the ministry by entrusting them to a team. Eventually the team structure helps reduce the pressure for constant contact on your part, and you can concentrate on resourcing and development.

Recognize the Tension Between Gifts and Interests: Many ministries place considerable emphasis on spiritual gifts inventories. This strategy may serve both as a blessing and a curse. On their own, inventories reveal interests and passions, but not always gifts and abilities. Listen to the recommendation of other team members, and use inventories as indicators, not final determinants for ministry.

Use Surveys Cautiously: A similar problem exists with surveys. They might be excellent ways to sample congregational interests, but they place implicit demands on leadership (particularly when Christian educators receive a positive response from someone they suspect may not qualify). Surveys should reach a large population, offer several levels of interest, and leave follow-up to leadership. Christian educators should be clear that the survey serves as a preliminary inquiry, not immediate recruitment for specific positions. Leaders advance best through developmental training where gifts and graces can be demonstrated within a monitored process.

Independent or Entrepreneurial Ministries: The best ministries often start spontaneously. Ministers need to observe the following cautions. First, make sure the initiator starts the ministry for the right reasons. Watch for "should" or "ought" language that may result in ministry that is viewed as indispensible. All new ministries should include a plan for review and evaluation after a trial start-up period. Second, entrepreneurs should locate sufficient resources (including people and funding) before they begin. Finally, entrepreneurs need to be prepared to perpetuate the ministry beyond their own leadership. Cultivating desire for this may take time; a good general rule is a requirement to secure additional leadership before the end of the first year to ensure continuity in ministry.

ESTABLISHING TEAMS

A leader's style of recruitment reveals the willingness to share ministry and the desire to empower others in their ministry calling. Team-based ministry offers a helpful view of shared leadership. The theological rationale for shared leadership in teams comes from our understanding of the relationship within the Trinity. Teams anchored in the triune relationship of Father, Son, and Holy Spirit covenant to seek God's missional vision through loving, trusting, collaborative relationships that both empower and enlighten the team through ongoing learning (Cladis 1999, 3-16). Teams can model a form of shared learning that bridges individual learning patterns with larger congregational learning and thereby assist churches to respond and adapt to changing culture (Hawkins 1997, 72-75). Not all teams are equal in relationship or ability. Team members must learn to trust one another, deal constructively with conflict, discover commitment, hold one another accountable, and pay close attention to the outcomes or results of their activity (Lencioni 2002). The mutual passion and discipline of team-based ministry releases leaders to embrace a sense of shared authority.

▶ MINISTRY COVENANTS

As noted in earlier chapters, covenants serve a primary role in educational ministry. One need not endorse a particular brand of covenantal theology to appreciate how covenants shape congregational commitments. John Wesley instituted a New Year's watch night covenant service that guided Methodist practice over the years, often serving as a means of reflecting upon baptismal vows (Parkes 1997, 35-58; Blevins 1999, 217-27). However, the concept of covenant relationships goes much further back. The Old Testament understanding of *covenant* (*berit* in Hebrew) possesses dual meanings. First, covenant functioned to bind two people (such as David and Jonathan; see 1 Samuel 8) or two communities (similar to the treaties established by Judah with neighboring countries). The second type, a *suzerain covenant,* was between the king and his subjects. The king would guarantee governance and demand certain acts of allegiance from his subjects either by protecting the land or by paying taxes (Anderson 1993, 138-39).

A review of the Bible will reveal many conversations on covenant: God's initial covenants with Noah and Abraham, the developed understanding in Leviticus and Deuteronomy of Israel's covenant, the challenge and invitation of the Old Testament prophets such as Ezekiel and Jeremiah, the new covenant announced by Jesus and explored in Romans and Hebrews.

One Old Testament covenant affirmation remains consistent: the promises of God and the call to the people to accept and live in the light of those promises. Even later prophetic challenges arise out of the people's tendency to take God's promises for granted rather than living to the fullness of those promises. A "covenantal people" describes a community, however small or large, bound together by what God does and will do. Living to the fullness of those promises means taking them personally, allowing them to be written on our hearts rather than assuming them as an automatic birthright. God's promises are given in community and received personally.

Jesus said little about covenant, but what, where, and how he said it has tremendous significance. During the Last Supper, Jesus spoke of the new covenant established in his blood (Matthew 14:22-25). God's promises were extended to all people through the death and resurrection of Jesus Christ. The new covenant was deeply personal, born out the grace of God through Jesus Christ and empowered through the activity of the Holy Spirit. This covenant is also deeply communal. Jesus announced the covenant during the first Communion with his disciples. Communion (or Eucharist), a sacrament that is expressly community-oriented, provides the context of the new covenant. People live in covenant relationship not only with God through Jesus Christ but also with one another as Christians.

Paul recognized this communal nature in the very act of sharing the bread and cup (1 Corinthians 11:23-34, esp. verses 33-34). Paul helps us understand that the covenant we have with Jesus Christ is also a covenant with the community of Jesus Christ, which is also called the body of Christ, the church. We are able to enter into covenantal relationship with one another because of the covenant Jesus has established with us in his death and resurrection. What had sometimes been mistakenly reduced to a birthright in the Old Testament is now understood as the grace we have received through faith in Jesus Christ.

MISUNDERSTANDINGS ABOUT COVENANTS

Covenants are often misunderstood because they are confused with contracts. Contracts, simply put, define if-then conditions. If the first party meets certain stipulations, then the second party must fulfill obligations. If either party does not meet its contractual requirements, then the contract may be canceled. Covenants, however, are based on more than the least common denominator of an agreement. Covenant language resembles the language of family. Covenants relate partners as whole persons (or whole communities) to each other, defining them as sisters or brothers. Covenants create flexible relationships where trust and faithfulness appear through the actions of the covenant partners, resulting in *because,* not if-then language. *Because* you are my brother or sister in Christ, I will minister with you. *Because* of what Jesus has done for me, I will encourage and assist you toward the Christlikeness that Jesus calls me to have in my life as well. Covenants are more enduring than contracts, and more empowering because of the fundamental trust that undergirds and flows from them. When people enter into covenant, trust builds upon trust.

A second major confusion about covenants involves the perception that *religion* is an individual endeavor, while the *church* is an institution. This view remains particularly prominent in North American culture, where rugged individualism reigns and yet big institutions are respected in the business and social worlds. Even church members tend to view the church as an institution, an abstract concept. Christianity, however, does not rely on concepts like individualism or institutions; the language of Christianity is both personal and communal and reminds us that we *are* the church. The Christian life is personal, touching each of us at the deepest level of our being. The Holy Spirit can permeate to the very core of who we are. Christianity is also communal, or community-based. The same Holy Spirit that reaches the core of our individual being connects us to other Christians. We are part of a community of believers throughout the world and in the specific place where we gather for worship, fellowship, nurture, and mission: the local church. We belong to God and we belong to one another. The Great Commandment from Jesus is clear on this: love God and love your neighbor as yourself (see Matthew 22:37-39).

The apostles certainly did not see the church as a collection of individuals, but as a body, with Christ as the head.

THE FUNCTION OF PUBLIC MINISTRY COVENANTS

Covenantal ministry embraces the particularity of each person through ministry profiles (not job descriptions) that clarify roles and responsibilities in educational ministry. In addition, covenants offer opportunities for public events that stress the mutual commitments between volunteer teachers and the local congregation, calling the lay teacher, the leadership of the church, and even the entire congregation into covenantal relationships. When congregations implement ministry covenants publicly (see appendix 23.1 for one version), these events may serve three different functions.

First, Recognition: Covenants recognize the commitment each person makes as a teacher, minister, and leader and the gifts given by the Holy Spirit to accomplish ministry. Covenants acknowledge the contribution that volunteer ministry makes to the church and express appreciation for and trust in that ministry. Covenants remind teachers that they are important to the work of Christ within the church; we, the body of Christ, recognize their important ministry.

Second, Reflection: Educator Donald Griggs is as a renowned workshop leader for teacher training (1980). He identifies five levels of ministry that many teachers, ministers, and leaders pass through:

1. *Committed:* having a basic desire to be in ministry
2. *Coping:* developing the basic skills for a particular age-level or ministry need
3. *Confident:* mastering the basic skills to the point that ministry (teaching) becomes much more natural
4. *Creative:* supplementing the basic skills with our own creative thoughts and techniques
5. *Constructive:* able to train and mentor others to become effective ministers, teachers, and leaders

Most ministers pass through each these levels at some point in their ministry, but they are not linear. A minister may repeat several levels when accepting a new age-group or ministry assignment. Even the most accomplished and creative adult educator can return to the coping level when placed in a classroom of six-year-olds! How well ministers negotiate one stage often influences how they accomplish future stages. Commitment, the fundamental desire to serve in ministry, remains central for teachers and for congregational support. Public covenants provide an opportunity to express personal and communal commitment; reflecting and affirming a shared desire to manifest holiness of heart and life while acknowledging that this can happen only because of the grace of God, through Jesus, by the power of the Holy Spirit.

Third, Reaffirmation: Reflection leads to the final function of public covenants. They serve to reaffirm ministry's heritage, activity, and hope. Covenants reaffirm God's will that the kingdom of God grow in size and depth and the call for all to participate in that growth. Covenants reaffirm that Jesus Christ will guide and empower all ministers as they allow the Holy Spirit to operate in their lives. Covenants reaffirm that no one ministers alone; all are part of a community that supports and trusts one another. Covenants reaffirm confidence in Jesus' call to ministry. Covenants are opportunities to celebrate, grow, and build trust that will flow through the ministry.

Used effectively, public ministry covenants are powerful reminders for the congregation. They offer opportunities to teach important biblical themes and create a congregational commitment anchored in the gospel.

▶ CONFLICTS AND CONFLICT RESOLUTION

Conflicts remain an inevitable part of leadership and community life. Some conflicts are unavoidable aspects of the natural development of the community. Other conflicts are not so inevitable or useful. They can be detrimental to the development of the congregation unless leaders both identify their sources and work to resolve them.

SOURCES OF CONFLICT

Not all conflict is negative; it can reveal differences that help people to move forward. Identifying the source of a conflict is often the key to resolving it.

Communication: Conflict often arises from simple misunderstandings in communication and communication style. Pausing long enough to understand both the intent and delivery of a message can reduce friction. Training in the various communication styles and raising awareness of them can be critical to the success of a ministry team.

Culture: People from different cultures may be offended or drawn into conflict because of misplaced perceptions of certain mannerisms and social customs. Culture also influences how people deal with conflict. Thomas Kochman notes that some cultures see dispassionate discussion as the best way to resolve issues while other cultures tend to view confrontation as healthy (1981). Cultural expectations may also be based on family history. Encourage sensitivity to cultural perceptions of gestures and mannerisms.

Power: Conflict often surfaces over issues of power, particularly when people do not share in decision making. People may be deeply invested in a position during a conflict. Fisher and Ury advise focusing on mutual interests rather than on positions or sides (1991). People sometimes resort to devious tactics or games to secure different forms of power: personal power, referential power, or implementation power (Berne 1996). Ministers need to be aware of power issues and where they stand in relation to them.

Conflicts sometimes surface indirectly. Ministers can find themselves in a triangle as the intermediary to relieve some unresolved anxiety between two antagonists (Richardson 1996). *Triangulation* can be subtle and insidious; it often indicates historic conflict that has raged within a congregation for a long time (Friedman 1985). Christian educators need to be aware of both process and content in communication. The *content* of a message may communicate one meaning, but the *process* of communication points to entirely different issues. Ministers, as helping professionals, risk becoming emotional safety valves for difficult relationships and must be vigilant, careful not to take sides in a difficult communication that may include hidden agendas.

Personality: Personal tendencies influence conflicts. What seems to be a major issue to one person might be minor to another. We all perceive reality differently, and this can be seen in the ways we work, how we internalize issues, and how we deal with conflict. People are socialized into specific modes of response to conflict by family history and cultural influence. None of these approaches is right or wrong in itself. Awareness of them and sensitivity to the conflict style of others can help keep small misunderstandings from escalating into serious conflict. Several typologies have been developed to describe these different styles. One, using animal imagery, describes five styles of conflict resolution that can be useful in addressing the mutual needs of achieving goals while maintaining relationships (Johnson and Johnson 1994).

- *The Turtle* (Withdrawing): Turtles withdraw into their shells to avoid conflicts, giving up personal goals and relationships, believing it easier to withdraw (physically and psychologically) from conflict than to face it.
- *The Shark* (Forcing): Sharks try to overpower opponents by forcing them to accept their solution to the conflict. Their goals prove highly important to them, and relationships are of minor importance. Sharks assume that conflicts are settled by one person winning and one person losing.
- *The Teddy Bear* (Smoothing): To teddy bears, relationships, not personal goals, are most important. Motivated by a desire for acceptance, they give up their goals to preserve the relationship.
- *The Fox* (Compromising): Foxes are moderately concerned with personal goals and relationships. Seeking compromise, they sacrifice part of their goals and relationships in order to achieve agreement for the common good.
- *The Owl* (Confronting): Owls value goals and relationships. They view conflicts as problems to be solved and seek a solution that achieves

both their goals and the goals of the other person. Owls see conflicts as a means of improving relationships by reducing tension between two persons. (332-39)

Some people cannot deal with conflict immediately. Leaders can provide a backdoor so that people can return to an issue later, even indirectly. Dealing with conflict is a significant challenge for any leader. The minister may need to disengage and create space to address the conflict before acting on crucial leadership issues.

CONFLICT RESOLUTION

Every conflict resolution is based on the answer to one basic question: Is it more important to be right or to be reconciled? Conflict resolution can involve mediation in either personal interactions (between individuals) or in situations that affect the whole congregation. While several texts offer elaborate models for intervention (Cosgrove and Hatfield 1994; Halverstadt 1991), leaders must think through how best to mediate congregational conflicts (there are often denominational guidelines), including circumstances when the leader cannot serve as the mediator. Appropriate procedures should be established in advance.

In personal conflicts, one effective strategy serves to diffuse the emotional investment. It is important to focus on behavior rather than on meaning or judgments. When you disagree with someone, describe the person's behavior (what you are struggling with) and your internal state: "When you _____, I feel _____." This allows the person to explain behavior without feeling immediately threatened. It opens dialogue that can lead to understanding rather than escalated conflict. Once you deal with the intent of behavior and emotional concerns, alternative strategies may be implemented: "I would prefer _____."

▶ THE CALL TO EDUCATIONAL MINISTRY AS FAITH DISCIPLESHIP

"Not many of you should presume to be teachers, my brothers and sisters, because you know that we who teach will be judged more strictly" (James 3:1). This verse serves as a caution to the church concerning dissension. It is interesting to review how the role of minister as educator has ebbed and flowed through the centuries. Paul and other apostles seemed to embrace the charge to teach as both a gift and a challenge. Many of the church fathers—Origen, Augustine, Athanasius, even Tertullian who seemed to want nothing to do with Greek and Roman schools—considered education a vital ministry. Theological treatises on education as ministry can be found in sermons and baptismal instructions. The demise of teaching as ministry did not occur until the Middle Ages when some leaders emphasized ritual mastery of the mass over the educational ministry of the church. Martin Luther, John Calvin, and then the Wesleys reinvigorated the role of education.

Luther launched one of the most ambitious educational programs of his day (under the watchful eye of Phillip Melancthon) that inaugurated public schools for girls and boys in Germany. Calvin stressed the primacy of the teaching office in Geneva, which Richard Osmer notes would (1) determine the normative beliefs and practices of the church, (2) reinterpret these beliefs and practices in shifting cultural and historical contexts, and (3) form appropriate educational institutions, processes, and material that could teach each new generation and help it deepen its faith as it matures and ages (1990, 115). To that end Calvin (like Luther) formulated catechisms for teaching. He also inaugurated the Academy of Geneva just before his death.

Wesley, as we have seen, wrote and organized extensive educational endeavors (whether or not they were all original is a modernist problem; Wesley borrowed as anyone would have in his day). All three Reformers demonstrated considerable insight and passion about education. Yet in some settings today, where these Reformers are revered as founders and inspiration, people and pastors in local congregations still question the value of educational ministry, faithful discipleship.

The problem is twofold: Pastors forget they are educators; Christian educators forget they are ministers. In North American settings, this divide surfaced during the revivalist era of the late nineteenth and early twentieth centuries. Preaching became exalted over all other pastoral functions, including pastoral care, leading in worship, organizing for the good of the body, engaging in compassionate ministry, and . . . teaching. Ministry became bound up in the personality of the preacher (Balmer 2000, 115-16). At the same time, the formation of the American Sunday School Union as a parachurch ministry placed Christian education outside the confines of the congregation. Pastors began to define ministry primarily, if not exclusively, as preaching, while education became an appendage rather than the lifeblood of the church. Christian educators became directors or program planners rather than ministers. Leadership was restricted to age-level subgroups, such as the youth ministers, which for years were known only as youth workers. Senior pastors began to view education as ancillary, something someone else did for them, or they trivialized education as a ministry function that one did if one had time. Ultimately, the educational ministry of the church was diminished, with disastrous results for discipleship.

One of our goals in this text is to restore the office of teaching to its proper place for the sake of the church and for the sake of Christianity. Central to this effort is our belief that teaching serves as important a role as preaching, though they fulfill different functions. *Preaching* is the proclamation of the Word of God, an event where we are encountered by the resurrected Lord and called to response. *Teaching* is the process of understanding the implication of those encounters through the daily life of the congregation. Teaching serves as the practical theology of a congregation, the collective working out of faith in the midst of life.

The evangelical church seems to have rediscovered worship and mission as central tasks, and they are vital to the life of the church. Christian education offers the informed and reflective engagement that ensures that the impact of worship moves beyond immediate emotional response and that mission is motivated by faithful discipleship, not manipulated by obligation. It is time that everyone called to ministry (even in the most senior roles) recognize the importance of Christian education as a distinctive and essential aspect of the life of the entire church. Ministers should embrace the potential that discipleship, as the teaching office of the church, can accomplish for the sake of the church. As pastors begin to see the power of learning environments, age-level ministries, and faithful leadership within a congregation dedicated in educational ministry, they will advance the call and response toward faithful discipleship.

▶ CONCLUSION

Leadership requires both developing leaders and resolving relational problems. It calls Christian educators to assess relational dynamics, attend to the vision of the congregation, reconcile, and encourage. Sound educational leadership also includes the stewardship of resources (planning and budgeting) and the formation of ministers. Leadership is more art than science as leaders discern how the Holy Spirit is leading and then work diligently to plan and participate in the actions of God.

▶ RESOURCES

Anderson, Bernhard W. 1993. Covenant. In *The Oxford Companion to the Bible,* 138-39. Ed. Bruce M. Metzger and Michael D. Coogan. New York: Oxford Univ. Press.

Balmer, Randall. 2000. *Mine Eyes Have Seen the Glory: Journey into the Evangelical Subculture in America.* 3rd ed., rev. New York: Oxford Univ. Press.

Banks, Robert, and Bernice M. Ledbetter. 2004. *Reviewing Leadership: A Christian Evaluation of Current Approaches.* Grand Rapids: Baker Academic and Brazos Press.

Bennis, Warren. 1989. *Why Leaders Can't Lead: The Unconscious Conspiracy Continues.* San Francisco: Jossey-Bass.

Berne, Eric. 1996. *Games People Play: The Basic Handbook of Transactional Analysis.* New York: Ballantine Books.

Bickimer, David Arthur. 1990. *Leadership in Religious Education: A Prehensive Model.* Birmingham, AL: Religious Education Press.

Blevins, Dean G. 1999. John Wesley and the means of grace: an approach to Christian religious education. Ph.D. diss., Claremont School of Theology. Ann Arbor, MI: UMI Publications.

Brafman, Ori, and Rod Beckstrom. 2006. *The Starfish and the Spider: The Unstoppable Power of Leaderless Organizations.* New York: Portfolio Hardcover/Penguin Books.

Carroll, Jackson W. 1991. *As One with Authority: Reflective Leadership in Ministry.* Louisville, KY: Westminster/John Knox Press.

Cladis, George. 1999. *Leading the Team-Based Church: How Pastors and Church Staffs Can Grow Together into a Powerful Fellowship of Leaders.* San Francisco: Jossey-Bass.

Cosgrove, Charles H., and Dennis D. Hatfield. 1994. *Church Conflict: The Hidden Systems Behind the Fights.* Nashville: Abingdon Press.

Fisher, Roger, and William Ury. 1991. *Getting to Yes: Negotiating Agreement Without Giving In.* Ed. Bruce Patton. New York: Penguin Books.

Foster, Charles R. 1986. *Ministry of the Volunteer Teacher.* Nashville: Abingdon Press.

Friedman, Edwin H. 1985. *Generation to Generation: Family Process in Church and Synagogue.* New York: Guilford Press.

Godin, Seth. 2008. *Tribes: We Need You to Lead Us.* New York: Portfolio/Penguin Group.

Griggs, Donald L. 1980. *Teaching Teachers to Teach: A Basic Manual for Church Teachers.* Nashville: Abingdon Press.

Halverstadt, Hugh F. 1991. *Managing Church Conflict.* Louisville, KY: Westminster/John Knox Press.

Hawkins, Thomas R. 1997. *The Learning Congregation: A New Vision of Leadership.* Louisville, KY: Westminster/John Knox.

Heitzenrater, Richard P. 1995. *Wesley and the People Called Methodists.* Nashville: Abingdon Press.

Hempton, David. 2005. *Methodism: Empire of the Spirit.* New Haven, CT: Yale Univ. Press.

Hersey, Paul, Kenneth H. Blanchard, and Dewey E. Johnson. 1969/2007. *Management of Organizational Behavior: Leading Human Resources.* 9th ed. Englewood Cliffs, NJ: Prentice-Hall.

Johnson, David, and Frank Johnson. 1994. *Joining Together: Group Theory and Group Skills.* 5th ed. Boston: Allyn and Bacon.

Kochman, Thomas. 1981. *Black and White Styles in Conflict.* Chicago: Univ. of Chicago Press.

Lencioni, Patrick. 2002. *The Five Dysfunctions of a Team: A Leadership Fable.* San Francisco: Jossey-Bass.

Osmer, Richard Robert. 1990. *A Teachable Spirit: Recovering the Teaching Office in the Church.* Louisville, KY: John Knox Press.

Parkes, William. 1997. Watchnight, covenant service, and the love-feast in early British Methodism. In *Wesleyan Theological Journal* 32, no. 2 (fall): 35-58.

Peters, Thomas J., and Robert Waterman. 1983/2004. *In Search of Excellence: Lessons from America's Best-Run Companies*. New York: HarperCollins.

Richardson, Ronald W. 1996. *Creating a Healthier Church: Family Systems Theory, Leadership and Congregational Life*. Minneapolis: Fortress Press.

Richey, Russell E., and Thomas Edward Frank. 2004. *Episcopacy in the Methodist Tradition: Perspectives and Proposals*. Nashville: Abingdon Press.

Appendix 23.1
A Ministry Covenant

The following covenant is a sample. It is designed to be used as both a personal document and a public litany. We would encourage you to adapt it to your congregational setting, with the goals of focusing on each individual's ongoing ministry *and* the mutual covenant of the entire congregation to support that ministry.

Sunday School Ministries Covenant
"But to each one of us grace has been given as Christ apportioned it"
(Ephesians 4:7).

Teacher/Minister/Leader

In response to the grace given to me by Jesus Christ and the confidence placed in me by the church in being selected as a minister, teacher, and leader within the Sunday school, I hereby covenant with this church and with Jesus Christ to continue to give my committed best:

- to follow to the best of my ability the responsibilities of this ministry
- to guide and empower individuals to be faithful disciples of Jesus Christ
- to maintain a high standard of Christian living as an intentional witness for Christ to others
- to cultivate my own personal growth and discipleship, to grow as a learner as well as a teacher

I covenant, as do all members of the body of Christ, to continue to regularly participate and support the community of believers in worship, education, stewardship, service, and mission.

"It was he who gave some to be apostles, some to be prophets, some to be evangelists, and some to be pastors and teachers" (Ephesians 4:11).

Discipleship Committee (or Sunday School Superintendent)

The Discipleship Committee, represented by the Sunday school superintendent and its members, affirms your faithfulness and ministry. We acknowledge the importance of your ministry and covenant with you and before Jesus Christ:

- to provide curriculum, resources, and supplies for your ministry
- to provide opportunities to expand and improve your ministry
- to provide a quality educational environment
- to serve as your advocate in the increase of your ministry

We covenant, as do all members of the body of Christ, to continue to regularly participate and support the community of believers in worship, education, stewardship, service, and mission.

*"To prepare God's people for works of service, so that the body of Christ
may be built up" (Ephesians 4:12).*

Congregation

We, the congregation, represented by our pastor and church board, acknowledge your faithfulness and ministry. We, too, seek to follow your example of pursuing Christlikeness and covenant with you and Jesus Christ:

- to uphold you in daily prayer
- to provide support for your ministry by encouraging church-wide participation
- to provide you with the environment necessary for your ministry and for personal growth

We covenant, as do all members of the body of Christ, to continue to regularly participate and support the community of believers in worship, education, stewardship, service, and mission.

*"Until we all reach unity in the faith and in the knowledge of the Son of God
and become mature, attaining to the whole measure of the fullness of Christ"
(Ephesians 4:13).*

CONCLUSION

Faithful Discipleship:
Practice and Becoming a Means of Grace

Throughout this book we have sought to provide a view of Christian education that is consistent with our Wesleyan-Holiness tradition. As we serve a particular tradition, we have explored the core definitions and key dynamics that influence faithful discipleship through that lens. In doing so we have explored the importance of the story of God, the Bible, the history of the church in discipleship, our core theological convictions, and our philosophical assumptions that envision ministry anchored in the means of grace. In addition we have explored how best to pay attention to people as they grow, learn, and come to faith by attending carefully to the life course, to the various dynamics that influence moral and faithful living, to key learning theories, and ultimately to our task in designing and delivering sound curriculum for Christian education. This review of the foundational influences that guide faithful discipleship brought us to a view of how this approach begins to reveal itself in daily congregational life and practice. Throughout, we have allowed John Wesley's categories, found in the various descriptions of the means of grace, guide our efforts as we envision faithful discipleship through the tasks of formation, discernment, and transformation. Our goal, like Wesley and others within our tradition, remains an educational ministry that results in holiness of heart and life—practicing the means of grace within Christian education in order to become a means of grace on behalf of the kingdom of God and for the sake of the larger world. How these efforts unfold within a given congregation involves the practice of faithful discipleship within learning environments that include Sunday school and small groups, within age-level ministries and families, and through careful shepherding of administrative tasks and leadership roles.

Embracing this approach is particularly Wesleyan, but it is ultimately Christian. While we have drawn clues from our Wesleyan heritage, we believe the core of our presentation has been true to the larger Christian tradition that began with the first church, which, by the power of the Holy Spirit, confessed and taught that "Jesus Christ is Lord, to the glory of God the Father" (Philippians 2:11, KJV). John Wesley did not invent a new Christianity; he merely attempted to draw out the best within Christian faith and practice for the renewal of the church and the redemption of the world. Our goal is the same. We do not aspire to form a discipleship of faithful Wesleyans; we aspire to see faithful Christians. We seek disciples of Jesus, followers of Christ, recipients of the Father's love, communities of the Holy Spirit, a people of God. When we work collectively to form people through God's loving grace, help them discern and participate in the activity of the Holy Spirit, and encourage them be transformed and to transform the world in the name of Jesus; we have met the task of faithful Christian discipleship. May God give us grace to be a means of grace in all of our efforts as Christian educators and as faithful disciples of Jesus Christ.